Culture/Contexture

Culture/Contexture

Explorations in Anthropology and Literary Studies

EDITED BY

E. Valentine Daniel
and
Jeffrey M. Peck

UNIVERSITY OF CALIFORNIA PRESS

Berkeley   Los Angeles   London

The editors wish to thank the University
of Michigan for its financial assistance
in the preparation of this volume.

University of California Press
Berkeley and Los Angeles, California
University of California Press
London, England

1 2 3 4 5 6 7 8 9

Library of Congress Cataloging-in-Publication Data

Culture/Contexture: Explorations in Anthropology and Literary Studies /
edited by E. Valentine Daniel and Jeffrey M. Peck.
    p.   cm.
    Includes bibliographical references (p.   ) and index.
    ISBN 0-520-08463-2 (cloth : acid-free paper). — ISBN
    0-520-08446-0 (pbk. : acid-free paper)
    1. Ethnology—Authorship.   2. Literature and anthropology.
    3. Anthropology in literature.   4. Culture.   5. Criticism.
    I. Daniel, E. Valentine.   II. Peck, Jeffrey M., 1950-
GN307.7.C85 1996
    306—dc20   94-3997
                                                      CIP

The paper used in this publication meets the minimum requirements of
American National Standard for Information Sciences—Permanence
of Paper for Printed Library Materials, ANSI Z39.48-1984 ∞

CONTENTS

PART II • IDENTITY MARKINGS

PART III • UNSETTLING TEXTS

ACKNOWLEDGMENTS

Grateful acknowledgment is made for permission granted to reprint several essays in this volume:

Clifford Geertz's essay is reprinted from his book *Works and Lives: The Anthropologist as Author* with the permission of the publishers, Stanford University Press. © 1988 by the Board of Trustees of the Leland Stanford Junior University. Permission to reprint also granted by Blackwell Publishers, Oxford, England.

Marilyn Ivy's essay is reprinted from her book *Discourses of the Vanishing: Modernity, Phantasm, Japan* (Chicago: University of Chicago Press, 1995). © 1995 by The University of Chicago. All rights reserved.

David Lloyd's essay is reprinted from the *Oxford Literary Review* 13 (Spring 1991): 62–94. Reprinted with permission.

Dan Rose's essay is reprinted from *Anthropological Quarterly* 64:3 (1991): 109–125, where the original title was "Elite Discourses of the Market and Narrative Ethnography."

Susan Stewart's essay is reprinted from her book *Crimes of Writing: Problems in the Containment of Representation*. Copyright © 1991 by Oxford University Press, Inc. Reprinted by permission.

The essays by Stewart, Lloyd, and Ivy have been slightly revised for their republication in this volume.

We owe special thanks to Marilyn Ivy, John Pemberton, Stephanie Hoelscher, and especially Margaret Hoey-Daniel, who helped us at various stages in the preparation of the manuscript.

Culture/Contexture:
An Introduction

E. Valentine Daniel and Jeffrey M. Peck

The presence of the literary in anthropology is best described as "uncanny"—a nonscientific drive lodged in the heart of a putative science, a presence both desired and dreaded, a Freudian *unheimlich*. For literary study, anthropology has for the most served merely as a source of the esoteric in theory and example. About fifteen years ago, the two fields found deeper significance in each other, which resulted in a flurry of publications heightening this awareness. In *Culture/Contexture*,[1] scholars from these two disciplines join, for the first time, to reflect on the antidisciplinary urge that has made this creative rapprochement both possible and necessary. The common urge springs from a common predicament. Both anthropology and literary study—and culture and writing—are alive to their extrinsic and intrinsic contextures; "contexture" being the term Hobbes used to connote both the texture that surrounds and the texture that constitutes. The themes by which the authors work through the fascination and fears that hold these disciplines together and hold them apart range from reading and race, nation and narration, and writing and representation to state and self, incest and violence, and travel and time. The resulting revelation is one of rich possibilities that each side, in its own contexture, holds for the other.

E. VALENTINE DANIEL: FROM AN ANTHROPOLOGIST'S POINT OF VIEW: THE LITERARY

In previewing my colleague's "Point of View" that follows, I was struck by the image he paints of scholars in literary study wanting to "get their hands dirty in the field." Some anthropologists today, with more than a century's hindsight, are more likely to identify with Lady Macbeth fretting about all the perfumes of Arabia not being up to snuff for sweetening her little hands.

1

For some of us at least, fieldwork is an act of "atonement," atonement for sins less sanguinary but more consequential than Lady Macbeth's, atonement for our conceits and the conceit of the West wherein our disciplinary interests originated. We provided the theory; they provided the cases. The more romantic among us have sought to make such atonements by getting to this unctuous word's radical etymology by achieving an at-one-ment[2] with the Other whom we have violated. But such attempts are condemned to fail even as the awkwardness of the decompounded word in question defies an at-one-ment with "atonement." The atonement an anthropologist is capable of making is at best an atonement *between* self and Other, almost never an at-one-ment *with* the Other.

Getting to know the Other has been anthropology's raison d'être. This Other has existed for anthropology in two modes. The first concerns another people, the second another form. The form in question goes by the popular appellation of the day, "the text." My emphasis in this introduction will be on the form that sustains the notion of the text, the literary. To appreciate anthropology's encounter with the literary, we need to briefly review anthropology's engagement with its other Other, another people. The Other as a people has borne various names throughout anthropology's brief history: primitives, natives, traditional peoples, tribes, and ethnic groups, to mention but a few. In short, anthropology has been enamored by that which is foreign to it. This Other with which anthropology has attempted to engage, and about which much has been written recently, is difference essentialized and distanced in time and space by a particular way of coming to know it.[3] Willingly or otherwise, this form of knowledge has abetted three strategies of engagement with difference: conquest, conversion, and marginalization (Connolly 1991: 36–63). The project is essentially Hegelian: how to reconcile the radical divide generated by the Enlightenment, the divide between subject and object, self and other, home and the world (Adorno 1973). Conquest and conversion, the stratagems of conquistadors and priests, respectively (Todorov 1985), played lambently on the methods and theories of anthropology. Broadly speaking, from its Tylorean beginnings in 1878 until E. E. Evans-Pritchard's 1950 Marrett lecture, anthropology's conquests advanced on the shoulders of the pumped-up brawn of positivist scientism in which reductionist explanations were the be-all and end-all. Insofar as the quest was for explanations rather than interpretations, laws rather than patterns, universals rather than particulars, the predictability of a naturalized moral order rather than the spontaneity of a moral[4] cultural field, the conquest of the Other lay in the imposition on it of such explanations, naturalized laws, and universals, with little regard to the historically specific scientistic culture to which these valorized goals belonged. Had the conquest in question, the conquest by imposition, been limited to *our* understanding of the Other, it would have been a partial one.

But to the extent that we may have succeeded in converting the Others to our point of view without reciprocity, in making them see themselves as we see them, our conquest is a resounding one. In many anthropology departments in India, for example, cranial indexes and nasal indexes, along with the concept of race, continue to preoccupy researchers. The high-precision calibrating instruments needed for such measurements are no longer imported from Europe but are locally manufactured. Archaeology, history, and folklore have become the instruments for constructing hoary traditions, antiquarian nations, and jealous national identities (e.g., see Ivy, this volume). And occasionally the point is made tragicomically vivid, as when Margaret Trawick's search for the Jackal Hunters' myth of origin ends at the door of the group's "chief native-informant" who informs her that the *ur*-text of the myth is to be found in none other than the little black box of a white man who had taped the myth some years earlier. Authorship, in its several senses, had been surrendered to a foreign white male who, in this instance, happened to be Trawick's own student (see Trawick, this volume).

But the opposite point needs to be made as well. The muscle of scientism and colonialism notwithstanding, and despite Edward Said's (1989) pessimistic picture of what anthropology had wrought, the Other has not only bent to but also resisted, frustrated, and transformed anthropological designs. That is, the asymmetry in the power relationship has not been consistently tilted in the anthropologist's favor. We certainly overstate the case when we attribute too much power to the anthropological account, interpretive or explanatory, in considering the dyadic relationship between the anthropologist and his or her Other. By and large, the Other's reality continues to exist, persist, grow, and change, independent of how that Other is reconstituted in anthropological reality. Times change, too. Consider Edgar Thurston, that British civil servant-cum-lay ethnographer of the early part of this century about whom Nicholas Dirks writes in his essay (this volume). Quite apart from "making much of" (in both senses) the "castes and tribes of South India," Thurston's seven volumes by that title became a paradigmatic text for the construction of South India's ethnographic reality and a veritable manual for learning about South Indian society. By contrast, the writings of most contemporary ethnographers lack that "reality-making" power. I can think of at least six reasons for such a state of affairs. First, contemporary anthropology has consciously attempted to disengage itself from both explicit and tacit collusion with the designs of the more obvious centers of power. Second, in the late twentieth century, anthropological productions do not matter as much to these centers and institutions of power as do the productions of economics, political science, psychology, and even sociology. Third, anthropology has come to possess self-doubts about its previous claims to explanatory authority (the kind of self-doubts sadly lacking in many of its sister social sciences). Fourth, anthropology's Other is not only distanced by space and time but, as often, by status and class as well, in which, as Dan Rose shows in this volume, the anthropologist is his Other's unequal. Fifth, a significant number of anthropologists have taken to heart Evans-Pritchard's claim (or at least parts of it) that if anthropology "studies societies as moral systems and not as natural systems, then it "is a kind of historiography, and therefore ultimately of philosophy of art. [It is]. . . interested in design rather than process, . . . seeks patterns and not scientific laws, and interprets rather than explains" (1962: 152). But finally and most significantly, anthropologists as well as those in literary study—inspired by the likes of Jacques Derrida, Raymond Williams, Michel Foucault, Mikhail Bakhtin, Walter Benjamin, and Antonin Gramsci—have realized that there are narratives, other than the available master narratives, that need to be drawn on to compose ethnographies. The writing of such ethnographies calls for the cultivation of an ear for discourses that are normally drowned out by hegemonic ones. Such discourses, or rather, "counter-discourses" (Marcus 1992), have made "culture" into an unsettled and unsettling thing, much like writing, or even more like "reading." The last point, reading culture, is amplified by Dirks in this volume. But we are getting ahead of our story.

If conquest and conversion are two interrelated operations employed by anthropology, especially in its engagement with the Other in distant lands, marginalization is the strategy employed by anthropology (as well as the liberal sectors of the society in which it feels mostly at home) in its engagement with the Other among us. The latter is most often expressed in the liberal idiom of tolerance without the awareness that toleration is but another form of marginalization and neutralization, a point elegantly brought out by David Lloyd in his chapter. The strategies of tolerating by marginalizing and marginalizing by tolerating are resorted to mostly in coming to terms with the stranger among us, who, in the argot of our time, is called the ethnic. Regardless of which three strategies are resorted to, and in whichever combination, the relationship between self and Other is embedded in a matrix of a kind of power: "the power over" rather than "the power to." A friend of mine, in a moment of alliterative weakness, opposed "othering" to "mothering." To continue this somewhat infelicitous pun, "mothering" is no less implicated in a relationship of power and can be construed in two ways. At the negative end, it rhymes with "smothering" and is found in various kinds of mushy universalisms, in a lovey-dovey "family of man" or Walt Disneyesque *Small World* and in Benetton ads with smiling faces of several representative "races." At its ideal best, it nurtures rather than smothers difference, it involves a power-to rather than a power-over: the power to bring out the best in the other or make a space wherein the other might find his or her identity and the freedom to express it.[5] But if that were to be the end of it, it would be paternalism under a different sign. Anthropology also urges us to open ourselves up to the Other so that the Other may reciprocate by bringing out the best in us. Such a reciprocity of recognition should not be confused with the liberal agenda of homogenization, or equated with the relegation of difference to an annual ethnic parade on Main Street. Rather, it pleads for a nonhierarchical relationship in which there will not only be the inevitable give-and-take but also the willingness to let differences be and, if need be, grow.

Now let us turn to anthropology's second Other, form. The form that we have called the literary must be presupposed if we are to appreciate its better-known manifestation as the text. To kidnap an expression from Julia Kristeva (1991: 191), the literary has been "the stranger within us" anthropologists. Let us enter our problem more broadly, by considering "other" disciplines in general. Given the relatively young field that anthropology was (and still is), many of its practitioners have had their primary credentials in foreign fields: biology, A. C. Haddon; classics, Sir James Frazer; engineering, Sir Edmund Leach; geology, Erminnie Smith; history, George Stocking and Francesca Bray; law, Robert Redfield and Max Gluckman; mathematics, John Atkins; medicine, W. H. R. Rivers; music, Frances Densmore; physical geography, Franz Boas; sociology, S. J. Tambiah. There are others for whom work in another field had a significant impact on later anthropological work. In this regard one thinks of Gregory Bateson and biology, Victor Turner and English literature,[6] Paul Radin and philosophy. Indeed, as one of the anonymous readers of the original manuscript of this volume reminded us, to this day most graduate programs in anthropology prefer students with backgrounds other than anthropology. Despite the full professionalization of anthropology by the 1920s by the second generation of anthropologists through the ritualization of fieldwork and the academicization of the discipline in university departments, the doors to the subject's interior have remained—relative to its sister social sciences—quite open, with the only proviso that the ritual of fieldwork be gone through. And thanks to this ritual, the discipline's center held, and its inner life was enriched with each stranger's entry.

Among the strangers who are at home in anthropology's arcane recesses, however, the literary has had, as I have indicated, an "uncanny" presence. The German word used by Freud for "the uncanny," *unheimlich,* signifies a breach of *heimlich,* which in its turn has the double meaning of homeyness and secrecy. In both the use and the denial of this second Other of anthropology, the same three strategies of engagement with the Other were brought to bear on the literary: to conquer and/or to convert and/or to marginalize. In a discipline nurtured in the hothouse of positivism, where "to see" was more than a metaphor, to admit to the literary was tantamount to admitting to the subjective, and the subjective was, unlike the objective, essentially blind.[7] For in an "objective science" such as anthropology, the literary, which after all belongs to the last of the triumvirate of logic, grammar, and rhetoric, with its attention and admission to style, had to be repressed. At no time in the history of the discipline, however, was the conquest of the literary as successful as it has been in certain other social sciences such as economics, political science, psychology, and even sociology. In fact, the rhetorical was the hallmark of many justly famous anthropologists. At the risk of excluding more than we include, those who come to mind alphabetically in this respect are Ruth Benedict, Sir Edwin E. Evans-Pritchard, Sir James Frazer, Clifford Geertz, Claude Lévi-Strauss, Bronislaw Malinowski, Ervin Meggitt, Hortense Powdermaker, Kenneth Reed, W. E. H. Stanner, and Victor Turner. The rhetoric of writing can often mask its politics. How easy it is to miss the politics for the rhetoric in the writings of two of our foremost women anthropologists, Margaret Mead and Ruth Benedict. Mead dared to write for *Redbook* magazine, compromising her chances of being taken seriously by the academic world. In the case of Benedict, we can appreciate the contrast between the diaries that characterize her vivid preanthropological phase and the neutralized voice of her academic writing only against the background of disciplinary politics. The politics of writing is far more obvious with respect to Franz Boas's two other students in whose work gender and race meet. Ella Deloria, the Native American author of the ethnographic novel *Waterlily*, began her career as Boas's student, research assistant, and informant. But neither her career nor her writings had any chance of breaking through and into the largely Eurocentric anthropological canons. Written in 1944, *Waterlily* was published only in 1988. The second of Boas's students whose writings—in particular, *Mules and Men*—remain excluded from the canons is the African-American ethnographer Zora Neale Hurston.[8]

Many are the closet novelists among anthropologists. A few (notably two, Saul Bellow and Kurt Vonnegut), fortunately or otherwise, had but a brush with anthropology, cut loose, and went on to become famous. Some anthropologists have opted to operate at the very edges where ethnography blurs into fiction. The most recent example of a work that has entered this no-man's-land from anthropology's side is Barbara Tedlock's *The Beautiful and the Dangerous*. Has the difference been effaced? And, if so, at what price? The jury of anthropological critics is out on this one. The South Asian novelist Amitav Ghosh, who holds a D.Phil. in social anthropology, returns to the margins of ethnography and fiction in his latest book, *In an Antique Land*, after having written two award-winning novels, *The Circle of Reason* and *The Shadow Lines*. Kirin Narayan has traversed in the other direction, from ethnography to fiction, in her recent novel, *Love, Stars and All That*; and so have Richard Handler and Daniel Segal in their study, *Jane Austen and the Fiction of Culture*. Scott Momaday's *House Made of Dawn* and Tillie Olsen's little jewel, *Yonnondio, from the Thirties,* represent two of the many more literary works that have drawn deeply from the well of ethnography. On any of these moves from the literary toward the ethnographic, there have been no adverse judgments and none likely. For ethnography is still seen as a repository of facts; even in our world of fiction, facts are highly valued.

Unlike prose, poetry's Otherness is seen as radical. The need to resort to poetry in the face of expressive inadequacy of prose is an only too familiar experience for those who have struggled to represent an otherwise eluding clarity of experience. Many are the anthropologists who have seen such a need as temptation and yielded to it in encloseted safety. But there are a number of exceptions; Edward Sapir, Margaret Mead, Ruth Benedict, Paul Friedrich, Dell Hymes, Dan Rose, Jerome Rothenberg, and Stanley Diamond, to mention only a few, went public with their poems. And Gary Snyder, like his counterparts in fiction, Bellow and Vonnegut, went "commercial," as they say. Dennis Tedlock has taken on himself the task of "transliterating" into poetry as a means of giving the Other voice. Giving voice is not merely letting someone else speak, for example, through transliterated and translated quotation. Giving voice is an art; the art of discovering the language of the Other. What Tedlock tries to show us is that this is an art that lies at the very core of linguistic understanding and translating skills. This was also what the late folklorist, linguist, and poet A. K. Ramanujan strove to achieve in his translations of classical Tamil poetry into English, trying to give voice to another language and another time. Derrick Walcott has done the same for St. Lucian English, revealing the inherent mimeticity of the English language and the English people. Unlike his fellow Caribbean, V. S. Naipaul believes in the existence of an original but is disappointed to find only mimicry in India—both in Indian English and among the English in India—and diagnoses his finding as degenerate by definition. Walcott goes beyond Naipaul, to reveal through his poetry that the English in England are mimics in their turn, no less than the Afro-Caribbean or the Englishman in India or the West Indies, transforming thereby the purported original into yet another simulacrum.[9] The Chicana lesbian writer Gloria Anzaldua also uses poetry and translation to give voice to a "borderland" of cultural heterogeneity and dynamism. Some anthropologists may find Anzaldua's book an explicitly autobiographical work that deserves to be appreciated as such and should not be confused with ethnography, quite apart from the fact that it is written in verse. But what ought not to be missed is the ethnographic impulse to be found in her attempt at giving voice not merely to her self but to a language, the language of her Borderlands—a language made up of English and Spanish, learning to be Indian in Mexican culture and being Mexican from an Anglo perspective, being lesbian among homophobes and a woman in a patriarchal social order.[10]

Unlike the expressive prose of fiction, however, poetry's radical Otherness has never carried the threat of being confused with ethnography. Poetry is seen as something that one does when one takes leave of one's ethnographic senses. Not to have access to its "angled vision and voice"—to borrow an expression from Ivan Brady (1991: 5)—is hardly seen as a loss and never as a failure. Despite Steven Tyler's (1986) call for a plurality of experimental ethnographies, none, to my knowledge, has attempted to write ethnography in verse, even though some poets could well serve as models for doing so; for example, Michael Ondaatje's *The Collected Works of Billy the Kid*. But how many ethnographers, when in their honest best, when they are most capable of reflecting on their struggle with their field notes against the winds in the field, will not consider Robert Frost's definition of a poem as "a momentary stay against confusion," equally applicable to ethnography? No master narrative there. And further, William Pritchard (1980: 175), writing about poetry, said, "Poetry will continue to count as a living force insofar as we keep the poems open, prevent their hardening into meanings which make them easier to handle only because they are no longer fluid, problematic, and alive." Substitute "ethnography" and "ethnographies" for "poetry" and "poems," and you have the means for judging good ethnography. Again, no master narrative here.

Nevertheless, the literary within anthropology, which has both widened and deepened this discipline's identity, has made its presence something to reckon with only since the field took its "linguistic" and, more recently, "reflexive" turn. Some may trace the attention and place given to language in ethnography to Malinowski's *Coral Gardens and Its Magic,* others to Franz Boas, Edward Sapir, and Benjamin Whorf. But the linguistic as harbinger of the literary awakening in anthropology did not occur until biology, an earlier ill-exploited guest, had been displaced. British structural functionalism of the twenties may have displaced Victorian evolutionism as pseudohistory, but biology continued to provide the dominant trope even for this new school of anthropology. In functionalism, the model was that of an organism's body. If the guest had been ill-exploited, his presence (the guest was "male") was also an uneasy one. If biology had empowered anthropology, it also overpowered it. For in a science that described itself as "cultural," the paradigm claiming regnance was "natural." With the linguistic turn came the euphoria of a coronation, anthropology's discovery of one it could claim to be its own. For who could deny, it was then thought, that language was anything but fully, centrally, definingly, and distinguishingly cultural. It was no mere metaphor; it was all-embracing and all-pervasive.

This turn of events either coincided with or was triggered by two other events: the animated activity initiated in language philosophy by Ludwig Wittgenstein's transformation from *The Tractatus* to *The Philosophical Inves-*

tigations and the rise in importance of Lévi-Strauss and his heralding of structuralism. The first of these drifted into what came to be called the "rationalism debates," which raised issues like the translation of one culture into another culture's terms, the universality of reason, relativism, whither reality, and so on.[11] In many ways, these issues and debates tilled the ground for a later, interpretive anthropology in general to take root and for ethnographic pluralism to flourish; they provided a means for the narrowly linguistic to expand into a broader interest in discourse in general and counterdiscourses in particular.[12]

The second kind of linguistic orientation in anthropology came with Lévi-Straussian (French) structuralism, which found its origins in the semiology of Ferdinand de Saussure and the phonology of Roman Jakobson and Nikolaj Troubetzkoy of the Prague school. Apart from displacing biologism in anthropology, French structuralism yielded two consequences of its own, one liberating and the other limiting. The former provided a clearing wherein anthropology and literary criticism found common ground. Not since James Frazer's *Golden Bough* had something from anthropology quickened the interest of literature as structuralism. An undergraduate thesis written by James Boon and published in 1972, *From Symbolism to Structuralism: Lévi-Strauss in a Literary Tradition,* remains one of the finest early examples of this link between anthropology and literature. Several more such bivalent works followed, channeling a respectable flow of ideas between the two fields. Furthermore, Lévi-Strauss himself was being read as much for his literary flair as for his anthropology. This was liberating. The second consequence, however, turned out to be limiting. The kind of semiology that Lévi-Strauss inherited from de Saussure was what Augusto Ponzion appropriately calls "code semiotics." Code semiotics has not only been incapable of dealing with the heteroglossia, plurivocality, ambiguity, and semantic-cum-pragmatic wealth of discourses but also reduced the task of interpretation to the act of decoding, which in the hands of lesser mortals than Lévi-Strauss, Roland Barthes, and a few other literary geniuses became bland reductionist exercises. A genuinely interpretive semiotic in which interpretation, unlike mere decodification, "is never final or guaranteed by appeal to a code with the function of prescribing the way in which signifiers and signifieds are to be exchanged" (Deledalle 1979: xii–xiii), did not make its appearance until the mid-1970s with the "discovery" of the writings of the other co-founder of modern semiotics, Charles Sanders Peirce. Milton Singer (1978), with different ends in mind than ours in this chapter, attempted to stress the difference between the de Saussurian version of the study of sign activity and its Peircean counterpart by calling the former semiology and the latter, semiotics. The attempted nomenclatural clarity, alas, has been largely ignored, and "semiotics" is indiscriminately used as a label to characterize both these and many other variants of approaches to the study of the activity of signs. Furthermore, Peirce's inherently dialogical semiotic itself began to be (mis)read in de Saussurian dualistic terms.[13] But even before the recovery of Peircean interpretive semiotics (or as Peirce preferred to spell it, "semeiotic"), code semiotics was beginning to be unsettled by another form of attention to language, the hermeneutics of Dilthey, Hans Gadamer, and Paul Ricoeur. Wilhelm Dilthey's influence on the anthropologists Geertz and Turner was considerable. Apart from being writers who paid special attention to style in language, revealing personalities, alert to life, in all of their sentences, they set "in motion," to adapt a line from Richard Poirier (1992: 66), "a beautifully liberating instability, a relativity rather than a 'relevance.' " Like Lévi-Strauss, Geertz and Turner were read and quoted by nonanthropologists in the humanities. Geertz, in particular, describing himself as a hermeneutician and a pragmatist (of the Jamesian variety), drove home the point that no longer could there be a point of view that wasn't a point of view. The objective scientist found his narrative to be part of a prejudicial world where every judgment, including his or her own, was a prejudgment. The best that anthropologists could hope for was not to escape prejudice in general but to be able to transcend their particular prejudices and thereby never lose sight of context and self. And it was this task that the anthropological narrative, the ethnography, was called on to carry out, painstakingly and reflexively.

In those heady days of liberation from the shackles of positivist conceit, some anthropologists wrote reflexive ethnographies that were so self-indulgent in their celebratory excesses that it was difficult even then, and harder now, to tell where reflexivity ended and self-indulgence began. It was forgotten that reflexivity, by definition, did not have to be expansive. It was forgotten, furthermore, that reflexivity and representation were mutually immanent categories. I, for one, held that the relationship between the two ought to be like that between the subjunctive and indicative moods of a proposition, where reflection is parenthetically embedded within representation (Daniel 1985). Perhaps mine was a mixture of overreaction and overcaution. But to call reflexive anthropology parenthetical was not to trivialize it. Johnson defined a parenthesis as "a sentence so included in another sentence, as that it may be taken out without injuring the sense of that which encloses it." When applied to ethnography, the first part of his definition holds, but the second does not. In this sense, ethnography is better likened to poetry than to prose. Consider those poets—T. S. Eliot, Emily Dickinson, Geoffrey Hill, for example—who give such importance to intercluding parentheses in their poems. Remove any one of them and the result would sound deranged. But, in the case of ethnography, one ought to close in on this metaphor of interclusion even further, to make it more snug than its manifestation as parenthesis.

I am thinking of the ultimate in intercluding marks, the hyphen. Reflexivity in ethnography can be brief, small, a particle in flight or a fleeting particular, a crepuscular detail, hyphen-like: holding together and holding apart, maintaining continuity and creating a breach, uniting and separating, estranging and binding, and most importantly, dividing but also compounding. (Daniel 1985: 247)

This more spartan form of reflexivity was to be found, not in the ethnographies of the self-declared reflectivists but among those who made the translation of cultural texts into contextured texts their central concern. Prominent among these are James Siegel's *Shadow and Sound,* Dennis Tedlock's *Popol Vuh,* A. L. Becker's *Writing on the Tongue,* and Lila Abu-Lughod's *Veiled Sentiments.* The irony is that, in a previous age, ethnographers such as Siegel and Tedlock would more likely have been philologists than anthropologists, reminding us that there flow currents from our "antiquarian" past that continue to irrigate our field and, at times, better than might the floodwaters caused by a passing tide. Philology is, after all, that nineteenth-century ancestor of both anthropology and literary study.

The reign of this kind of attention to the linguistically and reflexively situated in general may have helped both widen and deepen anthropology's identity, but it left it fundamentally untroubled. This fundamentally untroubling awareness of our linguisticality came to be best exemplified by the philosopher Richard Rorty. His *Philosophy and the Mirror of Nature* became the darling of as many literary critics as anthropologists, who were sympathetic to the turn to discourse and the questioning of all manner of foundationalisms, especially the belief that there were indubitable foundations to knowledge. This much-reviewed book gave (anti-)philosophical vim to Geertz's interpretive verve. The call was to replace the quest for "epistemological certainties" with "edifying conversations" between self and Other. In the eighties, with the rise of postmodern, post-structuralist, and feminist sensibilities, Geertzian anthropology, even if liberating of anthropology, in its turn came to be seen as issuing forth from a far too liberal view of life, culture, and the world—a view that was only possible from the safety and privilege of bourgeois comfort. The latter charge was especially directed at the easy hermeneutics advocated by Rorty—whom Geertz refers to with favor, a favor anticipated by Rorty (Geertz 1983: 222–224; Rorty 1979: 267). For the most part, such edifying conversations appeared to be thin ones, even thinly veiled monologic ones, blind to the structures of power that provided the ground on which such conversations took place. Foucault was to show us that even while conversing with the Other, as Bellow said somewhere, "one had to dig out from layers of discourse that had accumulated under one's feet." This difference with Rorty (and, by extension, Rorty's hero, John Dewey) is tellingly brought to our attention by William Connolly, who contrasts the "mellow metaphors" of Rorty et al. with those of Foucault:

Foucault's metaphors concentrate one's attention on the metaphorical character of conventional discourse which pretends to be literal; they incite a response stifled or cooled by the mellow metaphors conventionally used. Thus
he substitutes "surveillance" for "observation" in "probing" (a Foucauldian
term of art which replaces the more conventional "exploring") the relation of
the social scientists to object populations. He substitutes "interrogate" for
"question," "interrupt" for "pause," "production" for "emergence" (in talking
about the "origin" of the self), "penetrate" for "open," "discipline" for "harmonize" or "socialize," and "inscribe" for "internalize." . . . Foucault disturbs
and incites; Rorty comforts and tranquilizes. (1983: 134)

Even if Foucault's reality was a relativized one, it turned out to be hard,
densely and obdurately constructed by discursive and material practices, and
not one sustained by an easy conversation that could be written out into an
ethnography of equally untrammeled but aestheticized prose. With the expansion of "discourse" to refer to far more than the conversational context
intended by certain branches of linguistics and linguistic anthropology, "context" itself no longer remained a concept transparent to reflexive reverie or
pragmatic analysis but became a vexed one. As Michael Taussig (1992: 46)
has recently told us, "Context [is] not . . . a secure epistemic nest in which
our knowledge-eggs are to be safety hatched, but context is this other sort of
connectedness incongruously spanning times and juxtaposing spaces so far
apart and so different to each other." Context has to become contextured.

To have observed that the Other is anthropology's uncanny is both a
revealing and a misleading metaphor. If it reveals a fear or even an aver-
sion, it also misleads one into thinking that the Other is no more than
a projection of one's fears, which then ought to be cured by one's
"understanding" of one's self. Quite apart from the narcissism of the "truth
and method" involved in arriving at such a solution, it restores the illusion of an identity of coherence, an organic wholeness. The solution is
Hegelian, except that the *Geist* is individualized, and Hegel's philosophical imperialism is replaced by Freud's psychoanalytic one. In short, it
proffers an at-one-ment that denies its inherently hyphenated condition. The Hegelian riddle remains, the Other that resists reconciliation
remains, and so does the self that fails to reconcile. But none—neither
anthropologist nor informant, neither anthropology nor literary study—is
left out with identity intact. What of the hermeneutic hope wherein horizons of understanding merge in ever-expanding hermeneutic circles, purportedly in nonhierarchical patterns? This is perhaps where feminism's
contribution to poststructuralism is most apposite: identities, including
anthropology's and literary study's, are not sites of conjunction and concordance but sites of "multiple disjunctions that demand politicization
on the one hand as well as unities that enable life on the other" (Connolly
1991: 163). Two fine examples in this regard—and there are several

more—are Abu-Lughod's *Veiled Sentiments* (1986) and Behar's *Translated Woman* (1992).

JEFFREY M. PECK: FROM A LITERARY CRITIC/GERMANIST'S POINT OF VIEW: ANTHROPOLOGY

From anthropology, at least in its more reflexive form as practiced by Clifford Geertz, Paul Rabinow, Vincent Crapanzano, and others, we literary critics have learned to anthropologize our field, to ask questions about the way meanings are constructed under disciplinary conditions, and to reflect on our "situatedness." My own field, German, as part of the broader discipline of (foreign) literary studies, was always doubly predisposed (although unconsciously) to cultivate anthropological sensibilities. First, the principal task of a German department was to teach German language and literature. This is correspondingly true of any foreign language department. To German departments, culture was a concern, primarily in the form of *Kultur,* which was invoked, tacitly or otherwise, only to underwrite the importance of Germany's (and German's) intellectual and cultural contributions to Western civilization. Consigned to be mere background or context, the study of culture could be an attendant issue whose presence could enlighten the literary work or author but rarely be a subject in its own right. When culture is discussed in foreign language departments, it is subordinated to the more important and central work of the discipline, namely, literary interpretation or criticism. While German *Kultur* or French *civilisation* expanded a narrow notion of literature and its "criticism," it likewise collapsed two national (and competing) variations on culture under a generic concept.[14]

Second, foreign language departments in American universities are dominated by English departments. Because of their sheer size, status, and power, English departments have always represented, de facto, a hegemonic archdiscipline that incorporated all academic practices focusing on the literary text and the activities surrounding it, such as theory and pedagogy. Institutional, historical, and national factors have determined that English dominates literary criticism. It is easy to understand why many of those in English departments located in English-speaking countries come to assume that their relationship to English as a discipline is unproblematic and transparent. Entrenched discursive practices repress the problematization of their own ethnocentric position vis-à-vis the teaching of English or American literature, much less their responsibility to teach "culture." American studies, which has often had a very uneasy position in English departments, is the exception. But its interdisciplinary nature opened its practitioners to charges of dilettantism and superficiality. In Europe, however, American studies flourishes as the main vehicle for transmitting "American Culture" to the Dutch, Germans, and Scandinavians, as well as to the Eastern and Southern Europeans. A large and growing body of writing in English coming from Africa and South Asia is accommodated in some English departments under the rubric "Third World Literatures," in England under "Commonwealth Literatures," or in some universities in departments and programs of comparative literature. With the surge of social and political criticism in the eighties, the breakdown of the canon, and the exposure of white, Western, male, and heterosexist authority, English departments began to open up to "foreign" literatures and cultures (Native American, Afro-American, Latino, gay and lesbian literature) and to the different languages of popular culture (advertising, political pamphlets and speeches, newspapers and television), accommodating thereby a new subfield called "cultural studies." But they all remained under the privileged eye and authority of a dominant academic English (department) culture. And when and where the notion of "literary study" was redefined under these pressures, traditional critical activities in English moved toward appropriating the concerns and even the texts of foreign languages and literatures to the extent that they could—which, alas, has remained quite inadequate.

Thus it was left to foreign language and literature departments to make more out of their "foreignness." Some, however, chose to do so in ways that were not always the most productive. In German, an orientation called *Landeskunde* (the study of the country) focusing on general cultural background, including everyday popular cultural forms, rituals, and customs, was counterpoised to *Kultur*. Its demise was in part linked to its old-fashioned uncritically affirmative approach toward anything German that was signified by the antiquarian German term used to designate this field. In French the more worldly *civilisation* was used to describe the same activity. Cultural study as mere presentation and glorification of a country's grand memories and masterpieces gave way to more reflexive and critical approaches. It was often those in foreign language methodology (e.g., Claire Kramsch)[15] who addressed "cultural discourse" in more sophisticated ways. Those analyzing minority literatures as oppositional positions in their respective national cultures also made more out of the positive "alienation effect" of teaching a language, literature, and culture in a foreign environment. A special 1989 issue of the unique journal *New German Critique* was devoted to "Minorities in German Culture" and was edited, not surprisingly, by a Turkish, an Asian-American, and a Jewish Germanist.

Teaching German, French, or Hindi literature or culture in America was simply not the same thing as doing this in Germany, France, or India. The teaching of foreign languages (applied linguistics, as it is officially called) does not receive the respect that it deserves as the pragmatics of teaching grammar, reading, and writing is often subordinated to communicative competence (much like rhetoric and composition in English). Similarly, where literature and culture are concerned, those working on minorities, ethnic groups, and the oppressed and dislocated are often not taken seriously or are viewed as wasting their literary talents on second-rate literature or "interesting" yet "minor" subjects. The transmission of *Kultur* has remained the monopoly of those who taught the literature of Germany. While there are scattered academicians in foreign language and literature departments who take the "noncanonical" seriously, these departments still have not made a commitment to cultural study of a kind that combines the best of contemporary theory and what they themselves already know and experience from living, writing, and teaching about "other" cultures and peoples. In short, they have not made enough of the "foreign" and its anthropological and ethnographic relevance for the work that they have always been doing without reflecting on its dual nature (see Peck 1992).

Thus literary study, especially in the teaching of foreign language and literature, already has an anthropological component. It merely needs to be joined with the intellectual, theoretical, and cultural apparatus that anthropology has already conceptualized more deeply. To this one must add that the misconception among many in literature of anthropology as a field endowed with an undifferentiated and unproblematic notion of culture, on the one hand, and a single-sighted view of literature as only an aesthetic creation, on the other, offered little appreciation of an immensely problematized concept of culture and its representation in textual form.

Today anthropologists and literary types, joined by sociologists, political scientists, art historians, and scattered others, find themselves asking similar questions about culture and its many representations and are not satisfied by the answers provided for by their disciplinary paradigms. One of the consequences of this engaged encounter has been the creation of the field known as cultural studies, a field disdained by some members of both our professions and by others in the humanities and the social sciences. For the one side it is too hard; for the other, too soft. In between cohere (and at times incohere) intellectual interests that resist the hemming in by traditional disciplinary boundaries. For literary study, the clearing made by cultural studies has been a welcome one. And in this clearing our encounter with anthropology has been an exceptionally felicitous one. "Classics" such as James Clifford and George Marcus's *Writing Culture* and Marcus and Michael M. J. Fischer's *Anthropology as Cultural Critique* have significantly affected literary study's regard of itself. But some feminists have argued that in the advocacy of self-reflection these "classics" have slighted the existence of an entire tradition of reflexive ethnographies written by women. The more recent *Modernist Anthropology* by Eva Manganaro and numerous essays by feminist anthropologists are a partial corrective to this blindness.

For this American Germanist and literary critic, professional identities, institutional affiliations, and national traditions have become the dominating tropes for defining disciplinary attachments. The history of literary study, in fact, is an account of not only how language and literature departments emerged in the last quarter of the nineteenth century but also Germany's influence on this evolution. The German university's rigorous scholarly tradition and research methods as well as philology were transported to the United States as colleges and universities were established. In an attempt to legitimize the teaching of modern literatures, philology became the uneasy standard-bearer, "satisf[ying] the nostalgia for the past, especially for the European past and the Middle Ages, and at the same time the desire for facts, for accuracy, for the imitation of the 'scientific method' which had acquired such overwhelming prestige." Philology was a "worthy ideal . . . conceived of as a total science of civilization, an ideal originally formulated for the study of classical antiquity and then transferred by the German romanticists to the modern languages" (René Wellek, cited in Graff 1987: 68–69).

For philologists like the German Max Müller, a Sanskrit scholar and the first German philologist to be appointed at Oxford, "the study of linguistic roots demonstrated the unity of 'all Indo-European nations,' proving their membership in a 'great Aryan brotherhood'" (ibid., 69). Other respected philologists joined in the debate, which ultimately came to be about theories of race and national character. Franz Bopp, Joachim Boeckh, Wilhelm and Jacob Grimm, and Hippolyte Taine and Matthew Arnold were notable. Arnold, who became the standard-bearer for "high culture," was particularly interested in questions of national cultural identity, especially between the "Teutonic" and the "Celtic." Gerald Graff (ibid., 71) correctly concludes from these points, "One cannot minimize the importance of these theories of 'race' in the formation of language and literature departments in the 1880s. . . . The very decision to divide the new language and literature departments along national lines was an implicit assertion of pride in 'the English speaking race.'" Ultimately German dominance in philological scholarship was attacked for racial and nationalistic reasons. These hostilities were spawned by the increasing political tensions between England and Germany that would culminate in World War I. Ironically, it was England's colonial advances over Germany that drew would-be anthropologists, colonial officers, missionaries, and travelers to explore these unsurveyed territories and contributed to the professionalization of anthropology at the end of the nineteenth century and in the early decades of the twentieth century. Literature (at approximately the same time as anthropology) had been established as a credible academic field, but at the cost of nationalizing the discipline and of situating literature in a field identified with language and philological study, with an almost exclusive focus on literature.

Nowhere is this process to be seen more clearly than in the development of "comparative literature." Proclaimed as an advance in literary study that would encompass all of world literature by breaking down national boundaries, it often reinscribed national borders all the more forcefully by insisting its practitioners literally "compare" themes, characters, or authors in more than one national literature. However, it was in comparative literature where those in the various foreign language and literature departments could be exposed to Continental theory transported from the very national literatures whose uniqueness this field was intended to subvert. German hermeneutics via Dilthey and Gadamer and French semiotics and structuralism via de Saussure, Lévi-Strauss, and later Barthes had a crucial influence by introducing unfamiliar national traditions. For example, Schlegel, Heidegger, and, above all, Nietzsche became stock figures in French theory, ultimately producing "the new Nietzsche." Comparing literatures metamorphosed into comparing or applying theory on an international level. The constant crossing of national boundaries, first with literature and then with theory, also set the stage for a comparative cultural approach much more akin to anthropology than the practices of national literature fields. The foreign countries and international contexts through which comparativists traveled to situate their more theoretically informed readings could not but divert their attention to experiencing anthropological "otherness." It is not surprising that "comparative literature," the discipline that once represented reformist notions of literary study, has become a popular site for "cultural studies," the newest transformation of the discipline. Whereas comparative literature may be a site through which cultural studies has blown in as a new wind, cultural studies itself has received much of its challenges and inspiration from what we may call the hyphenated departments, programs, and fields such as Afro-American studies, Latino studies, Native American studies, and Asian-American studies. These are driven by a defiant spirit, which, unlike the one that inheres in the heart of the established departments of comparative literature, does not genuflect, tacitly or otherwise, before Eurocentric—even if not European—canons. It is such academic environments that insist that we turn our attention to multiculturalism while striving to resists its normalization. In this respect, cultural studies' greatest advantage is precisely this heterogeneity. Cultural studies is also opening up intellectual discourse to the social sciences, especially anthropology, whose concern with cultures and texts goes beyond only the "literary," engendering equally transgressive border crossings between national/ethnic as well as disciplinary divides.

Professional identities, whether Germanist, literary critic, or anthropologist, are constituted by a whole range of criteria, and naming itself is symptomatic. If a practitioner of anthropology is asked about what she or he does, the answer is usually "I am an anthropologist," and to this designation a subfield is added, cultural, social, biological, linguistic, archaeological, then a specific region, South Asia, Africa, or even Europe, and finally a particular theoretical orientation or specialization may be given, for example, economic anthropology or feminism. In literary studies, however, the response is not so straightforward. While one may have these same categories of subject, field, region, and theory, the definition of what one is based on what one does is not so clear. Today at American universities, those in departments of English, German, or Japanese are a mixture of philologists, literary critics, cultural critics, discourse analysts, and theoreticians. In short, our object of study is not necessarily literature, although the language is used for the naming of such departments and marks a relationship between language and literature that, as I showed, goes back to the discipline's professional roots.

Traditionally it was thought that anthropologists study anthropology, the cultures and nature of man [*sic*], and then write ethnographies describing, analyzing, and evaluating their observations and experience. Literary critics criticize, evaluate, and interpret literature. The distinction seemed simple and clear. Anthropologists traveled to another culture, practiced their requisite fieldwork for one or two years, came back to their home country, and "wrote up" their obligatory ethnography. The literary critic, the practitioner of literary study, or the professor of literature (the terms get increasingly tangled, as we strive to describe ourselves) might well go to another country to learn a different language and observe that culture, but she or he would only do so to enlighten the literary text, to enhance its context of understanding. Roughly stated, the anthropologist studies culture in order to write a text, whereas the critic studies the text in order to understand the culture. Before interpretive ethnography, the text was primarily a means of describing or explaining another culture; in literature, the critic concentrated on the *text* itself. The literary critic was not a writer but a critic of texts. At least as far as text-making went, the product of the literary critic was of a second order compared to the first-order products of the anthropologist. In the 1970s, drawing from the hermeneutic tradition (especially from Ricoeur's key essay "The Model of the Text"), Geertz and others began reading culture as text. The influence of poststructuralist revisions on what constituted the "literary text" came to have a telling effect on both fields. These rather parallel shifts that moved the respective disciplines toward each other and away from conventional notions of culture and text were decisive for both.

Poststructuralism and its insistence on textuality and feminism, its preoccupation with patriarchy and logocentrism and minority discourse/ ethnic studies, and its attention to power, authority, and hierarchies turned the activity of those who were trained in the literary disciplines into a revitalized project. It focused on what the anthropologically informed linguist A. L. Becker has called "text-building," rather than merely the translation, close reading, or criticism of the words in the literary text. While we have moved away from one aspect of philology, we have also drawn closer to its insistence on making broad cultural generalizations. This type of philologist, like the well-known collector of fairy tales, Jacob Grimm, hoped to draw together law, history, and literature; contemporary practitioners of literary study are likewise looking beyond literature to events, visual and cinematic representations, and written documents in their broadest sense, the "literary" being only one of many. They are interested in how the text is embedded in a political, social, and gendered network of relations that cannot be explained within a single disciplinary paradigm. Institutional and disciplinary history of the kind Foucault developed and more attention to pedagogy and the history and status of learning round out the field of literary study that understands itself as a dynamic and participatory activity rather than just a one-sided application of analytical methods to a literary work of art. From this constellation emerged a notion of literary study that instead of merely focusing on the text, as product of an authorial and authoritative subjectivity, encompassed an entire field of discourses that constituted meanings around and in the (literary) text. Once a disciplinary field of "literary study" freed literature from the constraints of criticism, it was opened to attend to the issue of culture that, at least in the foreign languages and literatures, was always present but never systematically addressed.

I have returned to the central concepts—culture and text—that I have designated as marking the shift and transformation of anthropology and literary study. Literary critics searching for alternatives to the exclusivity of high culture and its own canonized products were able to exploit the legitimacy, however disputed, of the discipline, however uncodified—which was in the "culture business." Culture became, in fact, an insignia for those in literary study who wanted not only to move beyond the literary text but also to make a place for counterhegemonic concerns and in many cases to translate their theoretical reflections into social or political practice expressed in feminism, minority and ethnic studies, pedagogy, and classroom practice. They were seeking, I think, access and connection to the clichéd "real world" of the anthropologist that she or he lived in and wrote about. In those areas that had at least traditionally been associated with civilization, gentility, and refinement, many in literature wanted to get their hands dirty in the field, at least metaphorically or vicariously, through their engagement with topics that would, especially in the isolated environment of the American university, bring them into the world. Although no anthropologists were advising the president (unlike "harder" social scientists such as economists and political scientists), there were public and political policy implications for what they were doing. Not blind to their own complicity in hegemony over the so-called primitives, or Third World, their work still concerned the oppressed, the displaced, and the less fortunate, as well as the urban, the corporate, and the well-to-do. In other words, they interacted with their subjects in ways that literary critics could only manage through contacts with writers, again one step removed from actual lived experience.

However, the work of the literary critic could approach the anthropologist's. The writing of the literary critic was elevated to a first-order exercise by theorizing rather than criticizing and by focusing on the operations, discourses, and practices producing cultural artifacts, literature as well as others. Once this shift took place, the practitioner of literary and cultural studies could achieve what the anthropologist had already achieved when culture was transformed into text. Thus textuality and the potential to textualize or read all situations as a text made it possible for anthropologists and cultural critics to meet in the same cultural domain, albeit using different resources and methods. Subjects such as the construction of national identity or gender, the representation of the subaltern, or the narrativity of states, societies, and selves engage both disciplines and establish the basis for a more productive and constructive notion of interdisciplinary study.

The invocation of the catchword "interdisciplinary" is a call to rethink the relationship of disciplines in light of the powerful and provocative influence of anthropology on literature, rhetoric and composition, (ethno)musicology, medicine, and law. But unlike those who would characterize interdisciplinary study as merely an assemblage of scholars from different fields around a particular subject, I would agree with Geertz's notion of "a third culture" (Olson and Gale 1991) or, in Barthes's words, "an object that belongs to no one" (Clifford and Marcus 1986: 1). When interpretive anthropologists redefine culture and literary critics reconceptualize text/textuality, a new version of interdisciplinarity emerges. This orientation recognizes how educating oneself in the rituals, discourses, and general habitus of a "foreign" discipline leads to a kind of boundary crossing that excludes neither the academic and disciplinary cultures that one has "grown up in" nor the influence of the one that has been newly introduced. Learning the ways of the anthropologist, the literary critic does not abrogate his or her disciplinary tenets but creates, as Geertz and Barthes suggest, a new scholarly domain in between the disciplines where collaborative work representing multiple voices can take place. If the polyvocality or heteroglossia of the cultural text is really a goal that we in cultural studies have in mind, representing a positioned and self-reflexive dialogic, between us and them, then collaborative writing, research, and publication, as we have in this volume, is a mainstay of such interdisciplinary work.

E. VALENTINE DANIEL AND JEFFREY M. PECK: THE CONTRIBUTIONS

In the opening essay, the anthropologist Paul Friedrich—as does Marilyn Ivy in a later essay—explicitly stakes his position in relation to literature. Be-

yond showing us that poetry is impacted with culture and culture with poetry, he employs poetry to argue against the "cryptopositivism"[16] of scientific
ideology that persists in anthropology. This argumentation is possible only
if we are willing to recognize that culture, like poetry—to quote Frost once
more—is but a "momentary stay against confusion" and not something that
can be fixed by positivist conceit or, we might add, by an essentializing discipline. Thereby, Friedrich's rejoinder "What good is anthropology?" to the
"cynical question" What good is poetry? begins to make sense. Moreover, according to Friedrich, it is this "scientific ideology that combines a tolerance
or feigned enthusiasm for the turn to poetry and other literary models (including performance anthropology) with the practice, particularly in dicta
and dogma for graduate students, that in effect rules out not only poetry but
bridges between poetry/poetics and anthropology that should yield enormous insight."

Friedrich indicts the scientific ideology for being reductionist. Reductionism, however, is not the insignia of the natural sciences alone but characterizes the practices of the human and social sciences as well. The
propensity to reduce finds its expression in the will to define. Thus we are
called on to define our disciplines and even our departmental boundaries.
Photographics, no less than analytics, constitute our understanding of definition. In Friedrich's call to turn our ear to the poetic, we find a sobering
reminder that the study of human life can neither be tamed by nor reduced
to enlightening definition; the field is lit also with sound.

In reading the essays of Friedrich, Trawick, Dan Rose, and Mary Layoun,
it is imperative to be attentive to the polysemy of "the field." The field is not
merely a place where a certain kind of "work" called ethnography is carried
out, nor is it only an area or branch of knowledge, be it anthropology or literary study. These authors also "field" questions and answers and, like good
cricketers, cannot afford to drop too many. Then there is the "field" of vision, a purview that is implicated in their methods, and beyond that a "field"
as a compass that sets limits to the expenditure of their symbolic capital—
as an American woman talking with a Greek-Cypriot refugee, or a white
woman mingling among peripatetic Jackal Hunters in South India, or an academic interviewing CEOs. And yes, a field-worker is *tethered* as much to
fields of knowledge as he or she is to class, race, and gender.

Race and class figure importantly in Trawick's and Rose's chapters, which
take the form of storytelling. The average literary critic who expects an
ethnography to be explicitly analytic, much like an essay of literary criticism,
may find these two anthropologists' essays somewhat disconcerting. Such a
critic has trouble even seeing how the recounting of the story so central to
the ethnography—what Rose calls narrative-digressive ethnographies—constitutes in itself the anthropological product and project. When scholarly expectations and standards are at stake, the literary critic may analyze stories,

but she does not write them. For the anthropologist, however, Trawick's narrative is fraught with an analytic point, that of self-reflexivity and inescapable irony. Hers is a story of a quest for *the* origin myth of the Jackal Hunters. Her quest reaches its end when she is finally told that the *authoritative* version of the myth was to be found in a little black box belonging to a young white man who had captured the story from the Jackal Hunters two years earlier. The young man in question turns out to be one of Trawick's own students and the little box, the field-worker's tape recorder. Rose and Trawick indicate by their stories and their own storytelling how the cultures of anthropology and literary study still differ regarding the freedom to construct stories appropriate to a subject matter.

In these two and several other chapters in this volume, the interview presents itself as the meeting point for scholar and informant, as well as anthropologist and literary critic. In the best of all possible worlds, a world that until recently some anthropologists had come to believe was attainable, the presence of a genuine dialogic was invoked as the determinant of a successful interview. Such a moment was seen as one in which the interview yielded to a well-rhythmed conversation of a give-and-take and hermeneutic depth. More recently, we have come to realize that the ethnographic interview, however dialogically ameliorated, is laden with power differentials. This is brought out from opposite ends of empowerment by Trawick, on the one hand, and Rose, on the other: Rose attempts to break up into power, and Trawick attempts to break down the anthropologist's own powerfulness to escape his or her power-stricken condition.

If Trawick and Rose are attentive to how a "good story" ought to be told by the anthropologist, Mary Layoun, a professor of comparative literature, and John Borneman, an anthropologist, attend to the manner in which the informant painstakingly constructs his or her story and appropriates narrative authority. Any narrative, whether that of the scholar or that of the informant, is subject to multiple readings and therefore brings with it its own set of problems and possibilities. A narrator who is sensitive to the formation of her own authority has an interest in proliferating and yet taming these multiple readings. In Layoun's words, her narrator "does not simply attempt to direct the reception of [a] narrative but to generate other narratives for which hers might provide a suggestive story and style." This is a fine and important point that ought to compel the attention of every ethnographer. Trained in Greek, Arabic, and Japanese, Layoun represents the potential of comparative studies (literary or anthropological) to set off difference, whether in national or disciplinary contexts, and for moving between these differences. Layoun exemplifies not merely the manner of moving between novels and interviews but also the deft back-and-forth movement over narrative and generic borders.

In her chapter, Susan Stewart offers a radical extension to the meaning of that unique kind of movement which we call travel, urging us to consider writing itself as a form of travel. She takes a text about travel clearly marked as literary—Hawthorne's *Marble Faun*—and interprets it so as to remind us that the "travel experience, in its endless search for meaning, must also be without irrevocable meaning—it must find a meaning in time, the very meaning of time implicit in such ideas of flight, escape, search, transgression, and reparation alternately at the center of travel narrative." In a poststructuralist reading, the travel narrative becomes an archetypal genre for Derridean deferral. Stewart invites us to see in travel writing forces that correspond to the ones that generate the key cultural impulse, the incest taboo. The marrying out in exogamy, with all its fears and desires, finds its analogue in the writing out in travel.

If Stewart reminds us that travel writing "offers us . . . a view too low to be transcendent and too high to be in the scene," ethnography strives to be low enough to be in the scene and high enough to transcend the chaos of particulars. Stewart's opening gambit—her invoking of Lévi-Strauss—is apposite. For not only were Lévi-Strauss's *Tristes Tropiques* and *Elementary Structures of Kinship* the two texts that drew literary attention to anthropology in the first instance and to the French theoretical scene more generally since then, they also helped catalyze a reaction against the degree of transcendence French structuralism offered over the field and raised questions regarding the inadequacy of "thick description"—to draw on an expression of Gilbert Ryle made famous by Geertz—that structuralist ethnographies allowed. One of those who articulated this reaction with the kind of suavity that was capable of catching the eye and ear of the English literary critic—for a second time within a decade—was Geertz, whose own boundary-crossing writing, criticism, and analysis made the exchange between anthropology and literature easier than it had ever been. We have chosen to end Part I with his essay "The World in a Text: How to Read *Tristes Tropiques*" from his recent *Works and Lives: The Anthropologist as Author,* not in order to let Geertz have the last word but to remind the reader that Lévi-Strauss's multilayered corpus—part myth, part history, part ethnography, and above all, as Geertz displays for us, dazzlingly literary—had already tilled the field and blurred the genres. And while Geertz's reading of Lévi-Strauss shows us how "the world in a text" creates an anthropologist as author (in itself a modernist enterprise), it behooves us to read this reading against Stewart's poststructuralist reflections on the master narrative of structuralism as well as the master narrator, the "founder" of modern structuralism.

The authorial voice aside, what of the relationship of ethnography to autobiography? From those who wish to hold, either sympathetically or otherwise, that the two genres are identical, we would, as intimated earlier, like to declare our distance. But there are similarities, at least two of which merit mention. First, Azade Seyhan, quoting Eakin, has this to say about autobiography: "The writing of autobiography is a second acquisition of language, a second coming into being of self, a self-consciousness." The writing of autobiography is not only a second but a multiple acquisition of language. In their conventional wisdom, the purists among anthropologists have insisted that the acquisition of a second language (in its widest sense) is also the first and most important step in doing ethnography. That this ideal is only infrequently met and that language ends as being more a tool to be used than a world to be entered into is unfortunate. The myth of the ethnographer going native, becoming those of whom she writes, may be just that, only a myth. But even if the acquisition of a field language need not be the same as "going native," the writing of an ethnography resulting from field experience ought to mark a new "coming into being of self, a self-consciousness" analogous to that which happens in autobiography. It is to this extent, then, that ethnography and autobiography are similar. Second, both autobiography and ethnography are translations/interpretations, and to that extent they deserve parallel meditations. Of autobiographies, Seyhan writes, "The personal narrative is no longer seen as an accurate record of a life lived, but as the text of a life constituted in writing and interpretation." Culture and biography are jointly thrown into clearest relief when autobiographies are written by immigrants, exiles, and refugees, where this genre and this experience are best summed up in the title of the Polish-Canadian émigré Eva Hoffman's novel *Lost in Translation: A Life in a New Language.* Translation is the literal metaphor for the experience of re-creating "self, space, and genealogy." The North American landscape is a terrain where these transformations are appropriately captured in their incompletion in that each of the immigrants (or children of immigrants) Seyhan discusses—Hoffman, Nicholas Gage, Richard Rodriguez, Maxine Hong Kingston, Amy Tan, and Oscar Hijuelos—are here, more than anywhere, hyphenated identities. Their conflicting worlds are bridged by the mark that gives them double selves, and the act of writing itself becomes the hyphen writ large, an attempt to come to terms with origins, pasts, and ancestors in a context that promotes their opposites.

The discourse of Seyhan, Arlene Teraoka, and Zita Nunes may be more familiar to those of us who are addressing the writing of texts emerging from within specific national traditions. Their work concerns the formation and dislocation of identities and the dialectic between these moves for both ordering/universalizing and dismembering those unities by disjunction and displacement. For Nunes, the place is Brazil, and she sees that country's literature trying to resolve the "problem" of miscegenation that was seen to threaten totalizing notions of purity and homogeneity. In short, questions of a universal white subject were difficult to maintain and sustain in a land filled with so many "mixed peoples." Brazil becomes a model for analyzing the assumptions of biology and racism and the construction of national identity.

Teraoka reminds us that Europeans have not done much better in resolving ethnic and national identity problems than have the Americans. Her focus is on the Turks in Germany. The exposé of Turkish-German conflicts based on the guest workers' anomalous situation in a country that essentially does not want them is by now commonplace. In her analysis of the ethnographic novels of Paul Geiersbach, Teraoka is concerned with a less-studied boundary crossing: the transgressions of a German ethnographer into the lives of Turks living in Germany. The tensions exist for her not only between the citizens and their invited "guests" but, more important for her, between the German ethnographer and his Turkish subjects as he tries, as any good ethnographer, to re-present his experiences living among them. The Turks speak back, and the construction of the Other is subjugated to the formation of his Self. Teraoka uses Geiersbach's mixed genre to illustrate many of the central concerns of interpretive ethnography today—narrative, representation, otherness—and adds the particularities of a German ethnographer's own brand of foreignness in a Turkish ghetto located in his own country. Teraoka embeds her analysis in a multitiered narrative of (even violent) demands and resistance of ethnographer as well as German, object as well as Turk. Like Trawick, Teraoka's German sociologist explodes the illusion of power-neutral context of fieldwork and representation. Borneman, like Layoun, uses stories in the form of interviews, exploiting this undervalued anthropological-literary genre to explicate complicated political relations constituting state and identity formation. In both cases, being Greek in Cyprus and Jewish in East Germany, genealogies and the incumbent historical process of constructing stories reinforce kinships necessary for survival. Whereas Layoun moves between novels and interviews, Borneman moves between theory and interviews. Borneman is concerned with the impact of hermeneutics, narrative theory, and the problem of representation on the ethnographical analysis of self and state. Following Hayden White, Louis Mink, and other narratologists, Borneman claims that narrative is " 'a primary and irreducible form of human comprehension,' an article in the constitution of common sense which fashions diverse experiences into a form assimilable to structures of meaning that are human rather than culture-specific."

Borneman's and especially Layoun's orientation draw attention to those whose identities are constructed and complicated by power relations of conflicting ideologies and interests, nationally, ethnically, religiously, and, of course, racially. Refugees, immigrants, and exiles are perhaps the most obvious and persuasive example—revealed on their persons and at the sites of cultural confrontation—where identities collide and are often oppressed. In taking up the issues of "minority discourse," the chapters of David Lloyd and Nunes, as well as Teraoka and Seyhan, remind us how the politics of identity draw anthropology and literary study even closer together. In these essays we find a response to Renato Rosaldo's call (1989) for ways in which we ought to shift our attention to such "borderlands" for expressive genres and voices that escape the Eurocentric ear and eye. Gloria Anzaldua's *Borderlands* is such a work in which autobiography, historiography, theory, and poetry combine to constitute what Behar calls "a new genre of personal ethnography."[17]

Lloyd's contribution makes us aware of the magnitude of the role that the master trope, the metaphor, plays in the making of our worlds. Thanks to the pioneering writings of Max Black, Thomas Kuhn, Paul Ricoeur, and others, we now know that metaphoric constructions are no less an integral part of science than of art. In effect, we may say that we are condemned to metaphor. What Lloyd does show us, however, is how we can go about making the best of such a condition, namely, to critique metaphor in each of its manifestations. He shows that metaphors assimilate in terms that may be aesthetic but also ethnocentric and are, therefore, excluding in their effects. This exclusionary aesthetic as well as teleology is most clearly brought out by Nunes's discussion of miscegenation as portrayed in Brazilian literature, which attempts to forge a Brazilian national identity as a cultural one in the same move. Miscegenation is a metaphor that has failed, "a perpetuation of a sickness." A "successful" metaphorization incorporates the Other by a method that is best described as "cannibalistic"—swallow and absorb what is useful and excrete what is not: the indigenous, the primitive, the black— but is in fact gnawed by its own inner disease, "a perpetuation of a sickness," a failure hidebound with its success.

In this regard it is worth noting not only the inadequacy of (metaphoric) representation but also, as Lloyd argues, the perniciousness and the power in this dominant form of representation that is still with us and that finds its roots in the "aesthetic culture" of eighteenth-century Europe. By means of an intellectual journey from Kant and Schiller and then to Freud, developing what he calls a "phenomenology of racism," Lloyd maintains that "crucial to this function of aesthetic culture is its formulation and development of a *narrative of representation,* by which is meant not only the representative narratives of canonical culture but also the narrative form taken by the concept of representation itself." He goes on to show how "within this narrative the same processes of formalization occur at every level, allowing a series of transferred identifications to take place from individual to nation, and from nation to the idea of a universal humanity. By the same token, the fissures and contradictions that trouble this narrative are replicated equally at every level or in every situation that it informs." For anthropologists, there is much to be learned about race from this unusually literate chapter. But this chapter also provides us with a beginning for a better understanding of the collusion of aesthetics, ethics, and logic in what we have called "identity markings" more generally, of which race is but a particular manifestation.

The final part of this collection, entitled "Troubling Texts," is introduced by Nicholas Dirks's chapter, "Reading Culture." Dirks's transfiguration of the title of Clifford and Marcus's widely read book *Writing Culture* into his own essay's title is serious play. As a practicing historian and anthropologist, he exhorts us "to read contexts as texts, even as we set out to read texts in terms of context." The anthropologist who hopes to "find" the "real" in context is also one who fetishizes "fieldwork." If one were to allow oneself a slip from the Marxian to the psychoanalytic sense of fetishism, one may ask the further question, What fears does this fetish conceal? What are the pretexts that the (con)texts hide? To pose the question in this manner is to open up a genealogy of representations that does not reach an "objective" end. For Dirks, the footnote is the key to the door that opens onto the vistas of pretexts and subtexts within which culture as text and texts on culture ought to be read. In contemporary South Asia, Thurston is such a footnote. As long as we continue to read South Asian culture and its texts—especially indological and ethnographic texts—without unlocking their major "footnotes," we read but in presentism's twilight and shadows.

His Majesty's civil servant and lay ethnographer, Thurston, who was bequeathed by his time and place the stylus and slate for inscribing a master narrative, forms the centerpiece of Dirks's chapter. Unlike Dirks's man on the spot, Michael Taussig's historian-hero is "a very old, very black, very blind man named Tomás Zapata" who lived until his death in 1971 in a very small town in southwestern Columbia. Much of Zapata's history is told in verse and commentary that cannot help but perturb the academic historiographer's confidence. This historian-poet-philosopher, who had never spent a day in school, must be seen not as one who does history but as one who *is* history. Unlike the professional historian, who is empowered by the illusion of standing freely above history arrogating to himself the right to choke off meanderings that could lead him astray from such "fine-sounding goals as the search for 'meaning' or design," Don Tomás is both a sign of history and a sign in history, a medium through whom "flow and mix" and "flow and swerve," streams originating from Western canonical sources such as Pythogoras, on the one hand, and complicated accounts of local history, on the other, meet. The professional historian or ethnographer writes "about" the past or "about" a people. Their representational conceit is to be found in the kind of "aboutness" they engage in. It entails a view that some form of mental content (that of a trained subject) is directed toward an object—the past or a people. Zapata is engaged in a very different kind of "aboutness," a man "going about" being-in-the-world. The former is about a way of knowing the world; the latter concerns a way of being-in-the-world.[18]

As alluded to earlier, the collusion of literature with ethnography is an old, even if an uncanny, one. As Ivy shows us, this collusion was not limited to Europe but was a much more general phenomenon, extending even to Japan. Ivy describes this relationship between literature and ethnography (mainly in the form of folklore) as complicitous and ghostly; the more diligently we search for their definitional contours, the more blurred their objects become. The object in question is a culture and a tradition that, if not already absent, never in fact existed. Ivy points out that "the disappearance of the object—folk, community, authentic voice, tradition itself—is necessary for its ghostly appearance in an authoritatively rendered text. The 'object' does not exist outside its own disappearance." Faced with such evanescence in the imaginary and the diversity of dialects in the real, the Japanese folklorist Yanagita, encountering the modernist imperative, attempted to write the uncanny specificity of local differences within the emerging constraints of a singular national language. Anthropologists and literary critics have, in their own ways, been no less free of this modernist imperative to fix in a language—the language of science in the case of anthropology, the language of method in the case of literary criticism.

If, as Borneman would have it, the impulse to narrate is pancultural, even more salient are those moments of "cultural poesis" alluded to by Friedrich, the "dialectical images" of Benjamin, and "the uncultured excesses" referred to by Valentine Daniel, which defy the will to narrate and occupy the even denser interstices of human life than those amenable to narrative. Daniel finds the crisis of representation in the human sciences and the humanities becoming manifest in its starkest form in the context of violence. He begins his chapter by sketching the relationship between the two fields that claimed culture for their own, the anthropological concept of culture over against the humanistic Arnoldian view of culture. The former appeared to triumph over the latter in the rise of cultural studies' and literary study's turn to the underprivileged, the oppressed, or merely the "ordinary." But Daniel finds culture in either of its representational modes to be far too Hegelian, far too trusting of the "reasonable," and far too indulgent of "the art of complaisance"[19] to be able to provide us with the perspective we need to understand the violence in and of culture. For Daniel, culture's significant Other is its "counterpoint," which he identifies as the blind spot that posits itself at the center of cultural understanding and into which the excesses of passion and violence flow, outwitting the gentle forces of reason and the aesthetic imagination that constitute culture, the very forces that make literature, ethnography, and narrative possible.

In wrapping up our introduction and in handing over these chapters to you, the reader, how should we characterize our offering? What readily come to mind are variations of "interdisciplinarity," "collaborative efforts," "boundary crossings," or even the now almost picturesque "blurred genres," all of which we have referred to in this introduction. But instead, turning a splinter of colonial vocabulary against those who once used it to exclude and to hurt, we would like to call this collection a "métissage." In colonial discourse, a métise referred to the colonial category of "half-bloods." But as Ann Stoler has so vividly argued, it took the métissage of French Indochina and the Netherlands Indies to threaten and undermine a great many imperial divides. Like the métise of colonial Asia, the essays in this collection "converge in a grid of transgressions." In so doing, they seek not only to subvert "the terms of the civilizing mission" of disciplinary thoroughbreds—be they anthropology, literary study, or literary criticism—but to introduce "new measures of civility" that enable the recognition of the robust movement between word and world, a recognition that refuses to perpetuate a curbed liaison under the civil pretext of interdisciplinarity (Stoler 1992: 550–551).

NOTES

1. Our attention to the somewhat archaic word *contexture* and its rich connotations was directed by Geoffrey Hill's little gem, *The Enemy's Country: Words, Contexture, and Other Circumstances of Language* (1991).

2. Defined by Geoffrey Hill (1984: 2) as "a setting at one, a bringing into concord, a reconciling, a uniting in harmony."

3. Joannes Fabian (1983) was the first to make this point in a grand way.

4. I use "moral" here, not in the weak, Durkheimian sense, but in the strong sense where moral choices—and hard ones at that, for which there may be no precedents—are made. See Evens 1982.

5. For an extended treatment of this distinction, see Wartenberg 1990: chap. 9.

6. See Turner 1990 for an extended account of Victor Turner's founding interests.

7. In E. T. A. Hoffmann's *Nachtstücke*, we find that the feeling of something uncanny is associated with the figure of the Sandman, that is, with the idea of being relieved of one's eyes.

8. I thank Ruth Behar for turning my attention to the place of these two writers in the scheme of things and especially to the writings of the Latina writer, Gloria Anzaldua.

9. See Terada 1992.

10. Anzaldua 1987; also see Rosaldo 1989: 196–224.

11. For a collection of early essays on this theme, see Wilson 1970.

12. For an intelligent updating of these philosophical issues in anthropology, see Thomas McCarthy's review (1992).

13. For a clear distinction between de Saussure's semiology and Peirce's semiotic and the impossibility of translating one into the other's terms, see Deledalle 1979.

14. For a more detailed and analytical discussion of this now-infamous distinction between *Kultur* and *civilisation*, see chapter 1 in Elias (1976: 1–64).

15. As just one example of Kramsch's work, see "The Cultural Discourse of Foreign Language Textbooks," in Singerman 1988: 63–88.

16. See Paul Friedrich, "Interpretation and Vision: A Critique of Cryptopositivism." *Cultural Anthropology* 7, no. 2 (May 1992): 211–231.

17. In her comments on the work of Gloria Anzaldua and Marlon Riggs at the meeting of the American Ethnological Society in 1992.

18. For a lucid elaboration of this Heideggerian point, see Dreyfus 1991: 68–69, 92–96.

19. For one of the earliest and richest expositions of "the art of complaisance"—which still is such an integral part of both senses of "culture" employed by Daniel—see the handbooks on proper conduct appearing in the Early English Books Series (1641–1700), which bear the title *The Art of Complaisance, or, The Means to Oblige in Conversation* (S.C. 1677).

REFERENCES

Abu-Lughod, Lila.
    1986.   *Veiled Sentiments: Honor and Poetry in a Bedouin Society*. Berkeley, Los Angeles, and London: University of California Press.
Adorno, Theodore W.
    1973.   *Negative Dialectics*. Translated by E. B. Ashton. New York: Continuum.
Anzaldua, Gloria.
    1987.   *Borderlands/La Frontera: The New Mestiza*. San Francisco: Spinsters/Aunt Lute.
Becker, A. L.
    1989.   *Writing on the Tongue*. Ann Arbor: Center for South and Southeast Asian Studies.
Behar, Ruth.
    1992.   *Translated Woman: Crossing the Border with Esperanza's Story*. Boston: Beacon Press.
Bellour, Raymond.
    1971.   *Les Livres des autres*. Paris: L'Herne.
Brady, Ivan, ed.
    1991.   *Anthropological Poetics: Savage*. Maryland: Rowman & Littlefield.
Clifford, James, and Marcus, George, eds.
    1986.   *Writing Culture: The Poetics and Politics of Ethnography*. Berkeley, Los Angeles, and London: University of California Press.
Connolly, William E.
    1983.   "On Richard Rorty: Two Views." *Raritan* 3, no. 1 (Summer): 124–135.
    1991.   *Identity/Difference: Democratic Negotiations of Political Paradox*. Ithaca: Cornell University Press.
Daniel, E. Valentine.
    1985.   "A Crack in the Mirror: Reflexive Perspectives in Anthropology." *Urban Life* 14, no. 2 (July): 240–248.
Deledalle, Gerard.
    1979.   *Theorie et pratique du signe*. Paris: Payot.

Deloria, Ella.
   1988.   *Waterlily*. Lincoln: University of Nebraska Press.
Dirks, Nicholas.
   1993.   "Is Vice Versa? Historical Anthropologies and Anthropological His-
            tories." In *The Historic Turn in the Human Sciences,* ed. Terrence
            McDonald. Ann Arbor: University of Michigan Press.
Dreyfus, Herbert L.
   1991.   *Being-in-the-World: A Contemporary on Heidegger's Being and Time. Division
            I.* Cambridge: M.I.T. Press.
Elias, Norbert.
   1976.   *Über den Prozess der Zivilisation.* Vol. 1. Frankfurt: Suhrkamp.
Evans-Pritchard, E. E.
   [1950] 1962.   *Social Anthropology and Other Essays.* New York: Free Press.
Evens, T. M. S.
   1982.   "The Concept of Society as a Moral System." *Man* 17, no. 2 (June):
            205–218.
Fabian, Johannes.
   1983.   *Time and the Other: How Anthropology Makes Its Object.* New York: Colum-
            bia University Press.
Frazer, Sir James.
   1890.   *The Golden Bough.* London: Macmillan.
Geertz, Clifford.
   1983.   *Local Knowledge.* New York: Basic Books.
Ghosh, Amitav.
   1986.   *The Circle of Reason.* New Delhi: Ravi Dayal.
   1989.   *The Shadow Lines.* New Delhi: Ravi Dayal.
   1992.   *In an Antique Land.* New Delhi: Ravi Dayal.
Graff, Gerald.
   1987.   *Professing Literature: An Institutional History.* Chicago: University of
            Chicago Press.
Handler, Richard, and Daniel Segal.
   1990.   *Jane Austen and the Fiction of Culture.* Tucson: University of Arizona
            Press.
Hill, Geoffrey.
   1984.   *Lords of the Limit: Essays on Literature and Ideas.* London: Deutsch.
   1991.   *The Enemy's Country: Words, Contexture, and Other Circumstances of Lan-
            guage.* Stanford: Stanford University Press.
Hoffman, Ernst Theodor Amadeus.
   1985.   *Nachtstücke.* Frankfurt: Bibliothek Deutscher Klassiker.
Hoffman, Eva.
   1989.   *Lost in Translation: A Life in a New Language.* Princeton: Princeton Uni-
            versity Press.
Hurston, Zora Neale.
   1935.   *Mules and Men.* Philadelphia: J. B. Lippincott.
Johnson, Richard.
   1986–1987.   "What Is Cultural Studies Anyway?" *Social Text,* no. 16 (Winter):
                38–80.

Kristeva, Julia.
    1991.   *Strangers to Ourselves.* New York: Columbia University Press.
McCarthy, Thomas.
    1992.   "Doing the Right Thing in Cross-Cultural Representation." Review essay. *Ethics* (April): 635–649.
Malinowski, Bronislaw.
    1935.   *Coral Gardens and Their Magic.* 2 vols. London: Allen and Unwin.
Manganaro, Eva.
    1990.   *Modernist Anthropology: From Fieldwork to Text.* Princeton: Princeton University Press.
Marcus, George.
    1992.   "The Finding and Fashioning of Cultural Criticism in Ethnographic Research." In *The Politics of Culture and Creativity: A Critique of Civilization,* ed. Christine Ward Gailey, 77–101. Gainesville: University of Florida Press.
Marcus, George, and Michael M. J. Fischer.
    1992.   *Anthropology as Cultural Critique: An Experimental Moment in the Human Sciences.* Chicago: University of Chicago Press.
Narayan, Kirin.
    1994.   *Love, Stars, and All That.* New York: Pocket Books.
Olson, Gary A., and Irene Gale, eds.
    1991.   *Inter(views): Cross-Disciplinary Perspectives on Rhetoric and Literacy.* Carbondale: Southern Illinois University Press.
Peck, Jeffrey.
    1992.   "Toward a Cultural Hermeneutics of the 'Foreign' Language Classroom: Notes for a Critical and Political Pedagogy." *ADFL Bulletin* 23, no. 3 (Spring): 16–29.
Poirier, Richard.
    1992.   *The Performing Self.* New Brunswick: Rutgers University Press.
Pritchard, William.
    1980.   *Lives of the Modern Poets.* New York: Oxford University Press.
Ricoeur, Paul.
    1971.   "The Model of the Text: Meaningful Action Considered as a Text." *Social Research* 38: 529–562.
Rorty, Richard.
    1979.   *Philosophy and the Mirror of Nature.* Princeton: Princeton University Press.
Rosaldo, Renato.
    1989.   *Culture and Truth: The Remaking of Social Analysis.* Boston: Beacon Press.
Said, Edward.
    1989.   "Representing the Colonized: Anthropology's Interlocutors." *Critical Inquiry* 15 (2): 206–225.
S.C.
    1677.   *The Art of Complaisance, or The Means to Oblige Conversation.* London: Printed for John Starkeu. (Microfilm)
Seyhan, Azade, Arlene A. Teraoka, and Russell Berman, eds.
    1989.   *New German Critique,* no. 46 (Winter). Special issue "Minorities in German Culture."

Siegel, James.
1979.   *Shadow and Sound: The Historical Thought of a Sumatran People.* Chicago: University of Chicago Press.
Singer, Milton.
1978.   "For a Semiotic Anthropology." In *Sight, Sound, and Sense,* ed. Thomas Sebeok, 202–231. Bloomington: Indiana University Press.
Singerman, Alan, ed.
1988.   *Towards a New Integration of Language and Culture.* Middlebury, Conn.: Northeast Conference.
Stoler, Ann.
1992.   "Sexual Affronts and Racial Frontiers: European Identities and Cultural Politics of Exclusion in Colonial Southeast Asia." *Comparative Studies in Society and History* 34(3): 514–551.
Taussig, Michael.
1992.   *The Nervous System.* New York: Routledge.
Tedlock, Barbara.
1992.   *The Beautiful and the Dangerous: Encounters with the Zuni Indians.* New York: Viking Press.
Tedlock, Dennis.
1985.   *Popol Vuh: The Definitive Edition of the Mayan Book of the Dawn of Life and the Glories of Gods and Kings.* New York: Simon and Schuster.
Terada, R.
1992.   *Dennis Wolcott's Poetry.* Boston: Northeastern University Press.
Todorov, Tzvetan.
1985.   *The Conquest of America: The Question of the Other.* Translated by Richard Howard. New York: Harper and Row.
Turner, Edith.
1990.   "The Literary Roots of Victor Turner's Anthropology." In *Victor Turner and the Construction of Cultural Criticism: Between Literature and Anthropology,* ed. Kathleen M. Ashley, 163–169. Bloomington: Indiana University Press.
Tyler, Steven.
1986.   "Post-modern Ethnography: From Document of the Occult to Occult Document." In *Writing Culture: The Poetics and Politics of Ethnography,* ed. James Clifford and George Marcus, 120–146. Berkeley, Los Angeles, and London: University of California Press.
Wartenberg, Thomas E.
1990.   *The Forms of Power.* Philadelphia: Temple University Press.
Wilson, Bryan R.
1970.   *Rationality.* New York: Harper and Row.
Wittgenstein, Ludwig.
1923.   *Tractatus Logico-Philosophicus.* London: Kegan Paul.
1953.   *Philosophical Investigations.* Oxford: Blackwell.

PART ONE

Narrative Fields

ONE

The Culture in Poetry and the Poetry in Culture

Paul Friedrich

According to a view commonly held in Tu Fu's time, much of the Book of Songs, *the most ancient surviving corpus of Chinese poetry, consisted of songs and ballads which had been deliberately collected from among the peasantry by rulers who wished to determine the temper of their people.*

DAVID HAWKES

OPENING GAMBIT: PLATH'S "WORDS"

Axes
After whose stroke the wood rings,
And the echoes!
Echoes travelling
Off from the centre like horses.

The sap
Wells like tears, like the
Water striving
To re-establish its mirror
Over the rock

That drops and turns,
A white skull,
Eaten by weedy greens.
Years later I
Encounter them on the road—

Words dry and riderless,
The indefatigable hoof-taps.
While
From the bottom of the pool, fixed stars
Govern a life.

This rarely cited poem illustrates some decisive connections between poetry and culture. As we start into the poem, "axes" seems to allude to the craft or craftsmanship with which the poet is fashioning something from the

This essay is dedicated to the living memory of Paul Riesman.

37

wood of a living tree. The echoes traveling off like horses are the crafted words going out into the wood to make it ring and into the world to make people listen. The sap welling from the tree is an extension of this conceit, like the human tears of the poet-craftsman, from which there is a sudden association to the water of the female sources of this poet's work that tries, in the face of vicissitudes, to reestablish the order of a mirror before transmutation into the strength of a rock and then the morbid but also regenerating image of the greens, the poet growing into new paths. Years later, the poet, now far along the road of life, encounters her words and poems and their sound, an encounter of reading and remembering except that they are now dry and riderless, on their own on their tireless hooves. In a final shift, the poet is plunged into or even identified with a pool's depths, another dimension of water symbolism, whose stars, the same as those above, govern and control her life and verbal creativity.

We see that "Words" is integrated in many ways. To begin, the rings of the tree resonate with the centrifugal sound waves of the echoes and also with the equally centrifugal ripples of the water that tries "to reestablish itself." A second, similar geometry takes us through a half-dozen angles and directions: (1) the oblique downward movement of the axes; (2) the outward movement of the echoes; (3) the inward movement of the water; (4) the horizontal plane of the water itself; and then (5) its downward motion and the words going off centrifugally, or perhaps intersecting on a tangent with the vertical, up-down that connects the stars in the pool with the stars in the sky; and, last and most, (6) the way the entire poem is governed by the figure of a whirlpool or vortex.

Since we are talking about a poem and since poetry, by one definition, forefronts the phonic shape of the message, is partly about the music of the language (Wright 1986), we should note that the poem as a whole is keyed on *ae* sounds ("axes, sap, taps," etc.) and an equal tissue of sibilant/shibilant (*s*) sounds (often working with *k* sounds). The above is the beginning of a partial—subjectivist and formalist—interpretation; other approaches would yield other generalizations. The longer we look at this masterpiece, in fact, the more meanings, coherencies, and subtexts we will find, until the philistine reader is moved to ask, "Yes, but what *good* is poetry?"

"What good is poetry?" is a cynical question that, explicitly or implicitly, we are confronted with often enough. We *could* rejoin, I suppose, with, "What good is anthropology?"

A PRIVILEGED ENTRY TO CULTURE

Students of culture, like poets, are engaged in constructing a worldview, whether sudden insights into "the mind of primitive man" or the vision in *Leaves of Grass*, the nitty-gritty of a "linguaculture" or the piecemeal induction of matrifocality from the archaeological remains of twenty Pueblo households. In these and other instances, the objective is not only to get a worldview but to get inside a worldview, to construct texts of one's own that reveal maximum empathy and comprehension. When looked at this way, the poems or songs that one finds, particularly when they are generally known and instantly understood by people, can constitute an incredibly swift and sensitive entryway. Eskimo poems and songs that deal with seal hunting, or the realities of old age, or the vulnerability of the single woman, or one's embarrassment or fear of embarrassment at forgetting the words of one's song, all seem to provide in distillate form some of the deep concerns, values, attitudes, and symbols of individuals or even of the entire community; one is often given the gist of the culture in a way that would be difficult or impossible to infer. These insights and intuitions are of singular value because they characteristically deal with and involve the emotions, the cultural experience as felt as well as understood—that is, in psychological terms, the phenomena of intention, identification, motivation, and affect that are often neglected in cultural analysis—including much of the recent research that combines an ideology of emotionality with practices that feature analytical instruments and objectivized data.

In societies like the Eskimo, a large body of oral literature is shared to a significant degree by everyone and is aptly and frequently cited by many persons; in other words, the poetry is a constituent as well as a vehicle of the culture and, more particularly, the linguaculture, that is, the "domain of experience that fuses and intermingles the vocabulary, many aspects of grammar, and the verbal aspects of culture" (Friedrich 1989: 306). Poetry in this sense is at once "data" for analysis and itself a body of generalizations about life that are at least as subtle as what the social scientist normally comes up with. These poetic data and insights in the interstices of culture are dealt with below with particular reference to Tu Fu and T'ang China.

There are many possible relations between a culture and its subcultures or between two or more subcultures (including the case of poetic subcultures). For example, the culture of Everyman (to the extent that there is one) may overlap or be coordinate with a/the poetic subculture—as in the case of the Polar Eskimo mentioned above. In other cases, there is considerable overlap and much agreement (T'ang poetic culture within national culture). In other cases, there is little overlap or consonance between the culture at large and a small enclave of socially alienated poetic specialists: witness the young Chicago bard who used to read his work in the entrance to one of the train stations—an island of postmodern poetry amid a stream of totally uninterested suburban commuters. But even this bard and the commuters, when interviewed about his poetry, would have provided a privileged entrée and an original angle on American values in the 1990s. We can shift our focus and see poetry as a way to establish better relations or as a sort of projective technique that will stimulate value-laden discourse among the people we are interested in. At a deeper level, poetry is a constituent of the imagination of any student of culture and, like other imaginative ingredients, will enter into the process of theory building, empathetic description, and the naming and classification of phenomena. The basic characteristics of most good poetry—economy, elegance, emotional condensation—will contribute to superior cultural studies. But let me consider in greater detail the pragmatic interweaving or, better, interpretation of poetry and culture.

POETRY IN CONVERSATION

Just as the language of conversation can inform poetry, so poetry can and often does inform conversation. This is partly because, at one level, conversation is always organized or at least channeled in terms of figures—irony, metaphor, chiasmus, and so forth—and to this extent conversation *is* poetry. At a more concrete level, actual words, phrases, lines, and even longer units may be components of conversation with high frequency and high symbolic import. The conversation of literate Chinese and even Chinese advertising is occasionally studded with fragments from Tu Fu and other poets (probably thousands of poets if we take into account the myriad minor and anonymous ones who have made their little contribution to the pan-cultural repertoire). Similarly, the conversation of Arab Bedouin is interspersed not just with words and lines but the fixed two-liner, the *ghinnawas*, hundreds of which are known by the ordinary speaker and used, above all, in emotional, liminal, intimate, and/or problematic situations. In many cultures, including modern, industrialized ones, entire classical texts may be widely known, voluminously memorized (especially in secondary school), and play an important role in conversation, ritual, and politics: the Koran in many Muslim countries (Caton 1990); the Bhagavadgita in India (at least Brahmanical India); Homer in Greece today; the Old Testament in Israel; contemporary poetry in Ireland (Coleman 1990); *Don Quixote* in the Spanish-speaking world; and a canon of classical poetry in Russia, notably, Pushkin, Tyutchev, Nekrasov, and the fabulist Krylov. These are not just corpora of texts but also underlying cultural charters, paradigms, precedents, and templates in terms of which to live, modest guidelines for the small individual who is having trouble on deck in the storms at sea that life contains. They are also poetic charters for political acts and attitudes of national or international import, such as territorial claims and counterclaims to Israel or at least Jerusalem and the West Bank. Despite this cultural and political-cultural dimension of poetry, the relatively prosaic nature of much American conversation, particularly that of social scientists, tends to carry over into the practice of ignoring the richly allusive poetic subtextuality of conversation in many cultures such as those just enumerated.

From yet another point of view, the ideology of a culture or a social class within that culture may be deeply embedded in its lyric charter poems—but so that it is partly or wholly hidden. There is complete agreement between Robert Frost's practical dictum to never say what you are actually talking about in a poem and the New Marxist claim that "what [a text] does *not* see, is not what it does not see, it is *what it sees*" (Althusser and Balibar 1970: 21). By the same token, the student of a culture's innermost symbolic values would get far by studying the gaps and silences in its key poetic texts.

Sets of poems, then, can function as a sort of ever-present verbal consciousness that "helps one to live," among other things (Pesman 1988). These poetic constituents of conversations, at one level, are like a well-turned phrase, an apt expression of needs and realities that are not necessarily poetic. In another meaning of "language," the meanings of these words and sentences can function as a sort of ever-present consciousness and conscience that underlies and partly determines the more superficial verbalizations. At yet another, deeper level, we have to think of "language" in some sense as continuously interpenetrating all levels of consciousness; in other words, language is a product of consciousness, but consciousness is also a product of language (Chomsky 1972; Lacan 1978). At any of its meanings or levels, the "language" in question may be the condensed, acute, and sensitized language of poetry and poetic forms. It is in these terms that the understanding, or better, the apprehension of individuals, culture, and worldviews, is clearly facilitated and goes hand in hand with sensitivity to the poetic underpinnings of conversation, politics, and ordinary life. To ignore these underpinnings is like someone trying to enter a house while ignoring the keys under the doormat.

METHODOLOGY (1): INEVITABLE REDUCTION

All known treatments of culture are guilty in the first degree of reductionism, be this to genealogical charts of kinship terms or to "bird song and laments," or even to local factionalism and the vendetta (Feld 1982; Friedrich 1987). These and other approaches reduce, apocopate, and select in skewed ways that reveal the author's prepossessions and obsessions. The inevitability of reduction stems in large part from the simplifying assumptions of all scientific practice and also art: whoever thinks that all-embracing Walt Whitman does not reduce drastically should read in nineteenth-century American economic, social, or intellectual history. What is striking is not the fact, or better, the variant of reductionism, in any given case but the way diverse students of culture claim that they themselves are avoiding it, whereas others are exemplifying it. As against such pros and cons, poetry "is good for something" because it apprehends, represents, and extracts something critical in a world out there and also the world in the mind of the member of the culture and in the anthropologist's own mind, and it does this with a diffuse sensitivity that not only complements other approaches but blocks many of the most extreme forms of scientistic reductionism. The many poetries alluded to in this chapter—notably, Eskimo poetry and the poetry of Tu Fu—deal with emotional and ethical matters intricately and comprehensively. They are "a morphology of feeling" in a way that is analogous to music (the phrase is Felix Mendelssohn's): the shape of realized poetry that is widely appreciated may be assumed to somehow reflect the shape of emotions that it symbolizes.

But this morphology of feeling—and this is one peculiarity of poetry among the verbal arts—is also like music in a way that bears not just on the representation of emotion in a given culture or tradition but on the representation of emotion by the student of culture in the larger sense: as suggested earlier, poetry is like music in its powerful rules for economy, condensation, and what Stevens called "the art of finding what will suffice." Because poetry is understandably grouped with the humanities, and because the criticism of poetry *has* to be so grouped, most people overlook or at least neglect how close poetry is not only to music but to linguistics and even mathematics (Sapir 1951: 159). The quality of elegance and the goal of extracting gist, neither of which can be captured by paraphrase, help to make poems and poetic lines part of the charters and ideologies of many cultures which the student of culture may want to deconstruct or at least examine with due thoughtfulness.

Being attuned to the poetic dimensions of culture necessarily means being alive to a very different network or texture of values, attitudes, and symbols. Going beyond "being attuned," one can take account of a great variety of phenomena, from the seven main connotations of "blue" in American student culture (which tend to be not only the same but hierarchized the same way) to the many meanings of "sentiment" in the emotional structure of a passionate Mexican leader (Friedrich 1987: 54–73) to the meaning of "shame" (that is, lack of Fulani-appropriate qualities) among the Fulani (Riesman 1977: ch. 7). It will often be difficult to deal with, to say nothing of analyze, these diffuse and extensive networks of meaning and feel, but that is precisely the point and the genuine issue. Being attuned to the poetic dimensions of language and culture, of linguaculture, by greatly expanding our "database" and the realism of our perceptions, effectively blocks or at least complements the familiar reduction or essentializing of culture to the graphs, paradigms, tables, and trees of social science ideology. Another way of saying this is that study based on ordinary language and ordinary experience runs the almost certain risk of being itself ordinary. A scientific consciousness, in contrast, that, as its goal, starts with the full poetic system cannot fail, in principle, to deal with the ordinary but also with a great deal more that is extraordinary, potential, possible, and still realistic. Sociocultural linguistics and the various cultural and social anthropologies should, on the analogy of politics, be "the art (and science) of the possible."

METHODOLOGY (2): CONSCIOUSNESS AND EMOTION

"Culture" can be used today as a convenient cover term for diverse ideas and phenomena, including the traditional archaeological and linguistic situations: what can one infer from a heap of shards and similar refuse, or from a set of texts in an extinct language? But even these empirical and concrete meanings overlap with many kinds of consciousness in the sense of general fields or associations of patterned perceptions, concepts, emotions, and motives or intentions that are relatively explicit, known, and articulated. In this broad and indeed sometimes tenebrous sense, we can speak of many kinds of consciousness, one of which is historical: what do Icelandic adolescents see in and construct from standard symbols of their cherished history, a Viking helmet, a patriotic poem (Koester 1990)? How does such historical consciousness contribute to Icelandic poetry, or political culture (e.g., regarding international fishing rights)? Alternatively, the consciousness we are concerned with may be dominantly emotional: how does the individual perceive the threat or even the advent of death, and how is death felt by the dying man or those at his side (Tolstoy 1978)? And again, how does this particular consciousness structure culture in a practical, engaged sense (e.g., the concern with MIAs or the reburial of American Indian remains)? Or the consciousness may be of social categories: rather than a set of terms that are defined with structuralist minimalism by their contrast with each other, what is the positive emotional content, what I used to call the "blood, sweat, tears, semen, and mother's milk" meanings of verbal symbols like "mother" and "brother" (Trawick 1990)? And again, how do these meanings of kinship terms bear on the observance of vendetta obligations (e.g., in the Caucasus cultures where the murderer tries to get at and kiss the nipple of any woman in the victim's patrigroup in order to establish "milk-brotherhood" and hence nullify blood vengeance obligations)? In the case of these three strong examples of a consciousness of national patriotism, feelings about death, and the texture of kinship, one good of poetry is that it gives us closer approximations of the sorts of consciousness that live in and animate a single person, a culture area, or even a historical period. More pointedly, so much poetry in so many cultures does involve "love and death" that the gist of a hundred or even a dozen death poems can in the optimal cases give us more insight than a great deal of the usual experience. Often these poetic intuitions seem to represent universal values: a haunting, deep similarity abounds in the world's poems about the death of a child, a son or a daughter. That, too, is part of the humanizing good of poetry: to suggest dimensions of common humanity that, limiting though they may be, qualify the heartlessness of one kind of extreme relativism and of many kinds of sociocentric New Marxism.

To illustrate the above contention, I include the following short poem. Like many poems of the stereotypically rationalistic, neoclassical, and verbally affected eighteenth century, this poem is, quite to the contrary, colloquial, emotion charged, and of universal import (Lonsdale 1984: xxxvii; this remarkable anthology dispells many stereotypes of the eighteenth century).

To an Infant Expiring the Second Day of Its Birth

> Tender softness, infant mild,
> Perfect, purest, brightest child;
> Transient lustre, beauteous clay,
> Smiling wonder of a day:
> Ere the long-enduring swoon
> Weighs thy precious eyelids down;
> Oh! regard a mother's moan,
> Anguish deeper than thy own!
> Fairest eyes, whose dawning light
> Late with rapture blessed my sight,
> Ere your orbs extinguished be,
> Bend their trembling beams on me.
> Drooping sweetness, verdant flow'r,
> Blooming, with'ring in an hour,
> Ere thy gentle breast sustains
> Latest, fiercest, vital pains,
> Hear a suppliant! Let me be
> Partner in thy destiny!

The poem was written in 1728, published in 1733. About its author nothing seems to be known except her name, Hetty Wright. In this anonymity she reminds us of the name-only Eskimo women who bemoaned their fate in lyrics captured on the wing half a century ago by that ethnographic giant in the earth, Knud Rasmussen.

> Why will people
> have no mercy on Me?
> Sleep comes hard
> since Maula's killer
> showed no mercy.
> Ijaja-ijaja.

Was the agony I felt so strange,
when I saw the man I loved
thrown on the earth
with bowed head?
Murdered by enemies,
worms have for ever
deprived him
of his homecoming.
Ijaja-ijaja.

He was not alone
in leaving me.
My little son
has vanished
to the shadow-land.
Ijaja-ijaja.

Now I'm like a beast
caught in the snare
of my hut.
Ijaja-ijaja.

Long will be my journey
on the earth.
It seems as if
I'll never get beyond
the foot-prints that I make . . .

A worthless amulet
is all my property:
while the northern light
dances its sparkling steps
in the sky.

Qernertoq, Copper Eskimo woman, Musk Ox Folk
(From Lowenstein and Rasmussen 1973: 19–20)

Such poems and their creation cannot be regarded as a social product pure and simple, as an output of purely social forces conceptualized by a purely sociocentric model; we should be able to recognize the absurdity of the claim by formalists such as Brik (Eagleton 1983: 30) and Tynyanov (1978) that had Pushkin never lived, *Eugene Onegin* would have been written by someone else. The social facts of lyric poetry raise in unavoidable form the significantly individual aspects of creativity, here verbal creativity. The biographical (life historical), psychohistorical, and individual stylistic approaches, far from being "positivistic," as some structuralists claim (Jefferson and Robey 1986), actually tend to involve or even entail a dissolution of the boundaries between poet and critic, subject and object, content and form (aside from the fact that the biographical approach antedates "positivism" by centuries, even millennia [Johnson, Vasari, Plutarch]). Close at-

tention to the individual and the individual creative process, while particularly fostered in the context of poetry and poetic criticism, leads not to treat-
ing nonpoets as poets, although it is worth trying, but to evaluating the
individual potter, mother, fisherman, or leader with full attention to, for example, the tropology of their language, the metaphors of action in their
construction of their lives, or what James Fernandez (1986: 28–73) calls "the
mission of metaphor." Poetry and, to a lesser extent, poetry criticism or poetics thus have a deeply humanizing influence on the study of culture and
cultural consciousness and in this sense are the unrecognized sister disciplines of personality psychology, Jungian psychology, and the whole field of
culture and personality.

METHODOLOGY (3): "METHODOLOGICAL INDIVIDUALISM" VERSUS POETRY AS SOCIOCULTURALLY DETERMINED

*The true locus of culture is in the interaction of specific individuals and, on the sub-
jective side, in the world of meanings which each of these individuals may unconsciously abstract for himself from his participation in these interactions.*

—E. SAPIR

Poems in folklore collections or in the texts of a dead language are rarely
individual in the sense of allowing us to infer an individual author, although
this has been possible in notable cases. The individual authors of Bedouin
two-liners as described by Lila Abu-Lughod (1986) are sometimes known,
although in general anonymous. But in all cultures, including primitive and
peasant ones, poems are to begin with created by one person and for a little while at least are known as a personal expression and may even be possessed inalienably, just as, to turn the tables around, the anonymous poem
is the exception in large, literate societies. These hard facts about poetic and
similar artistic creativity and productivity force the responsible student to
deal not only with the significantly individual sides of such phenomena but,
more generally, with the contention that all culture may be seen as, to a significant degree, a world of individual(ized) meanings, or, commuting the
Sapir quote above, the possibility that the individual agent or actor is our basic datum from which are constituted and from which we constitute our interpretation of such things as group, society, and nation. To illustrate this
point of "methodological individualism" with individual authorship in peasant society, I turn to a snatch of my own fieldwork:

> Of my five years of fieldwork, the majority (1954–56, 1965–67, 1970) have
> been spent among the Tarascan Indians of southwestern Mexico. I recall
> watching, sometime in 1967, a young man wander aimlessly in a field at high
> noon, and then I heard from him that he had been composing a story for me:
> "The Three Butterflies." This man was a linguistic virtuoso in his aptitudes but

also a mad poet in a familiar Spanish or American sense: the most prolific and obscene joker in harvest brigades; the man who knew the most stories in town; whose sentences were the longest and most complex, but whose scores on my tests for Tarascan grammar were the most deviant, and at times wild; who, in a brawl, used the fine, long jackknife I had given him to seriously slash his brother's hand; who, when his mother, a reputed witch, was being buried, leapt down into her grave and stood for a long time on her coffin, apostrophizing her and weeping piteously; who, when I had to go to a neighboring hostile village to get boxes for my wife's pottery collection, led me up the ravines where I would be in the least danger from sniper fire; who over-identified with me and, when I took a different virtuoso back to the States, suffered pathological jealousy and chagrin; finally, a thoroughly *macho* womanizer, who eventually joined the Mexican cavalry, where he did very well. Most Tarascan virtuosi I have known (in ceramics and guitar making as well) had similarly exceptional and emotional imaginations. (1986: 46)

Yet there is a flip side to this uniquely individual authorship and the corresponding tendency and temptation to embrace "methodological individualism." In the same way, while discussions of the culture/poetry interface usually focus on what poetry can bring to culture, or what poetics can bring to anthropology, it is just as rewarding to ask what culture and anthropology can bring to poetry and poetics. In one obvious sense, a lyric poem, whether it aspires to be significant to all humanity or to a local powwow, is as ensconced in society, culture, and history as any intellectual and artistic representation and, at several levels, cannot be understood without historical, philological, and anthropological contextualization (Benjamin 1989).

The phenomena of lyric poetry, while full of isolated, sociohistorically underdetermined genius, also abounds with cases of sociohistorical overdetermination, of clusterings of creativity that beg for causal explanation or at least an etiological interpretation: prime examples would be the century or so each of the High T'ang of China, of Elizabethan and Jacobean England, of the "American Renaissance," of the Russian Golden and Silver ages, of Anglo-American modernism, and Spanish *modernismo,* and of seventh- and sixth-century Greece. Most of these efflorescent ages arose in the context of some combination of most or all of the following five factors:

1. intense national, ethnic, or even local consciousness and often pride (e.g., the Greek city-state, Elizabethan England);
2. extraordinary primary and or secondary schooling in language arts (e.g., the T'ang entrance exams, the Russian aristocratic system of private tutors and adolescent university education);
3. encouragement of youthful precocity (e.g., adolescents welcomed into adult literary societies; Pablo Neruda in Santiago, Chile);
4. maximum prestige and valorization of poetry by the society, especially its hegemonic circles (e.g., the public schools and early colleges of six-

teenth- and seventeenth-century England—Milton and his friends; the high status of "poet" in society);

5. available aristocratic bureacratic lifestyle that allowed time for litera-ture (notably, in T'ang China and nineteenth- and early twentieth-century Russia).

The genesis and efflorescence of T'ang Chinese and Russian classical poetry, in particular, could be rigorously interpreted as the determined expression of the worldview of an ensconced nationalistic, linguistically hypertrained, poetically oriented aristocratic literati (Goldman 1964). (One speculates, incidentally, on just what social and historical factors are causing the extraordinary pluralism of form and content in American poetry today.)

All these factors suggest that lyric poetry, while inviting so-called method-ological individualism, also affords compelling and sweeping examples of lyric creativity as a social product in a New Marxist sense. One way to approach such social determinism would be through massive correlations using a world sample, as in A. L. Kroeber's extraordinary, pioneer analysis. In the one chap-ter that deals with poetry in his *Configurations of Culture Growth,* some of the variables I have just named are isolated and discussed. Yet most persons would correctly feel that reducing Tu Fu and Li Po to critical points on the top of a curve in an essentially statistical analysis is somehow missing almost all of the points that really matter. A second approach would be through the intensive study of one lyric poet in all the fullness of social and historical con-text, as in Walter Benjamin's also extraordinary, pioneer analysis of Baude-laire (1989), although, once again, most people would correctly feel that reducing the great symbolist poet to a product of the political economic forces of his time, to questions of production, distribution, and consump-tion, to what American poets include under "po biz," is missing most of what matters. A third approach, which I personally favor and which is partially illustrated here, is to triangulate (or quadrangulate or even sexangulate) be-tween a relatively small number of poets and/or poetries or poetic traditions that the given student can understand, "control," and even internalize with a modicum of sensitivity and thoroughness—in terms of knowing (even memorizing many of) the texts, mastering the intellectual history, and so forth; it is vital that these poets and poetries be selected judiciously (my own combination of Polar Eskimo, Arab Bedouin, T'ang Chinese, and, more in-tensively, modern American and Russian, has proven fruitful). With such tri-angulation one can generalize and synthesize for much of the world about such issues as poetic form; the creative process; intermedia relations to other arts; determinate relations with society and culture; the way poetry incarnates both culturally specific and universal, pan-human values, such as grief over a lost baby; and, last but not least, the possibilities of creative interaction between students of poetry and students of culture. The method of triangulation, adapted from Ralph Linton's method of triangulation in culture studies, has the advantages without the disadvantage of the extensive (e.g., Kroeberian) and the intensive (Benjamin-style) approaches.

PRACTICUM: TU FU

My original contention that poetry can provide an eyeopening entry to culture as a system of values and symbols is powerfully illustrated by the sorts of inferences that can be made from even a small sample of the poetry of Tu Fu: thirty-five poems in the canonical T'ang anthology (the same set used by Hawkes) comes from a total of over 1,400 poems by Tu Fu. This widely encompassing, if select, corpus touches on a great many themes, some of them Confucian in the conventional sense of respect and affection between primary relatives, or concern with the sociopolitical hierarchy and one's advancement within it. Out of a spectrum that includes these and other subjects, let us look only at what he appears to say about nature, or better, the relation between man and nature; one initial reason for doing this is that about half of his best poems, as anthologized by David Hawkes, *seem* to be dealing with nature. In reviewing some of these nature poems, let us keep in mind that Tu Fu's personal idiosyncratic view agrees to a considerable extent with three others: (1) those of the Chinese poetic tradition; (2) those commonly held in T'ang China; (3) specifically Confucian philosophic values. In what follows, incidentally, I depend heavily on the petite but brilliant study by Hawkes, supplemented by Yu-Lan Fung, William Hung, and Stephen Owen.

Tu Fu's worldview contains a philosophy of nature, or better, of the nature/culture relationship. To begin, nature is literally *animated:* trees and rivers are inhabited, even incarnated by spirits of many kinds. Thus in one poem called "From the World's End," we hear that "art hates a successful destiny [i.e., a too successful life], just as the hungry goblins in the mountains rejoice at the chance to gobble up a passerby." In another poem, "Dreaming of Li Po," one of several devoted to this deeply admired friend, Tu Fu expresses anxiety at the dangers presented by the tremendous distances that Li Po has had to cross to reach him in a dream and concludes with the warning (here in a "literal," word-by-word translation): "Watch deep, waves broad / Don't let water dragons get." These are not *primarily* figures of speech: Tu Fu and Li Po imagined really real dragons beneath the waters, really real goblins in the mountains. Nature, second of all, is seen as deeply analogous to society: nature in its parts is always tropological raw material for symbolizing relations among human beings, human mental states, and familiar human predicaments. One Tu Fu poem called "To the Recluse Wei Pa," opens with, "Often in this life of ours we resemble, in our failure to meet, / The Shen and Shang constellations, one of which rises as the other sets." In yet another poem called "To a Fine Lady," we hear that "the way people feel in this world is to hate what is decayed and finished / Myriad affairs are like a lamp flame flickering in the wind." And elsewhere in the same poem: "Even the vetch-tree knows when it is evening; / Mandarin ducks do not sleep alone," that is, the husband who has abandoned her should know when it is evening, time to return to her and a life in conjugal fidelity. These and other analogies between the human and natural world are often phrased in terms of a symbolism that had become partly formulaic in the T'ang Chinese poetic, where, for example, a solitary goose on the wing is a standard emblem of at least three things: autumn, a wanderer, a letter to or from an exile far from home. To take one example: "Here at the world's end the cold winds are beginning to blow. . . . When will the poor wandering goose [i.e., wanderer, letter] arrive?" The more or less formulaic equations, paradigms, and sets could channel and structure the creative process but also be played with and adapted in all sorts of ways. My impression is that the T'ang code of Tu Fu's time was not as explicit and comprehensive as that of Classical Tamil but that later, in the ninth century, this was indeed the case.

Third, nature is shared by two or more people or even all human society; it is as though reality required at least two persons and nature itself in interaction. This ontological, dialogical premise informs some of Tu Fu's most memorable lines and poems, where, for instance, "the moon is the same as that which shines down on our birthplace [i.e., morpheme by morpheme, Moon is old-home bright] / My brothers scattered in different places. The moon is only real as something shared by two or more people. Put aphoristically, nature is "out there" only if it is "in here" between us. This premise of a continuous relation between the socially, dialogically human and the natural does a lot of work in many of his most remarkable poems, and this dense interdependence between the dialogical and the natural deserves more critical concern than it has received so far.

Let us start to conclude with what is my fourth, and perhaps most obvious, contention about the poetics of the relation between man and nature, and that is, nature's anthropomorphic response to human beings and society. In "Spring Scene" we find the following: "Moved-by times flowers sprinkle tears / Hating separation birds startle heart" (i.e., the birds seem startled as with the anguish of separation). But these relatively simple-minded instances of the "poetic fallacy" are in Tu Fu encased in a much larger context where "Human nature have feelings tears wet blossom" (that is contrasted with "river-water river-flowers how come-to-end" [i.e., they go on forever]). Indeed, the deeper folds of what seems to be Tu Fu's tropological interweaving and even identification of man and nature is so continuous that there is no line between them. In one of his "Thoughts on an

Ancient Site," devoted to the tragic life of a court lady, "paintings have recorded those features that the spring wind caressed." In a second set of thoughts on an ancient site, a famous but failed statesman is likened to a single feather floating among clouds. The following poem "Night at Waj House," contains what some think is the best heptosyllabic couplet in the language:

> Fifth-watch drums-bugles sound sad-strong
> Three-gorges star-river's shadow moves-shakes (182)

Here the elaborated syntactic, semantic, and even numerical parallelism helps to establish the illusion of a sort of isomorphism between man and nature.

Perhaps the most profound apprehension of the continuous relation between the human and the natural is Tu Fu's "Ballad of the Old Cypress." In a long chain of mainly original metaphors and similes, the master incarnates the solitary old tree: "boughs are-like green bronze / Roots are-like rocks"; the "wide-encompassing, snake-like coil" of its roots grips the earth; the bitter heart has not escaped the ants, "but there are always phoenixes roosting in scented leaves." The old cypress becomes a cosmic tree and also a symbol of neglected genius in its old age.

To sum up provisionally, in the Tu Fuian view, nature is animated, analogous to society, only meaningful as part of a dialogue, and itself responsive or at least symbolically or indexically related to culture. The custom in criticism is to not address these issues as Confucian or to deal with them as Buddhist or Taoist deviation or part of the synthesis or at least coexistence of all three religions in T'ang times. It is my contention, which cannot be fully elaborated here, that these ideas about nature, while owning something to Buddhism and Taoism, are an essential and native Chinese part of Confucianism.

Through the poems there runs the generically Chinese but diagnostically Tu Fuian idea of cosmic space where man is neither central nor absent but only an infinitesimally small part of the cosmic whole. Our poet emphasizes this again and again in poems that descend from very general, abstract levels down to a final cathexis and poetic closure on a small, humble, and very human detail: the hatpin that his white hair is getting too thin to hold, the cup of muddied wine that he has to refuse, himself as a lonely goose or a solitary sandgull. The philosophy in these poems is the same as that of the numerous Chinese paintings where in the same nook or fissure in the midst of vast mountains and mist-filled gorges we notice a small man in his hut or his boat in his small human space.

There are many other aspects of nature that I could dwell on that may be just as important as those given: nature as unchanging or constant; nature as awesome, majestic, and full of divine power; nature as harmonic, in that its seasons and other natural cycles contrast with the irregularity of human affairs that can be destroyed by nature; between nature and ordinary human life there is the dream world with its dream logic (as in his dream poems of Li Po, so akin to his half-world of spirits and goblins, and, for that matter, the world of the imagination of all his poetry). These and diverse aspects of nature can be more fully apprehended by letting Tu Fu lead the way. His worldview, partly because of the great popularity he has enjoyed in such a large audience, may be thought of as highly meaningful in the Chinese tradition more generally, in the culture of T'ang China, and in the Confucian tradition. At least these three ambitious hypotheses would be worth exploring further.

Are many of the component values and symbols just discussed shared by many American and Russian poets? Yes, to some extent, but that enlarges rather than diminishes their partly universal significance. It also partly explains why, over twelve centuries later, they are meaningful and inspiring to Anglo-American readers, including sophisticated and often tired graduate students in comparative literature, anthropology, and related arts and sciences.

"The observer is part of the field of observation"

Tu Fu and Confucius influenced Emerson and Thoreau and, more recently, have inspired such American masters as Robert Bly and Gary Snyder (Faas 1978). I am a part-time participant in this tradition (e.g., going to high school in Concord, Massachusetts). The following poem (1990) came to me one cold winter morning five years ago, after biking to the office and working through David Hawkes's version, that is, through the ideograms, the transliteration, the literal translation, the rich annotation, and Hawkes's own literary translation of a Tu Fu "sonnet" (rhymed pentasyllabic eight-liner).

Early Hours

It is dark before dawn and the city is quiet
like the dead silence of a cave. Burglars
have gone home as I bicycle slowly through streets
you wouldn't recognize. Several crows start to caw
on campus as I pass. Then they rise from the tops
of the locusts to circle beneath the crescent
of the moon. It is cold enough to crack open
the essential remembrances:
Concord in winter
and the tracks of a blue jay in snow, or my run
through deep frost after midnight mass on Christmas.
But, when I finally get there, my office is warm
and by dawn I've deciphered the T'ang Chinese
of a Tu Fu "sonnet" in Regulated Verse:
between Heaven and Earth a Ring-Necked Gull.

In this poem, as I see it, the natural environment of crows and jays in the deep cold of a northern winter is melded with such thoroughly cultural and even urban components as burglars and midnight mass on Christmas, and everything is headed toward a cathectic closure on the small, personal act of trying to intuit the meaning of a poem by Tu Fu—before taking off again into the gull metaphor. At the time of the writing I was not aware that I was imitating Tu Fu; later that day I checked on "Gulls" in Roger Tory Peterson's *Guide to North American Birds* to make sure that I had the species right. I may have suppressed the connection to Tu Fu because of some jealous instinct of self-preservation, even some "anxiety of influence" à la Bloom. More probable a reason is the diametrically opposed meanings of his "sandgull" and my "ring-necked gull": his stands for personal isolation and loneliness amid social disorder and imagined personal failure as a writer, whereas mine stands for inspiration in a liminal space against a background of security in one's community and gratitude at some success with one's writing. In any case, it was only two years later when I got back to the poem, early on in the Hawkes volume, as part of teaching Comparative Poetry/Poetics, that I realized that my "ring-necked gull," which I had seen so often in the fall off the shores of Lake Michigan, was a local, Chicago-area response to the gull in Tu Fu, first literally translated as "sandgull" by Hawkes, but then, in one of his rare but critical errors of judgment, rendered simply as "seagull" in the poetic translation.

To fill out matters for the critical reader, I include here Hawkes's informed literary translation, and his literal translation of the last two lines.

Thoughts Written While Travelling at Night

By the bank where the fine grass bends in a gentle wind, my boat's tall mast stands in the solitary night. The stars hang down over the great emptiness of the level plain, and the moon bobs on the running waters of the Great River. Literature will bring me no fame. A career is denied me by my age and sickness. What do I most resemble in my aimless wanderings? A seagull drifting between earth and sky!

The literal translation runs as follows: "Fine grass slight wind bank / Tall mast lonely night boat / Stars hang down level plain vastness / Moon bobs-from-great river's flow / Name how literature famous / Office due-to age-sickness resigned /

7. *Piäo-piäo hé-suo sí*
Drifting-drifting what-am like

8. *Tiän-dí yí shä-oü*
Sky-earth one sand-gull

To belabor the obvious, if a poem or a poet provides us with an entrée into an exotic or at least different worldview, as I think is indisputable, then, given the universals of experience and of what some anthropologists call the pan-human aspect of culture, or better, life, those same poems should provide us with an entry or a new understanding of ourselves in the sense both of some subculture of America and of the unique particularity of each of us—whether or not the new insights and intuitions are necessarily jelled in a poem "after Tu Fu, after García Lorca, after the Eskimo."

RECURSION TO SYLVIA PLATH

We began with Sylvia Plath and now, after a long discussion of poetry and culture, let us return to her "Words" to see what we have learned. The body and mind of the poet are engaged in an act of sacrifice with an ax that makes echoes ring from the trunk of a tree, but this is less the Old Testament tree of the knowledge of good and evil than the giant ash tree of Germanic, specifically, Old Norse, myth. It is from this tree (and the alder) that the warrior-poet Odin (or Wotan) fashioned the first man. It is this tree that the poet must cut into to extract the words of his poems and from which "the sap wells, like water," like the primal fluids of both the poet and the tree with which she or he is identified. It is the tree of self-sacrifice on which Odin, the god of learning, poetry, and magic, hung himself for nine days and nights to acquire the lore of the runes and hence achieve wisdom for the gods. (The word for "write," that is, for Plath's fundamental act of putting words to paper, comes from the Proto-Germanic word for "scratch": runes were scratched on slabs of wood ["beech," was *bok*, from which comes our "book"]). Beneath this tree the water of Plath's sources is "striving to re-establish its mirror" over the rock of ages that turns into "a white skull eaten by weedy greens," which is the floating skull of the Norse god, Mimir. The most basic connection to Germanic mythology, however, is the pool with its "fixed stars," that is, of fate, that "govern a life," that is, the doom of Plath and of everyone, stars that lie at the bottom of the Well of Knowledge, that is, the Pool of Mimir, beside which stands the World Tree, Yggdrasil (Salus and Taylor 1970; Bellows 1957).

Thus we see that the main cultural subtext of "Words" is a complex skein of symbols from Germanic and, to some extent, world mythology (Eliade 1976); but more than that, it is one source of the poem's enormous imaginative thrust. In this it resembles the eponymous poem in her *Ariel* collection where, beneath an apparent symbolism of suicide and decadence, there roils a Germanic mythological symbolism of regeneration. Whether she got these mythic subtexts from her childhood readings or the stories of her myth-loving father in her (German-speaking) home, or whether they were mainly acquired in the many university English and German courses she took and taught is not our concern here. Nor is our concern the extraordinary irony and indeed mendacity of her most famous poem, "Daddy," in which her father, a warm-hearted if somewhat authoritarian Boston University botanist, is caricaturized as a jackbooted, Jew-butchering Nazi. This is one way to exorcise a beloved father who left you alone, an orphan. It is also one way to build a personal mythology and public relations image for college students and New York critics—to be "relevant" in the worst sense. But this is not our concern here.

Our main concern has been to enter into Plath's great poem "Words" and perhaps illustrate the degree to which poems are informed by culture, the degree to which culture is *in* language (commute the professional cliché of "language in culture"). All this is complementary to our earlier contention that poetry—poetic images, tropes, materia prima—informs, channels, and structures culture. The case of a major poet condensing the gist of a basic myth in her family and her subculture into one of her finest poems may be taken as a token of what happens all the time in more quotidian, humdrum, and even banal arenas of life.

REFERENCES

Abu-Lughod, Lila.
 1986.   *Veiled Sentiments: Honor and Poetry in a Bedouin Society.* Berkeley, Los Angeles, and London: University of California Press.
Althusser, Denis, and Étienne Balibar.
 1970.   *Reading Capital.* Trans. Ben Brewster. New York: Pantheon.
Becker, A.L.
 1991.   "Translating between English and Javanese." Ms.
Bellows, Henry Adam.
 1957.   *The Poetic Edda.* New York: American Scandinavian Foundation.
Benjamin, Walter.
 1989.   *Charles Baudelaire: A Lyric Poet in the Era of High Capitalism.* Trans. Harry Zohn. New York: Verso.
Bourdieu, Pierre.
 1985.   *Outline of a Theory of Practice.* Trans. Richard Nice. Cambridge: Cambridge University Press. Bloomington: Indiana University Press.
Caton, Steve.
 1990.   *The Peaks of Yemen I Summon.* Berkeley, Los Angeles, and Oxford: University of California Press.
Chomsky, Noam.
 1972.   *Language and Mind.* New York: Harcourt Brace Jovanovich.
Coleman, Steve.
 1990.   "Speaking Other People's Words." Ms.
Eagleton, Terry.
 1983.   *Literary Theory: An Introduction.* Minneapolis: University of Minnesota Press.

Eliade, Mircea.
    1976.   *Myths, Rites, and Symbols: A Mircea Eliade Reader.* 2 vols. New York: Harper/Colophon.
Faas, Ekbert, ed.
    1978.   *Towards a New American Poetics: Essays and Interviews.* Santa Barbara: Black Sparrow.
Feld, Stephen.
    1982.   *Sound and Sentiment: Birds, Weeping, Poetics, and Song in Kaluli Expression.* Philadelphia: University of Pennsylvania Press.
Fernandez, James.
    1986.   "The mission of metaphor in expressive culture." In *Persuasion and Performances,* 28–73.
Friedrich, Paul.
    1986.   *The Language Parallax.* Austin: University of Texas Press.
———.
    1987.   *The Princes of Naranja.* Austin: University of Texas Press.
———.
    1989.   "Language, ideology, and political economy." *American Anthropologist* 91(2): 295–313.
———.
    1990.   "Early Hours." *Mississippi Valley Review* 19 (2): 22.
———.
    1992*a*.   "Interpretation and Vision: A Critique of Cryptopositivism." *Cultural Anthropology* 7(2): 211–231.
———.
    Forthcoming.   "Catalysis and Synthesis in Life-Changing Dialogue." In *The Dialogic Emergence of Culture,* ed. Bruce Mannheim and Dennis Tedlock. Urbana: University of Illinois Press.
Fung, Yu-Lan.
    1948.   *A Short History of Chinese Philosophy.* Ed. Dirk Bodde. New York: Macmillan.
Goldman, Lucien.
    1964.   *The Hidden God: A Study of Tragic Vision in the Pensées of Pascal and the Tragedies of Racine.* New York: Humanities Press.
Hawkes, David.
    1967.   *A Little Primer of Tu Fu.* Hong Kong: Oxford University Press (Renditions Paperback).
Hung, William.
    1952.   *Tu Fu: China's Greatest Poet.* Cambridge: Harvard University Press.
Jefferson, Ann, and David Robey, eds.
    1986.   *Modern Literary Theory: A Comparative Introduction.* Totawa, N.J.: Barnes and Noble.
Koester, David.
    1990.   "Historical Consciousness in Iceland." Ph.D. dissertation, University of Chicago.
Kroeber, Afred L.
    1944.   *Configurations of Culture Growth.* Berkeley: University of California Press.

Lacan, Jacques.
    1978.   *Four Fundamental Concepts of Psychoanalysis.* Trans. Alan Sheridan. New
            York: Norton.
Lonsdale, Roger.
    1984.   *The New Oxford Book of Eighteenth-Century Poetry.* New York: Oxford
            University Press.
Lowenstein, Tom, and Knud Rasmussen.
    1973.   *Eskimo Poems from Greenland and Canada.* Pittsburgh: University of
            Pittsburgh Press.
Lutz, Catherine.
    1986.   "The anthropology of the emotions." *Annual Review of Anthropology*
            15: 405–436.
Owen, Stephen.
    1981.   *The Great Age of Chinese Poetry.* New Haven: Yale University Press.
Pesman, Dale.
    1988.   "Russian Poetry as Cultural Myth." Ms.
Plath, Sylvia.
    1972.   "Words." In *Contemporary American Poetry,* ed. Donald Hall, 246-247.
            New York: Penguin Books.
Plath, Amelia Schober.
    1975.   *Letters Home by Sylvia Plath.* New York: Harper and Row. pp. 12–25.
Riesman, Paul.
    1977.   *Freedom in Fulani Social Life.* Chicago: University of Chicago Press.
Salus, Peter, and Paul B. Taylor.
    1970.   "Introduction." In *The Elder Edda: A Selection.* Trans. Paul B. Taylor and
            W. H. Auden. New York: Random House.
Sapir, Edward.
    [1924] 1951.   "The Grammarian and His Language." In *Selected Writings of
            Edward Sapir,* ed. David G. Mandelbaum, 150–160. Berkeley and
            Los Angeles: University of California Press.
Snyder, Gary.
    1980.   *The Real Work: Interviews and Talks, 1964–1979.* New York: New
            Directions.
Tolstoy, Leo.
    1978.   "The Death of Ivan Ilyich." In *The Cossacks, Happy Ever After, The Death of
            Ivan Ilyich,* 99–163. Trans. Rosemary Edmonds. New York: Penguin.
Trawick, Margaret.
    1990.   *Notes on Love in a Tamil Family.* Berkeley, Los Angeles, and Oxford: Uni-
            versity of California Press.
Tyler, Stephen A.
    1984.   "The Poetic Turn in Postmodern Anthropology: The poetry of Paul
            Friedrich." *American Anthropologist* 86: 328–336.
Tynyanov, Yury.
    [1929] 1978.   "On Literary Evolution." In *Readings in Russian Poetics: Formalist
            and Structuralist Views,* ed. L. Matejka and K. Pomorska, 130–149.
            Ann Arbor: Michigan Slavic Publications.
Wright, James.
    1986.   "The Music of Poetry." *American Poetry Review* 15 (2): 43–47.

TWO

The Story of the Jackal Hunter Girl

Margaret Trawick

"There goes one of them now!" cried my companion, Lakshmi. "She's the same one I saw before! Go on! Go up and ask her!" She pointed in the direction of a barefoot woman striding through the bazaar.

Lakshmi was right; the woman was a Jackal Hunter. I knew she was a member of that caste, because she was dressed in the kind of outfit that only Jackal Hunter women wear. She looked about thirty. She was tall and strong, high-cheekboned and golden-skinned, like most of the Jackal Hunter people, and like most of them she had dirt on her arms and legs and her hair was dry and disheveled. Heart pounding, I approached her. Would she be able to tell me what I had been trying to learn for so long? Or would this be another dead end?

"Are you a Jackal Hunter?"

Of all the stupid questions. To ask a person's caste in urban Tamil Nadu is more than a little rude, especially among low-caste people, especially without even an introduction. Besides, it was obvious from her appearance what this woman was. But she would soon be gone, and I could not miss this chance.

The woman turned and smiled at my white face. I knew what she was thinking, or I imagined I knew.

"Buy some beads!" she exhorted me, pulling from her sack a dozen strands of multicolored glass and plastic beads. "Only thirty rupees for these black ones! Here! Take them! Thirty rupees!" She put the strand of black beads in my hand.

Mechanically, I took them and reached into my purse to get my wallet, an old habit, but as I was pulling out the money Lakshmi stopped me.

"Don't buy *anything*," she hissed into my ear. "Make her tell you the story first. Make her take you to the encampment."

I paused. Generally, Lakshmi's advice was wise. Without her help my life in Tamil Nadu would have been much harder. I had hired her as my cook many years before when I did not know how to cook for myself, and she had quickly moved into the role of research consultant and surrogate mother, ferreting out interesting informants for me and berating me tearfully when I ate poorly or turned a deaf ear to her words. She was smarter and took good care of me, but sometimes she protected me too much. Thirty rupees was too high a price for the beads—I knew at least that much—but I could spare thirty rupees and would have given many times that price just for the hope of getting a member of the Jackal Hunter caste to tell me the story of the Jackal Hunter goddess, Singamma. The woman standing before me could not be rich; surely she could use the money she asked for the beads. To buy them might show her that my interest in her had substance, might convince her that it would be worth her while to pay some attention to me. Or it might show her that I was like most other foreign visitors, my eyes set on things to buy and not on the people who sold those things. The woman was waiting.

"I'll buy the beads later," I said. "First could I talk with you for a little while? I want to know about your life."

The woman looked away. Her eyes darted around the bazaar, as though searching for someone else, like a person engaged in a boring conversation at a cocktail party, seeking an escape. "What is there to talk about?"

"Have you ever been through the city of Madurai?" I asked. The Jackal Hunters are nomadic scavengers. They travel by train like hoboes from town to town, never staying in one place for more than a few days. As long as they identify themselves through their dress and demeanor as Jackal Hunters, they are allowed to travel ticketless, a kind of ritual privilege afforded their caste in exchange for their being scavengers.

"I've been to Madurai many times," the woman answered, warming up some. A crowd was gathering around us. Singly, neither of us would have been an unusual sight. But a foreigner talking with a scavenger was strange.

"Have you ever been to a town called Melur, a few miles west of Madurai?"

"We're just coming from there."

What good luck! Melur, the site of the Singamma shrine, was a hundred miles away. I had searched all over Melur for Jackal Hunters, hoping to find the group with which Singamma was identified, hoping they could tell me their version of where she came from and what had happened to her. But the week that I visited Melur, the Jackal Hunters were nowhere around, and no one could tell me where they had gone or when they would be back. The high-caste people in Melur told me to give up my search. They told me that even if I found the Jackal Hunters, they would not be able to help me. The Jackal Hunters, they said, were dirty and dangerous people whom I should stay away from; moreover, according to the townspeople of Melur, the Jackal

Hunters knew nothing about Singamma, even though she had been a girl of their caste. Now, by accident, I had encountered Jackal Hunters from Melur camping out in this town of Tirunelveli, where I had come on other business. Here was my chance to ask them directly the questions that had been on my mind for years.

"Do you know anything about Singamma?"

"That poor girl. She died thirty years ago."

"Can you tell me her story?"

"She went to the Melur market to sell beads, and when she was returning to her family alone in the evening some high-caste men followed her and offered her food and then trapped her in a goat stall and raped her. Then she was murdered by her brothers. Her body is buried there in Melur."

This was the story I was looking for. At last my search was over.

I shall explain why my encounter with the Jackal Hunter woman on that day was so important to me. And before I relate the outcome of that encounter, I must provide some information about the place of Jackal Hunters in Indian society, about Singamma the Jackal Hunter goddess, and about myself and the nature of my research.

Since my first visit to India twenty years ago, I have admired the Jackal Hunters. Maybe it is my populism. Rich people bore me. People who have to live by their wits on the street somehow seem much more interesting, and the Jackal Hunters of southern India are street people like no others. In the cities of Tamil Nadu, they are highly conspicuous. Camping out at bus stands and train stations and near temples where festivals are going on, they live by telling fortunes and selling beads and small birds that they have captured and talismans made out of parts of the animals they hunt—peacocks' feet, bear claws, tigers' teeth, monkey eyeballs, jackal heads. The conservation-conscious Indian government has forbidden the hunting of some of these animals and the selling of items taken from them, but still the Jackal Hunters sell genuine-looking teeth, feet, and claws and swear by these items' wish-granting powers. They also sell medicines made from various plants and minerals that they gather on their rounds.

With the money they get from their sales, they sometimes buy rice and lentils, which form a part of their meals. But another important part of their diet consists of items that they have foraged from the city and the countryside. Jackal Hunter women may regularly be seen picking through garbage bins for things they can bring home to their families to eat. When higher-caste people have wedding feasts, Jackal Hunters will be there to gather and consume the leftovers from the leaves that the wedding guests have eaten off of. When there are vermin and animal pests in a neighborhood—snakes, cats, rats—the Jackal Hunters will be called on to capture these pests, which they then take back to their camps and eat. In the countryside they hunt and eat everything from sparrows to bears.

But their favorite food is jackal meat, hence their name. The nineteenth-century ethnologist Edgar Thurston reported that Jackal Hunter men captured their favorite quarry by imitating jackal calls so perfectly that they attracted real jackals, which they then netted and killed. Jackal Hunter men of the present still engage in this method of hunting jackals. When they do their jackal calls, they sound (to an American ear) like a chorus of wolves or coyotes.

It is remarkable enough that the Jackal Hunters have survived to the present within the arcane niche that they have carved out for themselves, adapting old hunter-gatherer ways to a modern urban environment, homeless, shelterless, always on the move, raising their children entirely on the street, living off garbage and vermin and still staying more or less healthy. More remarkable still is the strong pride Jackal Hunters take in their community and their way of life, given their status in South Indian society as a caste utterly beyond the pale of caste itself. Not only are they Untouchables to high-caste Hindus but within the ranks of the various Untouchable castes, Jackal Hunters are lowest of all. Even other Untouchables will not touch them.

Yet Jackal Hunters hold fiercely to the very customs that cause other castes to despise them. It is against Jackal Hunter caste law for men to cut their hair, for children to go to school, for a family to settle down in one place. Members of other low castes strive to imitate high-caste Hindus, in hope of improving not only the rank of themselves as individuals but, more important, the rank of their caste as a whole. But if a Jackal Hunter adopts the way of life of ordinary middle-class Hindus and, for instance, takes an office job, he must accept ostracism from the community into which he was born. In general, Jackal Hunters keep themselves aloof and observe what one educated onlooker called "a severe discipline." Unlike higher-caste Hindus, Jackal Hunters make no exceptions to the rule of monogamy. They strictly follow what Tamils call "the order of one man, one woman." Jackal Hunter women who go to the market to sell beads and trinkets must be back at the camp before sundown, or they will be driven from their families and their caste or even (in former times) killed. South Indian Jackal Hunters have their own deities and speak their own language, a mélange of North Indian and South Indian tongues unintelligible to people outside the Jackal Hunter caste. Jackal Hunter women do not wear the saris, tight jackets, and gold-colored jewelry that most respectable South Indian women wear but instead wear a multilayered calf-length skirt, a loose-fitting blouse, heavy metal ankle bracelets, and many strands of glass beads. Thus, in a variety of ways, the Jackal Hunters maintain their distinction from and show their disdain for the world of respectable Hindus whose garbage they eat. Or so they did until just about twelve years ago, when their life began to change. But I will say more about this later.

As an anthropologist with a belief in the power of the world's nonprivileged peoples, "the people without history," as Eric Wolf calls them, and with a special place in my heart for foraging communities, I had always been intrigued by the Jackal Hunters and longed to learn from them about their life. I never had an excuse to approach them, however, until a piece of information about them fell into my hands in 1984. During that year I was working in a village north of the city of Madurai, collecting life histories and songs from the people who lived there. About half the people in the village were Paraiyars, a major Untouchable caste with millions of members throughout Tamil Nadu, most of whom work as agricultural laborers. The Paraiyars were involved at the time in an intense political struggle to raise their economic and ritual status (the two tend to go hand in hand), through legislation, education, and private efforts to adopt the customs of higher-caste people, the very customs that higher-caste people used to justify their privileged status vis-à-vis lower castes. If the major differences in customs were erased, Paraiyars knew that high-caste Hindus would be deprived of an important ideological playing card. Hence the Paraiyars of that village at that time were scrupulously clean, dressed in the most respectable clothing, forbade divorce and widow remarriage, spoke the purest, most "civilized" Tamil, celebrated expensive weddings following the high-caste ritual style, went broke paying for these weddings and amassing large dowries for their daughters, and sharply distinguished themselves, on grounds of ritual purity, from castes even lower than they were. The Jackal Hunters were a kind of human being with whom the Paraiyars felt they had nothing in common. They liked to ridicule the Jackal Hunters and impugn their moral integrity, accusing them in folk songs of thievery, prostitution, brother-sister incest, and worse. They never thought of establishing an alliance with the Jackal Hunters in their efforts to revise the oppressive caste hierarchy of which both Jackal Hunters and Paraiyars were principal victims.

But one day I heard a song sung by a Paraiyar woman which seemed to express a different point of view. The song was addressed to the spirit of a Jackal Hunter girl named Singamma, and it told the story of this girl's life, her violent death, and her return as a goddess to demand recompense from the men who had murdered her. Essentially this song was a hymn in praise of Singamma, recounting her sufferings and her triumphs, and offered to her in the way that hymns of praise are commonly offered to Hindu deities. Woven throughout the song were a multitude of images of defilement, the state of ineradicable ritual pollution in which both Paraiyars and Jackal Hunters are considered (by higher castes) to be immersed. There also seemed to be a deep sympathy on the part of the singer for the unjustly murdered Jackal Hunter girl and a close identification with her. The song sung by the Paraiyar woman told this story.

A Jackal Hunter girl called Singamma lives with her five brothers and their wives. Singamma is kept secluded by her brothers and their wives, but one day she "puts on different clothes" and slips off to the local town market to sell beads. Still in town at dusk, she goes to a wedding feast, gathers up the saliva-polluted rice off of leaves discarded by the wedding guests, puts the rice in jars, and brings the jars of rice back home. To punish her for disobeying them and for coming home late, Singamma's brothers send her to stay alone in a hut in the forest. Then the brothers themselves enter the hut, pull the doors shut and lock them, and rape Singamma, telling her, "The sun has set on our good caste, we are excluded from caste."

After this, the brothers depart, leaving Singamma locked in the hut. But Singamma declares, "If my honor is destroyed, let the doors of the hut stay closed, but if my honor is undestroyed, let them open." Magically, the doors open, and Singamma flees to the arms of her mother. Her mother warns her that because she has been raped, she can no longer perform the tasks of an honorable woman, such as cooking milk and rice for a wedding feast, and that her brothers are going to kill her. Like a child seeking comfort, Singamma lays her head in her mother's lap. She then takes a louse comb in her hand and "assumes the form of louse eggs" [or perhaps she dreams this]. As she lies thus sleeping in her mother's lap, her brothers kill her, splitting her head with an ax. Then they dismember her body, bury it in the floor of the hut, and flee.

From Singamma's grave, a poisonous red oleander plant springs up, and an earthworm emerges from its flower. When one of Singamma's brothers returns to the grave site, the earthworm speaks to him, telling him to build a house for Singamma. As soon as lime is burned in preparation for its construction, the house grows up magically by itself. Subsequently, Singamma appears in a vision to a woman who comes there, identifying herself by name in response to the woman's query. Then, "rising high and speaking with unsheathed energy," Singamma addresses her eldest brother, saying, "You are the one who killed me, who saw my sin, who undid me. Tell me to rise up outside. Now I will stand up straight and show you." She leaves the house, she goes outside, they raise her up. And the final stanza of the song affirms, "As soon as they raised you up, Singamma, your house, too, stood up tall."

The story of Singamma is one of countless South Asian legends of virtuous, chaste women who are abused by husbands or male kinsmen, die violent, unjust deaths, and return to haunt the living as powerful and angry goddesses. The smallpox goddess Mariamman, worshiped by millions in Tamil Nadu, is supposed to have originated in such a way. Similarly, the great Sri Lankan goddess Pattini, the literary heroines Tankal and Nallatankal, and numerous regional and village goddesses share the attributes of long-suffering selfless devotion to husbands or brothers, spiritual power accumulated by dint of this devotion, violent death at the hands of villains, and postmortem apotheosis and revenge. The violation of sexual purity is

also a frequently occurring theme in South Indian goddess mythology.
Many South Indian women laboring under the burden of a sexually oppressive society, made more onerous still by the weight of poverty, identify
with the goddesses about whom such stories are told and draw comfort
from the promise of ultimate justice and empowerment that they offer. In
Tamil Nadu, the possession cults that grow up around these goddesses tend
to cut across caste boundaries, emhasizing not caste hierarchy but solidarity
among women in similar situations of distress. Typically in South Asia, it is
a young, recently married woman who is most likely to become possessed
by a goddess or some other spirit. This is because the role of the new
daughter-in-law is perhaps the most oppressive of all social roles in India.
Removed in her early teens from the home of her parents and siblings, married to a stranger and living in the house of strangers, treated as a servant
and burdened with a workload much greater than any she has ever borne
before, clumsily deflowered and required to submit to frequent sexual intercourse with her stranger-husband so that she will quickly become pregnant, knowing that if she does not become pregnant within a year she may
be reviled, beaten, sent back in disgrace to her parents' house and never
given a second chance at motherhood, the young daughter-in-law can easily break down. When a spirit enters her, she does not, cannot, act herself,
for the spirit controls her speech and movements. The girl may dance
wildly, may hurl obscenities at her in-laws, may refuse to work: all this is the
possessing spirit's doing. The spirit may demand special foods, special
clothes. When these demands are met, the spirit departs. Meanwhile, the
daughter-in-law has gained a brief respite from work, a chance to let out her
feelings, and perhaps also some nourishing and tasty food and attractive
clothing, without being held responsible for her strange behavior. Some
women gain greater freedom and power still by becoming professional
spirit mediums and healers. In this capacity, they serve only their spirit fa-
miliars; husband and children must take second place. If a spirit medium is
successful, she may earn a substantial income and will become the undisputed ruler of her family.

The politics of spirit possession is nothing new to anthropologists; the
patterns just described have frequently been reported by observers of the
lives of poor people over the decades. Spirit possession happens throughout the world but seems to be especially prevalent in South Asia, where
literary texts document its occurrence from the beginning of the first mil-
lenium B.C. Like the story of the suffering-woman-turned-angry-goddess,
with which it is often combined, spirit possession is an ancient, well-
established way for South Asian women to cope with the most oppressive
aspects of their lives, without actually setting themselves against the system
(family/village/state/society) that oppresses them but on which they are
dependent for their survival.

Thus, when I returned to Tamil Nadu in 1990 and visited Melur, I was not surprised to learn that a possession cult had grown up around the shrine of Singamma and that most of the people who became possessed by Singamma's spirit were (in the words of a man living near the shrine, who claimed to have helped build it) "recently married Paraiyar women who are having problems with their families." At least within the specialized context of this possession cult, it seemed, the antipathy between Jackal Hunters and Paraiyars was suspended.

In 1984 when I first heard the hymn to Singamma, I was nearing the end of a busy period of fieldwork and did not have time to visit Melur and learn more about the cult. So I took the song home and studied it together with other materials I had recorded that year, looking forward to the time when I could go back and hear different versions of the song that had been performed so movingly by the Paraiyar singer. Most of all I wanted to know what the Jackal Hunters themselves could tell me about Singamma. Did they worship at her shrine? Was she an established deity of their own? Had they introduced her story to other castes, who liked it and adopted it? Did they have professional spirit mediums who served her? Did Jackal Hunter women gain power in this way? I had a feeling that the "historical" Singamma had lived and died not so long ago. Perhaps there would be some older members of the Jackal Hunter community who had actually known her and could tell me about the events of her life and death as they remembered them. Then I could document the growth of the cult from its beginning in an actual human life tragically ended to its culmination in the birth of a goddess. This would be a good example of a truth I had come to see as archetypal, how in India the power of Womanhood always triumphs, even as countless real Indian women needlessly meet early deaths.

But because I had pressing concerns at home, the years slipped by without my finding a chance to return to India. At last in 1987, I phoned Barnie Bate, a young graduate student friend of mine who was just departing for Tamil Nadu, and asked him if he would visit the Singamma shrine in Melur for me. I explained that I was trying to find a Jackal Hunter rendition of the hymn to Singamma. "If the shrine has a priest or a shaman," I said, "ask him or her to tell you the story of Singamma. Tape-record the shaman's version if you can." I assumed that the people in charge of the Singamma shrine would themselves be Jackal Hunters, since this goddess might represent to the world at large a strong image of their proud caste.

A year later, I got a package from Barnie, containing a tape cassette, a transcription of the cassette's contents, some photographs of the Singamma shrine, and a long letter describing his experience in investigating the shrine. It had been difficult, he wrote, because the exorcist who worked at the shrine—his name was Vellaccami—did not understand why Barnie was there and felt intimidated by him.

"The recording session lasted about two hours," Barnie wrote.

Vellaccami sang directly into the microphone, and when his eyes were not closed he looked at the dancing L.E.D. lights on the machine. We stopped several times and discussed the tape, the machine, and if we could hear it. . . . At the end I attempted to ask some questions of him about his family and upbringing. My questioning and timing were sloppy and he clammed up. I decided it wasn't the time or place. He was so conscious of the machine and tightened up when the red light indicated it was on. He relaxed noticeably when it was off.

After the aborted interview I attempted to calm him down a bit by engaging in light conversation. Again, failure. I asked his wife if she were afraid that her husband dealt with ghosts. She said something I didn't catch, so I repeated, "Does it frighten you to listen to this song?" She said, "*You're* the one that frightens me!" She then went on to express her fears that I was some kind of police and that I would force her husband to stop working.

Nevertheless, the song on the cassette was a fine performance. It was also quite different from the performance I had collected from the young Paraiyar woman, Cevi. Whereas Cevi's song was addressed directly to Singamma and the events were narrated largely in the second person, Vellaccami's narration was in the third person entirely. Vellaccami's song identified precisely the site of Singamma's death and the manner in which she was killed, while Cevi's song was vague on both counts. Cevi's song contained numerous magical and mythical elements: a talking worm, a building growing up by itself, the heroine before her death assuming an animal form. Vellaccami's song was dramatic but unmythologized; all the events it described could have been historical fact. While Cevi dwelled on Singamma's goodness and virtue, Vellaccami dwelled on her seductive beauty. Cevi's song climaxed at Singamma's apotheosis. Vellaccami's song climaxed at the rape scene, which it described in long and cinematic detail, comparing the trapped Singamma to a frantic sparrow captured in a net. In Cevi's song, Singamma was raped by her own brothers; in Vellaccami's song, she was raped by two higher-caste men. Vellaccami's song also contained a long description of the possession of the rapist's daughter by Singamma's ghost and the role of the exorcist in identifying and placating the ghost. In the middle of his song, Vellaccami suddenly changed voices to simulate the market cries of a Jackal Hunter girl inviting customers to buy birds and strings of beads, jackal bones, and healing oils from her: a wild rhythmic chant that sounded partly human, partly jackal, partly bird. These were the cries that Singamma's ghost was supposed to emit through the mouth of her victim. Cevi's song contained none of these elements.

What could account for all these differences between the two songs? Until I had a chance to go back to India myself and ask, I could only guess. Since

Vellaccami evidently made part of his living as an exorcist at the Singamma shrine, it would make sense for him to stress in his performance the important role of the exorcist in dealing with Singamma's ghost. Low-caste men sometimes did become goddess mediums, dressing in women's clothing and speaking and acting like women when they went into trance and received the spirit of the goddess. Some anthropologists have argued that these men are acting out a kind of Oedipal fixation. Perhaps Vellaccami was a medium of this sort. Perhaps this was why he emphasized, indeed dramatized, the sexuality of the goddess.

My visit to Melur in 1990 deflated this last hypothesis and was in other respects also rather disappointing. Vellaccami was not a medium of Singamma, nor did he become possessed by her or identify with her or consider himself her devotee. Rather, he was an exorcist who in the past ten years had cornered the market on Singamma's ghost, exorcising her for a fee from spirit-possessed young women. The demand for his services as an exorcist being irregular, he had other businesses, too, including a regular business as a fortune-teller in the Melur market. He was not a Jackal Hunter but a Kallar, the Kallars being one of the more powerful landholding castes in the area. I judged from his well-made clothing and his new bicycle that in general he was doing pretty well.

Vellaccami remembered singing for Barnie. When I approached him, he seemed not afraid but rather like he did not want to be bothered with me. He said that since he had already sung the Singamma story for Barnie and since I had the tape, there was no point in doing the same performance for me. Barnie, he said, had promised I would come and pay him for his performance. I doubted this was true but gave him twenty rupees all the same.

The people in charge of the Singamma shrine, that is, the building itself in which she was said to be housed, were also Kallar men. They told me they were devotees of Singamma, whose shrine used to be at the base of a nearby banyan tree. When the banyan tree fell over a few years ago, they pooled their money and built this shrine. They all were local residents, but this was not anyone's home village, they told me. Until ten years ago, the place had been a wasteland where nobody lived. Then a cotton mill had been built there, and a village had grown up around it to house the workers. Singamma's grave site was inside the cotton mill grounds, but I could not visit it. The grounds were enclosed in barbed wire and only mill workers were allowed in. The guard at the gate to the mill sternly enforced this prohibition.

Why had they bothered to build a new shrine for the ghost of a Jackal Hunter girl? "As an act of devotion, an act of merit," one man answered. "Singamma is a powerful spirit. In return for our devotion, she will protect the village and the mill."

Did Jackal Hunters ever come and worship at the shrine? "Occasionally," the man answered. "When the Jackal Hunters pass through here, they offer worship to Singamma just as everyone else does. But they have no special connection with her."

How did the spirit of Singamma attack people? "Here is how it happens," a younger man said. "A young girl will be walking down the road, past the shrine. At the time she passes the shrine, something will startle her. Perhaps just a sudden loud noise. When she is startled, then the ghost of Singamma will attack her, but the girl will not realize it at the time. She will return to her own village. Years later, after she is married, when there are some troubles in her marriage, that is when she will become possessed. Then they will call in an exorcist, and the ghost will identify itself as Singamma. Then the girl will be brought here, and the ghost will be dispelled."

When a young woman was possessed by the spirit of Singamma, another man told me, she would start chanting the market cries characteristic of Jackal Hunter women selling their beads and small birds at festivals. She would demand to be dressed in Jackal Hunter clothing and to be fed jackal meat. The clothing would be bought for her and the meat procured, and she would be led dancing down the road to the Singamma shrine. Vellaccami would lead her along the way, keeping her moving to the beat of his drum. When they reached the shrine a cock would be sacrificed and the spirit would depart. The depossessed woman would put on her old clothes and leave the Jackal Hunter outfit as an offering at the shrine. I wondered when I learned the details of this exorcism ritual whether some higher-caste women might secretly envy the mobility, the defiance, and the flamboyance of the Jackal Hunter people. Possession by Singamma might allow a hardworking and respectable village daughter-in-law to be a dirty runaway Jackal Hunter girl for a while. The cult of Singamma might give village women a context in which to think deeply about joining hands with Jackal Hunter women.

"Who are the girls who become possessed?" I asked. "Has this happened to local women? May I meet any of them?"

"No," the men answered. "It is mostly Paraiyar women from other villages."

But one man who looked about fifty years old volunteered, "My wife was possessed by Singamma, many years ago. But that was before they built the shrine, before Vellaccami came here."

Could I meet his wife? "No, she has gone to her home village."

I left the shrine and the village and walked back to the Melur market, where I had been told there might be Jackal Hunters. I was feeling discouraged. It seemed as though the Jackal Hunter goddess Singamma, in whose fate I had come to feel I had an interest, had been entirely appropriated and circumscribed by middle-caste, landowning men. Vellaccami controlled her spirit, the cotton mill owned her body, and the shrine builders managed her public image. No landless person, no overworked woman benefited from her power, except perhaps the young Paraiyar wives who were "attacked" by her, and whatever they gained seemed fleeting.

I hunted through the Melur market for the Jackal Hunters I had been told might be there, asking many people, but my search was futile. They were gone. I might catch a bus to the Alagar temple where a festival was going on; a child had told me they were probably there. I was exhausted from my miles of walking through the midafternoon heat. I decided just to go home and headed for the bus stand.

While I was waiting for the bus, an old man dressed in white khadi hailed me. "I hear you're interested in the Jackal Hunters," he beamed. "I can tell you all about them; I'm a social worker, involved in the Society for the Advancement of Jackal Hunters."

Better than nothing, I thought, and followed him to his house. It was a small one-room place near the bus stand, half office and half home. The old man spoke for what seemed like a long time, while I listened, not needing to say much to keep him going. He began by citing Thurston's description of the Jackal Hunters. He told me that there were several nomadic tribes in the Madurai area. Some, such as the Lambadis, were fierce, but the Jackal Hunters were gentle people. They were monogamous, he said, as if proud of them for this, and they did not steal. Prior to India's independence, some Gandhian social workers had taken an interest in them, hoping to help them, but most of the Jackal Hunters were not interested in being helped. One orphaned Jackal Hunter boy was adopted by these social workers, raised and educated and married by them to an orphaned girl of another caste. Then when he was an adult, he was sent back to his own people to help organize them and educate them. He failed in this task: the Jackal Hunters ostracized him because he had cut his hair and adopted high-caste Hindu ways and, worst of all, had married outside the community.

Later, the old man said, another Gandhian social reformer took it on himself to develop the Jackal Hunters. He bought land for them and built houses and schools for them, and he himself had even married a Jackal Hunter woman. He had a hostel for Jackal Hunter children in Saidapet, where he also lived with his wife and child. Scores of Jackal Hunter children had been taken away from their parents and lodged at the hostel, where they were taught to read and write and to be vegetarians and were given vocational training. One such child had even gone on to get a Ph.D. in engineering, the old man told me. Great advances had been made.

I thanked the old man and left for home, feeling even more uncomfortable than before. On the one hand, I felt nothing but admiration for Gandhi and his followers, whose main aim had been to instill in the Indian people, especially Untouchables and women, enough confidence in their own strength and courage to demand independence. As part of his program of nonviolence, Gandhi was a vegetarian, and I had become a pacifist and a vegetarian myself partly because of his influence.

On the other hand, to try to transform hunter-gatherers into vegetarians for purely philosophical reasons seemed to me to be a problematic pursuit. And the old man's description of Jackal Hunter children being taken away from their parents, kept in a boarding school, and made to adopt the way of life sanctioned by the dominant culture reminded me of an account I had once read by a Hopi woman who had been taken from her home as a child and forced to live in a government school. Native Americans did not feel they had benefited from these kinds of "educational" programs. Were the nomadic tribes of India faring any better?

A short while later, I found myself in Madras and went to visit close friends who knew the neighborhood where the Jackal Hunter hostel was supposed to be located. Yes, they knew of this hostel, they said. It was famous; everyone in town knew where it was. The man who ran it was a member of their own caste, Reddiars. His name was Raghupathi. One of my friends thought he had married a Brahman woman named Jnana Sundari. And yes, indeed, the children they had taken in were being improved. Recently, the children had given a concert at the Jackal Hunter hostel. They were adorable, my friend said. They sang very sweetly in perfect Tamil long songs that they had memorized, and they were impeccably clean and well mannered. You would never have known they were Jackal Hunters, she said. My friend was angry that at the beginning of the concert the children were introduced as Jackal Hunters. She said it made them dirty, it made the performance dirty, to call them by that name. Someone else had argued with her, saying that it was important to say what caste these children belonged to, to show to the world that even Jackal Hunter children could come this far.

The Jackal Hunter hostel was in a hollow behind the main bus stop at Saidapet. There was one large concrete building containing the school on the first floor and the beadwork factory on the second. Next to that was a smaller concrete building housing the main administrative office. Behind these two buildings were two rows of concrete houses. In front of the building complex was about an acre of open space containing several large banyan trees. Camped beneath the banyan trees were what appeared to be several families of Jackal Hunters. They did not look up as I walked by them to the main office.

"I've come to see Jnana Sundari. Is she in?"

"She's gone to a wedding. She will be back later this morning."

"May I wait here for her?"

"Certainly. Would you like some tea?"

As I waited, I looked around the office. People working behind desks. Typewriters. Newspaper clippings framed and hung on the wall. Twenty minutes passed.

"While I'm waiting, may I look at that newspaper article on the wall?"

A young office worker brought it to me, together with a scrapbook containing other magazine and newspaper clippings. One article in the Indian Express discussed the "problem" of the Jackal Hunters' refusal to be reformed. In its efforts to improve the lot of scheduled tribes, the Indian government had made gifts of houses and land to the Jackal Hunter community, so that they would have an opportunity to convert from a foraging to an agricultural mode of subsistence. But the Jackal Hunters had abandoned the property granted to them and insisted on continuing their itinerant way of life. Why? According to the author of the article, Jackal Hunters have a strong belief in spirits and ghosts. They will not stay in a place where a person has died, for fear that the spirit of the dead person, tethered to the site of its death, will haunt them. If the Jackal Hunters remain in one place for too long, eventually a member of their community dies there. Then they must abandon that place and move on. (If this is true, I wondered, could it be the reason why the Jackal Hunters do not lay claim to the shrine of Singamma?)

Another article talked about Raghupathi and his decision to devote his life to the Jackal Hunters. In his youth he had seen the corpse of a Jackal Hunter who had died of smallpox, lying festering near a train station. Nobody would touch the corpse because it was double polluting: it was the body of a Jackal Hunter, and it was killed by smallpox. Raghupathi had taken the corpse away and burned it himself. Later he saw a Jackal Hunter woman giving birth at a bus stand. No one would come near her, not even her own kin, because of the birth pollution, so Raghupathi himself assisted in delivering the baby. Shortly after it was born, the mother picked up the baby and went begging around the bus stand. These two experiences shocked and disturbed Raghupathi so much that he decided he must do something to improve the Jackal Hunters' condition. On the day that he saw the new mother go begging, he determined to make the development of the Jackal Hunters his life's work. So he moved in with a band of Jackal Hunters and started holding classes for the children. Subsequently, he decided that he could not sincerely devote himself to the Jackal Hunter community unless he married one of its members, so he began a search for a Jackal Hunter girl who could be his bride. Since the Jackal Hunters were unwilling to give any of their young daughters in marriage to a man from outside their community, and since Raghupathi himself, despite his decision to marry across caste, still insisted that his bride be educated, vegetarian, and previously unmarried, it seemed unlikely that a match would ever be made. Eventually, however, Raghupathi made the acquaintance of the Jackal Hunter man who had been raised and educated by the Gandhian social workers, and he married this man's daughter. Her name was Jnana Sundari.

"Until Jnana Sundari comes, is there anyone else I can speak with? May I speak with the Jackal Hunters outside?"

The office worker seemed accustomed to such requests. "Will any of them do?" he asked.

"Yes."

He went out and came back a minute later with a young woman and a ten-year-old girl. The woman was chewing betel. She spat out the door.

"This child has run away from the hostel many times," the office worker told me. "Her mother," he said, glancing coolly at the insouciant woman, "does not discipline the child for running away. She is the reason they will not be corrected."

I followed the betel-chewing woman out to the foot of the biggest banyan tree, where six or eight people were sitting.

"Do you know what this is?" I asked in Tamil, showing them my portable tape recorder.

"It's a Panasonic cassette recorder," one of the children answered. "How much did it cost?"

I turned on the tape recorder. "Have you ever heard of a goddess called Singamma? She lives in Melur. They say she was one of your people."

Blank stares all around. "No, we don't know."

I wondered where I should go from here. It would be nice if I had time to stay with them longer. But I had to board a train that night.

"Can you tell me anything about the deities you worship?" I felt foolish. An old man standing by rattled off a list of names of deities, starting with Kali.

"Do you like your itinerant way of life?" I asked him, hoping to ease into the question of why the Jackal Hunters would not stay on the land that had been given them.

The old man pulled a pile of battered postcards from his pouch. "We've been all over India," he said, smiling broadly. I looked at the postcards. Delhi. Benares. Agra. Bombay. Srinagar.

"You've been as far as Srinagar?" I asked incredulously.

"I've been as far as Srinagar," he responded with obvious pride.

"But do you *like* traveling all the time?" I asked. "Would you settle down if you could?"

The old man did not answer. It was as though he could not understand the question, which was possible. "We've traveled all over India," he repeated, showing me the postcards again. I turned back to the young woman.

"Would it be possible for you to tell me the story of your origin?" Since the Paraiyar version of the story of Singamma was told as an explanation of why and how the Jackal Hunter caste had "fallen," I thought the Jackal Hunters might have a related account.

"Or could you tell me the story of any of your gods?" I asked. It was a long shot, certainly, since I had just arrived that morning and was a total stranger, but the Jackal Hunters did not seem suspicious of me, as Vellaccami had been. They had probably been interviewed in this same fashion by more than one newspaper reporter, if one were to judge by all the newspaper clippings the office worker had shown me.

"We should tell the story in our traditional way," the young woman said to me.

"That would be good," I answered.

She summoned a young teenage girl to come help her, then seated herself on one of the more elevated roots of the banyan tree, while the girl sat down at her feet. The woman commenced a formal narrative, in verse, in what I took to be the Jackal Hunters' own language. I could not understand a word of it. At intervals, the girl at her feet would inject a question, keeping to the meter, and the woman would respond. It seemed like a sort of catechism, with the elder woman acting as instructor, the younger as student or novice. In the middle of this performance, the office worker interrupted us.

"Jnana Sundari has come," he said to me. "She invites you to her house for lunch."

"Come back as soon as you finish eating," the Jackal Hunter woman told me. "There will be more of us here at that time, and we will be able to answer your questions better."

"Be sure to visit our beadworking factory before you leave," the office worker said.

I mounted the stairs to Jnana Sundari's apartment. She was a small, round, serious woman, dressed with impeccable modesty. I could understand why people would take her for a Brahman. She told me that the best person to talk to about the Jackal Hunters was her husband. He was the founder of this establishment and could explain things to me better than she herself could, she said. But she became friendlier when she saw that I could understand Tamil. I explained to her about my interest in Singamma. She was intrigued.

"I was born and grew up in Melur," she said, "But I have never heard of this goddess." I told her about the way that young Paraiyar women were possessed by the spirit of Singamma and spoke in her voice. As I spoke, Jnana Sundari's eyes grew wide. "They speak in the Jackal Hunter tongue?" she asked.

"Singamma speaks through them," I answered. I then told her the story of Singamma, about how she had been murdered by her brothers because of the loss of her chastity.

"The Jackal Hunters of that time practiced a severe discipline," Jnana Sundari commented, after she had heard the story. I thought I detected a hint of pride in her voice. These were, after all, her own kinsmen.

Jnana Sundari cooked and served lunch (vegetarian, of course) to me and a cousin of Raghupathi's who was visiting. We all sat together at a table and talked as we ate, Western-style. I asked the cousin what Raghupathi's family had thought about Raghupathi marrying a Jackal Hunter girl. They were all in favor of it, the cousin said to my surprise. There had been many cross-caste marriages in that family. Their tradition of social activism went way back. Old leftists, I realized with delight as he spoke. A whole family of radical utopians.

Raghupathi entered, smiling cheerfully. Jnana Sundari introduced me and repeated what I had said about Singamma. "When girls become possessed by her, they speak the Jackal Hunter language," Jnana Sundari told him. Raghupathi made no comment.

He was a handsome man with eyes burning fiercely above a well-kept salt-and-pepper beard. He wore a green turban and a green shirt, which he explained to me were signs of his membership in the local Green Party. He said, "I hear there is an organization called Greenpeace in America. I would like to write to them but do not know their address." I promised I would send him the address when I got back home, as I often received mailings from that organization.

The betel-chewing woman whom I had started to interview before was at the door, summoning me. "All the people are gathered out under the trees now," she said. "We're ready to continue telling you the story."

"I'll be there in a few minutes," I said, "as soon as I've finished talking with Jnana Sundari and Raghupathi."

"The people outside can't wait for you," the woman replied. "They all have to leave again in a little while. Give me the tape recorder and I'll record the story for you and bring it back to you before you leave."

I started to hand my tape recorder to the woman, but Jnana Sundari stopped me. "Don't let them use the tape recorder," she said. "If you want to make a recording of the things they say, you should operate the machine yourself." I glanced helplessly at the betel-chewing woman, who shrugged and started back down the stairs.

"They will never be corrected," said Jnana Sundari. It was a statement I heard several times in the course of the day.

Raghupathi had agreed to let me interview him, and so after lunch we went up to the roof where there was less noise and Raghupathi thought the acoustics would be better. He spoke for about an hour, telling me about his encounters with the corpse and the parturient woman, essentially the same accounts that had been written up in the newspaper some years before, and then telling me his future plans. He hoped to start a school in which the children would be taught to live in a natural way.

"All you need is a tree," he said. "All you need is to sit in the shade of the tree and eat the fruit that the tree provides. You do not need electricity. You do not need civilization. You do not need science." He hoped to teach the Jackal Hunter children under his protection to live in this fashion.

"But don't the Jackal Hunters already lead a natural life?" I asked him.

"They lead a *kind* of natural life," he conceded. "But their food habits are very bad. They eat all kinds of meat."

I left Raghupathi's house feeling somewhat reassured. The Jackal Hunters were not required by law to send their children to his school, and the families of the children in the school could easily fetch the children away if things got too uncomfortable for them. Raghupathi was a gentle, courageous man who meant only good for the children he had taken under his wing. He had given the Jackal Hunters another option and had probably been instrumental in improving their economic situation.

And yet I also felt there was something wrong. Clearly, Raghupathi's values conflicted on many accounts with those of the Jackal Hunters themselves, and I wondered how practical his idea of living under a tree really was. The Jackal Hunters knew what it was like to live under a tree. How much had Raghupathi's dreams been influenced by the realities of Jackal Hunter life? It was the kind of question that could not be answered in one afternoon's conversation. What would happen if the Jackal Hunters became what Raghupathi wanted them to be? They would probably be better off in many ways, at least for a while. But a way of life would disappear, knowledge would be lost, foraging as a survival option for human beings would be rendered still less viable than it had already become. We might need that way of life, that knowledge, that option someday soon. Did Raghupathi know this? He seemed to be an incurable idealist, to romanticize the natural way of life. Or was I the romantic? It seemed to me that Raghupathi, as a high-caste male, was appropriating the Jackal Hunters to his own utopian purposes, just as Vellaccami had appropriated their goddess for the sake of his livelihood. But was I not appropriating the two of *them,* incorporating them into my research design?

As I left the apartment of Raghupathi and Jnana Sundari, thanking both of them for all their kindness and all their help, the young office worker whom I had met in the morning approached me. "Please come and visit our bead factory before you leave," he said, repeating his earlier invitation. I followed him to the bead factory, which was on the second floor of the building next door. There in glass cases were necklaces and belts and earrings and seated on the floor were six or eight well-dressed young adults working at making more beaded jewelry. A sign above the door proclaimed, "Au-

thentic Gypsy Beadwork." The Jackal Hunters of Tamil Nadu are often referred to as gypsies.

"Are you all Jackal Hunters?" I asked the young workers. They did not
look it. But they politely said they were. I examined the things on display
and bought a belt and some earrings and many strings of necklaces, partly
to please the manager of the factory who had brought me there and partly
because I like beads.

By now it was late afternoon and I knew I had to get back to my hotel
room and pack my suitcase for my journey that evening. I was hoping to continue my interview with the Jackal Hunters outside, even if the woman I had
originally spoken to was gone, but as I left the beadworking factory, I saw
that there were only a half-dozen people beneath the banyan trees now, including one well-built middle-aged man standing naked under the largest
tree pouring water over himself. No, I will not try to interview him during
his bath, I decided, and continued on my way to the bus stand. That night,
Lakshmi and I took the train to Tirunelveli.

I had work to do which kept me from exploring the town, but a few days
after we arrived in Tirunelveli, Lakshmi reported to me that she had found
a group of Jackal Hunters camped near the train station. When we went to
the place where she had seen them, they were no longer there. The station
master had driven them away, we were told. But Lakshmi took me to the
bazaar to a place where she had seen one of the women selling beads, and
there that woman was again.

"Take us to your home," Lakshmi said. She meant the place where the
group of Jackal Hunters was staying while they were in Tirunelveli. Funny
that she called it their home.

The woman stopped at an empty stall in the bazaar and said, "Sit down.
I can tell you the story here." But Lakshmi commanded her to take us to
where the other Jackal Hunters were staying. The woman seemed not to
want to do it. I guessed that she wanted to keep me, as a potential customer,
to herself. It was probably hard making a living selling beads.

Reluctantly, at Lakshmi's insistence, the woman led us over the foot-
bridge to the other side of the railroad tracks. There in an open lot next to
the tracks about a hundred people were sitting scattered about. When they
saw us coming, a dozen or so of them crowded around us. There was much
talking in what must have been their own language with some Tamil mixed
in. I heard the words *muppatu varusham* ("thirty years") and *ate katai* ("the
same story"). The woman was trying to explain to the others what I wanted.
A train rumbled by on the tracks twenty feet away, drowning out all other
sounds. A turbaned man broke through the crowd pressing in on me. Except for his turban and some amulets hung around his neck, he had on only
a loincloth. In carefully enunciated English he said to me, one word at a
time, "Where are you come from?"

"I come from America," I answered him in Tamil.

"Ahhh," the whole crowd said in unison, whether responding to the content of my answer or to the language in which it was couched, I did not know.

"How do you perform your weddings?" another woman said in Tamil, looking not at me but at the other people in the crowd, as though answering a question rather than asking one. She had guessed the nature of my business and was predicting the kind of thing I would say next.

This woman, whose name I learned later was Jagathamba, was now told once again by the woman who had led me to the encampment that I was interested in the story of the girl who had died in Melur thirty years ago.

Jagathamba told one of the children to go fetch a straw mat. The child brought the mat, and Jagathamba laid it down by the side of the road.

"Sit down," she said, touching me on the shoulder. She touched me again and again as she spoke to me. "Do you want us to tell you the story in our own language, or in Tamil?"

"Tell it first in your own language," I answered. "Then tell it in Tamil."

"Ahhh," said the crowd again.

Jagathamba and the first woman seated themselves facing each other on the mat, and I placed the tape recorder between them. They began a performance that was not unlike the pedagogical one I had seen in Madras, a kind of formal rapid-fire dialogue, one speaking and the other responding. The first woman would say a few sentences in the Jackal Hunter language, and Jagathamba would then repeat them in Tamil. After a while, the alternation of languages broke down, and the first woman interjected many comments in Tamil, as though wanting to bypass the formalism of speaking first in a language I did not know. I translate here the Tamil portions of the performance.

"A girl went to town, it is said, to beg something to eat."

"They invited the girl, saying, 'I'll give you food. Come to my house.' With these words, they invited her, it is said."

"On both sides, they closed the doors, it is said."

"She was a grown-up girl, and they invited her to secretly have intercourse, it is said."

"They stuffed a cloth in that girl's mouth, it is said."

"Then they raped that girl and wasted her, it is said."

"Then they closed that girl out of the house, it is said."

"She had six brothers, it is said. Those six brothers . . . "

"She said to those six brothers, it is said, to those six brothers, 'If you keep me, keep me, or if you leave me, leave me, or if you kill me, kill me, in whatever manner."

"The youngest brother said she had committed a sin. The oldest brother said, 'One must not commit a sin. We must not keep her.' "

"Then the boy said, 'I will marry that girl,' it is said. 'I will keep that girl, and give you twelve rupees brideprice, and marry that girl.' So he spoke, it is said. But those brothers did not agree, it is said. 'We don't want you. You may leave us. You must not marry her. You must not perform a marriage, leaving your own caste, and going to another caste asking. You must not keep that girl.' That is what those brothers said to that farmer boy."

"Then the brothers brought that girl away, telling her to lie across their thigh, and with a hammer, an iron hammer, beating her with that hammer, they killed her."

The woman who had been telling the story in the Jackal Hunter language while Jagathamba translated, now slipped into Tamil, saying, "Then she became a ghost."

"That girl became a ghost," Jagathamba repeated.

"Then having become a ghost, in order once again to be born, she went to a girl among those people who graze cattle and goats, and she seized her, it is said. Having seized her, she said, 'Only if you bring oil and a buck or bull and give them to me will I come out.' "

"What does she do, they say? 'Give earrings, corn gruel, a sari, a mat, like this one, a mat, a bottle. Leave all that.' "

Another woman interjected, "She asks all of that, because of what happened."

The narration continued, and Jagathamba translated, "Having become a ghost, that ghost will seize a woman, no? Then the people of that caste will die. She goes and becomes a ghost, and a farmer girl, someone who is out grazing cattle and goats, she will attack her. Then what will she ask? 'Give me gruel, give me earrings, give me corn, give me a mat, give me a bottle, give me jewels and bangles.' So she asks, it is said. That farmer girl. She is the one who becomes a ghost and inhabits that shrine. Then she will seize *you*. You must go there and ask, they say. In Melur. They say you have asked. When he beats his drum, that exorcist, when you ask him, he tells you directly. 'In this way, people of the Jackal Hunter caste, they sell beads and needles, a goddess [*sakti*] went by, in this way five or six people raped her and killed her, then she herself came and seized someone. Now she wants jewelry, earrings, a mat, gruel, jackal meat . . . ' "

"Jackal meat?" I asked.

"Jackal meat," Jagathamba repeated. "They won't eat all that, but if the ghost seizes that girl she will ask for that, and she will eat it, they say. She will ask for it and eat it."

More narrative came now in the Jackal Hunter language. Jagathamba translated, "When that was finished, the six brothers had six wives, it is said. They all wept, it is said. Having wept, the six of them cut up the girl and buried her and went to another town."

"And that boy who had invited her to have secret intercourse, that boy who invited the sparrowlike girl to have secret intercourse, they captured her [*sic*] in a tape, it is said, and the one who punished her by killing her, they captured the two men in the tape, the music, the sound, that house, that road, there is a little road, he took her along that road, that grown-up girl, to take her along the road they captured her in the tape. And afterwards . . . "

"Whatever farmer girl wearing flowers goes along that road, for desire of the flowers she will sit upon that girl. She will turn to a ghost. She dances, she sings, if the ghost lights upon the girl who wore flowers, it is said, she speaks the language of our caste. Then they take her to an exorcist. Banana, green chilies, onions, millet gruel, corn gruel, she will ask for all that, it is said. Jackal meat, she will ask for that to eat, it is said. That's the story," said Jagathamba.

"That's the story!" I echoed, breathless and laughing.

"That's what they captured on the tape, it is said," answered Jagathamba. "They captured it on the tape and went from town to town wearing roses and dancing. It's on the tape, they say. To raise the habit of nonviolence, just one woman, she went to every single town. A devotee of god, she became a devotee of god."

"They captured it on the tape?" I asked.

"They captured it on the tape. There, in Melur."

"Who?"

"That temple. In Melur there is a temple, no? Right in that temple, they captured it on the tape, it is said. Standing there in the temple, she wept, it is said."

"Standing right near the temple, she wept, it is said," the other woman affirmed.

"Those brothers . . . ," someone else put in.

Jagathamba continued, "She weeps within the temple, it is said. 'Oh God, you killed me in this way. They raped me, and my brothers killed me, and my sisters-in-law wept. And their children wept. What am I to do?' Like that she wept right near the temple, it is said. There is the bus stand in Melur, you know? And near the bus stand there is a temple, a big temple. Near that temple she wept profusely, it is said. She weeps within the temple, it is said. Near that temple, she wept profusely, it is said. In that very place he captured her, the tape-person."

Me: "Who wept?"

J.: "That girl, the girl who died."

Me: "Singamma?"

J.: "Singamma, Singamma. Her name is Singamma. Thirty years have passed. On this day thirty years have passed."

Someone else: "Thirty years, but she lives in that tape still."

J.: "Okay, now I will tell you a story."

Me: "Tell it."

J.: "I will tell you a story. A girl of our caste went to the farmers. She became a teacher. A girl of Madurai."

Me.: "Where?"

J.: "Madurai. Madurai. In Madurai, a girl of our caste was studying. While she was studying, a person, he was a Pillaimar . . . "

Me.: "From where?"

J.: "From Madras. No, he was a Reddiar. A Reddiar came and asked for a girl of our caste in marriage. And we said, 'Get lost, Mister! You should put mud in your mouth! What are you asking to marry a girl of our caste for?'

" 'No, mother,' he said, 'I am well bred. I too am an important man. I have studied enough to be a teacher myself. If you give a girl to me, an educated girl, I will marry her,' he said.

" 'We'll give you something, all right,' we said. 'Mud to put in your mouth. We will never give you a girl of ours. We will never do it.' And so they were talking, in our caste.

"But that man said he would not give up. 'What girl in your caste has studied?' he asked.

"In Madurai, there was a girl who was studying. Jnana Sundari. The girl whose name was Jnana Sundari. Raghupathi, his name was Raghupathi. He went. He went to MGR [M. G. Ramachandran, former chief minister who encouraged cross-caste marriages and presided over them en masse] and did the marriage. They did the marriage, and he gave her jewels and everything. They got married and she has two children, two girl children. A girl child, in our caste she became an important matter. She has taken our children and educated them."

Me: "Where is she?"

J.: "In Madras. In Saidapet. A big hostel. And in Kalyanamkundi. In Conjeevaram. Thevaraneri, where our Jackal Hunter colony is, on Sanjavaripuram Road. In our Jackal Hunter colony is a school, a big school. That one lone woman went and married that man, and wherever the people of our caste are, those children she educates to the eighth or the tenth or the twelfth grade, and now she is a fine, big, rich woman. Wherever she casts her eyes, there she buys land."

Me: "And now she's in Saidapet?"

J.: "Saidapet. Yes. Raghupathi."

Me.: "Have you been there?"

J.: "Yes. Our children have studied there. Those children, and these children [pointing some out], all of them are educated children, children who have studied to the eighth grade, the tenth grade . . . "

A young man interjects: "I'm an M.A.! M.A.!"

Me: "You're an M.A.? Having studied this far . . . "

Young man: "I am not working."

Me: "You're not working."

Young man: "The government gave me no work."

J.: "I'm just telling you. These children have studied. These girls. This boy. They have all studied. That girl. They have all studied. With Raghupathi."

Me: "Okay, you all have land . . . "

J.: "We have land. We have houses in Thevaraneri. In Thiruchendur on Sanjavaripuram Road. [She and the young man speak harshly to the noisy children in their own language, hushing the children up.] Please listen. In Thiruchendur on Sanjavaripuram Road. Our colony is at Thevaraneri. Hey! Karunanithi! [another chief minister]. Karunanithi gave us 140 houses, a schoolhouse, a radio office, a water tank, a school for the children to study, all the conveniences he gave us."

Me: "Okay, I have a question."

J.: "Yes."

Me: "You have gotten all these conveniences, yet still . . . "

J.: "We still live in this way?"

Me: "You wander from town to town."

J.: "There is no water. We have no water for farming."

Me: "Oh."

J.: "Only if the rain falls is there a harvest. If it doesn't, there isn't. In a year, there may be a harvest, or there may not be. They give us loans, the government. Loans. Six thousand per person. They give us six thousand. They gave it. We took the loans and we bought beads and sold them at Sabari Malai [a major pilgrimage center], and in this way we survived. But now they have stopped giving loans. Sometimes we do well, and sometimes we go hungry. Our children who have been to school have no work. We will do any kind of work, manual labor or office work. We do not steal. We do not tell lies."

The talk went on in this vein for some time. At one point I asked Jagath-amba, "Do your people still hunt? Can you get food in this way?"

She answered, "We used to hunt, but we don't so much any more."

"Why not?" I asked.

"Where's the forest?" she answered. "There is no forest anymore so how can we hunt? We still catch jackals and rabbits and sparrows and so forth. But we can't live on that."

"Where are you from?" the man with the M.A. asked me.

"America," I told him again.

"Tell the people of America we need a bore well," he said loudly into the tape recorder.

"Listen," I said, "I'm not the president of the United States."

"Ahhh," the whole group of them responded in unison, as before.

"I'll do what little I can," I said, "But please don't expect too much."

I told them that I wanted to hire one of their educated children to help me transcribe the tape we had just made, and perhaps we could take things from there. It was getting late in the afternoon and we all had other work to do, so we agreed to meet the following morning, to make further plans for the transcription.

As Lakshmi and I walked back to our hotel room, my mind was busy try-ing to absorb and make sense of all the things I had learned in the past two hours. Everything I had thought about the Jackal Hunters was turned around. I had had a vague sense, previously, that by studying the cult of Singamma, tape-recording the songs of the cult, analyzing them and pub-lishing my analyses, I was in a certain way appropriating, swallowing, and di-gesting a thing that belonged to the Jackal Hunters. If I was not harming the Jackal Hunters by doing this work, I was nevertheless inevitably distorting the information conveyed to me, merely by putting it into a publishable frame. But now I was made aware of an interesting twist to this chain of events, for now I saw that the Jackal Hunters had appropriated my act of ap-propriating them. They had taken the news of Barnie's tape-recording the story of Singamma in Melur and had incorporated this news into their retelling of the Singamma legend, embroidering on the "facts," to be sure, so as to fit the event to their own understanding of what Singamma was and so as to make the new episode in the legend redound to Singamma's glory. If Vellaccami the exorcist had "captured" Singamma in his song, and if my friend Barnie had in turn captured Vellaccami's captive version of Singamma on his tape cassette, then the Jackal Hunters had captured this whole scene in their new version of the Singamma story. It was like the car-toon picture of a fish eating a fish eating a fish. And here I was taking the form of the biggest fish and capturing the Jackal Hunters themselves, I thought wryly. But I had better keep an eye on my tail.

In another way, also, my new friends had surprised me, for they, the hunter-gatherers, had forced me, the anthropologist, out of my quaintly folkloristic and unprogressive frame of mind. I had come to them looking for a Jackal Hunter "version" of what I had come to think of as "the" Singamma story: a mythic ideal type, or else an actual historical event, whose pristine image I thought I could reconstruct more or less accurately if I col-lected enough versions of the tale. I saw Singamma herself as an example of the eternal Hindu goddess: tragic victim of brutal oppression, whose rage from the other side of death helps keep murders and rapists from doing it too often.

Jagathamba and her friends had seen what I wanted and had cheerfully complied with my request. They told me a story. Then they had doubled the ante, by telling me a second story, hard on the first. They had scarcely drawn a breath between the end of one story and the beginning of the next. They had not given me time to think that I was moving into a different category of ethnology, from myth and religion to political economy, from traditional thought to modern. They had just set the two stories side by side, given them a roughly parallel structure, and left it to me to weigh their relative values. The main formal difference between the two stories was that the first had an ending, the second did not.

In the first story a Jackal Hunter girl had gone out begging. Offering her food, a boy of an agricultural caste had raped her. After this, the girl had let her brothers decide what to do with her, giving them three choices: abandon her, keep her, or kill her. The boy had asked for the girl's hand in marriage, offering her kin a brideprice. The brothers had refused. They had killed the girl, their wives had wept, and the girl had come back as a ghost to haunt the living daughters of higher-caste men. Now she had achieved the stature of a goddess, but from the Jackal Hunters' point of view her story was over. Her life ended thirty years ago. Her hungry ghost was contained in a shrine; her weeping voice was contained on a tape. Only the hunger and the weeping would be eternal.

In the second story a Jackal Hunter girl had gone to school. A young man of an agricultural caste, desiring an educated Jackal Hunter wife, had asked to marry her. Suspecting the worst, the girl's kinsmen had at first refused, but the young man protested that his intentions were honorable, and the girl had married him. He gave her wealth, and she used it to buy land and houses for her own people and to educate their children. In Jagathamba's hands, Jnana Sundari's story had become a new myth, a new ideal for her daughters and sons to emulate. The Jackal Hunter girl who got a college education and married outside her caste had achieved the status of a heroine, but her work was far from complete. She was still teaching more children, still buying more land. And there was the big problem of finding jobs for the Jackal Hunters. A long, uphill battle awaited them all. Only the days of caste separatism were over.

I missed my appointment with the Jackal Hunters the morning I said I would visit them again. As I dozed through the misty dawn, I woke just long enough to tell myself they would probably forgive this lapse of punctuality. I instructed Lakshmi to wake me at 5:00 A.M. the next day, to accept no excuses. Lakshmi did as I asked and at 5:35 A.M. the day after I said I would visit them, I stumbled out the hotel door to visit the Jackal Hunters. I got to the bridge that went over the tracks just as the sun was rising. I mounted the bridge and looked down on the place where I had talked with them before. Not a soul was there, not a trace of there even having been an encampment. I realized with dismay that I should not have slept through my appointment the day before. Overnight, the Jackal Hunters had moved on.

THREE

Fresh Lima Beans and Stories from Occupied Cyprus

Mary N. Layoun

I will tell you something about stories,
[he said]
They aren't just entertainment,
Don't be fooled.
They are all we have, you see,
all we have to fight off
illness and death.

You don't have anything
if you don't have the stories.
—LESLIE MARMON SILKO, *Ceremony*

The Lebanese women and children had left the apartment across the yard. Able to afford a couple of months respite in Cyprus—away from water short-ages and electricity outages, car bombs and gun battles in the streets—they had now gone back to Lebanon. I had come to know the tall, dark-eyed woman in particular. She would sit on the narrow balcony of their apart-ment, clutching her hands and looking out over the dusty park next door. She had knocked quietly on my door late one morning to tell me she had heard me talking to my children while I hung out the clothes; she thought I sounded Lebanese; her next door neighbor had told her I was writing a book about refugees; she thought I should hear what had happened to her. I did, over coffee or orange juice on mornings when I did not leave early for the library or one of the archives. And our kids played together, trading their own stories of life in the midwestern United States and in Beirut. I thought I had to let her know that I was not writing about Lebanon or even about refugees in particular. She insisted it made no difference. She would visit and tell me about her neighbors and neighborhood in Beirut, her fam-ily elsewhere in Lebanon, the other women and children who had come to Cyprus with her. And she would ask about how I lived in the United States, what I was doing in Cyprus, how I came to teach literature, about my fam-ily, neighbors, and friends.

Now standing in her place on the balcony was a thin old woman dressed in black. She watched me closely as I hung out the clothes, a little surprised when after a while I greeted her in Greek.

"You're from America, aren't you? A teacher, right, who's writing a book?" (Information circulated rather efficiently in the neighborhood.) And then, after a short pause, "I have to talk to you."

In a few minutes, she came over carrying a large plastic bag. When I offered her coffee, she smiled and asked for orange juice instead. (Later she laughingly admitted that she was not sure at first whether I knew how to make Cypriot coffee, so orange juice seemed a safer choice.) She introduced herself as the owner of the flat across the yard, in Nicosia on a five-day "leave of absence" from her enclaved village in the north.[1] I introduced her to my mother-in-law who had come to spend a couple of months with us in Cyprus. While I got coffee and orange juice, they talked about daughters-in-law, about the effects on younger women of their access to education, and about the lace tablecloth that my mother-in-law was crocheting. As I reentered the room, the old woman called out.

"So, your mother-in-law makes lace, you make books, is that it?"

This pleased my mother-in-law, Eleni, immensely for she is the daughter of a village schoolteacher and proud of her six years of formal education. In a strong Cypriot dialect, the old woman proceeded to describe the school that her sons and daughters had attended in their now-enclaved village on the Karpassian peninsula in the Turkish-occupied north of Cyprus. She was in Nicosia to see her daughter and grandchildren and get medication for her husband who was too ill to make the long bus trip to the south. She rather matter-of-factly cataloged life under Turkish occupation—the harassment and daily indignities, the shortages of basic necessities and inaccessibility of medical care, the isolation and loneliness of being cut off from family and friends who had left or been forced out of their village, the frequent cancellations of their monthly passes to unoccupied Cyprus. With the help of substantial government subsidies for resettling refugees, her children had purchased the apartment across the way for her and her husband. But the old couple had never moved south to the unoccupied half of the capital city. They had had different plans; at this point in her story, tears quietly began to creep down the old woman's wrinkled brown face.

"In the beginning, we old folks thought we would stay in the villages to take care of things, to defend what was ours. Until everything went back to the way it was. It wouldn't be long, we thought. The [Cypriot] government urged us to resettle in the meantime, assured us that there would be a quick resolution by the U.N. to the 'Cyprus problem' and that all refugees would then return to their homes. But [unlike the younger villagers] we didn't have children to send to school, work to take care of. We had our pensions, our gardens with vegetables and an orange tree or two. So we stayed. We tried to keep things up. And we managed in the beginning. But we were already old to start with, and fifteen years have gone by. Now we can barely manage. Me, of course, I'm younger than my husband."

Here the old woman smiled faintly, with a touch of pride.

"Fifteen years ago, we thought . . . we would hold out against the invaders. We old folks would be the 'front line.' "

She paused for a moment and smiled again, a little more sadly this time.

"Then we stopped talking so much about everything going back to the way it was. We knew anyway. And the oldest of us started dying off. We had trouble preparing and burying the dead. It got harder to take care of our houses, of the vegetable gardens that we depended on."

The old woman stopped again and looked at me almost fiercely.

"Are you going to put this in your book? Will you remember? You write that we weren't fooled. We knew. We knew things weren't going back to the way they were before. But we stayed anyway. No matter what the [Cypriot] government said; we told them we would hold out in the north. No matter what the Turkish military authorities threatened; we told them we were old and could cause them no harm, that they had nothing to gain by forcing us out. No matter how much we would rather have been close to our children; we told them we would wait for their return to our village. And we weren't wrong. Or maybe we were. But we weren't fooled. We knew."

She broke off for a moment, wiping her eyes almost angrily. And then she began again, telling us now about her house, her children, her family and co-villagers, the things they had and the way they lived before the invasion. Looking often at my empty hands, she punctuated her story with "Do you understand me? Will you remember what I say?" My mother-in-law—feeling, I think, compelled to defend the absence of tape recorder or paper and pencil—reassured the old Cypriot woman that I had a great memory, that I could remember telephone numbers and addresses from years ago. And then, pointing out her own experiences in the Balkan wars, World War II, the Greek civil war, the dictatorship(s) that followed, and the loss of virtually everything that she had known as a young woman, my mother-in-law added that nothing is the way it was before. Old people have only their memories of a better time. At this the old Cypriot woman straightened up in her chair and answered firmly.

"The memories aren't just ours. We have to think it was a better time. We have to say it was a better time. We have to keep telling the younger ones stories about that better time." (She cast a meaningful look in my direction.) "And maybe it will be that [better time] for them in the future."

With that she drew her plastic bag close and pulled out a bag of fresh hulled lima beans.

"Now I've told you what I have to say to you. Wouldn't you like some fresh limas? I grew them myself—beans from occupied Cyprus. Two liras a kilo. Here, just look at what fine beans they are."

We laughed; I bought the beans. And she went back to her enclaved village two days later. Though we made arrangements to meet the following month when she hoped to be allowed to return to the south, I never saw her again. Six weeks later her flat was rented out to an old Lebanese couple and their grandchildren.

The old Cypriot woman's conversation is suggestive testimony: to the simultaneous though not uncontradictory telling of personal and official history; to the crucially gendered matrix of the telling and its audience; to the imbrication of private—home, family, village—and public—the political, the state and nation, the Turkish invasion of Cyprus and resistance to it; to the "ethnographic" aspect of presumably nonethnographic, archival research.[2] I will return to this last notion. But there are two facets of the old woman's narrative that seem particularly significant in the present context. One is her insistence on her own authority in the narrative present in which she tells her story. What seemed most important to her, what she emphasized over and over, was her ability in the narrative present to tell the larger story as well as her own past experiences—and the preferred manner in which she told both. In the retelling of her narrative, I privileged, as she seemed to do in the telling, her claim to and distinctive style of narrative authority. Of course, her story or, more properly, stories were important to her telling. They were set in two past moments separated from one another by the Turkish invasion—life in her village before the invasion, her home and possessions then, her relationships with family and co-villagers then *and* life in her now-enclaved village in the occupied north of Cyprus, (the creeping loss of) her home and possessions, her relationships with her family and co-villagers, most of whom are now separated from her by death or by exile as refugees in unoccupied Cyprus. But as important as her stories was her strategic construction of narrative authority. It was this authority, the perspective from which she could and did tell her own and the larger stories, that she insisted most adamantly I be able to remember. Accordingly, her narrative authority and strategy included the attempt to carefully and relatively directly implicate her audience in the telling. The implication of her audience (in this instance, my mother-in-law and me) was not simply an attempt to direct the reception of her narrative but to generate other narratives for which hers might provide a suggestive story and style. She, as many of the other women with whom I spoke, was concerned not just to relate her own story but to question the reasons for and influence the context of what she thought might be my retelling of her story.

And so, I remember her strategic authority here perhaps because she insisted on it—a variant claim to some sort of narrative realism on my part. But more important because it suggests what became overwhelmingly apparent in the more textual focus of my rereading of nationalism and the consideration of the larger stories of the nation(s) in nationalism. That is in spite of, or at least simultaneous with, the "boundary fixations" that specific nationalisms-in-crisis would call forth, the peoples of the nation often negotiate that nationalism and its boundaries in far more various and inventive ways than they are given credit or apparent narrative license for. It was the specifics of those literary and cultural negotiations and their implications that I wanted to trace. Those negotiations and their implications suggest that—in the consideration of relations between the state and its societies and, more specifically, between culture and the state or oppositional and dominant cultures—to look only at official or ruling party or governmental or international proclamations, laws, documents, or statements of intent and to read them literally, as statements of fact, is to forget the ways in which they construct "fact." But more to the point, the suggestion here is that the very folks whom those proclamations and documents and laws claim to and undoubtedly *do* partially represent[3] do not read, live, or theorize them as statements of literal fact. They then suggest the importance of paying attention to the ways people narrate the stories in which they are involved and the stories that they tell. My retelling of those stories, my attempt at antiliteral readings of official and unofficial stories, does not neatly coincide with either their tellings or their readings. More likely, our various answers to the question of what is or was happening bump against each other uneasily.

At first, the conversations over midmorning or late afternoon coffee seemed to me simply a gendered part of living in the neighborhood; I welcomed the company and was familiar enough with the ritual among women of coffee, gossip, jokes, and personal and social concerns. And then I was an object of neighborhood "fieldwork" as well: I was a curious transitory member of a neighborhood community that was only too familiar with passers-through. Later, I came to think of the women's stories as a way to check that what I thought I saw in political and cultural texts was not only a figment of my desire or imagination. But it became increasingly clear that these were also and simultaneously occasions for other women to speak their piece ("to say what I have to say to you") to a marginally familiar and arguably trustworthy outsider. And to mark the privilege of my position as someone who could come and go, who could gather stories or read texts and retell them to a different and differently powered audience. There was no recrimination in their pointed observations about that privilege, only a relatively direct request to communicate something of their own determination, resourcefulness in duress, and expectations for change. My reading or listening and retelling, then, cannot "re-present" or substitute for theirs. But I would invoke as trope their narrative strategies to suggest that the battle over who gets to tell the story of what happened—and in the telling critically shape the what-happened itself—is a complex and variously waged one and, finally, perhaps only provisionally won. In that battle, however apparently decisive its outcome, counternarratives (whether alternative or conservative) of what happened do not just give up and go away. They sometimes manage not only to survive but even to insinuate themselves in the dominant narratives, though that is scarcely an inevitable or unwaveringly predictable possibility.

The literary precedent for these observations was that participants in a literary narrative or complex of narratives do not perform that narrative and their roles within it in precisely the ways that the narrative structure would appear to direct. This suggests that in the construction of nationalism as a narrative, the role of the state and/or dominant political organization as authoritative narrator is constantly under assault. Not just from without—from other, competing narratives—but from within—from other, competing tellings of (not quite) the same story. The old Cypriot woman's narrative account contradicts the notion that narrative theorizing and potential narrative alteration (and, more arguably, structural transformation) are unavailable to narrative characters or narratees within the narrative. For she articulated in performance, in the telling, a complex and strategic theory of narrative. She accounted for the nonidentical calls of the Cypriot government, the Turkish occupation forces, and her family and co-villagers and her necessarily nonidentical responses to those calls. She recognized and participated—or was forced to participate—in various narrative accounts of her place in the dominant order of things. And implicated variously in those narratives, she constructed from within a position from which to strategically narrate back. In the process she iterates her own agency as partial narrator, not just as victimized character, in a narrative not entirely of her own making. The apparently incontrovertible and fixed order of a military occupation, a national(ist) government, a village society, or the Cypriot family is at least disputed and arguably even controverted. And, obviously, she attempted to account for her audience as well.

The "order" of a literary or at least written narrative is here interestingly implicated by the "order" of an oral narrative—an order that resonates for the audience/reader as much as for the teller/writer and "text." The retelling of oral narrative is virtually always a variation on a theme; it is not the exact duplication of the theme and its order. The authoritative text of a narrative with irrevocably positioned narrator(s), narratees, and characters is putatively far easier to maintain as an abstract category in a written text between the two covers (a mark of our own fetishization of the word as book-object perhaps). But, in fact, even there—written out and contained between two covers—the firm ordering of narrative is not as firm as it might appear.[4]

The second suggestion of the old woman's conversation that I would like to foreground is her assertion of the necessity of telling stories—stories of "a better time," of a different time, in the past—in the hope of making possible a better future. It is, with distinct urgency, to hold out for the possibility of things being different, of there being something other than the endless repetition of the same in the present. On the one hand, her insistence on her own narrative authority in telling stories concedes an agency in the narrative present in retelling narratives that would not seem to grant her license for that authority. On the other hand, the stories of the past (or pasts) and their telling in the present point to, hold out for, a future of something better and different when neither the narrative present nor the stories past would seem to allow that authority either. Here, then, telling stories is not just a way of constructing an arguably renegade authority in the present or of nostalgically remembering a better past; it marks the desire for, the attempt to point at (but not necessarily to represent or narrate), a different future. It also marks the desire for what, lacking a better word, I will call "confrontation." That is to resolutely bring to the fore, to get in the face of the audience with, an ignored story and/or narrative perspective on a story in which the audience is implicated. Thus, as the old Cypriot woman insisted, not just the narrator and her characters but the narratee, the implied reader, the real reader and listener are variously implicated in the telling. It is the construction of narrative authority and the implication of the narratee/reader in that construction that is of equally paramount concern in Rina Katselli's literary narrative, her novel, *Blue Whale*.[5]

Katselli's *Blue Whale* is another point of entry—powerful, if troubling—to what is familiarly referred to in Cyprus as "the Cyprus problem" (*to Kypriako*). It is as much a disturbing *performance of* as it is eloquent *testimony to* the contradictions of the Greek Cypriot position(s) on and in "the Cyprus problem." First written "from exile"[6] in the Cypriot capital of Nicosia in 1976, the novel was revised in 1978 and published later that year. Katselli, like the unnamed male narrator of *Galazia falaina*, is from the northern port city of Kerynia, from which she and thousands of others were forcibly driven when the mainland Turkish army used that city as a point of entry for its invasion in July 1974. Her novel opens in Nicosia a year and a half after that invasion.

Katselli's autobiographical account of her initial enclavement in Kerynia's Dome Hotel and subsequent flight to the unoccupied south of Cyprus is recorded in *Prosfugas ston topo mou*/ (Refugee in My Homeland).[7] *Galazia falaina* is not, then, Katselli's first narrative account of the uprooting of a third of the Cypriot population from their homes during and following the invasion. In fact, the differences between these two narratives provide an interesting commentary not just on ethnic boundaries in Cyprus—though both narrators are distinctly Greek Cypriots—but also on gender divisions within the Greek Cypriot community. For the first-person narrator of *Prosfugas ston topo mou* is clearly designated as Katselli herself or, at a minimum, as a distinctly female narrator. The narrator of *Galazia falaina*, in contrast, is a forty-two-year-old Greek Cypriot man, a once prosperous landowner and chicken rancher in Kerynia who, with the devastation of the invasion, loses everything except his penchant for "culture" and "art." His often bitterly ironic account of his fall from the "grace" of wealth and property to his status in the narrative present as a dispossessed and penniless refugee is in distinct contrast to the anguished urgency of the narrator of *Prosfugas ston topo mou*. That narrator tells a story of violent displacement from home, everyday life, friends and family; of missing relatives; of dead bodies strewn in the streets; of long days of enclavement waiting for the defeat of the invading army and, when it becomes clear that that will not happen, of international assistance to flee to the south; of emotional exhaustion and personal loss. If the narrator of *Blue Whale* also speaks of personal loss, of missing family and friends, of displacement, his story is rather more distinctly distanced and reframed by the irony of the narrative present rather than the loss and confusion of the story time itself. This difference is, I would suggest, not just some predictable transformation in perspective with the passage of time but, at least equally, a performance of implicit gender boundaries in Katselli's narratives. The bitterly ironic tone, the self-absorbed concern, and the almost-categorical political, social, and literary pronouncements of the narrator of *Blue Whale* are not available to the narrator/author of *Refugee in My Homeland*. It is, instead, the pressing concern for the narrator's community of family and friends, for their survival and safety, for an effective communal and personal response to the violence and violation of the Turkish invasion that dominates *Prosfugas ston topo mou*.

Galazia falaina opens in an apparently less urgent tone with a short verse-form dedication entitled "Text for/to 19 friends," enigmatically signed "D.G.C." ("X.E.K."). If *Prosfugas ston topo mou* openly addresses a wide audience, the dedication of *Galazia falaina* conspicuously foregrounds its own more constrained appeal. The limitations of that appeal are reiterated throughout the narrative, as in the opening when it offers an authorial dedication for only one copy—its own. The other copies are to be inscribed by the nineteen friends with their own dedication or invocation in a blank space provided by the author. But such constraint notwithstanding, there is an explicit, if ironic, attempt from the beginning of this "manuscript" to implicate, to provoke the participation of, what is that severely delimited audience. And yet the designated narrative response site for the nineteen readers of D.G.C.'s manuscript is as circumscribed and impinged on by the narrator as the refugee life of D.G.C. himself.

Divided into thirty-nine short, if architectonically constructed, sections,[8] *Galazia falaina* does not invoke the urgent immediacy, weariness, and fear of what are presumably the journal-entries-written-during-catastrophe of *Prosfugas ston topo mou*. The opening of section 1 is a letter, written in casual, almost leisurely fashion.

Friend,

I'll write first of the blue whale. Not because I want to justify the title of my manuscript, but, well, if you don't like the rest of these pages, or if they strike you as untrue, or—even if you believe them—if you find that they damage the favorable opinion that you have of the world, or if you are like me a displaced Greek Cypriot[9] and you're tired of saying the same thing over and over, or, finally, if you are a member of a powerful country and think you aren't in danger of being served the same dish of injustice that was offered to me, hold onto this page. And you'll have a short handbook about her (the blue whale) whose life is as moving as the lives of all the others who are mentioned below.

Now then, the blue whale before they made her extinct. . . . (5)

This is followed by almost two pages of detail about the size, weight, eating and mating habits, and so on, of the blue whale. Each time a specific figure is given in reference to the blue whale, the number is written first in letters and then in parenthetical Arabic numerals in what is almost a caricature of precision in scientific writing.

. . . one hundred (100) feet long, . . . two hundred (200) tons, . . . it would take thirteen (13) elephants to equal her. . . . She easily travels eighteen (18) nautical knots an hour. (5–6)

In spite of the discreet analogy proposed by the narrator between the blue whales of the title and opening section and the Cypriot refugees—they are, at minimum, both "moving" stories—the repeatable precision of scientific knowledge proves an impossibility in framing and telling the refugee story. There is no simple and direct narration of the "facts" of his refugee story.

The thwarting of his desire for precise and objective narration becomes apparent as the narrator accounts for the context in which he learned his facts about the demise of the blue whale—a program aired on Cypriot national television immediately following the Turkish invasion. His response to that program is to "step out onto the balcony and cry, feeling unbearably ashamed of my sudden sentimentality" (7). Repeated precision cannot be marshaled for the "blunt account of our dismantling." There is, in fact, a double failure of analogy here between the narratives of the blue whale and the Cypriot refugee. Not only is the language and style—putatively precise and scientific—of the blue whales' story unavailable to D.G.C.'s telling but the narrative perspective of the television documentary—omniscient, third person—is an impossibility as well, at least as he narrates his own story. (Narrating *their* own story is, presumably, an impossibility for the blue whales. The television account and then D.G.C.'s narrative account represent them instead.)

D.G.C.'s proposition of an analogy between the *stories* of the Cypriot refugees and the blue whales elides the disjuncture, the absence of analogy, between the two as *narratives.* It is precisely the language and perspective of the narrative of the blue whales that pose a continuous threat to the narrative of D.G.C. and, by extension, of Cypriot refugees in general. The omniscient or at least impersonal third-person narrative perspective—that of, say, an international commission on refugees or even a governmental refugee report—and the precise language of statistics—"two hundred (200) tons"— are the opponents against which D.G.C. marshals his irony and first-person narrative perspective (however limited). At the same time, like his response to the television story of the blue whale, the narrator's ironic first-person account is threatened throughout by a lurch into "sudden sentimentality" or—more often, though scarcely as self-consciously—into fierce ethnoreligious chauvinism.[10]

But if the narrator can recite the "facts" about the blue whales in section 1, he most decidedly cannot do so—or at least, not any longer—about himself. And so, not surprisingly, section 2 opens with the question, "Who am I?" The narrator confides, "Sometimes I answer in verse, sometimes with curses" (8). This section concludes, however, with neither verses nor curses but with the reproduction of the narrator's refugee identity card. Like his "baptismal name," which has been replaced by the ID number on his refugee registration card and the initials D.G.C., the narrator's choice of verses or curses has been resolutely impinged on by definitions and answers to the question "Who am I?" that are distinctly out of his control. Whatever "facts" he might once have been able to deploy in answer to that question were (scientifically?) disputed by the Turkish invasion and occupation of Cyprus. The remaining thirty-seven sections of *Galazia falaina,* then, are the narrator's attempt to regain or reconstruct some of that control both by telling selected new "facts" about his situation and self and by writing in a suitable audience for those "facts."

In a movement reminiscent of the narrative of the old Cypriot woman recounted above, the narrative of the unnamed D.G.C.[11] moves back and forth between two topoi and times: the lost (if retrospectively ambiguous) plenitude of a time and space before the Turkish invasion and occupation of Cyprus *and* the narrative present and refugee camp space of a literal uprooting and exile. His is an unavoidably motley narrative—bitterly ironic, pieced together from fragmented stories, marked with inconsistencies, unanswered questions, and sardonic observations. The narrator's language as he tells his stories is similarly pieced together: from demotic Greek, the flyleaf of the novel includes a note on "Orthography," identifying the accents used in the text as the system of the University of Thessaloniki (in mainland Greece); from ancient Greek, with Heraclitus as the narrator's preferred philosophical site; from the Cypriot dialect, with a glossary appended to the novel; from the flowery language of artists like the narrator's cousin, excerpts from whose work the narrator includes in his own text. The rupture that necessitates a patchwork of history and quasi-autobiography also, it seems, necessitates one of language.

In this fashion, then, the narrator of *Galazia falaina* attempts to proceed with the telling of his story as he proceeded with the "orderly" life that befell him in Kerynia before the invasion. While his initial answer to the question of his identity is to present his refugee identity card, he subsequently cites historical precedents for his status as exile and refugee—the Armenians and Greeks of Asia Minor who fled the Turks, the Jews who fled Hitler, the Palestinians who fled the Israelis (sec. 3). He describes his wife's ridicule for his preoccupation with writing instead of with heroism (sec. 4). But, in spite of her ridicule, he describes and then rejects (sec. 5) the autobiographical realism and descriptive detail of his earlier writing, noting his aborted attempt to represent life in Kerynia before the invasion—an attempt he bitterly refers to (pace Proust) as "A la Recherche du Pays Perdu" (Remembrance of a Homeland Past). But his refutation of realist description notwithstanding, he then engages in considerable descriptive detail about his present condition: his relations with his wife (sec. 6), the (sexual and psychological) "madness" that allows him to survive his present situation (sec. 7), the potential destruction of the world and the worthiness of the human race to survive.[12]

The narrator then recounts his "unorthodox" political beliefs derived, he claims, from reading history books. And he concludes this account of putative unorthodoxy with a request to be buried in the orthodox "position of an Orthodox Christian corpse, with [my] hands crossed in front of me." Later (secs. 10 and 14), fearful that it will be forgotten in the turmoil of the invasion and occupation with the many dead who must be buried, he describes the "traditional orthodox" burial position and procedures. This juxtaposition of apparently disjunct narrative segments suggests another unwritten (and unwriteable) narrative for which the narrative present of *Blue Whale,* in all its *un*orthodoxy, will have ended. For that future narrative, the narrative present is cast as that which will have been rather than that which is. In this context, the narrator's concern with the moment of narrative closure—of his own death but also, at least for him, of the end of unorthodoxy as well—will have been signaled by his own orthodox burial position and funeral rites. And thus he will presumably transcend the narrative present to another narrative space and time (an Orthodox afterlife?).

The rapid succession of scarcely subtle series of oppositions in these sections—sane and mad, normal and deviant, legal and illegal, orthodox (Orthodox) and unorthodox, past and present—would, then, certainly seem to privilege the initial term in each set. There is an implicit, if uneasy, postulation of relation among those initial terms: past, orthodox/Orthodox, legal, normal, and sane. But the move to link that cluster of signs as synchronous and almost inherently related is dubiously based on the narrator's ironic pride in his authorial productivity in the narrative present. And that narrative present is grounded in and even generated by the second term in the string of oppositions—in unorthodoxy, illegality, deviance, and madness. If it is some future narrative for which the present will be concluded that the narrator desires, it is very much in the narrative present that he articulates that desire. The narrative present, with all its associations of rupture and deviance, provides access to that narrative future. The serial construction of opposing terms that point at the past and present aspires to neither. Rather it aspires to a future narrative moment and its perspective for which the narrative present will be past. It is that projected future moment, its narrative(s), and, most important, his own correct and orthodox position, to which D.G.C. as narrator struggles to accede. For that future narrative, his (dead) body and his affairs (including his manuscript, the *Blue Whale*) will be in "orthodox Christian" order. It is in this light that he proceeds, then, from burial rites to the contents of his "official" will, legally recorded but inaccessible in now-occupied Kerynia. So he provides the text of his revised, if legally "unofficial" and unrecorded, will.

Having thus provided for the orthodox order of his narrative closure (his will, burial position, and funeral rites), the narrator turns to the demands of the narrative present—his manuscript for nineteen friends, the pages of which he seeks to fill "responsibly," urging his readers to do likewise with their pages. Section 12 introduces the narrator's cousin, also a refugee and writer, and their argument about the purposes of art. In a gesture that presages one of the pivotal contradictions of Katselli's novel, the narrator's text is interrupted by his cousin's insistence that he include *her* text in his.[13] He acquiesces, if grudgingly, and follows the excerpts from her work with his own ruminations on the purposes of art. In closing, the narrator enjoins his readers to fill the remainder of the page he has left blank with *their* thoughts on the subject. Here again the narrator's directive is as noteworthy for its circumscription as for its solicitation of his reader's response.

Section 13 warns his nineteen readers, especially those who live outside of Cyprus, of the difficulties of contacting the narrator to register their (*un*-solicited and *un*circumscribed) responses to his manuscript. "I have no telephone in my shack." Nor is contact through the mail likely: "My location here in the desolation of state-owned land in Leukosia is too difficult to find for the person who delivers mail." So, too, attempts at contact by newspaper, radio, or television announcement are all futile; the message will never reach its destination, the narrator warns. Still, almost perversely, he urges the readers of his manuscript, "Write me an unrestrained account of your opinion; you have nothing to fear from me." D.G.C.'s narratees are here implicitly implicated in a double bind very like the situation of D.G.C. himself: write if you want, but it will not reach me or have any effect on what I am doing. Or: respond only here, in the carefully demarcated spaces that I provide for you. (The threat of a reader who does not confine herself to the demarcated spaces for response is made clear in the closing lines of the novel.) D.G.C. thus reiterates for his audience something like the conditions that impinge on his own situation. The spaces for his responses to the refugee narrative in which he finds himself are equally constricted and constricting. In fact, he longs for silence but fears that, if he falls silent, he will become yet another symbolic martyr. "And so, I'll continue, describing some human types that I know or, at least, I knew" (47). And he proceeds to outline the correct procedure for burying the dead (especially for himself when he dies) in section 14.

Subsequently (secs. 15–24), the narrative shifts to the narrator's friends and acquaintances—Cypriot and foreign—and the various ways in which they have come to terms with, responded to, the occupation of Cyprus. This series of vignettes concludes in section 24 with the narrator's decision *not* to tell the story of "some women from Kerynia who've become like blue whales, extinct like Our Lady of Chrysoglykiotissa. . . . [To narrate their stories] would take a great deal and I feel it's better that they hold a special place in my heart rather than a page here" (70).

The parallel in this passage between women of Kerynia, virtually extinct blue whales, and the Virgin usurped-from-her-throne suggests a problematic equation that implicitly informs much discussion of the "Cyprus problem." Baldly stated, the formulation of implicit equivalencies runs something like this: the properly "enthroned" and "housed" Virgin is (or should be) the marker for (Greek) Cypriot woman who is (or should be) similarly accommodated in her own house.

But this religious and familial order has been violated—invaded—and that space occupied. The Virgin who once "sat on her throne" has been "uprooted from her home, ravaged, and her house made into a mosque" (70). And thus, according to this formulation, both Virgin and woman— here, specifically, "some women from Kerynia"—are, like the blue whale, made extinct. This postulation that the woman uprooted from her home is the woman extinct resonates ominously in terms of this narrative, not to mention of post–1974 Cypriot society and culture.[14] Here, in the narrator's rhetorical construct, the reference to the *dis*order or rupture of the configuration Virgin/woman/home results in a refusal (or inability) to narrate.[15] The narrator breaks off his own story of disorder and displacement in a gesture strangely evocative of his representation of that other orderly narrative—of "enthroned" Virgin and "housed" (Greek) Cypriot woman—broken off by the Turkish invasion and occupation. It is the latter that, perhaps perversely, generated his own narrative in the first place. And so his refusal to narrate is a sort of negative testimony (by self-imposed silence) to the highly charged and threatening power of the formulation that constructs as parallel the unhoused Virgin, Cypriot women, and extinct blue whales.

It is at this moment of narrative disjuncture that our narrator turns from the people around him to "more abstract concepts and how they operate in our times." With bitter irony he discusses the "Disunited Nations" and the betrayal of its goal and purpose (sec. 25); the operations of propaganda (sec. 27); the proximity to everyone of disaster in the age of nuclear weapons, regardless of spatial distance, with a diagram of a compass provided for the reader's "precise orientation" to danger (sec. 28); the fate of his home and possessions in Kerynia (sec. 29); the desire of some refugees for "compensation" for their losses (sec. 30); the nonrefugee wealthy whom the narrator sees as largely undisturbed by the occupation (sec. 31); the nonrefugee poor who are, for the narrator, unquestionably "rich" if they still live in their own neighborhoods, villages, or towns (sec. 32);[16] the narrator's violently angry refusal of an aspersion on his refugee "identity"—the praise of an acquaintance that, in improving his lot as a refugee, he (the narrator) has displayed a steadfastness and tenacity that was his all along (sec. 33); his fear of man as more overwhelming than his fear of God (sec. 34); a television performance of the ballet of Romeo and Juliet and the unbearable future (sec. 35);[17] the (future of the) narrator's children, the week of the coup that preceded the invasion, the narrator's outline for an unfinished play about extraterrestrial beings (sec. 36); the "ancestral" practice of cursing while crossing a bridge, with a blank space for the reader's insertion of her favorite curses (sec. 37); and, finally, the necessity and problem of endings, here accomplished with a dedication from the narrator's dead friend and a quote from Heraclitus (sec. 38). The concluding section (39) is set in different type and entitled "Afterword." It recounts the return of the manuscript to the narrator by his dissatisfied nineteenth reader—"an old acquaintance of mine, a quiet, almost boring woman who loved to read." In response to the narrator's query as to whether she returns his manuscript because it is too "fiery" (*apsi*), she answers,

> —On the contrary, I found it lukewarm. It's ridiculous for a [grown] man to pretend to be a blue whale. I thought more highly of you than as an animal who submits to his fate and wants to strike an existential pose. Now that you don't have your property and factory you try to impress and overwhelm your acquaintances with literature. We knew that you had that inclination from the time you were a small child; it wasn't necessary for you to remind us again, now that things are so bad here.
>
> —It's not my fault if things are bad.
>
> —For there to be such misfortune, it means that every one of us is to blame [*o kathenas mas ftaei*]. It's not just those who commit the crime but those who didn't stop it [who are responsible]. And we didn't do anything significant to stop it. Now you come to us again, pretending to be a family man, the good Christian, trying to convince yourself that you've made it instead of raising your head and fighting the evil in your country and the world. And on top of that, you write about people as blue whales. (99)

The nineteenth reader of D.G.C.'s manuscript drops it in his lap and "runs off, before [he] had a chance to say anything else" (100). And there, without "a chance to say anything else," the novel ends. In a gesture that parallels the complaints of the narrator's wife, the intrusive (female) text of the narrator's refugee cousin, and the ominous extinction of "unhoused women" and the Virgin, it is again an unhoused refugee woman who disrupts and here terminally silences the narrative.[18]

In addition to its suggestive gesture to the implied reader in general, there is a peculiar resonance to this exchange between writer/narrator and reader/narratee in the context of the rhetoric of post-invasion Cyprus. The response of the Cypriot right wing to the accusation that it was precisely the right-wing military coup that provoked, or at least provided a pretext for, the Turkish invasion and occupation of Cyprus was the protestation, "We are all to blame." The extent to which this claim gained circulation is attested to not least of all by the conclusion of Katselli's novel when the nineteenth reader of D.G.C.'s narrative echoes that statement.[19] But even if the obfuscation and leveling of such a statement is bracketed, even if we agree for the moment that the narrator is no doubt liable for at least some of the charges made against him by his nineteenth reader, the marshaling of this phrase in particular in the conclusion of this masterfully ironic and poignant account of Cypriot refugee life gestures back to that event which precedes the opening of the novel and its story of invasion, uprooting, and displacement. That is the short-lived right-wing Cypriot coup itself, an incident figured in the *Blue Whale* in a peculiarly revealing fashion.

In contrast to the statement, "We are all to blame," to which the novel gives currency in closing, there are two images that the novel assiduously does *not* foreground. But, juxtaposed, they serve as silent markers in *Galazia falaina*. One is an almost incidental reference to the narrator's clean white shirt. He wears that spotless shirt during the week before the Turkish invasion—the week of the right-wing coup that overthrew the elected president of Cyprus. That the narrator was strikingly exempt from the coup's immediate and organized attempt at the elimination of its many opponents[20] is attested to precisely by the fact that his shirt remains spotless during that week. And it is attested to by the narrator's observation that the coup and its imposition of house arrest (another kind of "order") "gave [him] the time to put [his] books in order, a job that [he'd] been putting off for three years" (92).[21] It is to this moment—with a clean white shirt and ordered bookshelves as its predominant images—as well as to its more commonly understood reference that the phrase "We are all to blame" could be brought to bear. That "clean white shirt" with the outline of a "futuristic play" in its pocket stands as a crucial and contradictory signpost in and of D.G.C.'s narrative. The absence of marks (*deigmata*) on that shirt during the week of a coup, whose violent repression and imposition of house arrest results in nothing else for the narrator than an opportunity to put his books in order, is surely as indicative as the later condition of the shirt.

The day of the Turkish invasion the narrator puts on that same shirt "with trembling hands, while overhead Turkish airplanes whistled as they dropped flames [firebombs]." And then the shirt is transformed.

> That shirt underwent all of the misfortunes of the invasion and the first week of my becoming a refugee, accumulating signs of whatever most tragic could exist in my life: dead members of brave young men, branches of executed savory and myrtle, blood-spattered earth, the sweat of struggle, heroic battle, self-sacrifice, forced flight, the tears of women, men and children, my own tears. . . . When I went to take it off it bore a fearful resemblance to my soul.[22] I examined it from all sides and decided to wash it only when we returned to Kerynia. (92)

The narrator's shirt is inscribed by and then read by the narrator as a text of the Turkish invasion and his own subsequent displacement as refugee. It is a poignant trope. Still, his graphic shirt-text here is indicted by the earlier blank text of the same shirt—"clean" and "white." And thus the promise of a future return of the clean shirt resonates more than a little ominously, given that earlier context in which the blank shirt-text and Cypriot society were presumably "in order." For the narrator, there is no text of, no inscription or marking from, a violent and repressive internal (though clearly externally influenced) coup. That series of events is unremarkable and unmarked. Nor is there any intertextual relation between the coup and the Turkish invasion that followed. For the narrator, his shirt, his bookshelves, and by extension, Cypriot society, are only being corrected, put in order, by the coup.

It is this imposition of (textual and military) order that weighs so heavily on D.G.C.'s narrative in retrospect—perhaps also on Katselli's *Galazia falaina* as well. For D.G.C.'s narrative, the carefully orchestrated implication of the reader/narratee in his equally carefully constructed narrative chain results in the refusal and return of his manuscript by his nineteenth reader. The ironic undertone of D.G.C.'s narration, of his attempt to order and relate the stories of being a Cypriot refugee, is thoroughly called into question by that nineteenth reader. But the nineteenth reader's challenge to D.G.C.'s irony and her call to "direct action" ambiguously echoes the defensive rhetoric of the same people who engineered the coup in Cyprus and its putative order. The untantalizing opposition here would appear to be between the almost smug irony of the narrator and the aptly critical but disturbing call to direct action of the narrator's nineteenth reader.

In a similar fashion, the narratee/reader of D.G.C.'s manuscript is presented with a series of circumscribed (and inconsequential) choices in response to the (ironically consequential) questions the narrator asks: In the

face of injustice, war, and destruction, is the effort to continue the human
venture (*anthropini peripeteia*) worthwhile?

> If you want, answer [the question] yourself, friend, with a single syllable in the
> box below: yes or no? (28)

Or, again in ruminating on the destruction of one small country, Cyprus,
and the potential destruction of the entire planet:

> In the small space which I leave, write something yourself, friend, something
> about the human race. A rough draft of a memorial placque or something
> better. . . . In order to help you, I am tracing a border. (51–52)

There is apparently room here for little more than monosyllabic, circumscribed answers. And yet, of course, in the face of circumscription and
radically delimited possibility, the narrator himself manages more than
a single syllable or an inscription within a narrowly defined boundary. So,
too, his implied readers and narratees can exceed the boundaries traced
for them. Within the narrative, some of them do, of course, most notably,
the nineteenth reader but also the narrator's wife and his cousin. And yet
the alternative readings that they enact are little more compelling than the
writing of the narrator or the reader responses his narrative solicits. The alternative readings and writing of the narrator's cousin are set off in italics
and framed by the narrator's dismissive commentary. The alternative readings of the narrator's wife are relegated by his narration to the margins of
his stories; she may be an efficient caretaker of daily affairs, but she is an intrusive aggravation to his narrative. And yet one of the audiences to whom
he addresses his narrative is precisely such women. This is most conspicuously the case with the nineteenth reader to whom he gives his manuscript,
but his audience is also clearly the other "unhoused" women who "read"
(and threaten) his refugee text. For D.G.C., their readings must necessarily
be contained and defused—a narrative task that the narrator only temporarily manages.

   D.G.C.'s narrative is a narrative of the refugee story—and of the foreign
invasion and occupation that created that refugee status for the narrator
and thousands like him—not only through the stories of its content but also
in its reenactment of another sort of "invasion and occupation." That is, of
the narrator's text by his (female) narratees. If, for D.G.C. in *Galazia falaina*,
the image of the unhoused woman is the trope of choice for representing
the invasion and occupation of Cyprus, it is equally but more subtly the predominant trope for representing a grave threat to his own narrative. That is
the threat of interruption, of potential silence, of narratees who read his
story differently and who, in their turn, are potential (or actual) narrators
telling other and different stories. For much of his narrative, D.G.C. masterfully fends off that threat. The counternarratives (of ethnochauvinism, of

"sudden sentimentality," of right-wing "order" and "correction," of women who read and write against the grain of his narrative) that seep into his narration of refugee stories strain against the carefully drawn boundaries of his own account.

Ultimately, in the concluding section of his manuscript, those boundaries are less violently transgressed than just worn down. "You're crazy; you're absolutely mad,"[23] he tells the nineteenth reader breathlessly. And then, minutes later, " 'And I, what do you think I should do anyway?' I asked hoarsely."

It is with this question that I would like to return for a moment to the narrative of the old Cypriot woman with which I began. Hers, too, was a narrative of a refugee story and its aftermath. She also paid careful attention to the construction of her narrative authority and accordingly attempted to speak certain spaces for her audience: "Do you understand me? Will you remember?" As narrator (of her various stories) and as narratee (of the Turkish invasion and occupation, of the Cypriot governments' responses to the Turkish presence, etc.), she, too, attempted to answer the various questions posed to her by other narratives and stories in which she is figured—her family's, her villages.

But while she shares to some extent the positions of D.G.C. as narrator of (and character in) his/her own story and as narratee of other stories and narratives, the old woman's narrative style—or her ordering of her narrative present, her stories, and her audience—is not shared with the fictional chicken rancher from Kerynia. Of course, hers was an informal, oral account to a transient stranger in her neighborhood and the stranger's mother-in-law. D.G.C.'s narrative and manuscript are the pretext of a polished literary text. But that substantial difference being duly noted, her posing of questions and her attempted answers assume a different and instructive stance toward complexity, contradiction, and variation than that of D.G.C.'s manuscript.

It is to suggest this play in the notion and narration of "order" that I juxtapose here her narrative of the refugee story to that of D.G.C. in Katselli's *Galazia falaina* (and to the literary text of *Galazia falaina* itself). It is surely this aspect of narrative "order" and not just shared stories and narrative present that links anthropological and literary narratives. Of course, since this chapter is also a narrative construct, a linking and ordering of literary, linguistic, and historical elements, more than a few of the connections between the old Cypriot woman's narrative and Katselli's novel are of my making. They arise from a determination to pay attention to the literary and narratological but also political questions of who tells the story, who listens, and how. And then there is the citation of a shared historical and social context—nationalism in crisis, the cultural and historical situation of the period of the right-wing coup and the Turkish invasion and occupation of Cyprus. Those are relatively conspicuous connections. But there is another more intricate set of relations between the literary text (Katselli's novel) and the transposed oral account (the Cypriot woman's story) and between the two narratives—of D.G.C. and the old Cypriot woman. And it is precisely the order and style of their narratives and texts that suggest a narrative future—the desire for, the attempt to suggest, something other than the narrative present. That future for the old Cypriot woman is one that must necessarily be informed by stories of a different past. In her account, only in juxtaposing such stories to the narrative present is there a conceivable possibility of change, of a different future. There is no postulation of a return to the difference of stories past, unlike the return to the unmarked white shirt (the cleanliness and "order") of the past as preferred telos in D.G.C.'s narrative. Both narratives, both the literary text and the old woman's oral testimonial, articulate a desire for change from the present order of displacement and foreign occupation.[24] But the change that they envision is scarcely shared. And it is the differences between their projected futures that is as crucial to a reading of their narratives as the fact of a shared desire for change. This projected future, the end to which the desire for change aspires, is articulated in their narratives in the retelling of stories past and the account of the narrative present. But it is also structurally suggested in the "order" that the narrative imposes on its narrator, its narratees, and implied audience, its stories. For if narration is the linking of events and elements in a construction of meaning, that linking is equally a spatial and temporal ordering of those elements or events. The narrative designates and systematizes. And it is not just the "what" but also the "how" of those processes that are crucial for the narratives of anthropology and of literary studies. Perhaps for any narratives. Attention to how a narrative designates, organizes, and tells its stories is less a reiteration of structural narratology or anthropology than a suggestion that that careful reading/listening might make us more efficacious audiences and storytellers in turn: of stories that attempt to ward off rather than invoke again sickness and death, displacement and war. Of stories that attempt other endings. And perhaps a pot of fresh lima bean stew as well.

NOTES

1. The Turkish military authorities occupying the north of Cyprus agreed, under pressure from the United Nations, to allow enclaved Greek Cypriots (but not Turkish Cypriots) a "leave" of five days a month to travel to the unoccupied south of Cyprus to see their families, conduct whatever business affairs were necessary, and so forth. In fact though, as my visitor reiterated, the monthly leave was subject to frequent and unexplained cancellation. This was the first time the old woman had been able to cross the "green line"—the boundary between occupied and unoccupied Cyprus—for five months.

2. I bracket for the moment the way in which (the story of how) a "textual" project—rereading literary and nonliterary texts of nationalism in crisis for mainland Greece (1922), Cyprus (1974), and Palestinian culture and society (1982)—grew to include oral histories and testimonials. That story, though, is probably no less appropriate to the "anthropology and literary study" of the present collection. It is certainly one of the ways in which I was called to account as "reader" audience and future "narrator" of others' stories.

3. Taking due note of the double sense of "representation" that Gayatri Spivak points to in her suggestive discussion of Marx's *The Eighteenth Brumaire* and the double "representation" of *Vertreten* and *Darstellen* (276–279): "Can the Subaltern Speak?" in *Marxism and the Interpretation of Culture,* ed. Cary Nelson and Lawrence Grossberg, 271–313.

4. The vacillation of that "order" is forcefully indicated by Rina Katselli's *Galazia falaina* (Blue Whale) (Leukosia: Chrisopolitissa, 1978), discussed below.

5. Rina Katselli, *Blue Whale,* trans. Mary Ioannides (Leukosia: Chrisopolitissa, 1983). Although I have consulted the Ioannides translation with interest, all translations are my own unless otherwise noted.

6. Literally, *prosfugia* is "the state of being a refugee" rather than the spatial designation that "from exile" suggests. Katselli, like her narrator, is still in Cyprus but not in her home city of Kerynia, which is occupied by the Turkish military and to which she is not allowed to return.

7. Katselli, *Prosfugas ston topo mou* (Leukosia: Chrisopolitissa, 1975).

8. Curiously, Ioannides's translation omits several significant passages and words and eliminates the final section (39) of the novel altogether. In that last section, one of the 19 readers utterly rejects the manuscript and returns it in disgust to the narrator/author, challenging him to find a more appropriate way to confront the uprooting of the Cypriot people. The omission of that conclusion is even more baffling than the selective deletion of passages earlier in the novel, since the conclusion so clearly gestures back to and is a critical comment on the overall shape of the novel.

9. The "D.G.C." of the invocation.

10. If the narrator's response to the story of the blue whales' demise is a rehearsal for the response of the narratee or implied reader to *his* narrative, the implications are grim indeed and the critical necessity of other responses to D.G.C.'s narrative clear.

11. Which is finally specified on his refugee identity card as an acronym for "displaced [or, more literally, "unhoused"—*xespitomeno*] Greek Cypriot."

12. To this last question, he asks the reader to respond by writing "yes" or "no" in a small box. The permissible range for reader response here would seem to be fiercely restricted.

13. Implicitly, her text is the "feminine" antithesis of his narrative: "her experiences of the Turkish invasion of Cyprus and displacement" (*xespitomo*/unhousing), which he hastens to characterize as inadequate and unsatisfactory. After reproducing its opening lines, he edits her "small book" with the comment, "Like the woman that she is, she babbles on about insignificant things." He concludes the fragments excerpted from her text with the statement, "I found this book of my cousin's lukewarm and many other refugee acquaintances of mine agree" (39–40).

14. Some of the implications, literal and metaphoric, of this equation—a woman "unhoused" is a woman "extinct"—are being pursued in greater detail in a work now in progress.

15. This moment has been foreshadowed in an earlier moment of narrative disjuncture—again, specifically, a refusal to narrate—in the conclusion to section 12. There, as mentioned earlier, the narrator grudgingly acquiesces to the insistent requests of his cousin who wants to insert *her* literary narratives into *his* text. In this, something of the threat of the displaced/unhoused woman and her narratives would seem to be explicitly figured. And then, too, there are the persistent criticisms of his writing by a similarly "unhoused" woman, the narrator's wife. Her criticism of him is also an attempt by her to disrupt, to read differently, his story. Thus the response of the narrator's nineteenth reader—another "unhoused" woman who, in the closing lines of the novel, disrupts his narrative both by reading it differently and by forcibly returning it to him—is clearly prefigured.

16. The protestations of and demonstrations by the nonrefugee poor that their needs have been and continue to be ignored in favor of virtually exclusive aid for the refugees casts an interesting light on this assertion of the narrator. See, for example, Tassos Tsapparellas, "Unacceptable Living Conditions," *Haravghi* (Nicosia, Cyprus) 15 Oct. 1989: 10.

17. A parallel in closing to the television documentary on the blue whale that provided the opening trope for the novel.

18. It is interesting, and puzzling, that this section is not included in the English translation of the novel.

19. See Peter Loizos, *The Heart Grown Bitter: A Chronicle of Cypriot War Refugees* (Cambridge: Cambridge University Press, 1981), especially 133, for an account of the crucial elision that the currency of this phrase makes possible.

20. This, the coup's attempt at "cleanliness" and order.

21. This analogic sense is accentuated by the fact that the word in Greek is *diorthoso,* literally, "I correct/rectify/remedy." In an arguably similar sense, the coup proposed to correct or remedy or rectify the putative disorder of Cyprus under the president, Archbishop Makarios.

22. Literally, to the perceptible (*noete*) side, to my own perception, of my soul.

23. The idiomatic phrase is literally, "*Eisai yia desimo*" (You should be tied up). In the penultimate lines of the novel/manuscript, the idiom is interestingly echoed in the narrator's reference to his vehemently rejected manuscript as *desmi*—a bound "bundle" or "packet" of papers. Perhaps his manuscript is gendered female and "crazy"—"fit to be tied" in the English idiom—like the nineteenth reader and the other women of his text?

24. It is this shared concern with change that Didier Coste, in his *Narrative as Communication* (Minneapolis: University of Minnesota Press, 1989), notes as the common, or at least contiguous, terrain of narratology and anthropology. For both take up "the production, transmission, and exchange of information on change and simulacra of change" (5).

FOUR

Narrative Ethnography, Elite Culture, and the Language of the Market

Dan Rose

INTRODUCTION

The ethnographer who employs narrative strategies in writing the text has available a number of resources for configuring the results of inquiry. Here the chronotope of the road encloses a story line with digressions and excerpts from an interview with the former chief executive officer (CEO) of Deere and Company, the world's largest manufacturer of farm machinery. By using a language game derived from Bronislaw Malinowski, the effort is made to focus on language use in market culture from the perspective of elites. A closing critique of the interview helps us understand the way the leaders of America's most substantial corporations locate themselves in an unself-conscious, individualistic community of companies that make up a significant part of the contemporary world market. A central aim of this chapter is to theorize narrative—whether or not of market culture—and to invite the reader to theorize it as well. The theorizing draws from devices developed by twentieth-century authors of the multigenre novel.

THE EVENING OF 6 SEPTEMBER 1988

At dusk William A. Hewitt turned his Rolls Royce left onto Highway 100. Behind him, the gravel driveway disappeared in the trees up to Rondelay, his home now hidden on the hilltop. Rondelay was a large house that faced south above the Brandywine River valley in southern Chester County, Pennsylvania. That evening Hewitt had glanced over the tops of the green hills toward Delaware; the mist that had hung in the air during the summer days and offered its rich humidity to the greenness of the rounded hillsides was now giving way to the dryer days and cooler nights of early fall.

The car was a two-tone, metal-flecked brown, and as it moved quietly down the road the tall London plane trees sped across the fenders and doors in deformed reflections. Hewitt had meant the color of the paint to resemble the rusted Cor-Ten steel that had been used to frame the headquarters of Deere and Company in Moline, Illinois, which Eero Saarinen had designed in the late 1950s in close consultation with Hewitt, then chairman of the board.

> Deere and Company is proud of its mid-western farm-belt location and of its strong, handsome farm machinery. The proper character for its headquarters' architecture would reflect the big, forceful, functional character of its products. Its architecture should not be a slick, precise, glittering glass and spindly metal building, but a building which is bold and direct, using metal in a strong basic way.[1]

As Hewitt turned and drove south, three other men were each driving toward Chadds Ford in their own, less imposing automobiles to meet with him: Tony Parrotto, a businessman who had his own advertising and publishing business; Larry Taylor, a physicist who served the executive office at Sun Company as an internal consultant; and Dan Rose, an ethnographer who set up the meeting with Hewitt and taught at the University of Pennsylvania. During the previous six months, Parrotto, Rose, and Taylor had been meeting fortnightly to discuss matters of mutual interest, mostly in the realm of ideas of moment to each of them, at times making formal presentations to one another. They convened the gatherings over dinner, at Parrotto's country club, or in one restaurant or another on Philadelphia's Main Line. There was an air of exploration in their conversations, the not-quite-articulated interest in putting together something like a think tank that would, one more time, link some particular portion of the world of business with university-generated ideas. Prior to moving to Sun Company, Taylor had worked for a number of years administering the University of Pennsylvania physics department and had contacts in both industry and academia.

> The canoes glide slowly and noiselessly, punted by men especially good at this task and always used for it. Other experts who know the bottom of the lagoon, with its plant and animal life, are on the look-out for fish. One of them sights the quarry. Customary signs, or sounds or words are uttered. Sometimes a sentence full of technical references to the channels or patches on the lagoon has to be spoken; sometimes when the shoal is near and the task of trapping is simple, a conventional cry is uttered not too loudly. Then, the whole fleet stops and ranges itself—every canoe and every man in it performing his appointed task—according to a customary routine. But, of course, the men, as

they act, utter now and then a sound expressing keenness in the pursuit or impatience at some technical difficulty, joy of achievement or disappointment at failure. Again, a word of command is passed here and there, a technical expression or explanation which serves to harmonize their behavior towards other men. The whole group act in a concerted manner, determined by old tribal tradition and perfectly familiar to the actors through lifelong experience. Some men in the canoes cast the wide encircling nets into the water, others plunge, and wading through the shallow lagoon, drive the fish into the nets. Others again stand by with the small nets, ready to catch the fish. An animated scene, full of movement follows, and now that the fish are in their power the fishermen speak loudly, and give vent to their feelings. Short, telling exclamations fly about, which might be rendered by such words as, "Pull in," "Let go," "Shift further," "Lift the net"; or again, technical expressions completely untranslatable except by minute description of the instruments used, and the mode of action. (Malinowski 1923: 311)

My agenda in those routine meetings with Parrotto and Taylor had been directed toward increasing my ability to conduct ethnography as close to the top of American market culture as possible. Ethnographers have for the most part routinely neglected the study of the highest reaches of American and world societies, in part because it is less demanding to study the powerless. One of the ways of practicing ethnographic inquiry is to want something, to desire, to long after someone or a state of affairs, and from such destabilizing interests one is propelled toward those who can best offer what it is one longs for. My curiosity, a mimesis, undoubtedly, of the insatiable desires of a consumer society, is about that which is less available to our knowing and at the same time highly ideologized, the locus of money and power, where momentous, obscured decisions are made in our capitalist culture of consumption. In making contact, the world opens slightly around the space desire has formed.

> I have sometimes thought of constructing a system of human knowledge which would be based on eroticism, a theory of contact wherein the mysterious value of each being is to offer to us just that point of perspective which another world affords. In such a philosophy pleasure would be a more complete but also more specialized form of approach to the Other, one more technique for getting to know what is not ourselves. (Yourcenar 1954: 14)

Through the fissure of the social fabric delicately or not so delicately parted by meeting, purchasing something, importuning someone, offering someone something, the ethnographer catches a first glimpse into the workings of a world formerly opaque. My undisguised and, since 1975, growing interest in American market culture has been shaped by the eros of wanting to study closely while at the same time protectively resisting those with inherited wealth or those who married them and those who made money in

the country's largest corporations. The scholarly aim is to contribute to a
growing interest in the culture of market economies (see, e.g., Appadurai
1990: 1–32; Fox and Lears 1983; Frykman and Lofgren 1987; MacCannell
1989; Macfarlane 1987; McCracken 1988).

The men fish in the calmer waters of the lagoon. A says, "Pull in," and he
and another try to haul the net in. Something stops their effort, perhaps the
catch is too heavy. B then adds, "Let go," and just as they let it go a bit, C
speaks out, "Shift further," and D seeing they have found an advantage, exclaims, "Lift the net!"

Although we could imagine that this was an entire language game, it does
not help us to understand much what lies beyond the immediate context of
the situation, just the situation in which the immediate words occur here
fishing in the lagoon. The context of the exclamations and directives each
fisherman exchanges with the other must be expanded, something like:
Fishing so the family members will have something for dinner and some
extra to dry in the sun for when the fish are not running.

I just said, "It does not help us," and by that I meant that in returning to
Malinowski's essay on the meanings of a primitive language in which he
shows us that it must be understood in its wider social contexts of utterances
for purposes of translating words and sentences into English, the situation
itself is not sufficient to understand the uses to which we put language.

These reflections on Malinowski's paragraph diverge from his intention
and are employed to dramatize another objective, which is definitely not to
make translations based on the discovery of native meanings in the use of
phrases. The idea is to go back to the kernel notion within Malinowski's *context of situation,* which he revealed in the paragraph quoted above, and to let
the phrases which I have placed into the mouths of A, B, C, and D in the co-
ordination of their fishing efforts, direct our thought toward solving a certain puzzle or confronting a particular challenge; that challenge, in a small
way addressed here, is to characterize and understand the use of language
in the contemporary culture of the market. The inquiry begins with the assumption that the world market now pulls human language into itself so
that newness will be endlessly created by means of effective discourses, often using images to produce products, advertising, and services. The utterances that feed into the exchange possibilities of the market are a pragmatic
rhetoric in which statements are relentlessly made, day in, day out, of steps
to go through again and again, the speech of algorithms and heuristics, that
is, imaginative, practical talk about assembling some sort of mundane project no matter how minute or extensive; and the analysis of the way to put
things together, such as planning a Deere and Company combine factory
for China, is also meant to persuade those persons working on complex
tasks toward aiding in forming some sort of marketable assemblage. A key

assumption here is that the market pulls our speech from us; it demands a pragmatic shaping of mutual current and subsequent activities. It can be argued that we now act unconsciously in relation to this vast market in the (concealed) interests of a larger humanity that benefits however directly or indirectly from our discursive labors (and from whose linguistic exertions we also gain), whether we identify with those distant others or not.

The Delaware Valley, Philadelphia with its old money (much written about) and Wilmington, Delaware, with the rich and populous du Pont family (also much written about), stimulated the inquiry in the first place and offered itself as a site of possibility. The way I would formulate it now would be to say that I have tried to find the high altitude in American life from which the world is viewed as if from the top down and outward to a world of peers, as if dwelling on a promontory from which are visible others on their promontories and then figuring out what the bonds are between those available to one another. With highly stratified class relations that are painfully evident in America and increasing in extent worldwide with the formation of new elites controlling fabulous wealth,[2] it is not difficult to think of society in spatial imagery, such as viewing downward. The objective I have evolved is to study down (and up there, to study sideways), to invert Laura Nader's phrase, "studying up." Except for a handful of books and articles on dynastic families or their fiduciaries by anthropologists, or on upper-class leisure and aesthetic pursuits (Marcus 1983, 1990; McDonough 1986; Miller 1987) and that perennial interest by sociologists in the interlocking directorates thought to directly influence American business life,[3] there has been little enough face-to-face investigation in the higher latitudes beyond the formal interview.

As a result of its central role in the formation of the Atlantic market economy in the seventeenth century and the American industrial revolution in the nineteenth, the Delaware Valley is a vast laboratory for any ethnography—or any archaeology—of the culture of the market. It has a history of white settlement dating to the colonial period (Warner 1987) and like the mid-Atlantic region in general, quickly became ethnically and racially heterogeneous (Golab 1977), heterophanous, and highly stratified; it has an extensive working class and a rather large, insular upper class of old and new money (Baltzell 1979). The economy of the region replicates that of the country in a shift from manufacturing toward services; and in terms of settlement patterns, the middle classes of the area have suburbanized like those of other U.S. cities in ways that only vary locally. It would seem that all of the readily visible, hidden, or partially or fully obscured workings of modernity are more than amply represented in this location (Dorst 1989), a site in which the transactions of the world market are locally fascinating as examples of global processes.

The fishermen have lifted the nets heavy with fish into the canoe and have decided to paddle back to shore. As they arrive a number of children help them carry the catch to the huts, where some of them are given to their wives and mothers. Others are placed in overnight storage. The next morning they hang remaining fish on racks to dry in the sun. Half of these will be kept for later use in the women's cooking; the other half will be taken to the village quay where they will be sold. We could now trace where the sold fish will be taken, how they will be processed, packaged, distributed, marketed, and purchased, say, in Singapore. All along this value-added process, this extended journey of the fish after they left the water, we could record the speech of the men and women who have something to do with them, including the meal in the Singapore apartment during which they are quickly consumed. There we would abandon speech-connected-to-fish. The route of the fish through the production process necessitates speech to coordinate their flow to market, purchase, and consumption. This is the context of situation that I wish to point toward, the worldly and endlessly pragmatic discourses of the market.

If humans evolve verbal praxis that intimately binds their routine activities to a world market, how ought we to inquire into their operations? Our intellectual questions require an approach. We now have more than a century's worth of ideas for addressing the understanding of language. Do we want to understand language? Not per se; not since Malinowski was joined to structural linguistics by sociolinguists. Language, in the example of the fishermen, pushes us beyond itself [words → fish] and we are taken farther than the words as uttered; it is toward this beyond-itself that we initiate our inquiry into the discourse of the market.

My interest enclosed within this ethnographer-framed story line lies in a kind of opportunistic ethnographic inquiry into the upper reaches with the aim of writing ethnographic narrative accounts.[4] By beginning with William Hewitt leaving his driveway in his car to drive down the road for a meeting, an interview, really, with three other men, I wanted to evoke in the reader a sense of place, time, and character, each of which is associated with the story. The interruption in the narrative, the quote from Malinowski, reveries on that language game, and acquainting you briefly with the three men moved toward a nonnarrative description of ethnographer's intention coupled to a brief statement about the site of inquiry. The textual form of the account, thus far, is narrative → digression, where the digression serving as revery or explanatory interlude provides an intellectual framework, background, and context and motivates the story on two levels, issues of narrative and enduring interests in the discourses of modernity—here applied to the marketplace. In a moment I will end the digressions and return to the story line.

The overall feature of the narrative strategy I am using is narrative + digression + narrative + digression; this allows for story and analysis, text and context, evocation and interpretation, to inhabit the same textual space. As a literary practice, it has been central to the development of the twentieth-century novel and short story and can be used effectively in the further expansion of techniques available for authors of narrative ethnographies. The narrative-digressive mode enables the author to insert a variety of genres into the flow of narration, thus enriching, explaining, commenting on, subverting, or creating a parallel discourse to the story line (Kundera 1988). One of the points of this chapter is to illustrate that writing tactic; another is to reflect on an absence at the zenith of the American culture of capitalism which we can witness based on discursive analysis. Hewitt's conversation with the three men—in part chronicled below—takes the form of a complex narrative made up of brief stories that illustrate points he wishes to make. From the accounts, the ethnographer may map the topoi of the market and address what appears to be missing through negative analysis. That absence can be described as a characteristic omission, a discovery through comparison of what American business culture lacks. Obviously, I am now getting too far ahead of the story.

Hewitt had just finished dinner in the dining room and watched for a moment the sun setting over the piedmont hills across the Brandywine River, well above the stone house and outbuildings that belonged to the painter Andrew Wyeth. The Jamaican cook had broiled his steak the way he liked it, and a Jamaican servant served him alone at the table. Hewitt's wife, Tish, had brought the servants back to Chadds Ford, Pennsylvania, from Kingston when he returned as the American ambassador, and up Highway 100 to the right, she had bought a house for one of the families that they immediately set to painting a bluish purple trimmed in red.

After he retired as chairman of Deere and Company, Hewitt served in Jamaica under Secretary of State George Schultz early in the Reagan presidency, and he and Tish, at her insistence, had then moved from Moline to Chadds Ford. He would rather have returned to the Napa Valley in California where he grew up and had inherited a vineyard.

With dinner this evening he sampled a glass of the family Cabernet from that very vineyard, and, on a small California knoll there among the trellises surrounded by the carefully cropped vines, the architect Kevin Roche had designed for him a large U-shaped house. One of the ideas was to extend the living space with capacious awnings for evening entertainment. The architect's model for it was in the living room.

His closest friends lived on the West Coast, and the idea of building a house there stated in material terms that it was *there* he wanted to be, but Tish was interested in her horses and the friends she rode and partied with, on the opposite edge of the continent.

PRAGMATIC DISCOURSE. It leads to changes in the material-social life of one or more of the conversationalists and others who are not present.

A man and a woman shop at Bloomingdale's. The woman holds up a sweater and asks her husband, "What do you think of this one?"

"I rather like it," he replies. "Why don't you try it on?"

She tries it on. He admires it again.

She takes the sweater to a clerk who asks, "Cash or charge?"

The woman hands the clerk an American Express charge card, and after the transaction the couple leaves. That evening they entertain another couple over a light dinner on the deck overlooking the ocean. The woman wears her new sweater, and her husband and the other couple comment on it appreciatively.

This vignette sketches the form of pragmatic discourse I want to identify as a nucleus of capitalist-effective conversation. Two people talk at a transaction site where there is material for sale—*the effect of which* as a *result*, one makes a purchase. They buy a physical item, then take it home and wear it to the accompaniment of further talk.

Pragmatic discourse effects a different state of affairs through subsequent speech and action: it can create the new.

What is interesting about this little story is that the pragmatic discourse is not restricted either to the *event* of a conversational encounter (event as speech act or conversational turn taking) or to the utterance or exchange of utterances at a given conversational moment but is played out over several events—a discussion about a purchase, the purchase, and the later wearing with further comment, embellishment, whatever. The men converging in the autos on Chadds Ford were intent on a form of pragmatic discourse. Hewitt's reminiscences of his corporate governance were thought by the three others to be valuable for their own pragmatic thinking.

Frolic Weymouth had talked Tish into buying and remodeling Rondelay, and in a sense it was more her house than her husband's, just as Roche's designs for the house in the vineyard were more his than hers. Frolic, who was full of pranks and laughter, was one of the people Tish enjoyed most, a charismatic member of the du Pont family from Wilmington, a sportsman, and the founder and chairman of the board of the Brandywine River Museum and Conservancy.

THURSDAY, NOVEMBER 25, 1976—
NEW YORK—CHADDS FORD, PENNSYLVANIA

Andrew Wyeth, Jamie's father, was there. Frolic Weymouth was there, a neighbor—who's Andrew Wyeth's niece had just left him for an antique dealer or something after lots of married years—he's a du Pont—and he was depressed, so he was over for dinner. And Andrew's two sisters, one nutty who looks like she drinks and paints. . . .

FRIDAY, NOVEMBER 26, 1976—CHADDS FORD
Went with Jamie to the Brandywine Museum and we were photographed and had a press conference. Went back to Jamie and Phyllis's and there were cocktails. . . .
SATURDAY, NOVEMBER 27, 1976—CHADDS FORD
Went in the carriage again. This time Frolic had his carriage out, too. He was drinking all day. He took his drinks onto the wagon with him and he was riding around drinking. Jamie took me to his aunt's house to see a 5' doll house. It was like an old-fashioned Christmas.
(Warhol 1989: 1–2)

Frolic had intended that the museum house mainly the art of Andrew Wyeth and include members of the Wyeth family and, more broadly, the Brandy-wine school of illustrators and landscape painters. Frolic himself was a skilled realist painter and had done commissioned portraits of notable people in Europe and America as well as landscapes along the Brandywine (Rose 1989).

Tish, Frolic, and others from northern Delaware and southern Chester County raced in their horse-drawn coaches along the river and paraded, formally dressed, laughing and drinking, behind their high-strung horses at racing events, large parties, and fund raisers. Tish served as one of the directors on Frolic's Museum and Conservancy board and was caught up in the life of her rich neighbors who pursued polo and thoroughbred racing. She rode to hounds at times, not regularly, with Mr. Stewart's Cheshire Foxhounds (Rose 1990*b*), but Hewitt would have none of it, was uninterested in the horsey set, and was critical in conversation of Frolic's playful lifestyle and the way he managed his duties as board chairman of his nonprofit company. Hewitt was far more fascinated by David Rockefeller, with whom he was friends. After weekends spent together, Hewitt would develop the pictures he had taken and send duplicates of them to the Rockefellers as mementos. Frolic, for his part, tended to deride Hewitt for what Frolic thought was his exaggerated interest in the Rockefellers. He said that the picture taking was sycophantic.

When Hewitt was the CEO at Deere, the Hewitts had installed a tatami room on the top floor of their Moline home, a displaced borrowing from the Japanese. Along the walls in floor-to-ceiling closets, Hewitt had kept in hundreds of trays well-organized 35 mm slides of his and Tish's growing family—two daughters and a son—and their world travels.

In the interests of a common humanity, it would be worthwhile to imagine humanist-scientific comparative studies of the largest world corporations as pragmatic persuasive discursive structures. It would be valuable to treat them as a set, companies in their complex dealings with one another and with governments and countries, and to think of them as being inhabited by citizens, to consider them as being cultural institutions; and it would be instructive to monitor their rapid contemporary formations and the moral worlds that they provide for themselves and the people who work for them and the kind of possibilities they afford the human communities that depend on them. In part, the agenda for such a comparative inquiry would be the aim to further humanize these great structures that are now indispensable to the well-being of humanity and the very health of its citizens and the planet itself.

The interest here would in part be shifted from nations, societies, and cultures to great world corporations as a community of companies, but all those other notions—of polity, economy, environment, culture, social justice, stratification, gender, language and rhetoric, human rights, democratic principles—would be brought to bear for understanding the formation of the ultra-large capitalist community of companies, as a (speech) *community* whatever its complex character turns out to mean. We would examine, too, their inscriptions on the landscape, the ongoing reconfiguration of the earth and the physical transformations they induce on the planet.

Two miles down the road at the junction of Highway 100 and U.S. Route 1, Hewitt turned the car to the right and without glancing to his left, passed the buildings of the Brandywine River Museum and Conservancy. He sat behind the wheel with an easy military erectness, his posture seeming to reflect his service in the navy during the Second World War. There always seemed to be an air of pleasantness about him when he was not talking, a hint of a smile on his lips. When he sat in a chair, whether receiving strangers or visiting intently, he never crossed one leg over the other or squeezed himself together in a defensive or nervous posture; driving, talking, making a tough point with his directors on the Deere board, he exuded relaxation in a way no one else in the room could quite duplicate. Time seemed to slow down and swirl around him as if his air of pleasant abstraction took the anxiety, if not the immediacy, out of the most difficult problems.

Just beyond the museum parking lot next to the heavily traveled Route 1, Hewitt had bought a large old house with Tish; it was their office building, made over, remodeled, the interior decorated in Victorian Americana patterns by Tish herself. They rented out the second story as office space and on the first floor Tish's blond, placid Jamaican secretary sat all day long, every weekday, surrounded by high-technology machines, computers, phones, a fax machine, and photocopiers.

In the next room, Hewitt had installed a large desk with books he meant to read piled in the corners. Whenever he sat there, he faced a wall of selected pictures of his tenure as ambassador and his service in Washington on various boards and roundtables made up of America's most notable business leaders. Since Truman's presidency he had been photographed with each of the succeeding heads of state. That was all there as visual souvenir, constant reminder to himself, and a source of conversational openings with visitors.

In a space reserved for him he parked the Rolls Royce and entered the office building to inspect the receiving room. He arranged the chairs slightly. The three expected guests arrived almost exactly at the same moment, at 7:30 P.M. They introduced themselves: Anthony Parrotto (TP), Dan Rose (DR), Lauren Taylor (LT), Bill Hewitt (BH). Hewitt adjusted the air-conditioner, and they sat comfortably in the overstuffed furniture. Rose turned on the cassette tape recorder.

BH: I went to work for Deere and Company in 1948, and I became CEO in 1955 and remained CEO until 1982. John Deere started the company in 1847, and the son Charles Deere expanded it, and his son-in-law William Butterworth expanded it some more. Butterworth had no children, so Charles Deere's grandson, Charles Wiman, headed the company.

I was the fifth head of the company in 145 years when I left. The company always had successful heads of the company who made it grow.[5] The company was doing about a 130 odd million dollars a year in sales when I became CEO in 1955, and I expanded it to almost five and a half billion; then I said good-bye. I wrote the retirement rules myself.

[The other three men laughed.]

BH: That's just establishing credentials. Let me ask you, Dan, what are we talking about tonight?

DR: Our agenda for the evening is to talk about the role of the CEO and the board inside the company and the relations of the CEO to the wider environment that the CEO operates in. So I think it is both within the company and outside the company that is our interest. We have questions that we can fire at you.

BH: Questions are fine, because the only justification for this evening is to talk about things you want to talk about if they are in my orbit. I'd be delighted to talk about them. How do you want to start it?

DR: I wouldn't mind kicking it off.

BH: Sure.

DR: My interest is in the way the world capitalist system is organized. Now that is just for starters. According to theoreticians today, there is a lot of talk about the socialist system as having to operate on world markets, therefore operating in a capitalist manner. We all know that Russia does not have a stock exchange and so on, so they are not *very* capitalist. Nevertheless they have to work on a pricing mechanism the same way we do.

BH: Let's look at it this way; our system is not totally unregulated. Private enterprise is not totally unregulated. The socialist system acting [in] capitalist ways means that they're *considerably* more regulated than we are. They are finally seeing the light: that the ultimate in socialist government—the dictatorship of the proletariat—never really existed, and it never will. In the Soviet case, the idea of the five-year plan never really worked, as population grew it just became absurd. Let me illustrate it, call it a joke if you will.

When the secretary of agriculture of the United States was trying to explain the American free enterprise approach from the farmers' point of view in relation to the Russian farmer working on a farm commune, the American secretary of agriculture said, let's take a pig farmer—this is so old I think you probably have heard it—he said, pigs are subject to certain diseases; they are curable. An American pig farmer, his pigs get sick in the middle of the night, he's going to get up and inoculate [them] or do whatever is necessary to help get them better. In a Communist state who the hell wants to stay up all night with the state-owned pigs?

[A little laughter.]

BH: The point obviously is the American farmer is in a sense staying up with his pigs and in another, staying up with his pocketbook. That's an incentive, and you hear it over and over again—*market forces*, which aren't always pleasant and happy. Basically, they keep things in balance better than a relatively few people in a country of 275 million, trying to crank out one five-year plan after another to keep things in balance. It just absolutely doesn't work.

DR: My further interest lies in—If you would take an American CEO, AT&T, Deere, General Motors, there are obviously a number of associations that you belong to by which you get acquainted with other people in your sector, in your industry, across a variety of industries, you meet banking CEOs, do business with them, you meet competitors, probably under a variety of circumstances, like on boards somewhere else, you sit on other sector boards as you did AT&T. What I am wondering about is, What are those associations that a CEO is a member of that creates a community—or if it does or if it doesn't—of people who are in touch with one another, who understand one another's interests, who talk the same kind of language, that kind of thing? Now is that a function of the Business Roundtable? Is it a function of associations you belong to, such as the association that presidential candidate Bush addressed a few months back of presidents and CEOs of large midwestern companies? This is one of the questions I had, What is your operating environment outside the company?

BH: I think we're leading up to a minor question. I don't think that's major. I think its helpful but not material, really, to build a foundation on. Also I believe that there is no simple formula; I could tell you something, and it would be good for certain segments of the business community, but not for all of them. I think that humans tend a lot to oversimplify. . . .

LT: You, you were on the board of AT&T?

BH: For twenty years.

LT: Was that a significant experience for you?

BH: I think so, yes. . . . James O'Toole wrote a book called *Vanguard Management,* and he made a study. The way it turned out for him was he selected ten companies and wrote about those ten companies. Deere and Company was one of them. Levi-Strauss was one of them. The chairman of Levi-Strauss and I were roommates in college; his name was Walter Haas. He's a descendant of Levi-Strauss. O'Toole uses the term—instead of shareholders being the important people—he uses the word, stakeholders. *Stakeholders* means several categories of people: you're a stakeholder of a corporation if you're an employee; you're a stakeholder if you're a shareholder; you're a stakeholder if you're a customer; you're a stakeholder if you're a supplier; you're a stakeholder if you're a member of a community in which the operation employs a lot of people. His point was that to be an overall good CEO and manager you had to give considerable consideration to shareholders, employees, customers, suppliers, and people in the communities where you work.

And why not?

In spinning these threads, you have to jump back and forth a little bit. You've heard for a long, long time that earning a profit is the most important thing because if you don't earn a profit you're either very sick or you're dead. And none of us CEOs are going to say that earning a profit is not important.

Earning a profit on an ongoing basis is *essential.* [Here he deliberately drew out and emphasized each word.] *It is not the whole game.*

It's not the whole game just to earn a profit. Because how long are you going to be able to continue earning a profit if you don't pay attention to other things which you're supposed to be paying attention to?

What is important? I may repeat it ten more times: Earning a profit is absolutely essential to the health of the company that wants to say in business. I am not going to argue against that set of facts for a second. It's not the whole game. You have to pay attention to your employees, to your customers, to your suppliers, to the communities that you work in, to the whole worldwide scene.

LT: Also to competitors?

BH: The answer is yes and no. The yes part of it is, of course, you have to pay attention to what your competitors are doing, and um, I'll have to tell you something that maybe is a little unorthodox but I just simply, personally am not the kind of a guy that feels that you have to trample your competitor and grind your heel in his neck to try to win the game. I think the world is big enough for both [!] of us. If you don't have any competitors you've got a monopoly and then you've got other problems. I never have felt it was a winner-take-all game. That's not my personal attitude.

I've always enjoyed being a friendly adversary of competitors. Adversary? Yes, of course, you're an adversary. That doesn't mean you have to hate 'em. So that's my answer on competitors.

At this point in our interview, I began to write down on the page opposite the notes I had been making my reaction to the tack he was taking in relation to the agenda I had suggested: "I think his response reflects a profoundly American, limited cultural attitude, something to the effect that the CEO is the highest authority in a company and the rest of the culture, government, competition, etc., is a constraining or facilitating environment. I'm concerned with something more interesting: Germany, France, Sweden, Japan, Taiwan, China, U.S., each has different sorts of relationships between corporate leaders, across sectors of the economy, across financial, manufacturing, service, and governmental units. My larger interest is the relationships between corporate leaders and their companies in world competition. Example: Roger Smith, CEO of General Motors, buying a computer company [Ross Perot's Electronic Data Systems, Inc.] to internalize expertise to GM. Why couldn't the auto industry have equal access to state-of-the-art computer technology expertise for autos to make them more competitive with Europeans, Japanese, and Koreans?" (Lash and Urry 1987) The very complex answer to this question cuts to the heart of the American ideology of business, to the heartfelt assumptions that operate in the portion of everyday life that takes place after working hours, and to the utterances that characterize the pragmatic possibilities in the minds of corporate and national leadership.

BH: I was CEO for twenty-seven years, and I *knew* that I had to guide the company from having a family member be the head of it to a transition period of having a professional manager and nonfamily member be head of the company. . . .

BH: At the end of World War II, Deere and Company was virtually only a producer—designer, manufacturer, and distributor—of farm machinery for the domestic U.S. market with a small export business; no overseas manufacturing. International Harvester had been manufacturing overseas for years, Massey Ferguson, for years, and they were big in it. Henry Ford had started building Fordson tractors in Ireland in 1918.

One of the first big decisions I had to make as a new CEO was this: Let's make a conscious decision of what we are now—that we are domestic producers and distributors of farm machinery, period. Is that what we want to be? Let's answer that question either yes or no.

In 1948, the year my wife and I were married, we took a vacation trip to France and we rented a Citroen automobile and drove ourselves from Paris over to Brittany and Normandy and down to the southern edge of France along the Mediterranean and up the east coast of France and back to Paris.

In northern France we saw—almost all the farm equipment we saw—was pulled by large horses and in southern France pulled by large oxen. There were forty thousand tractors in France at that time, and potentially there could be a million tractors.

The Marshall Plan had been bailing out Europe at that time, and Europe had low-cost labor relative to the United States; and it had the Marshall Plan building up its manufacturing strength. There was absolutely no protective tariff on the import of farm machinery from Europe to the United States. I looked at it and I said, Okay, there's a big potential market here for our growth in Europe, just taking France. I didn't realize it but France was the second largest country in agricultural production in the free world. The first was the United States in acres and total land in farm use, the second was France. France!

I thought, My God!

Going to the University of California I was a free trader; I didn't want protective tariffs. I still don't want them. Okay, we're not going to fight the protective tariffs; this is a growth opportunity for us to start manufacturing in Europe for growth there and as a hedge against French and European countries exporting their lower-cost labor products against our low tariff barrier here. Kill two birds with one stone and start producing over there. So we did.

LT: Have you had any international interest in the Soviet or Chinese markets?

BH: The answer is yes, and it's a long story. I was a member of the U.S.–USSR Business Council for many years and made many trips to Moscow and made good friends with various Russians. My favorite Russian, a youngish guy, who was one of the undersecretaries of agriculture over there, he used to visit this country. He is one of the relatively few individuals who have the medal, Hero of the Republic. He was nineteen years old and a soldier in the Russian army when Berlin was taken. He just had the wonderful good luck to be walking around somewhere near Berlin in his uniform and out of nowhere comes a German officer and he wants to surrender to somebody. He's got to surrender to somebody. So he surrenders about a thousand guys to my friend Boris. Boris leads them in. Any one of us could have done this.

[The men laugh.]

BH: Boris becomes a Hero of the Republic, and he's got a medal to prove it.

Boris was granted some special privileges. One of the *best* was right after World War II, as a young guy interested in agriculture. I have no ideas how it happened but he was sent to the United States to Ames, Iowa, where the Iowa State agricultural school is, one of the best in the United States, and he lived there for a year. He lived with an American family and studied, and he speaks good English. What a good benefit that was for him. He just got to know and understand the idioms and enjoyed the experience.

When I met him it was much later. He had this official position. We would see each other at these meetings in Moscow. Then I'd see him in Washington. Then one time I had to go to Moscow, and he is the only Russian who invited me to his apartment for dinner in Moscow. He and his wife and his twenty-one-year-old son and an opposite number from another ministry and that guy's wife and myself—he told me everything. He said, I make 650 rubles a month and am taxed 17 percent income tax, but I have a car and a driver, part-time use of a dacha, and I travel to the United States all the time.

We had a nice dinner, and then after dinner he pulls out a cassette player a little bit bigger than that one. He likes American music, especially show tunes. You know, *Oklahoma, Carousel.* That kind of thing. Here we are sitting around the table in the dark after dinner, all of a sudden, coming from his cassette player I hear the theme from *Doctor Zhivago,* and I said, "Boris, you're not supposed to be listening to that kind of music."

You know what he said to me? He said, "It's okay, Bill, I like the music and I don't listen to the words."

[Loud laughter.]

BH: I said, that was early glasnost.

LT: Tricky glasnost at that.

BH: But I like him. I'd enjoy it if he walked in the door right now.

LT: Is there any market there?

BH: That's a sad story. There are two problems—this has been changed recently—they have a minister of agriculture and a minister of farm machinery production, a minister of parts distribution, a minister of agronomy, and there's a fifth one I can't remember, but generally, these ministries, instead of cooperating, are fighting for their own turf all the time. That screwed up our ability to do business with them. You know we send machines over for the Moscow machinery fair and end up selling the machines we sent there as samples. We never really did get rolling with them the way you would expect to.

Finally, finally, we thought we had a breakthrough. They asked us to modify one of our best model tractors, which was of the large size, and modify it by making it lighter weight and faster on the road, so it would do the work they wanted. They don't have motor trucks and pickups the way we do, so they needed it to go from here to there.

We did it. According to their specs we did it, and they tested it for thirty-five hundred dollars. They were amazed, and *we* were amazed that they had no problems with it. They were on the verge of placing a big order—this almost sounds phony, it's so sad but true—but right at that point a man named Jimmy Carter declares a boycott and hit that thing on the head right there. It was an asinine thing to do.

I'll tell you another Chinese story. In 1972 there was a series of Ping-Pong games, and my wife and I actually contributed money to those Ping-Pong games. Oddly enough, it triggered Richard Nixon opening up relationships with China. Kissinger and Nixon went over there, and in 1973 a fellow named Fred Dent who was secretary of commerce—his family had a textile mill in the South somewhere—appointed a board of directors for a new organization called the National Council for U.S.–China Trade. I was appointed to be on the board of directors of that and went to Washington, and Fred Dent told us all, he said, "Here I am a member of the government appointing this board of directors and there are going to be no government people on the board; it's going to be strictly private sector!"

In 1973 we all went to China, established contact with our counterpart, with the head of CCPIT, which is China Council for the Promotion of International Trade, the English words, Mr. Wong Yung Deng, champion mai tai drinker in China.

[Laughter.]

We had a *wonderful* trip around China with him and his people. Then he came over to this country, and we gave them a trip they'll never forget. They traveled in corporate jets all around the United States with one exception—two exceptions—from Moline to Chicago, we had a private train from the Santa Fe, and from Dallas to Los Angeles, we thought they should see what American airlines were like so they traveled that way. When they visited Moline we took them to visit a farm of a thousand acres run by a man and his son and one hired hand; they had 250 head of cattle, and they raised corn and soy beans. We pitched a great big yellow and white striped tent there and had a good old American lunch of corn on the cob and apple pie and ice cream.

[Much laughter.]

After lunch we went out and showed them how this guy and his son and one hired hand were running it. Time for the cow to have lunch, and there were these silos with different kinds of grains and the conveyor pipes going down to the mixing building. Push these buttons, pull those levers, and then the mixture's all done and it goes on a conveyor belt, and there's this row of feeding troughs going down here [he gestures with his hands to describe the area] and the feed comes in on the overhead going down into sort of a V-shaped slot like this so that all the cows don't bunch up at the head of the feeding trough.

Pull a lever, and the feed comes down right along the whole trough at the same time and the cows just wander up.

They couldn't get over it!

[More appreciative laughter.]

Then eventually they wanted to license and manufacture John Deere combines in China. We said, "Sure." We were aware of the pitfalls, we thought. Part of the contract is that all of the machines that you make you cannot sell them outside of China. You're going to make these machines, and any improvements or changes come through future negotiations. It was a pretty good deal.

We had two kinds of combines, one made in the United States and one made in Germany. The growing conditions in Germany are slower climate-wise than they are here, and that means the grain grows taller and you have more chaff to get rid of—when you cut the wheat it goes through the com-bine, shakes out the grain, and throws the chaff out the rear end. They chose that one because it's quite suited to their conditions.

I went over to Europe to meet with them and the combine manufactur-ers in Germany, and we had a good session with these Chinese. After it was all over and they agreed they were going to do it, we were having a kind of a bull session, and I sort of digressed a little bit in this way: I have a couple of suggestions, I have some unsolicited advice for you. Two points: one is that any kind of machinery, I don't care who makes it, and it's a brand-new manufacturing facility, there's going to be some bugs in these machines. No matter how good you are and how careful you are, there are going to be some bugs! For that reason in your initial production, distribute them in a relatively small radius, then you can get out there and service them more quickly. You come from a *very* big country. Don't scatter them all around the country. Point number two, as you build these new machines don't just build a bunch of machines. Start building parts as you go along. Set aside parts to be used as parts because machines are working hardest when they're needed the most in the planting or harvesting season, and that's when a ma-chine's going to break down. That's when you're going to need it the most. You gotta have the parts ready; don't trust to luck that the machines won't break down.

They listened very patiently and attentively, and then the response came. The response was very polite. "We agree with what you've said. I'm sorry to say we cannot follow your advice because this factory belongs to all the peo-ple of China and we have to distribute them equitably around the country. Part number two we have nothing to do with the parts distribution: that is done by the town councils."

"Okay fellas, don't say I didn't warn ya."

Corporations seem to be infinitely extended structures of persuasion. It is not difficult to arrive at the idea that corporations are rhetorical structures; they exist to persuade.

The entire interior, from the president all the way down to entry level, *begets persuasion*. But also, corporations impel their customers, existing and potential; and companies competitively seek to persuade, so the whole culture rides on a rhetoric of inducement to direct action for making things into the market for exchange transactions: operant discourse.

The interpreter and hearer or audience does not merely interpret the utterance for understanding but interrogates the utterance for how to assemble a next activity so as to make that activity successful or accomplish something or make material changes or whatever. At its most general, people who grow up in a universe of discourse dominated by daily pragma interrogate their world—what they see and hear, even a TV commercial—for how to dress, act, speak, think, respond, and gesture, and what to use and how to use it and in what portions or proportions. A speaker's pragmatic utterances contain a use-value for the hearer's subsequent modifications of the world-at-hand.

I want to make two points based on the material presented here, an interpretation of a portion of Hewitt's monologue and a brief addition to the discussion on writing narrative ethnography. First, I want to point out again William Hewitt's diegesis as a strategy of topic management within pragmatic discourse. He refused to discuss in *any* systematic or serious anecdotal way the ambience of the CEO outside the corporate confines. This forces the listener or reader to construct an image of the American executive, and by extension, the American firm, as preeminently looking outward from itself to discrete points of contact and gazing downward into its own business. Hewitt put off the invitation to discuss the networks through which he was articulated into a wider system of relations with other corporate and government leaders, except as by-products of his stories about his role in the company. For him, the communal relations of the firm from the perspective of the CEO included employees (!), customer, suppliers, and the settlements where employees lived. The ideological formation—certainly his agenda—in his evening monologue was aimed at discoursing on the governance of the firm in which Deere and Company seemed to stand almost autonomous, even in international dealings. Obviously, this is not the only way American business leaders think of corporate activity, and surely a different interview would have elicited a much different response from him, particularly concerning, say, company relations with the banks in Manhattan where he borrowed capital for expansion or retooling; however, he did have the opportunity, and we are attending the text transcribed from his conversation.

The anecdote of his industrial, but inadvertent, ethnography undertaken while traveling through France with his new bride and thereby discovering the potential European market for farm equipment is the tale of the lone corporate decision maker who finds new market potential. The firm, under his direction, then, in pragmatic follow-through, realizes the vision.

I came away with an overpowering visual image, a metaphor, of the entire American landscape as a collection of very large corporate enterprises, each distant from one another, like farms in the Midwest—rural Illinois seen from the air at 10,000 feet—each punctuating the sky with their white or dark blue silos another mile down the road. The image resembled Frank Lloyd Wright's Broadacre City model with its one-acre suburban farms and, despite a residential tower and sports arena, no urban focus. It was as if America's midwestern settlement patterns and utopias each inscribed versions of one another; one on the landscape, the other on an architect's model and published in photographs. It was as if in Hewitt's narrative representation the whole corporate community were atoms or individuals whose connections with one another or counterparts in other nations were at best informal networks and entirely contingent relationships and, more important, as if the whole set of individuals could not be conceived of as having dealings together as a larger, self-realizing unity, or even in whole subsets, as if each entity were such a thing in itself, that its main connection to any of the others was purely through the market but not by means of either profound knowledge of one another's existence or through awareness of the larger American community of collective enterprise that these companies made up (Prestowitz 1988). America's narratives of itself among its highest-level corporate leadership can offer us a complex and rich story of nation-based notions of the possibilities or impossibilities of collective enterprise. It is here that the rationale for ethnographic inquiry seems most eloquent, for despite the voluminous outpouring of writing about business, the serious work of assembling knowledge from face-to-face relationships with American decision-making elites would potentially offer a more profound, reticulated, pervasive understanding of the culture of the market. In a very real sense, a rich understanding coupled to a critique may help provide an agenda to further the humanization of the corporate order.

As a result of that evening, it seemed that the evolution of the American market culture became more, rather than less, problematic and that life in the highest strata, rather than revealing itself, was self-mystifying, heavily loaded with a tacit ideology, one that implicated the fabric of the entire American social order. Particularly absent were anything other than anecdotal relations between corporations and government. Relations remained invisible between companies in America and those in other nations except for stories of fortuitous involvement between companies and people, and it was as if the larger American corporate polity were composed of only tangentially connected corporate citizens. I would say that connectivity was not so much denied as ideologically, as well as narratively, kept invisible to the key players. To impute too great of degree of self-consciousness in this process would be, I believe, wrong; I do not think that capitalists obscure their corporate order as wittingly as some of their critics would like to imagine.

Through his arbitrary management of topic—I am certain it was culturally determined—Hewitt portrayed the individual CEO and the singular company he governed as the apex of a system; above, or even on that level, there was no coherent (communal?) order between units that he was willing or, perhaps, able to discuss *as such*. Although I want to point toward a topic of vital interest, the *community* of corporations, how companies through their officers interact at the national and international levels to produce the world as we know it, community, as can be witnessed in Hewitt's American story of the firm, can only be considered as a double problematic: what it may mean to the set of all the CEOs of America's largest corporations; and what it may portend for the academic ethnographer who attempts to investigate just those firms in their not yet fully understood relationships as they engage the world market. My provisional conclusion, however, is this: American executives, presidents, and highest-level vice-presidents of the largest U.S. companies tend not to understand their immediate business world as a *we*, but as an us-them competitive, adversarial set of freestanding institutional units. And by *us*, I mean, a company's officers: they do not think at all easily about the communal, the sectorial, the national, much less the interests of all humanity, in their day-to-day decision making, nor as far as I can tell, routinely—much less first—in their strategic planning. At best, there are networks through key individuals to other autonomous companies, or companylike formations in China and Russia, but collective action outside the firm itself seems, except rarely, impossible.[6]

Second, the emplotment of this narrative resembles, distantly, the novel of the road, usually a route, as here, through nonexotic space (Bakhtin 1981). The character leaves, in this case, the domestic site, takes a short and familiar trip to his work site, something happens—a conversational transaction in the male world that in miniature emulates the corporate setting— and the character returns. The journey encloses reveries on contemporary market discourse, the genre *interview* that contains within it oral anecdotes and miniature narratives as well as the frame of question-and-answer discourse, one of the pragmatic discursive forms on which modern capitalist practices relies (Rose 1990*a*).

The chronotope of the road, with its axes of space-time, is a narrative convenient for the ethnographic author. And with the insertion of digressions, it is possible to take up a counter-discourse that seeks to frame for understanding the stories of a person who has spent his life directing his considerable portion of the American culture of the market. The stories themselves each transcend the coordinates—that is, the physical setting in Chadds Ford—in which they are told; the walls of the room seem to fold down for a moment, and the storyteller takes the listeners on market-related side trips to Russia, France, or China, those evoked presences in remote space but nearby time to which the listener would not have otherwise gained access except through these stories.

The narrative, whether told by the ethnographer or recounted by the person with whom the ethnographer speaks, when digressively interrupted for commentary, interpretation, resituated within a body of literature, or critique, is contradicted, subverted, and ultimately relegated to a role of lesser importance. Even though these digressions are set inside a story line that originates the text (and not vice versa) and in a few more lines will return to the ending of the story, which demands in our novel and cinema-drenched sensibilities a formulaic closure, they reach beyond, transcend story by seeking to relegate its status to illustration, example, or part of the semiotic apparatus of narrative itself.

In its competition for space in the scholarly work, narrative remains deeply problematic, because we have to decide if we are going to write narrative, demystify its subtle productions of reality in the reader, or both. In particular, this issue remains confused because scientific inquiry has reduced the story line in its scholarly genres and, in most of the physical and biological sciences, has banished it altogether.

More than two hours after their conversation began, the four men stood up to begin to take their leave. Hewitt seemed the most reluctant to end the evening and walked into the darkened room that held the shadowed form of his desk and the now-invisible pictures on the walls and brought out articles on Deere and Company from architectural journals and magazines. He pointed out several pieces on the Deere headquarters building and the landscape designed by Sasaki Associates which included a Henry Moore sculpture that reclined at ground level on a small island in an impoundment of water just outside the executive dining room in front of the building. Behind the building, Sasaki had drafted another landscape for the headquarters complex. After Hewitt returned from visits to Japan to purchase an engine production facility, he had asked Sasaki to design a Japanese garden in back, and five large stones were flown in from Kyoto to complete the project. He had caused to be inscribed on the grounds formal Eastern and Western landscapes mediated by the Deere corporation headquarters building. In a sense, the iconicity of landscape and of architecture were themselves a visual pragmatic, in part to impress both his Japanese partners and the corporate employees of the international reach of the firm. He had a passion for superb design and through significant landscape compositions, registered a cultural connectivity that replicated his narratives at the level of personal stories rather, I would say, than incisive awareness of the larger scope of an international community of corporations rapidly forming during the postwar period.

The four men took their leave from one another. Hewitt turned out the lights, locked up, and drove home.[7]

NOTES

A somewhat different version of this chapter appeared in *Anthropological Quarterly* 64 (1991): 109–125.

1. From comments by Eero Saarinen quoted in a brochure entitled "Deere & Company Administrative Center." The economist Joseph A. Schumpeter, in his influential *Capitalism, Socialism and Democracy* (1975: 126), comments, "There is the capitalist art and the capitalist style of life." William A. Hewitt embodied and lived Schumpeter's observation.

2. The business weeklies and monthlies in America routinely run stories on the world's richest people. For a recent rundown on the compensation for chief executives of America's "most valuable publicly held U.S. companies," see *Business Week*, 19 October 1990; Saul Steinberg, generous donor to the University of Pennsylvania and CEO of Reliance Group Holdings headquartered in Philadelphia, in 1989 received in salary and bonuses more than 6.2 million dollars; *Fortune*, 10 September 1990, "The Billionaires: Ranking the World's Richest," and *Forbes*, 1 October 1990, "The World's Highest Paid Entertainers."

3. Since the turn of the twentieth century, American social scientists have sought to prove the coercive, controlling power of interlocking corporate directorates. For a recent example, see Herman (1981) and Useem (1984). These books are merely recent examples. It would be useful to know what effect the direct and indirect relationship between directorates had on American business and culture and what indeed they *meant*. My sense is that the *culture* of the American CEO is such that we do not need necessarily to rely on a theory of collusion-by-face-to-face-contact but that CEOs buy into a very similar set of values, beliefs, discourses, and practices such that they can replicate similar behaviors having the same effects on the market and the wider society without having to necessarily discuss it among themselves as if there were some capitalist cabal. In this I am not too far from the class interests detailed by Marx in *The Communist Manifesto*, except that I would substitute cultural formation rather than relying too closely on the well-worn, reductionist notions of class.

4. The ethnographers who wish to write narrative ethnographies find themselves plunged into schizophrenic practices: narratology breaks the diegesis into its analyzable components, while the novelist, nonfiction writer, screenwriter, or cultural journalist explores new possibilities for crafting story features of the text. The narrative ethnographer demands both. Historians have over the last twenty years debated the value of narrative historiography over against nonnarrative—usually under the influence of scientific models—approaches to the discipline. Ethnographers are now confronted with similar choices between narrative and nonnarrative writing about those they study. The schizophrenia, however, arises when ethnographers tell the story of people, or feature the stories people tell about themselves, and at the same time wish to critically examine the narratological strategies that the people use in creating effects in their listeners or readers. It would seem that within the confines of the same textual production, a scholarly article, for example, writing an evocative story and producing the critique of narrative form at best a very uneasy alliance. Here I am confronting that uneasy alliance with a finely split personality and a prosaic narrative structure. For a virtuoso review of the debates concerning narratology, narrative in history, and the philosophical developments addressing time, see

White (1987). John Van Maanen, in his *Tales of the Field: On Writing Ethnography* (1988: 103), offers a warning to narrative ethnographers; and George Marcus (1986: 191) comments, "Rather than attempting to represent the system or major events by an orderly account of them, to which realism is partial, the modern essay permits, or rather sanctions, the ultimate hedge—it legitimates fragmentation, rough edges, and the self-conscious aim of achieving an effect that disturbs the reader."

5. Hewitt married into the Deere family and guided the firm. This is not at all uncommon in world business, but as is well known, once a firm becomes ultra-large, the family falls by the wayside, no longer producing members eager for very large-scale corporate leadership, particularly not if they must begin somewhere near the bottom and spend twenty-five years in apprenticeship working their way to board chairmanship. By way of heuristic to address such phenomena, I have been reading two historical documents that with the passage of time serve as something more than historical verity for me—more as fables that can be used to provoke thought about what I am observing when studying chief executive officers, top management, and the varieties of the Anglo-American firm. Hope Botti (1990), in her study of Pirelli, used M. Yourcenar's novel *Memoirs of Hadrian* as a metaphor for thinking about the Latin type of corporate organization.

The first document is the legal incorporation of the London Company of Merchants Trading to the East Indies, chartered by Queen Elizabeth in 1600. The more than two hundred men who formed this joint stock company—one of the most significant institutions in the history of market formation and the relations between the West and the East—were unrelated to one another, and no principles of near-kinship were operating as predominant in the organization for their trading ventures (Birdwood and Foster 1893). Also terrifically useful to stimulate thought about the continuity and discontinuity of the Anglo-American firm from 1600 to the present are the 1621 *Lawes or Standing Orders of the East India Company,* republished in 1968 by Gregg International Publishers in England.

The other document is Machiavelli's *The Prince,* which I have carried with me and even read aloud from when interviewing a board-level executive. My reason for reading *The Prince* in conjunction with my fieldwork is to stimulate my thinking about the remnant role kinship continues to play in the management and control of the great American, and certainly world, corporations. These two documents, then, are two axes along which the very largest corporations continue to play out their destinies: kinship and purely nonkin forms of relationship at the apex of the capitalist order. These two enduring forms of enterprise have been widely recognized by historians; see Rice (1970: 43).

6. The question of community raises the issue of the role of trade associations and their lobbying effectiveness at the state and national legislatures; but also at issue is the place of trade associations at the service of companies in a sector in regard to international competition. In America, the trade association attempts to represent, ideally, all the major corporations in a sector for purposes of concerted action in matters of direct relevance to their interests.

Research consortia in the United States, for example, have a tough time collectivizing the interests of relevant corporations. The focus in the American business press underscores the point I am making about Hewitt's executive worldview, and in reporting the successes or failures of collective enterprise efforts, entrepreneurial individualism is foregrounded above concerted, intercorporate efforts. " 'If You Control . . . Computers, You Control the World,' " *Business Week*, 23 July 1990, 31. For a similar article on the efforts to establish a national-international computer network, or information infrastructure, as it is called, see John Markoff, "Creating a Giant Computer Highway" (1990). The entire article is phrased in relation to an entrepreneurial talent, Robert Kahn's "vision of a national network of information."

The discourse of the leadership of America's largest firms, the organization of manufacturing and capital corporations in relation to themselves and government, has come under scrutiny and criticism as never before mostly in relation to competition with Japan; see the *Harvard Business Review* for September-October 1990. Indeed, economists now realize that Japanese capitalism resembles very little the classic theories of Adam Smith. For a running account one can monitor the business weeklies, for example, Blinder's, "There Are Capitalists, Then There Are the Japanese" (1990: 21).

As an ethnographer I remain interested in the research issues that continue to be phrased as, What kind of international corporate formation as a real nexus of firms is now occurring, and how may we study it at its apex, whatever that may turn out to be? The particular national communal manifestations are themselves subsets of, but politically engaged in actively shaping, a world order and subject to face-to-face inquiry.

7. As a final note let me add that this landscape—of Rondelay, the overlook of Andrew Wyeth's house, the drive along the Brandywine, passing the Brandywine River Museum and Conservancy, to Hewitt's made-over office building and the return—is a part of a much larger study of the concealed American landscape with studious attention paid to the Brandywine River basin. This chapter fits as part of a jigsaw puzzle with chapter 5 in Rose (1989; see also 1990*b*). Although published in fragments, each contributes to the study of a locality but based in the larger American culture of the market. This last addition, a mere footnote, however, has already undercut the claim that the narrative closure would effect a kind of finality to the prose, that is, the authentic and comforting termination to our conventional prose accounts. A mere footnote has done in the proper sense of an ending.

REFERENCES

Appadurai, Arjun.
　　1990.　　"Disjuncture and Difference in Global Cultural Economy." *Public Culture* 2: 1–32.
Bakhtin, M. M.
　　1981.　　*The Dialogic Imagination*. Trans. Caryl Emerson and Michael Holquist. Austin: University of Texas Press.
Baltzell, E. Digby.
　　1979.　　*Puritan Boston and Quaker Philadelphia: Two Protestant Ethics and the Spirit of Class Authority and Leadership*. New York: Free Press.
Birdwood, Sir George, and William Foster, eds.
　　1893.　　*The Register of Letters &c. of the Governour and Company of Merchants of London Trading into the East Indies, 1600–1619*. London: Bernard Quaritch.

Blinder, Allen.
  1990.   "There Are Capitalists, Then There Are the Japanese." *Business Week*
          (8 October): 21.
Botti, Hope.
  1990.   "Conversations with Parodi: A Research Tale." Paper presented to the
          XII World Congress of Sociology, Madrid (July).
Dorst, John D.
  1989.   *The Written Suburb: An American Site, An Ethnographic Dilemma.* Philadel-
          phia: University of Pennsylvania Press.
Fox, Richard Wightman, and T. J. Jackson Lears, eds.
  1983.   *The Culture of Consumption: Critical Essays in American History, 1880–1980.*
          New York: Pantheon.
Frykman, Jonas, and Orvar Lofgren.
  1987.   *Culture Builders: A Historical Anthropology of Middle-Class Life.* Trans.
          A. Crozier. New Brunswick: Rutgers University Press.
Golab, Caroline.
  1977.   *Immigrant Destinations.* Philadelphia: Temple University Press.
Herman, Edward S.
  1981.   *Corporate Control, Corporate Power.* Cambridge: Cambridge Univer-
          sity Press.
Kundera, Milan.
  1988.   *The Art of the Novel.* Trans. L. Asher. New York: Harper.
Lash, Scott, and John Urry.
  1987.   *The End of Organized Capitalism.* Madison: University of Wisconsin Press.
Maanen, John Van.
  1988.   *Tales of the Field: On Writing Ethnography.* Chicago: University of
          Chicago Press.
MacCannell, Dean.
  1989.   *The Tourist: A New Theory of the Leisure Class.* New York: Schocken.
McCracken, Grant.
  1988.   *Culture and Consumption: New Approaches to the Symbolic Character of
          Consumer Goods and Activities.* Bloomington: Indiana University Press.
McDonough, Gary Wray.
  1986.   *Good Families of Barcelona: A Social History of Power in the Industrial Era.*
          Princeton: Princeton University Press.
Macfarlane, Alan.
  1987.   *The Culture of Capitalism.* Cambridge: Blackwell.
Malinowski, Bronislaw.
  1923.   *The Problem of Meaning in Primitive Language.* Supplement I. In *The
          Meaning of Meaning,* eds. C. K. Ogden and I. A. Richards. New York:
          Harcourt, Brace and World.
Marcus, George.
  1983.   "The Fiduciary Role in American Family Dynasties and Their Institu-
          tional Legacy." In *Elites: Ethnographic Issues,* ed. G. Marcus, 221–256.
          Albuquerque: University of New Mexico Press.

———. 1986. "Ethnography in the Modern World System." In *Writing Culture: The Poetics and Politics of Ethnography,* eds. James Clifford and George E. Marcus, 165–193. Berkeley, Los Angeles, and London: University of California Press.

———. 1990. "The Production of European High Culture in Los Angeles: The J. Paul Getty Trust as Artificial Curiosity." *Cultural Anthropology* 5: 314–330.

Markoff, John.
1990.   "Creating a Giant Computer Highway." *New York Times* (2 September).

Miller, Benjamin.
1987.   "The Colonial Polo Club: An Examination of Class Processes in the Suburban-Rural Fringe." In *Cities of the United States,* ed. L. Mullings, 198–218. New York: Columbia University Press.

Prestowitz, Clyde V.
1988.   *Trading Places: How We Allowed Japan to Take the Lead.* New York: Basic Books.

Rice, Eugene F., Jr.
1970.   *The Foundations of Early Modern Europe, 1460–1559.* New York: W. W. Norton.

Rose, Dan.
1989.   *Patterns of American Culture: Ethnography and Estrangement.* Philadelphia: University of Pennsylvania Press.

———. 1990*a. Living the Ethnographic Life.* Newbury Park, Calif.: Sage.

———. 1990*b.* "Quixote's Library and Pragmatic Discourse." *Anthropological Quarterly* 63 (4): 155–168.

Schumpeter, Joseph A.
1975.   *Capitalism, Socialism and Democracy.* 3d ed. New York: Harper.

Taylor, Lauren.
1987.   "Management: Agent of Human Cultural Evolution." *Futures* (October): 513–527.

Useem, Michael.
1984.   *The Inner Circle: Large Corporations and the Rise of Business Political Activity in the U.S. and the U.K.* New York: Oxford University Press.

Warhol, Andy.
1989.   *The Andy Warhol Diaries.* Ed. Pat Hackett. New York: Warner.

Warner, Sam Bass, Jr.
1987.   *The Private City: Philadelphia in Three Periods of Its Growth.* 2d ed. Philadelphia: University of Pennsylvania Press.

White, Hayden.
1987.   *The Content of the Form: Narrative Discourse and Historical Representation.* Baltimore: Johns Hopkins University Press.

Yourcenar, Marguerite.
1954.   *Memoirs of Hadrian.* Trans. Grace Frick. New York: Farrar, Straus & Giroux.

FIVE

Exogamous Relations:
Travel Writing, the Incest Prohibition,
and Hawthorne's *Transformation*

Susan Stewart

INCEST

One must travel to find a mate. That is, one must not look too closely, and one must not look too far afield. This aphorism links two projects—travel writing and the prohibition of incest—that have to do with the articulation and maintenance of cultural boundaries in time and space. If we in fact look to the notion of such a "link," we find a rule of metaphor: a point of comparison must be articulated within an acceptable field, yet must be novel enough to be "striking," to make a sign of difference. Such a rule of metaphor is thereby also a rule of writing, or marking, which must be recognizable to others and meaningful to one's kind.

Let us begin by considering some of the ways in which the prohibition of incest operates, not so much in culture as in cultural thought, on the bounds—not quite out of bounds—of this rule of metaphor. First, as Claude Lévi-Strauss has explained, the incest prohibition is the cultural rule appearing at the limit of cultural rule—that is, the one most resembling the oxymoronic possibility of a rule of nature.

> Suppose that everything universal in man relates to the natural order, and is characterized by spontaneity, and that everything subject to a norm is cultural and is both relative and particular. We are then confronted with a fact, or rather, a group of facts, which, in the light of previous definitions, are not far removed from a scandal: we refer to that complex group of beliefs, customs, conditions and institutions described succinctly as the prohibition of incest, which presents, without the slightest ambiguity, and inseparably combines, the two characteristics in which we recognize the conflicting features of two mutually exclusive orders. It constitutes a rule, but a rule which, alone among all the social rules, possesses at the same time a universal character.[1]

Thus the incest prohibition appears as the vehicle of an impossible trans-
latability between nature and culture, a vehicle motivated by a kind of deferred tenor—a position that must always appear as an unarticulatable given
of a cultural order irremediably with us. Dramatically, of course, we immediately realize that such a cultural order must then constantly be reinscribed
by its own gesture of self-consciousness as something natural and universal.

Furthermore, the incest prohibition extends in all directions of time
and space. As Lévi-Strauss contends, all exceptions (Egypt, Peru, Hawaii,
Azande, Madagascar, Burma, etc.) are "relative": for, "from another's perspective, [the incest prohibition] might be temporary or ritual marriage
allowed."[2] The prohibition has its "real" and "metaphorical" forms in that
one can be prohibited from marrying a parent, for example, and prohibited
from marrying someone old enough to be one's parent, or, inversely, one is
prohibited from violating minors.[3] The prohibition is simultaneously en-
dogamous (defining those within the marriageable pool) and exogamous
(defining those without it). The prohibition extends spatially to the boundaries of social groups and temporally through the organization of generations. It can be articulated positively as the scope of claims of entitlement
and eligibility, and it can be articulated negatively as the renunciation of a
privilege, as E. B. Tylor expressed in a well-known conclusion: "marry out or
be killed out."[4]

There are many ways in which this natural rule of the cultural, appearing
as it does as the cultural rule of the natural, is made suspect, but none of
them serve to eliminate it. For example, the current explosion of debate
surrounding the increased reportage of the violation of minors and
parent/child incest in the industrialized West takes as its point of attack the
formulation of Freud, who contended that violation of the rule was imaginary rather than real in most cases.[5] The debate does not attack the formulation of the incest prohibition itself. The rule is not subject to attack. And
it is not subject to attack precisely because there are no grounds of intelligibility for reproduction outside of its reign. In other words, the prohibition
of incest and consequently the articulation of kinship are both descriptive
and classificatory—hence what contradicts them still falls within their
rule and hence what falls outside their rule is promiscuity, anarchy, wild-
ness, and nonmeaning.

Exogamous relations therefore pose a contradictory set of cultural solutions. On the one hand, they define one's membership and by completing
one's needs for otherness pose an imaginary wholeness, a completed gaze
or circuit. But, on the other hand, as in Tylor's "be killed out," they define
one's subjection, the renunciation of "spontaneous" desires, the "castration" one experiences under the rule of all cultural law and the reinscrip-
tion of all novelty into the domain of tradition. Obviously, I am borrowing
here a formulation from Jacques Lacan—the necessarily separating func-

tion of the visual and the alignment and articulation of subjectivity under the rule of Language. Specifically, I want to borrow this theory of the visual and the spoken to examine the rhetoric of a particular form of literature—the writing of travel—in order to study the negotiation of cultural meaning and the "staking" of intelligibility in such writing. And even more specifically, I want to use this problem of the stake of intelligibility as a pretext for a reading of Hawthorne's enigmatic *Transformation*, the novel we know as *The Marble Faun*—to "go the long way around" to arrive at a reading of a novel that meditates on the relation between exogamy, gazes, resemblances, and formlessness in a systematic attempt to elide the cultural rule of the incest prohibition.

WRITING TRAVEL

It is by now something of a commonplace within the theory of travel writing to acknowledge the ways in which travel is a form of writing and writing a form of travel. Travel, as the traversal of a space, calls forth notions of memory propelled by desire and of the movement of a body through a landscape that is called on to mean. Michel Butor reminds us of flags planted, the markings of arrival and the "thick tissue of traces and marks" by which the movements of travelers leave their inscription on nature.[6] And as for the second notion—that writing is a form of travel—we acknowledge the exodus of all writing into the undifferentiated whiteness of the page, writing as sign of habitation and movement, a kind of territorial marker like the bent twigs and bread crumbs left by others on the paths before us.

Yet to see travel and writing as metaphors for each other is also to note the relentless metaphorizing nature of thought. In fact, the churning of one thing into another within an acknowledgment of difference is perhaps the central task of travel writing as the inscription of views both familiar and strange. And though such views may risk unintelligibility, the writing of them may not. Just as the movement of writing takes place within a history of forms and possibilities for excursus, so does the movement of travel have its pregiven genres: the one-way and the round-trip, the stopping by wayside, the return home, the journey into outer space and the journey around one's room, the business trip and the holiday, the pilgrimage and the march to the sea. Similarly, the resting places of significance in travel are either those centers of mixing and dialogue and consequently danger—the inn and the crossroads—or those places of seclusion and silence where one confronts an interior consciousness made of external censors: the forest, the holy site, the shrine, and the temple.

Now in this tension between public and private we see a fundamental problem in the writing of travel, and that is its necessary and founding disjunction—a disjunction that, on the one hand, locates us all the more squarely within the necessarily liminal world of travel and a disjunction that, on the other, makes the very idea of a theory of travel writing suspect. For travel writing reminds us of its own temporality: it always balances its metadiscursive properties, its aphorisms, against the contingencies of the next experience. It offers us the view of a person on the road—the mounted view, a view too low to be transcendent and too high to be in the scene. If one of the most vivid moments in Goethe's *Italian Journey* is the description of the girl in Catania who runs beside the mule of the *vetturino* "chattering and spinning her thread at the same time,"[7] it is because this talking picture is moving at the speed of, and alongside, the traveler—presenting us with a dream of the end of mediation, a dream nevertheless merging with the accomplishment of distance. Hence she represents a perfected form of temporal exogamy, perfectly poised between this side and that and moving with us—all at the same time.

The ways in which the inscription of a gaze results in a writing of the self are recapitulated in the very history of travel writing. Between the eighteenth and nineteenth century, the paradigm for travel writing shifted from supposedly "disinterested" observation to biographical narrative.[8] Another way of accounting for this is to say that a literature of exploration, involving the cataloging of curiosities, surrendered to a literature of travel, involving the transformation of a subject via firsthand experience. The latter is the kind of travel writing we find described by Mikhail Bakhtin when he writes that "the author's own real homeland serves as an organizing center for point of view, for scales of comparison," and that "the hero of such a work is the public and political man of ancient times, a man governed by his sociopolitical, philosophical, and utopian interests. . . . [Here] biography is the crucial organizing principle for time."[9]

But this public figure is without his or her public. The home culture is under assault at the same time as it is a unit of measurement, and so we find the travel writer imagining, in his or her isolation from home, an intimate and domestic audience. The epistolary form of the travel piece, ranging from the imagining of letters to family or friends to the frequent American convention of sending travel letters to one's hometown newspaper, thus satisfies a need here that the seeming disinterestedness of the journal or note form does not. The product of too much cultural noise is loneliness. Thus the traveler is caught between his or her desire for self-transformation, for the search for wider horizons of consciousness (consciousness being, of course, a landscape) and the desire to be a faithful witness, a steady point of comparison and accountability. Thus travel experience, in its endless search for meaning, must also be without irrevocable meaning. It must find a meaning in time, the very meaning of time implicit in such ideas of flight, escape, search, transgression, and reparation alternately at the center of the travel narrative.

In the American travel writing of the nineteenth century which serves, for our purposes, as a backdrop to Hawthorne's project, we find a rich discussion of these paradoxes of the traveler's biography: the problems of coming too close or going too far, the problems of staying too long or leaving too quickly, the problems of rigidity and provinciality, on the one hand, and promiscuousness and contamination, on the other. Margaret Fuller's tripartite typology of the servile (or gluttonish), the conceited (or unchanging), and the thinking (or admirable) tourists obviously prefers the thinker whose knowledge augments and enriches those selective experiences to which he or she is subject.[10] Similarly, Henry Theodore Tuckerman makes the following suggestions in his "Isabel; or Sicily, A Pilgrimage" of 1839.

> In truth, no ideas can be more false than many of those which it requires at least one sojourn of an American in Europe to correct. There is a vague notion prevalent among the untravelled, that abroad there are many and peculiar means of enjoyment. In one sense this is true: but is it enough borne in mind, that the only worthy pleasures peculiar to Europe, are those of taste, and that to enjoy these, a certain preparedness is requisite? The truth is the legitimate gratifications of Southern Europe are eminently meditative. They are alike incompatible with a spirit of restless ambition or gainful passion. They address themselves to the imaginative and enthusiastic, to the contemplative and intellectual, . . . to those who have faith in the refining influences of art and culture.[11]

One is reminded of Edward Gibbon's lengthy instructions in his *Memoirs* for preparing one's self for a visit to Rome. Gibbon suggests one begin with indefatigable vigor of mind and body and then progress through knowledge of classics, history, and music to the possession of a flexible temper and independent fortune to a knowledge of all national and provincial idioms as well as all arts of conversation.[12] The complete tourist would be so completely cultured that he or she would not need the corrective of culture contact. Indeed, he or she would become the place itself. We should consider at this point the fate of the idealized European tourist, the Count di V——, described in James Fenimore Cooper's 1838 *Excursions in Italy*. Cooper explains that

> in this age of cosmopolitanism, real or pretended, so many people travel that one is apt to ask who can be left at home; and some aim at distinction in this era of migration by making it a point to see everything. Of this number is a certain Count di V——, whom I met in America just before leaving home. This gentleman went through the United States, tablets in hand, seeming to be dissatisfied with himself if he quitted one of our common-place towns with an hospital unexamined, a mineral unregistered, or a church unentered. It struck me at the time that he was making a toil of a pleasure, especially in a county that has so little worth examining.

Cooper concludes this anecdote by noting that the Count traveled all over the world and that he eventually "lost his life by falling into a boiling spring on the island of Batavia."[13]

The fetishistic activities of the Count di Vi— and his fall into nature make his story a parable of the problem of traveling too far. The Count's venture into the wild contrasts sharply with the travel activities of nineteenth-century Americans journeying to Europe. The predominant number of such Americans—Protestant preachers, lawyers, doctors, businessmen, society women, educators, abolitionists, actors, health seekers, and young wanderers—were searching for culture and a matrix within which to articulate a new American identity.[14] Thus their travels are marked by activities of comparison and judgment and a frequent fear of conversion. This fear is particularly evident among Protestant travelers to Italy. By relentlessly aestheticizing Italian life, these travelers were able to protect themselves from the full implications of the contexts of Italian art. The ways in which many Protestant travelers still prefer to think of Italy's churches as museums testifies to the endurance of this aestheticizing gesture. By making all travel experiences metonymic to aesthetic experiences, travel writers could separate themselves from dialogue and the obligations of reciprocity, with the latter forms of the spoken thereby saved for an audience of cultural peers. Furthermore, the late-eighteenth-century and nineteenth-century American's view of Italy was already mediated by British aesthetics of the period—from Gothicism to romanticism, Italy represented what might be called a contaminated site of representations ranging from classicism to Catholicism to revolution.

SPEAKING PICTURES

Although there obviously are many suggestive aspects to the attempt of travel writing to appropriate and contain cultural forms and values, I would like to focus here on the ways in which a central problem of eighteenth-century aesthetics—the relation between the plastic arts and writing—comes to be renegotiated in the tension between description and narration in this travel writing. And more significantly, in the tension between aestheticism (and the separating function of the gaze) and ethics (and the implicating function of the dialogic) reflected in the stasis of depiction and the moving judgment of language as it is uttered in time. Thus the formal tension of travel writing as the temporal inscriptions of views and scenes is what suits it so well to the thematic of forging identity and the critique of cultural relations motivating such accounts in the first place.

The subtext here is Lessing on the Laocoön and, consequently, Schiller. In fact, along with the Apollo Belvedere, the Capitoline Venus, and the

Dying Gladiator, the Laocoön was one of a handful of classical works familiar to American artists thanks to casts brought to New York at the turn of the
century and later copied in Philadelphia as part of Charles Wilson Peale's
attempt to make Philadelphia "the Athens of the West."[15] The problems
posed by the Laocoön—the impenetrability of static art and the temporality
of verbal art; the temporality of one's viewpoint; the silence, even indifference, of history—are central to the traveler's experience of nineteenth-
century Italy. The Laocoön is a work that casts its shadow strongly on texts
we will focus on: Rembrandt Peale's *Notes on Italy, Written During a Tour in the
Year 1829 and 1830,* David Dorr's 1858 volume, *A Coloured Man Around
the World,* Washington Irving's *Tales of A Traveller* (1835), and, finally,
Hawthorne's *The Marble Faun* of 1860, formed during his sojourn in Italy in
1858 and 1859 and heavily indebted, especially in what we might call its de-
partures, to the structure of his *Italian Notebooks.*

These texts are quite self-conscious about the problems of travel writing
as a narrative of the self. Perhaps not so coincidentally, Hawthorne's famous
description of a romance as the product of a romancer who can "dream
strange things and make them look like truth" is presaged by Rembrandt
Peale's insistence on the dreamlike character of "his" Rome. *The Marble
Faun* begins with a well-known passage claiming, "Side by side with the mas-
siveness of the Roman past, all matters that we handle or dream of nowadays
look evanescent and visionary alike . . . this dreaming character of the present, as compared with the square blocks of granite wherewith the Romans
built their lives."[16] When the Napoleonic wars kept Peale from going to Italy
in 1807 and again in 1810, he became obsessed with seeing Italian paintings
in England, Paris, and America. "Italy," he writes, "which was my reverie by
day, became the torment of my dreams at night,"[17] adding, "the idea that
my dreams of Italy were never to be realized seemed to darken the cloud
which hung over the prospect of death itself."[18] Once Peale had arrived, he
contended that Rome "is indeed a delicious dream, but a dream that must
be repeated by the artist until its impressions are confirmed into records of
truth and usefulness."[19] The problem then becomes, as it is in managing any
dream, the subjection of the ego to the demands of the law, the testing of
the daydream against reality and of idealizations measured against practice,
and most significantly, the posing of issues of reproduction and representation. If such a problem speaks to the situation of the relation between the
New World, which is, as the Count di V—discovered, all Nature and newly
articulated Law, not yet subject to experience, and the Old World, which is
by now a Land of Pictures, an archaeological site with so many shifting and
fusing layers of meaning that all is art rather than rule, we have dreamed
this dream before. And perhaps as much as any other feature, this artistic
dream is characterized by its vagueness, its refusal of cultural definition. For
the most part, the picture is Italy and not a celebration of particular works

or paintings. When the Pennsylvania Academy opened in 1807 many of the "Old Masters" came without labels and the Peales had some trouble attributing them.[20]

Contemporary tourism markets its views as compositions of ways of life and thereby exaggerates the leisure of the tourist as he or she observes others working. From this retrospective viewpoint, one of the most startling aspects of nineteenth-century American traveler's accounts of Italy is how squarely they are framed within the paradigm of the aesthetic view. Yet we are also made aware of how relentlessly these discourses explore the implications of the problems of representation arising out of the picturesque: What do these views stand for? What do they mean? How will their history be completed? What stance should the viewer take with regard to them? These are the problems plaguing Peale and the problems arising from the aesthetic issues addressed in Hawthorne's *Italian Notebooks*, later played out in the condensations and displacements of *The Marble Faun* itself. For Peale, trained in the realistic genres of historical painting and portraiture, a Protestant moralism led to a taste for allegory, as in his most successful painting, *The Court of Death*. And since this viewpoint would preclude a Catholic reading of the Old Masters, turning to landscape as painting, even a painting that only referred further to painting, was a likely move.

Just as the landscape is conceived as an allegorical canvas within this literature, so does the notation of Italian types call for moral conclusions. In his 1858 volume, *A Coloured Man Around the World*, Dorr recorded the following observations regarding the connection between volcanoes and immorality: "I don't think that one contented man can be found in the whole city of Naples, with its 450,000 souls. Every time this growling, burning mountain roars it jars the whole city; organ grinders give themselves as little trouble about Vesuvius as any other class, and the streets are full of them. . . . Naples is yet the most wicked city on the face of the globe . . . To see a club-slain man in Naples is no object of pity . . . [T]heir mind is forever placed on wholesale calamities."[21] In the prostitution district of Naples, Dorr's lazzaroni gives twenty-five cents to a group of women in payment for exhibiting themselves: "as many as wished to claim stock in the 25 cents commenced showing their nakedness, to the horror of man's sensual curiosity. I saw fifty women show what I had never legally seen before. I must end the chapter and commence another."[22] Dorr's anxiety is the anxiety of volitional sight: to have license to see is also to claim a responsibility for seeing. To claim that one has seen is to posit one's originality, that one is not merely recognizing.

Yet the innocence of the picturesque view is always suspect, already framed by another picture. This travel writing is thus relentlessly intertextual. Dorr's narrative, for example, borrows directly from James Fenimore Cooper's, particularly in its historical descriptions of the Palantine. And it is difficult to believe that Cooper had not read Rembrandt Peale when we compare their passages on quack doctors. Peale records "an eloquent quack doctor, who proclaims his skill from the seat of his carriage, or witnessing the dexterity of a dentist who, on horseback, draws teeth."[23] Cooper writes of a quack doctor who "extracts a tooth from a peasant without dismantling,"[24] thus condensing Peale's image. And whereas Cooper has derived his impressions of "picturesque-looking bandits" (who later turn out to be friendly peasant-farmers) from Washington Irving, Irving's picture of "The Italian Banditti" in his *Tales of a Traveller* (1835) has no doubt come from Mrs. Radcliffe:

> They wear jackets and breeches of bright colors, sometimes gaily embroidered; their breasts are covered with medals and relics; their hats are broad-brimmed, with conical crowns, decorated with feathers, or variously-coloured ribands; their hair is sometimes gathered in silk-nets; they wear a kind of sandal of cloth or leather, bound round the legs with thongs; . . . a broad belt of cloth or a sash of silk net, is stuck full of pistols and stilettoes; a carbine is slung at the back; while about them is generally thrown, in a negligent manner, a great dingy mantle, which serves as protection in storms, or a bed.[25]

The prostitute, the quack doctor, and the bandit, representing in this empire of signs the profusion of a semiotic outside the boundaries of law and expectation are at the same time already written, always inscribed by a previous view. They thus promise exogamy within the constraints of an already written order.

There is no virgin sight or site: the slippery types at the edge of the Law are symptomatic of a writing whose referent will not remain fixed or pure. Goethe sees his friend Kniep substitute for the middle and foreground of an "awful" view an "elegant and delightful set borrowed from Poussin" and writes, "I wonder how many 'Travels of a Painter' contain such half-truths."[26] And we are similarly struck when we read, without attribution, Laurence Sterne's account of the Spanish pilgrim weeping over his donkey: "A poor ass fell down under a heavy load, cut its side, and dislocated its hind leg. As soon as the poor man, who led him saw this, he looked sadly, then sobbed aloud, and burst into the most piteous grief and lamentations." Although the origin of this incident seems to lie in the Indian folktale of the washerman and the Queen, we might see the intertextual allusion to travel characters as the more likely one here.

Thus, ironically, the traveler finds that, although firsthand, his or her experience is all the more inscribed in an already written order. Hawthorne notes in *The Marble Faun* "a party of English or Americans paying the inevitable visit by moonlight [to the Coliseum], and exalting themselves with raptures that were Byron's, not their own."[27] Peale suggests, "I have preferred the simple task of describing only those things which I saw, as they may be seen by other persons in my situation, and have pretended no opinions or judgments but such as forced themselves upon me."[28] But he is unable to sustain this benevolent and passive relation to his sense of realism and nature. It is as if the tiny figures in the shadows of Piranesi's monuments had become gigantic and thereby too vivid. The prostitute's nakedness; the shifting rhetoric and obliviousness to pain of the quack doctor; the almost feminine deadliness of the gaudy bandit—these present the traveler with a surplus of information, a type exceeding the bounds of its own cultural propriety, its own cultural landscape. Such vivification is thus a reminder of the customshouse and of the worldliness of exchange. And it is also a reminder, then, of the darker side of exchange—the side of contagion and contamination. The traveler, like the characters in Tuckerman's *Isabel* and like Peale entering Naples, was frequently subject to quarantine, and so the themes of decay and disease signified a quite literal threat as well as a metaphorical reading of the breakdown of an old order.

Furthermore, death results from the sacrifice the picturesque makes in diminishing its subjects. In an inversion of the Galatea story, the Italians surrounding art and occupying the landscape are either aestheticized within it or purged from it. When Peale observes contemporary life in a scene near Michelangelo's David, he has an interest in creating a disjunction between life within the view and life outside it: "These objects of fine art are daily seen without emotion by the greater part of the people who pass or frequent the place, occupied with bales of goods near the custom-house, bargaining for straw hats or horses; surrounding a foolish buffoon, or a set of dancing gods."[29] Tuckerman's hero Vittorio says, "How unutterably sad . . . that so fair a heritage, should be so unhappily peopled—that superstition and ignorance should overshadow so rich a domain."[30] The aestheticization of context enables the traveler's interpretation of the work of art to gain a kind of formal integrity. Hence what is made original is not the work but the view of the traveler. And it is not accidental that the native view must be thereby suppressed. Hawthorne has Kenyon give a little speech in the Coliseum, claiming, "The Coliseum is far more delightful, as we enjoy it now, than when eighty thousand persons sat squeezed together, row above row, to see their fellow creatures torn by lions and tigers limb from limb. What a strange thought that the Coliseum was really built for us, and has not come to its best uses till almost two thousand years after it was finished!"[31] Yet following our discussion of the respective anxieties attending propinquity and distance, we can see that such writers were attempting to contain and articulate a kind of American originality. What would it mean for Americans to produce an art that was not a mere reproduction, or cast, of a previously completed European corpus? How could such an art acquire qualities of novelty, animation, and authenticity? For Hawthorne, the remedy for such a problem lay in a tension between fidelity to nature (although a nature to be found in art as much as anywhere else) and a kind of spiritual animation, an animation arising from a particularly Protestant notion of the individual view.

In this sense, the art of the past is always liable to improvement, including the improvements effected by reproductions and copies: American imitations of European masterpieces are hence seen to reawaken their spirituality, now drowned in the malaria of a corrupted European context. The narrator explains that Hilda's copies are valued because she does not attempt to reproduce the whole of a masterpiece but only "some high, noble, and delicate portion of it, in which the spirit and essence of the picture culminated." He adds,

> If a picture had darkened into an indistinct shadow through time and neglect, or had been injured by cleaning, or retouched by some profane hand, she seemed to possess the faculty of seeing it in its pristine glory. The copy would come from her hands with what the beholder felt must be the light which the old master had left upon the original in bestowing his final and most ethereal touch. In some instances even . . . she had been enabled to execute what the great master had conceived in his imagination, but had not so perfectly succeeded in putting upon canvas.[32]

Hawthorne's *French and Italian Notebooks*, as well as *The Marble Faun* itself, are preoccupied with negative judgments of European art. The Trevi Fountain is "absurd" and full of "artificial fantasies, which the calm moonlight soothed into better taste than was native to them";[33] Hilda "began to suspect that some, at least, of her venerated painters had left an inevitable hollowness in their works, because, in the most renowned of them, they essayed to express to the world what they had not in their own souls. . . . A deficiency of earnestness and absolute truth is generally discoverable in Italian pictures, after the art had become consummate"; the narrator suggests "who can trust the religious sentiment of Raphael, or receive any of his Virgins as heaven-descended likenesses, after seeing, for example the Fornarina of the Barberini Palace, and feeling how sensual the artist must have been to paint such a brazen trollop of his own accord, and lovingly?"[34] Elsewhere in *The Marble Faun*, criticisms of Guido's archangel and Titian's Magdalen are offered. Thus Hilda's metonymic relation to the Old Masters becomes a technique that Hawthorne valorizes for any "copy," including the selective relation between American and Italian culture. His proposal is that the Old World not be reproduced but rather selectively copied so that the spiritual can be excised and remade under the conditions of a Protestant novelty. And Hilda, whose whiteness is itself metonymic to an abstracted spirituality, twice removed from nature as an aestheticization of the aesthetic, herself becomes the figure most copied in the book: she is copied by other copyists as she spends her days in the picture galleries; and her white hand is copied by Kenyon.[35]

Now the latter case brings to mind the relation between copying and metonymy in the "novel" as a whole. For the novel is often copied out of Hawthorne's travel notebooks, we noted above. And the impressions of the traveler in those notebooks are themselves largely formed by previous travelers' accounts. Furthermore, Hawthorne copied his characters from life: Kenyon is, of course, based on the American sculptor William Wetmore Story; and Hilda herself is based on Hawthorne's wife, Sofia, whose work as a painter was supposedly limited by her proclivity to copying the works of Salvator Rosa and others. The characters in the novel are copies of art as well: Miriam's self-portrait resembles Guido's Beatrice (which, the novel claims, could not resemble the real Cenci so much as Hilda's spiritualization of the portrait does); and, of course, Donatello wavers between a copy of Praxiteles' faun (which the Murray guidebook Hawthorne used would have identified as a copy of a Greek bronze original) and a copy of a real (that is a mythologically natural) faun. And just as the assembly of the buried archaic Venus in the chapter "A Walk on the Campagna" (a Venus who is "either a prototype or a better replica of the 'Venus of the Tribune' ") falls apart, becoming "a heap of worthless fragments," once Kenyon's thoughts turn away from art and toward the consequences of a "human affection," so do the pieces of *The Marble Faun* ultimately refuse closure. This chapter is, in fact, importantly mimicked by the final elements of the novel's "structure," for Kenyon integrates the statue by putting a head on it, characterizing it thereby. And yet on second look its artificiality compels his gaze to disassemble; analogously, the narrator of the novel becomes a character in the novel itself, meeting and wandering with the characters in the novel's closing sections, and in this gesture the narrator completes the outside/in movement, the recapitulating functions of copying, which the novel takes as its subject—hence underscoring the romance and dream aspects of the form and at the same time emphasizing the novel's celebration of abstraction and attack on sensuality and nature.

In this attack on secularism and naturalism, *The Marble Faun* is quite typical of American travel writing's refusal to acknowledge the contexts of Italian art and its distaste for any art imitating a grotesque nature. Especially revealing are Peale's remarks on the waxworks in Florence's Museum of Natural History: "I expected to find the waxworks representing the plague which depopulated Florence large and anatomically correct—On the contrary, they are in three small boxes, each with a sheet of glass in front, and containing figures only a few inches long, arranged in groups to produce the effect of pictures, and expressly calculated to excite horror in the imagination rather than to represent truth. It is a disgusting exaggeration, the toy of a demon and a gossip's tales."[36] To understand that Peale's quarrel is with the representation and not with death itself, we might remember his father's innovative experiments with taxidermy and his only mention of a souvenir or relic—from his trip to the Catacombs of Santa Maria della Vita near Naples: "The flesh of fifteen hundred years was still of such tenacious though pliant fibre that it required a sharp knife to cut off a piece. The guide showed us the heads of some of these early Christians with the tongues still remaining in them, but would not permit us to take them away."[37] In contrast, when Cooper observes waxworks in Bologna, he says they have a "horrible truth [yet] are odious as spectacles in their disgusting accuracy."[38] Finally, we should recall that both the figure of Donatello and the plot of *The Marble Faun* turn real at the moment when the model is killed. The model's murder is effected by Miriam's glance and by Donatello's acting on a scene he can no longer stand to view. Later, the dead model reappears as a kind of awakened waxwork, a corpse made lifelike that it horrifies as an overly real representation as much as a matter of evidence of the crime. This is in fact another point at which Hawthorne both uses and reflects on the concept of metonymy to great effect. For the feet of the corpse become for Kenyon quite literally feet of clay, "Those naked feet!" said he. "I know not why, but they affect me strangely. They have walked to and fro over the hard pavements of Rome, and through a hundred other rough ways of this life, where the monk went begging for his brotherhood. . . . It is a suggestive idea, to track those worn feet backward through all the paths they have trodden, ever since they were the tender and rosy little feet of a baby, and (cold as they now are) were kept warm in his mother's hand."[39] Thus these worn feet, soiled by time and the corrupted dust of Rome, lead the sculptor, retrospectively, to a hand that will become the white hand of Hilda—a hand he has "photographed" by heart (just as Hilda "photographed" the portrait of Beatrice) and then kept from contamination in an ivory coffer. These traversing metonymical images (for, of course, the coffer then moves forward/backward to the "grave" of the Venus, with the "dirt between her lips," in the campagna chapter)[40] thus become symptomatic of Hawthorne's design for an art that copies, and so isolates itself from chaos, and that also abstracts a spirituality from a prelapsarian version of art—an art before materiality, and hence an art destined to vanish by its closure.

For Hawthorne especially, everyday life might be picturesque from a distance, but it appears too vivid, even stained, on firsthand examination. Representations can therefore suffer from a surplus of reality. Emblems of nature in *The Marble Faun*, such as the buffalo calf accompanying Kenyon on his walk across the countryside, the distilled sunshine wine, the traditionary peasants of carnival, all are emphatically denatured. As the title of *Transformation* makes clear, history will not allow nature to remain unemblematic; allegory resounds.[41] And it is impossible for an American artist, literally compelled by the morality of allegory, to see nature in any other way.

When Hawthorne continually claims that nature imitates art and, second, when he valorizes the notion of copying, he has taken from travel writing two strategies that are in perfect accord with his aims as an artist. And, in the metonymic traversals outlined above, he as well claims his victory over time: the victory of the "consummate artist" Kenyon is not, an artist who distills a spirituality out of fragments beyond the claims of nature and beyond the claims of any art merely reproducing nature.

It is obvious that that nature which imitates art is already another form of art: a nature of cliffs, valleys, crags, and other uneven space. The landscape appears as a canvas; even the built environment seems to be a form of sculpture.[42] In fact, we might attribute the taste for Rome and the Roman campagna by moonlight stretching in touristic discourse from Piranesi to Edith Wharton to the desire to solidify such masses and to excise the distractions of their contemporary context—as well as, of course, the desire for a meditative epiphany in the style of Gibbon's late-night inspiration for his masterpiece.[43] According to both Peale and Cooper, English-speaking tourists spent a great deal of their recreational time playing at charades, tableaux vivants, and other speechless theatrical entertainments—all of which can be seen as another level of "playing" at the nonreciprocity, silence, and visual closure of the touristic experience.[44]

Some scenes of nature imitating art. From Peale: "During our ride to Borelli, I remarked effects of atmosphere, such as I had never seen in nature before, but recognized as true in the picture of Claude and Vernet—a hazy horizon—masses of mountains resembling clouds in colour pale and grey—the front objects more and more distinct." Peale complains that there are not enough peasant cottages for sketchers to rest in.[45] Tuckerman's characters similarly see art everywhere they look. In Messina, "the broadly undulating shapes of the Sicilian mountains come clothed with the vivid verdure of the lemon and orange trees, and the darker evergreen of the olive. On their tops, at intervals, volumes of pearly mist reposed, and elsewhere the edge of their summits was marked with the distinctness of a chiselled line upon the clear background of the horizon." When Tuckerman's character Clifford Frazier sees an old woman's face near Etna, "it reminds him of some of the Dutch portraits he had seen in the collections of Italy."[46] And when a peasant fetches chestnuts for Isabel, the heroine, "she wished there had been time to sketch the curious picture."[47] Cooper often shows the pervasive influence of Salvator Rosa and the Poussins in his descriptions, and he sees the background to Bologna as "the view . . . which the old Italian masters sometimes put to their religious subjects."[48]

In our postsnapshot age, it is perhaps difficult for us to see how relentlessly writing and drawing were connected for these authors, particularly in the temporal/spatial conflation brought about by joining these two activities. Peale had written in his 1835 textbook, *Graphics*: "Writing is little else than drawing the forms of letters [just as] drawing is little more than writing the forms of objects."[49] We might remember Goethe noting in his *Italian Journey* that one evening he found himself using his sepia drawing ink for writing.[50] This mixture of the sketcher's and writer's art is particularly served by the notion of nature as itself a kind of painting, now copied within the temporal movement of the line. Hilda's most successful copy, her drawing of Guido's Beatrice, is accomplished by writing with her eyes. Since "the Prince Barberini" forbids copies of the painting, "I had no resource but to sit down before the picture, day after day, and let it sink into my heart. I do believe it is now photographed there. . . . Well, after studying it in this way, I know not how many times I came home, and have done my best to transfer the image to canvas."[51] Beatrice's "red-rimmed gaze" reminds us of the historicity of sight. It is impossible to look afresh: all seeing is contaminated by knowledge; all seeing is a form of action. Hence the intertwining of a panoply of "scenes": the scene of original sin, the scene of the crime, the scene of the painting. Throughout *The Marble Faun*, seeing/reading becomes a matter of the consequences, or effects, of impressions—their contaminating possibilities, their capacity for implication, their linking of gazes and actions, their relation to originality and authenticity.

We arrive once again at the crucial issue of copying for these American tourist/aesthetes. The aestheticization of Italy—her language a music, her people a caricature, her landscapes a painting—was part of a very generalized tracing of an aesthetic genealogy from the classical world, more specifically, the classical world now traversed by a Christian and democratic myth seeming to run backward from Rome to Athens to Jerusalem. Peale concluded his travel account,

> In leaving Milan, I may bid farewell to the arts of Italy! An Italian, not exempted from bigotry, discovered a new world for the emancipation of man. May America in patronising the arts, receive them as the offspring of enlightened Greece, transmitting through Italy, where their miraculous powers were nourished in the bondage of mind. Let them in turn be emancipated and their persuasive and fascinating language be exalted to the noblest purpose and be made instrumental to social happiness and national glory![52]

Any marriage between America and Europe depended on a separation of generations and a translation of classicism into indigenous terms. Peale, born on Washington's birthday, the son of the painter whom he calls "the first painter of the Western world," traveled through Italy carrying his own portrait of Washington. He displayed the portrait throughout his trip to dignitaries and artists, and he had given instructions that if he died during the journey he was to be buried with the portrait placed on his coffin. Peale himself appears, therefore, in his search for culture as a case of nature imitating art.

But we should look more closely at this portrait, which shows Washington through a perforated screen of ornamented stonework, beneath a Phidian head of Jupiter. This perforated screen through which we view the "father of our country" is strangely reminiscent of several other screens: the golden, even erotic, one through which Goethe observes the statue of the virgin in the side altar of the church at Monte Pellegrino, outside of Palermo (Goethe refers to her as a "beautiful lady who seemed to be reclining in a kind of ecstasy," an almost willful refusal to "read" her native meaning, especially considering the presence of a "cherub, fanning her with a lily").[53] And, further, two examples from Hawthorne: the "iron lattice of a prison window" through which Kenyon seems to observe the Carnival at the close of *The Marble Faun* and the iron grating of the Vatican sculpture gallery through which Hawthorne observes the Laocoön for the first time.[54] The *Notebooks* record three views of the Laocoön—this first, hurried view; a second, where Hawthorne compares the sculpture to the "tumult of Niagara, which does not seem to be a tumult because it keeps pouring on, forever and ever"; and a third, derivative view at the Uffizi, where a copy of the sculpture does not impress Hawthorne "with the sense of might and terrible repose . . . growing out of the infinitude of trouble" he had felt in the original.

If American culture was to copy Italian culture, the challenge would be to avoid being a mere valorization of the original, as the Uffizi statue seemed to be. There is a moving scene in Irving's travel narrative when he tells of his feelings on seeing the statues in the Pitti Palace, for his father had had etchings of them in the house when he was growing up: "The views, the wrestlers, the dancing faun and the knife-grinder, four of my oldest acquaintances on paper, now stood before my eyes, looking like living beings."[55] But the risk taken in bringing the statue to life is its irreversibility—that very feature which makes it no longer a representation but rather something subject to mortality is what will come back to haunt us.

TRANSFORMATION, OR *THE MARBLE FAUN*

The Marble Faun, as a novel of glances and resemblances, plays out this paradoxical desire for an artistic animation of history as a tension between the morality of allegory (the possibility that the signs of art can be made to cohere within judgments regarding the ethical) and the neutrality of aestheticism (the play of resemblances as an unending and empty comparison). In "Scenes by the Way," a chapter key to this theme (though importantly, quite minor to that minor player in Hawthorne's romance— the plot), we find a passage exemplifying this tension between the allegorical and the aesthetic, the American and the Italian. First, the narrator writes, "A pre-Raphaelite artist might find an admirable subject in one of these Tuscan girls, stepping with a free, erect, and graceful carriage. The miscellaneous herbage and tangled twigs and blossoms of her bundle, crowning her head (while her ruddy, comely face looks out between the hanging side festoons like a large flower), would give the painter boundless scope for the minute delineation which he loves." He then explains, a few sentences later, "Nothing can be more picturesque than an old grape vine, with almost a trunk of its own, clinging first around its supporting tree. Nor does the picture lack its moral. You might twist it to more than one grave purpose, as you saw how the knotted serpentine growth imprisoned within its strong embrace the friend that supported its tender infancy and how (as seemingly flexible natures are prone to do) it converted the sturdier tree entirely to its own selfish ends, extending its innumerable arms on every bough, and permitting hardly a leaf to sprout except its own."[56] Of course, to "twist" the picture to this grave purpose would be to be condemned to repeat it.

At this point, the American sculptor Kenyon, who will ultimately find what Hawthorne poses as an American form of happiness by marrying Hilda the copyist, thinks of how "the enemies of the vine, in his native land, would here see an emblem of the remorseless gripe which the habit of vinous enjoyment lays upon its victim."[57] Hawthorne seems to abandon this passage by changing the subject in his next paragraph. Yet on closer look, Hawthorne has in fact reinscribed that problem he has borrowed from Lessing—the relation between imitation, indication, and action, implicit in the contradiction between the stasis of the view and the temporality of narration. This relation between seeing and acting is further emphasized by the contrasts between Miriam and Kenyon. Miriam becomes emblematic of the fluid and temporal medium of paint; Kenyon becomes emblematic of the static and permanent integrity of marble. Miriam's gaze ties her to the literal "execution" of her model. In contrast, with a verbal command, Kenyon is able to have his assistants bring stone to life.

It is part of the studied brilliance of *The Marble Faun* that this gripping image of the vine is only glancingly a repetition of the Laocoön, as are the whole series of central problems in the novel: Donatello's achievement of life through his break with resemblance and the wrong action of the murder; Miriam, whose crime is, as the conclusion puts it, "after all merely a glance," weighted by the novel's closure with the full ethical implications of a meaningful look; the facility and superficiality of the copyist's matching and distanced perception; and the active relation between hands and eyes that produces, for Hawthorne, a genuine art. Finally, the little passage on the vine mimes Lessing's point regarding tragedy—that we enter into a view of the struggle with the serpent in the moment before the cry and that as well we already know the narrative and are powerless before it.

Hawthorne weaves this narrative from the story of original sin and the theme of incest. Critics have attended to the Cenci theme in *The Marble Faun* as an allusion to Shelley's "Cenci," as an allusion to Byronic legends of incest, as an allusion to Hawthorne's own supposedly incestuous relation with his sister Elizabeth ("Ebe"), and retrospectively as itself an allusion in Melville's *Pierre*.[58] But as *The Marble Faun* itself demonstrates, mere allusion does not suffice outside of a sphere of intelligibility and structure within which allusion is able to "resonate." Furthermore, allusion severed from its grounds becomes gratuitous detail. Thus I would conclude by remarking on the ways in which the Cenci portrait is, for the novel, a kind of indeterminate center of overdetermination.

We should begin by noting that the Cenci portrait is now considered to be neither Beatrice Cenci nor a work by Guido.[59] But for Hawthorne, and for Sophia, the portrait was a central point on a tour of Roman art. Hawthorne records in his *Notebooks* that in his visit to the Barberini Palace, he passed quickly by Dürer's picture of *Christ Disputing with the Doctors* "and almost all the other pictures, being eager to see the two which chiefly make the collection famous.—These are Raphael's Fornarini, and Guido's portrait of Beatrice Cenci. These we found in the last of the three rooms; and as regards Beatrice Cenci, I might as well not try to say anything, for its spell is indefinable, and the painter has wrought it in a way more like magic than anything else I have known."[60] The picture, in Hawthorne's view, clearly achieves the goal of abstracted spirituality that he states as an aim throughout *The Marble Faun*. He describes the figure in the portrait as "like a fallen angel, fallen, without sin. It is infinitely pitiful to meet her eyes. . . . It is the most profoundly wrought picture in the world; no artist did it, or could do it again. Guido may have held the brush, but he painted better than he knew. I wish, however, it were possible for some spectator, of deep sensibility, to see the picture without knowing anything of its subject or history; for no doubt we bring all our knowledge of the Cenci tragedy to the interpretation of the picture."[61] Now here we find the traveler's wish for a completely aestheticized context—a land of pictures unburdened by the stories of history—that links Hawthorne's project to the central problematic of incest as a relation between the overly propinquitous and the overly alterior.

Beatrice, in fact, is the perfect emblem for this problematic since she has taken up both the position of acted upon and actor, since she has suffered from the temporal reflexivity of being too close to her mate, and since she has suffered from the spatial reflexivity of being too far from her kin. The contamination of incest and the estrangement of fratricide and parricide are the axes thereby of a circle of Western culture that finds its narrative origins in the story of original sin with its account of too much knowledge and too much estrangement and the story of the founding of Rome with its incestuous mixing of nature and culture and its analogous coda of fratricide.

The Marble Faun imitates, then, an anxiety regarding consummation. Incest, travel, and art are linked as actions that threaten a closure that would mark the end of reproduction. It is rather easy to see the biographical import of this theme for Hawthorne. Once one attends to them, the most particular details in the text have the most general resonance. Consider, for example, the feet of the murdered model, which we earlier mentioned as a symbol of both experience and the worn trajectory of all paths in Rome. The symbol of the feet is readily linked to Hawthorne's earlier story of guilt and expiation, "The Ancestral Footstep," to Hawthorne's visit to the legendary "bloody footstep" at Smithell's Hall in London, to Hawthorne's own lame foot in his youth, to Byron's affliction, and metonymically then, to Byron's experience of incest and thereby to Oedipus's swollen foot as a mark of incest and patricide. We are reminded of other places in Hawthorne's fiction where to "dream strange things and make them look like truth" becomes a device for the conflation of act and symbol; for example, "The Birthmark," the story of an infant hand that reminds the bridegroom of a connection with animals. Or the moment in "Alice Doane's Appeal" when Leonard Doane, looking down at the face of the man he had murdered, Walter Brome, sees his dead father's face. Leonard has killed Walter because Walter has brought about the "shame" of Leonard's sister Alice. But Walter, it turns out, is also Alice's brother; Leonard has thus committed, in more or less literal and metaphorical degrees, incest, fratricide, and patricide.[62]

All of Hawthorne's work, including his life, of course, is concerned with an inheritance of sin, with the reading of stains, with the consequences of views. Yet to reduce *The Marble Faun* to biography or anything else is to refuse the very problems of determination the novel works to present. A consummate art would have no story to tell; in this sense, Hawthorne is struggling at the margins of such a possibility. Yet he is also presenting us with the particular ways in which such a possibility must necessarily fail. To travel in a land of pictures is to trade a being in time for a spatial illusion. The Laocoön itself is only intelligible because of the narrative Virgil has provided for reading it. And its perfected spatial form is thereby constantly put into motion by its representation of a punishment delivered in retribution for an unlicensed prophecy. We are not surprised to learn at the end of the novel that Hilda and Kenyon have in fact abandoned art. Without the risk of contamination by narrative particularity, on the one hand, the unintelligibility of abstraction, on the other, the transformations effected by the aesthetic have no meaning.

As is the case with the experience of the Laocoön, the site to which all roads, including this one, lead, we have a relentless critique of aestheticism within a proclamation of the triumph of aestheticism. Although it may seem that Hawthorne aligns America with moralism and Italy with aestheticism, we find that he has in fact presented a devastating critique of the limitations of both—the sterility, the impossibility of closure and production, found whenever art and action refuse one another. If Hawthorne rather gloomily reminds us that to stay too long in Italy and away from America would lead to a "kind of emptiness," for we would "defer the reality of life, in such cases, until a further moment . . . and by the by there are no future moments—or if we do return we find that . . . life has shifted its reality to the spot where we have deemed ourselves only temporary residents,"[63] he as well reflects on the meaning of the metaphors of emptiness, that emptiness of all travel writing that has as its point the redemption of actions now subject to view.

NOTES

This chapter is reprinted, in slightly different form, from Susan Stewart, *Crimes of Writing* (Oxford and New York: Oxford University Press, 1991): 173–205.

1. Claude Lévi-Strauss, *The Elementary Structures of Kinship*, trans. James Harle Bell, John Richard von Sturner, and Rodney Needham (Boston: Beacon Press, 1969): 8–9. (Jacques Derrida, "Structure, Sign and Play in the Discourse of the Human Sciences," in *Writings and Difference*, trans. Alan Bass. [Chicago: University of Chicago Press, 1978]: 278–294, discusses the paradox of this passage in light of Lévi-Strauss's entire oeuvre.) Lévi-Strauss focuses on *elementary* structures of kinship (those systems that prescribe marriage to an "almost automatic determination of the preferred spouse") as opposed to *complex* structures based on a transfer of wealth or free choice. But he points out that "even in elementary structures there is always some freedom of choice," and "on the other hand no complex structure allows a completely free choice, the rule being not that one can marry anyone in the system, but only those not expressly forbidden" (xxiii). Clearly issues of intelligibility come to the fore in situations of complex kinship in which the set of marriageable persons is less articulated than the set of those who are expressly forbidden.

2. Lévi-Strauss, *Elementary Structures*, 9.

3. Ibid., 10.

4. Quoted in Lévi-Strauss, *Elementary Structures*, 42, 43. See also Jack Goody, "A Comparative Approach to Incest and Adultery," in *Marriage, Family and Residence*, ed. Paul Bohannan and John Middleton (Garden City, N.Y.: Natural History Press, 1968): 21–46. Goody cites Malinowski's treatment of incest, as the prohibition on sexual intercourse, and exogamy, the prohibition on marriage, as "being but two sides of a coin" (22). He finds this position unsatisfactory, for he claims that it does not account for the asymmetry between in-group marriage rules and intragroup marriage rules, nor does it account for the asymmetry between marriage, which "affects the alignment of relationships between groups" and sexual intercourse, which when conducted in "semi-secrecy" does not affect such alignments (43–44). Although Goody's argument makes a strong methodological point regarding the anthropological study of incest and exogamy, this chapter must necessarily deal with codes that are not "semi-secret," and so exogamy and incest are treated as cognitive offenses and not "merely" sexual offenses.

Other standard readings on incest can be found in Emile Durkheim, *Incest, the Nature and Origin of the Taboo*, trans. Edward Sagarin (New York: Lyle Stuart, 1963); E. B. Tylor, *Researches into the Early History of Mankind and the Development of Civilization* (London: T. Murray, 1870); "On A Method of Investigating the Development of

Institutions, Applied to Laws of Marriage and Descent," *Journal of the Royal Anthropological Institute* 18(1888): 245–272. John T. Irwin's *Doubling and Incest/Repetition and Revenge: A Speculative Reading of Faulkner* (Baltimore: Johns Hopkins University Press, 1975) provides a valuable paradigm for thinking about the relation between time, space, repetition, and repression. Other studies of the thematic of incest in literature include Sandra Sandell, *"A Very Poetic Circumstance": Incest and the English Literary Imagination, 1770–1830* (Ph.D. dissertation, University of Minnesota, 1981); William Goetz, "Genealogy and Incest in *Wuthering Heights,*" *Studies in the Novel* 14, no. 4 (Winter 1982): 359–376; and W. Daniel Wilson, "Science, Natural Law, and Unwitting Sibling Incest in Eighteenth-Century Literature," *Studies in Eighteenth-Century Culture* 13 (1984): 249–270.

    5. See Sigmund Freud, *Dora: An Analysis of a Case of Hysteria,* ed. Philip Rieff (New York: Collier, 1963); Jane Gallop, *The Daughter's Seduction: Feminism and Psychoanalysis* (Ithaca: Cornell University Press, 1982); Charles Bernheimer and Claire Kahane, eds., *In Dora's Case: Freud—Hysteria—Feminism* (New York: Columbia University Press, 1985).

    6. Michel Butor, "Travel and Writing," *Mosaic* 8(1974): 1–16.

    7. Johann Wolfgang von Goethe, *Italian Journey,* trans. W. H. Auden and Elizabeth Mayer (San Francisco: North Point Press, 1982; reprint of Pantheon Books ed., 1962): 273.

    8. See Charles Batten, *Pleasurable Instruction: Form and Convention in Eighteenth-Century Travel Literature* (Berkeley, Los Angeles, and London: University of California Press, 1978); Michel de Certeau, *Heterologies: Discourse on the Other,* trans. Brian Massumi (Minneapolis: University of Minnesota Press, 1986): 69–71; Percy Adams, *Travel Literature and the Evolution of the Novel* (Lexington: University Press of Kentucky, 1983); George B. Parks, *The English Traveler to Italy.* I. *The Middle Ages to 1525* (Stanford: Stanford University Press, 1954).

    9. Mikhail Bakhtin, *The Dialogic Imagination,* ed. Michael Holquist and trans. Caryl Emerson and Michael Holquist (Austin: University of Texas Press, 1981): 103.

    10. Quoted in Allison Lockwood, *Passionate Pilgrims: The American Traveler in Great Britain, 1800–1914* (Rutherford, N.J.: Fairleigh Dickinson University Press, 1981): 150.

    11. Henry Theodore Tuckerman, *Isabel; or Sicily, A Pilgrimage* (Philadelphia: Lea and Blanchard, 1839): 15–16.

    12. Edward Gibbon, *Memoirs of My Life,* ed. Georges A. Bonnard (London: Thomas Nelson, 1966): 135.

    13. James Fenimore Cooper, *Excursions in Italy,* 2 vols. (London: Richard Bentley, 1838), 1: 47–49.

    14. For a survey of these texts, see Harold E. Smith, *American Travellers Abroad: A Bibliography of Accounts Published Before 1900* (Carbondale: Southern Illinois: University, 1969).

    15. James Thomas Flexner, *The Light of Distant Skies: History of American Painting 1760–1835* (New York: Dover, 1954): 160.

    16. Nathaniel Hawthorne, *The Marble Faun, or The Romance of Monte Beni* (New York: Penguin, 1961): 13–14.

    17. Rembrandt Peale, *Notes on Italy, Written During a Tour in the Years 1829–1830* (Philadelphia: Carey and Lea, 1831): 4.

18. Ibid., 5.

19. Ibid., 137.

20. See Flexner, *Light of Distant Skies*, 161.

21. David F. Dorr, *A Coloured Man Around the World, By a Quadroon* (Cleveland: Printed for the author, 1858): 104–105.

22. Ibid., 106–107. Here Dorr's complaints about morality echo those of Stendahl, who wrote of the lazzaroni, "A sense of duty . . . has no hold on the heart of the lazzaroni. If, in a blind fit of anger, he should chance to kill his best friend, yet still his God, *San Gennaro*, will grant him forgiveness." See Stendahl, *Rome, Naples and Florence*, trans. Richard N. Coe (New York: George Braziller, 1959).

23. Peale, *Notes on Italy*, 205.

24. Cooper, *Excursions in Italy*, 4–5.

25. Washington Irving [pseud. Geoffrey Crayon, Gent.], *Tales of a Traveller*. (Philadelphia: Cary and Lea, 1837): 48.

26. Goethe, *Italian Journey*, 272.

27. *The Marble Faun*, 117.

28. Peale, *Notes on Italy*, 3.

29. Ibid., 205.

30. Tuckerman, *Isabel*, 31.

31. *The Marble Faun*, 118.

32. Ibid., 50.

33. Ibid., 109.

34. Ibid., 244.

35. For discussions of *The Marble Faun* and Hawthorne's views of aesthetic response, see John Dolis, "Hawthorne's Metonymic Gaze: Image and Object," *American Literature* 56, no.3 (October 1984): 362–378; Thomas Brumbaugh, "Concerning Nathaniel Hawthorne and Art as Magic," *American Imago* 11 (1954): 399–405; Jonathan Auerbach, "Executing the Model: Painting, Sculpture, and Romance-writing in Hawthorne's *The Marble Faun*," *ELH* 47 (1980): 103–120; Rita K. Collin, "Hawthorne and the Anxiety of Aesthetic Response," *The Centennial Review* 4, no. 1 (Fall 1984): 28–29 and 94–104; Carol Hanberry Mackay, "Hawthorne, Sophia, and Hilda as Copyists: Duplication and Transformation in *The Marble Faun*," *Browning Institute Studies* 12 (1984): 93–120; Paul Brodtkorb, "Art Allegory in *The Marble Faun*," *PMLA* (June 1962): 254–267.

36. Peale, *Notes on Italy*, 211.

37. Ibid., 52.

38. Cooper, *Excursions in Italy*, 17.

39. *The Marble Faun*, 140.

40. See Henry Sussman, "*The Marble Faun* and the Space of American Letters," in *High Resolution* (Oxford: Oxford University Press, 1989): ch. 6, 129–151, for a discussion of the significance of this "goddess" as part of Hawthorne's "fictive program, in which the image is the source of energy and illumination" (148). Furthermore, the story of Kenyon's miraculous discovery echoes that of the miraculous discovery of the Laocoön. Here "uncovering" the art of the past is a form of animation more powerful than copying. Felice de Fredi, who discovered the Laocoön among the ruins of the Baths of Titus on January 14, 1506, has his good fortune recorded on his tombstone at the Aracoeli church.

41. The standard formulation for this problem remains Paul de Man's "The Rhetoric of Temporality," in *Interpretation: Theory and Practice*, ed. Charles Singleton (Baltimore: Johns Hopkins University Press, 1969): 173–209.

42. William Gilpin, "On Picturesque Travel" (1792). Reprinted in *Eighteenth-Century Critical Essays*, 2 vols., ed. Scott Elledge (Ithaca: Cornell University Press, 1961), II: 1060–1064, 1063. See also Elizabeth Wheeler Manwaring, *Italian Landscape in Eighteenth-Century England: A Study Chiefly of the Influence of Claude Lorrain and Salvator Rosa on English Taste 1700–1800* (New York: Russell and Russell, 1965), for material regarding the background to these views.

43. See Gibbon's *Memoirs*, 136: "In my journal the place and moment of conception are recorded: the fifteenth of October 1764, in the close of the evening, as I sat musing on the Church of the Zoccolanti or Franciscan friars, while they were singing vespers in the Temple of Jupiter on the ruins of the Capitol." The "surprise ending" of Edith Wharton's "Roman Fever," is in fact a pun on Gibbon's legend of "conception." See "Roman Fever," in *Roman Fever and Other Stories* (New York: Charles Scribner's Sons, 1964): 9–24.

44. See Peale's account of a "scenic exhibition" of the *Tragedy of Desdemona* (161–163) and "the contrivance and exhibition of living pictures" at "the residence of a Scottish gentleman of fortune" (164–165) and Cooper's account of "an entertainment" involving the caricature of various "national traits" at an English residence in Tuscany (50–51).

45. Peale, *Notes on Italy*, 188.

46. Tuckerman, *Isabel*, 32.

47. Ibid., 36.

48. Cooper, *Excursions in Italy*, 23.

49. Rembrandt Peale, *Graphics: A Manual of Drawing and Writing for the Use of Schools and Families* (New York: J. P. Peaslee, 1835).

50. Goethe, *Italian Journey*, 125.

51. *The Marble Faun*, 54.

52. Peale, *Notes on Italy*, 304.

53. Goethe, *Italian Journey*, 227.

54. Hawthorne, *The French and Italian Notebooks*, ed. Thomas Woodson (Columbus: Ohio State University Press, 1980). *Centenary Edition of the Works of Nathaniel Hawthorne*, vol. 14, 86.

55. Irving, *Tales of a Traveller*, 43–44.

56. *The Marble Faun*, 212–213.

57. Ibid., 213.

58. See Diane Long Hoeveler, "La Cenci: The Incest Motif in Hawthorne and Melville," *American Transcendental Quarterly* 44 (1979): 247–259; Frederick Crews, *The Sins of the Fathers* (London: Oxford University Press, 1966); Philip Young, *Hawthorne's Secret: An Un-Told Tale* (Boston: David R. Godine, 1984); Gloria C. Erlich, *Family Themes and Hawthorne's Fiction: The Tenacious Web* (New Brunswick: Rutgers University Press, 1984).

59. This point is mentioned in Young, *Hawthorne's Secret*, 42. Carol Hanbery Mackay (116, n. 5) cites the following texts as questioning both the identity of the figure and attribution to Guido Stuart (New York: Boni and Liveright, 1925), II: 280–288; and Isabel Stevenson Munro and Kate M. Monro, *Index to Reproductions of European Paintings* (New York: H. W. Wilson, 1956).

60. *Notebooks,* 92.

61. *Notebooks,* 93.

62. *Hawthorne's Short Stories,* ed. Newton Arvin (New York: Alfred Knopf, 1961): "The Birthmark," 177–193; "Alice Doane's Appeal," 411–422. We should note that as the passage ends, Leonard decides to carry Walter's body: "that the face still wore a likeness of my father; and because my soul shrank from the fixed glare of the eyes, I bore the body to the lake, and would have buried it there. But before his icy sepulchre was hewn, I heard the voices of two travellers and fled" (417).

63. *The Marble Faun,* 330.

SIX

The World in a Text:
How to Read *Tristes Tropiques*

Clifford Geertz

The advent of structuralism ("advent" is the proper word; it came as a sudden unriddling announced by an improbable presence) has done rather more to alter anthropology's sense of itself than its sense of its subject. Whatever becomes of circulating women, mythemes, binary reason, or the science of the concrete, the sense of intellectual importance that structuralism brought to anthropology, most especially, to ethnography—in which Lévi-Strauss once declared he had found nothing less than "the principle of all research"—will not soon disappear. The discipline had worked its way, here and there, into the general cultural life before: Eliot read Frazer; Engels read Morgan; Freud, alas, read Atkinson; and, in the United States at least, just about everybody read Mead. But nothing like the wholesale invasion of neighboring fields (literature, philosophy, theology, history, art, politics, psychiatry, linguistics, even some parts of biology and mathematics) had ever occurred. So precipitate a move from the edge of things to their center has turned greater heads than ours, and the effects—despite my irony, not altogether bad—will be with us, I think, more or less permanently.

What is most striking, however, in all of this is that, using the word in its uncensorious sense, it was an essentially rhetorical accomplishment. It was not the odd facts or the even odder explanations Lévi-Strauss brought forth that made of him (as Susan Sontag, who is in charge of such matters, called him) an intellectual hero.[1] It was the mode of discourse he invented to display those facts and frame those explanations.

The reanalysis of the Oedipus story only partly aside, the particular findings of structuralist anthropology have had scarcely more effect beyond the borders of the discipline than those of functionalism, culture and personality studies, or social evolutionism; quite possibly, even less. What changed the mind of the age, as none of those ever did, was the sense that a new language had appeared in which everything from ladies' fashions, as in Roland Barthes's *Le Système de la mode*, to neurology, as in Howard Gardner's *The Quest for Mind*, could be usefully discussed.[2] It was a cycle of terms (sign, code, transformation, opposition, exchange, communication, metaphor, metonymy, myth, structure), borrowed and reworked from the lexicons of science and art alike, that defined Lévi-Strauss's enterprise for those whose interest in Australian section systems or Bororo village shapes was at best limited. More than anything else, he cleared an imaginative space that a generation of characters in search of a play rushed to occupy.

Again, I should make it clear, especially in the light of my own admitted skepticism toward the structuralist project as a research program and my outright hostility to it as a philosophy of mind, that I regard this construction of an entire discourse realm from a standing start as a stunning achievement, altogether worthy of the attention it has received. Lévi-Strauss is clearly one of the true "authors" in anthropology—if originality be all, perhaps the truest. The fact that I myself am not attracted to write in the tradition he authored, preferring less ambitious strategies, is quite beside the point. To characterize someone as writing with world-making intent is not to accuse him; it is to situate him.

It is, at any rate, from such a perspective, appreciative and unconverted, that I want to approach Lévi-Strauss as a Barthesian "author-writer." He is, or rather his work is, a peculiarly illuminating case in point for the proposition that the separation of what someone says from how they say it— content from form, substance from rhetoric, *l'écrit* from *l'écriture*—is as mischievous in anthropology as it is in poetry, painting, or political oratory. The investigation of how a Lévi-Strauss text, or more exactly how *Tristes Tropiques*, the finest of his texts and the one that most illuminates the whole of his work, is put together takes us into some of the most intractable instabilities of what (borrowing a term, and some ideas as well, from the linguist Alton Becker) one may call text-building strategies in anthropology.[3]

Of course, the most immediate value of such a "lit-crit" approach to Lévi-Strauss is that he is very difficult to read; and not only, as has sometimes been argued, for flat-footed Anglo-Saxons. He is difficult not just in the recognized sense that his by now famous rain-forest prose—dripping with steamy metaphors, overgrown with luxuriant images, and flowered with extravagant puns ("thoughts" and "pansies," "ways" and "voices," and perhaps, considering the text at hand, even "tropes" and "tropics")—is so easy to get lost in. He is difficult in the deeper and more serious sense that although, stylistic extravagances aside, his books look like ordinary anthropological works, even at times like rather old-fashioned ones, Bureau of American Ethnography monographs reincarnated, they are not. They are another genre under the sun. To approach *Tristes Tropiques* with reading habits formed by experience with *We, the Tikopia* or *Patterns of Culture* or even with what might seem a better model but is really a worse one, *The Golden Bough*, is rather like the little old lady in the Thurber vignette who found *Macbeth* lacking as a detective story because it was clear whodunit from quite early on.

But the main reason for regarding Lévi-Strauss in a literary way is not the exegetical one, structuralism made easy, but that his works, *Tristes Tropiques* most particularly, form excellent cases on which to train such a regard.

The innocence about text-building that I have ascribed to our profession in general certainly does not apply to him. Were he any more self-conscious, he would transport to a higher plane. In the whole of anthropology there are no works more self-referential—works that point as often to themselves as artifacts, and deliberately, as they do to what they are ostensibly about—than *Tristes Tropiques*. It is a classic example of the book whose subject is in great part itself, whose purpose is to display what, were it a novel, we would call its fictionality; a painting, its planarity; a dance, its comportment: its existence as a made thing.

If one reads, say, Meyer Fortes's *The Tallensi* or E. E. Evans-Pritchard's *The Nuer*, one can and usually does feel that one is looking through a crystal window to the reality beyond. The devices, the construction scars, the brush marks are all more or less invisible, at least to the unwary eye. In *Tristes Tropiques* (and, for that matter, in *La Pensée sauvage* and *Mythologiques* as well) the devices are foregrounded, pointed at, flourished even. Lévi-Strauss does not want the reader to look through his text, he wants him to look at it. And once one has, it is very hard ever again to look through, at least with the old epistemological nonchalance, anyone else's.

What is critical, however, is that such a how-is-this-text-built approach to *Tristes Tropiques* leads on to a somewhat unstandard interpretation of Lévi-Strauss's work, both of the parts that make it up and of the by now largely unfolded totality those parts constitute. Or to put the matter less generally, we can counterpose to the two approaches usually taken to the *oeuvre entière* a third one that gives to that *oeuvre*, and thus at least indirectly to structuralism, a rather different look. Tracing out the strategies of so strategical a book is not (to employ a familiar libel) just a literary exercise. It is a revisionary one.

Of the two usual approaches to Lévi-Strauss's work as a whole, the more common, because it seems so simple and familiar to historicistic Westerners, is to see it as a linear development: a view Lévi-Strauss himself, as a bit of deliberate mystification in my opinion, considering his famous hostility to all forms of historicism, has in fact promoted.

This view is, as linear views tend to be, essentially a Whiggish one. The great structuralist enterprise begins with *Les Structures élémentaires de la parenté* in that most standard of anthropological domains, kinship, in which it makes its first real, halting steps. But it is mired down by the social actuality of it all: the mind sunk in materialities. Then, the story goes, in "The Structural Study of Myth" and in *Totemism*, it begins to shake free of this social dross to get more directly at its proper subject, the formal play of the human intellect. This approach is then codified, systematized, and turned into a veritable science, like Marxism, geology, or psychoanalysis, in *La Pensée sauvage*, after which it is carried to triumphant culmination in the great four-volume record of the mind gamboling freely in the fields of its own imagery, *Mythologiques*.

It would take us too far from our subject to trace out here the difficulties of this view of Lévi-Strauss's work as describing a rise from nature to culture, behavior to thought, matter to mind. It is actually plausible only so long as one doesn't look too closely into chronology or, even more important, into the intertextual relations that actually obtain, independently of sequence, among the various works. *Les Structures élémentaires*, with its tracing of logical transformations across vast geographic spaces, stands in many ways closer to *Mythologiques*, two decades further on, than does *La Pensée sauvage*, with its theoretical cavalry charges, methodological set pieces, and *Rive Gauche* quarrels, which was published only a year or two earlier than *Mythologiques*. One of his most recent books, *La Voie des masques*, a sort of tailpiece to the *Mythologiques*, was published in 1979 but conceived in 1943, before his first one, *La Vie familiale et sociale des Indiens Nambikwara*. And his whole argument is, in bare-bones terms, already there in the thirty pages or so of "The Structural Study of Myth," written in the 1950s. The rest is an enormous footnote.

Because the problems of Whiggism in connection with so achronic a writer as Lévi-Strauss are, once one gets down to cases, so obvious (even his individual books do not march directionally through their subjects like proper monographs, beginning at the beginning and ending at the end, but circle, hovering, around them like avian meditations, remote and brooding), another approach to his work has seemed to a number of people more promising. This is to see it, so to speak, recursively, each phase of it, or even each work, being concerned with training the constant, unchanging, structuralist gaze on one or another domain of anthropological research; a huge rotating searchlight, lighting up first this dark corner, then the next.

In this story, Lévi-Strauss, fixed of mind and sure of purpose, scatters one after another the academic ideologies blocking his path. *Les Structures élémentaires* takes on the Warner/Radcliffe-Brown/Murdock kinships controversy, displacing the whole axis of dispute. *Totemism* upends Durkheimianism and Radcliffe-Brown's vulgarization of it. *La Pensée sauvage* tilts with Sartre, epistemology, and the idea of history. *Mythologiques* dismantles and reassembles, bricoleur-style, the Boas/Müller/Frazer schedule of issues. And the rhetoric of the argument shifts appropriately as the wheel of attention turns. It is Maussian (men communicating through gifts of women)

in the Australian–Southeast Asian work. It is British functionalist (though
with the signs changed, "good to think rather than good to eat") in *Totemism*.
It is trans-Marxist and high-linguisticist (*imagines mundi* and animal
metonyms) in *La Pensée sauvage*. And it is a mélange of aestheticism ("overture," "coda," "the bird nester's aria," "the fugue of the five senses," "opos-
sum's cantata") and Enlightenment encyclopedism (ARAWAK to ZAPOTEC)
in *Mythologiques*.

I will not go, here, into the problems of this approach either. It is better
in some ways than the first (at least it avoids the myth of progress). It is worse
in others (complete stability in the structuralist program from 1949 to 1979
is, to put it mildly, difficult to establish). The critical point is that, as my failure to mention it in describing them suggests, both approaches have difficulty accommodating *Tristes Tropiques* at all. It seems like a mere sport, even
an embarrassment: a reflective, rather pointless pause in the long march toward intellective purity in the linear case; a mere personal expression, an indulgence best overlooked, in the recursive one. As I have pronounced it the
key work, the center around which the whole pivots, I need to take a quite
different tack.

To my mind, Lévi-Strauss's work is organized neither linearly, a progress
of views, nor quantumly, a series of discontinuous reformulations of a fixed
and single view; rather, it is organized, if you will, centrifugally. It is possible, I think, and profitable as well, to look at all of Lévi-Strauss's works, except *Tristes Tropiques*, even those works that, in publication terms anyway,
predate it, as partial unpackings of it, developments of particular strains present, embryonically at least and usually much more fully than that, in this,
the most multiplex of his writings.

Whether or not this cosmic egg view of *Tristes Tropiques* is the last word on
the subject is surely debatable; but not, I should think, until it is first explored. Looking at *Tristes Tropiques* in text-building terms as the arch-text
out of which the other texts are, in a logical sense, generated—Stevens's
"parakeet of parakeets that above the forest of parakeets prevails/a pip of
life amid a mort of tails"—can lead one into a better grasp of Lévi-Strauss's
thought that can seeing it either as an advancing series of etherealizing
visions or as a static and obsessive iterating theme.

From this perspective the first thing to be said about *Tristes Tropiques*, and in
some ways the last as well, is that it is several books at once, several quite different sorts of texts superimposed one upon the other to bring out an overall pattern, rather like a moiré.

"Superimposed" is, however, not exactly the right word. For what we
have in *Tristes Tropiques* is not a hierarchical, surface-to-depth arrangement
of texts, the one hidden beneath the other, so that interpretation consists
in deeper penetration as one strips away the layers. What we have is

co-occurring, competing, even sometimes mutually interfering texts existing at the same level.

The book is a virtual analogue of Lévi-Strauss's kaleidoscope image of "concrete thought": a syntactic conjunction of discrete elements, played out horizontally along what Roman Jakobson called the plane of contiguity, rather than a paradigmatic hierarchy of continuate elements, played out vertically on what he called the plane of similarity.[4] *Tristes Tropiques* is an ideal-typical Russian/Czech formalist poem: meaning constructed by projecting the analogue axis of paradigmatic substitution, Jakobson's "metaphor," onto the digital one of syntactic combination, his "metonymy." It is, to put it more casually and in a language less special, a manifold text *par excellence*: several books at once all jammed together to produce . . . well, we shall come back to what is produced later. First, it is necessary to look at the component elements, the thin books wildly signaling to get out inside this fat one.

In the first place, it is, of course, and despite the ironic and self-reflexive denial of the famous opening passage, a travel book in a very recognizable genre. I went here, I went there; I saw this strange thing and that; I was amazed, bored, excited, disappointed; I got boils on my behind, and once, in the Amazon . . . —all with the implicit undermessage: Don't you wish you had been there with me or could do the same?

An invitation to dreams of adventure and escape, and even a dream itself. He can be as superior as he wants to be about lantern-slide lectures, stories about the ship's dog, or descriptions of seagulls swirling about; but just listen to him on Fort de France:

> When the clocks struck two in the afternoon Fort de France was a dead town. There was no sign of life in the oval-bordered "main square," which was planted with palm-trees and overrun with rampant weeds—a patch of dead ground, one would have thought, in which someone left behind a statue of Josephine Tascher de la Pagerie, later Beauharnais. [That is Napoleon's Josephine, of course.] No sooner had the Tunisian and I checked into the deserted hotel than, still shaken by the events of the morning, we hired a car and set off toward the Lazaret, with the intention of comforting our companions and, more especially, two young German women who had led us to believe, during the voyage out, that they would be unfaithful to their husbands just as soon as they could get properly cleaned up. From this point of view, the business of the Lazaret was yet another disappointment to us.[5]

Which is both crude enough and sufficiently arch for any lantern lecture.

Or hear him, even, much farther on, approach the Tupi-Kawahib across the mid-Amazon plateau:

> I had left Cuiba in June, and it was now September. For three months I had wandered across the Plateau, camping with the Indians while my animals had

a rest, or pushing on interminably from one point to the next, asking myself the while what it would all add up to in the end. Meanwhile the jerky motion of the mule gave me sore places so atrociously painful, and yet so familiar, that I ended up feeling they were a permanent part of my anatomy and I should even miss them if they were not there the next morning. Boredom got the upper hand of adventure. For weeks on end the same austere savannah would unroll before me—a land so dry that living plants could scarcely be distinguished from the dead stumps that marked the place where someone had lately struck camp. And as for the blackened remains of bush-fires, they seemed merely the culmination of a territory where it was the destiny of everything, sooner or later, to be burnt to a cinder.[6]

"My Life among the Headhunters" or "Two Years in Darkest Africa" could hardly be better, or worse, than this Richard Burton/T. E. Lawrence sort of tone. Actually, there are French referents for this that would be more appropriate. The Third Republic *haute vulgarisation* popular culture was pockmarked with this sort of thing: Gide's *Voyages au Congo*, the intensely read romantic travelogues of Pierre Loti, or even such a classic mandarin figure as André Malraux, at least in his archaeological–Far Eastern phase, seem the prototypes of the attitude, and the style, Lévi-Strauss is adopting here. A systematic attempt to connect *Tristes Tropiques* with the French travel literature he was supposedly reacting against, though actually reincarnating and even exploiting, could be extremely revealing.

In any case, whatever the models, the image of the hardy traveler, sorely beset but terribly *interested,* never leaves the book, and it connects his account to a type of social consciousness—vulgar in the root, not the tendentious, sense of the word—that this almost classic *normalien* (even though he was, as he very carefully points out in *Tristes Tropiques,* by his own choice, not literally one) would never admit to and indeed has spent much of his career distancing himself from.

Second, the book is, however oddly looking a one, an ethnography. A controversial ethnography perhaps, and more than a bit overfocused; but the affirmed and affirmed pose of the ethnographer, like the disclaimed and disclaimed one of the tourist, never leaves the book. Indeed it often becomes, in its shrill insistence, a bit thick:

> An antinomy, therefore, which we have as a profession on the one hand, and on the other an ambiguous enterprise, oscillating between a mission and a refuge, hearing within itself elements of both and yet always recognizably one rather than the other. Anthropology has in all this an especially favored place. It represents the second alternative [that is, the "refuge"] in its most extreme form. The ethnographer, while in no wise abdicating his own humanity, strives to know and estimate his fellowman from a lofty and distant point of vantage: only thus can he abstract them from the contingencies particular to this or that civilization. The conditions of his life and work cut him off from his own

group for long periods together; and he himself acquires a kind of chronic up-
rootedness from the sheer brutality of the environmental changes to which he
is exposed. Never can he feel himself "at home" anywhere: he will always be,
psychologically speaking, an amputated man. Anthropology is, with music and
mathematics, one of the few true vocations; and the anthropologist may become aware of it before ever he has been taught it.[7]

The anthropologist, as here, venturing where lesser souls—his café intellectual friends in Paris; the orchid-elite of French Quarter São Paulo;
his shallow, novelty-pursuing Brazilian students; and you, dear chemist,
philosopher, or art historian, enfolded in your laboratory, study, or museum—dare not go, and penetrating forms of existence they can only read
about: this note too runs continuously through the book. The mystique of
fieldwork that Malinowski founded and Mead proclaimed finds its apotheosis here, significantly enough in someone who has not done all that much
fieldwork and who would deny its experiential authority, as he does in *Tristes
Tropiques*, as a bit of "shopgirl philosophy."

Unlike the travel text, however, which is, as such texts are by nature, one
damn thing after another, the ethnographic text has a thesis, the thesis in
fact that Lévi-Strauss has pursued for the quarter century or so since:
namely, "the ensemble of a people's customs has always its particular style;
they form into systems." The "overture" and the "coda" to *Mythologiques* are
perhaps more powerful statements, "The Structural Study of Myth" a more
systematic one, and the fourth chapter of *Totemism* a clearer one. But Lévi-
Strauss has never been able to put capital-S Structuralism in so neat a nut-
shell as he was able to in *Tristes Tropiques*:[8]

> The ensemble of a people's customs has always its particular style; they form
> into systems. I am convinced that the number of these systems is not unlim-
> ited and that human beings (at play, in their dreams, or in moments of delu-
> sion) never create *absolutely*; all they can do is to choose certain combinations
> from a repertory of ideas which it should be possible to reconstitute. For this
> one must make an inventory of all the customs which have been observed by
> oneself or others, the customs pictured in mythology, the customs invoked by
> both children and grown-ups in their games. The dreams of individuals,
> whether healthy or sick, should also be taken into account. With all this one
> could eventually establish a sort of periodical chart of chemical elements anal-
> ogous to that devised by Mendelier. In this, all customs, whether real or merely
> possible, would be grouped by families and all that would remain for us to do
> would be to recognize those which societies had, in point of fact, adopted.[9]

Third, besides a travelogue and an ethnography, the book is a philosophical text. It is a philosophical text not simply in the man-in-the-street
sense that it is flamboyantly reflective—the mute-exchanges-of-forgiveness-
with-a-cat sort of thing—and full of dark sayings—"Marxism and Buddhism
are doing the same thing, but at different levels." It is a philosophical text

in the scholarly sense that it addresses itself, with some resoluteness, to a central issue in Western thought: the natural foundations of human society. Not only does Lévi-Strauss hope to find Rousseau's Social Contract alive and well in deepest Amazon—and so counter such theories of the origins of sociality as Freud's primal parricide or Hume's conventionality—but he thinks that, among the Nambikwara, he has actually and literally done so:

> The evidence of the Nambikwara runs, to begin with, clean counter to the ancient sociological theory, now temporarily resurrected by the psychoanalysts, according to which the primitive chief derives from a symbolic father. . . . I should like to be able to show how markedly, in this regard, contemporary anthropology supports the thesis of the eighteenth century *philosophes*. Doubtless Rousseau's schema differs from the quasi-contractual relations which obtain between the chief and his companions. Rousseau had in mind a quite different phenomenon—the renunciation by the individual of his own autonomy in the interests of the collective will. It is nonetheless true, however, that Rousseau and his contemporaries displayed profound sociological intuition when they realized that attitudes and elements of culture such as are summed up in the words "contract" and "consent" are not secondary formations, as their adversaries (and Hume in particular) maintained: they are the primary materials of social life, and it is impossible to imagine a form of social organization in which they are not present.[10]

Lévi-Strauss does not merely think that he has found the Social Contract *in vivo* (a claim, a bit like saying one has discovered the country where Plato's Ideas or Kant's Noumena are stored). He wants to bring back to respectability Rousseau's *societé naissante* model, which sees what we would now call the neolithic as, quoting from Rousseau, "un juste milieu entre l'indolence d'état primitif et la pétulant activité de notre amour propre" (the middle ground between the indolence of the primitive state and the questing activity to which we are prompted by our *amour propre*). Better we had never left that world, which we need now to reconstruct and which we can reconstruct because Rousseau's model is eternal and universal.[11] By knowing other societies, we can detach ourselves from our own and build, on the basis of an ideal beyond space and time, a rational social order, one, Lévi-Strauss says, in which man can live.

And this, in turn, leads to the fourth sort of text *Tristes Tropiques* is: a reformist tract. There has been an enormous number of indictments by now of the West for its impact on the non-West, but there are few, no matter how radical their authors, with the devastating bitterness and power of Lévi-Strauss's *Tristes Tropiques*. He makes Frantz Fanon sound postively genial.

The passages are famous. The descriptions of the dilapidated "former savages" spoiling the view around São Paulo; the diatribes about empty beer bottles and discarded tin cans; and the intense hatred for industrial civilization that keeps breaking through: it is unnecessary to requote them here. What needs to be noted is that they connect with a distinctive strand in nineteenth- and early twentieth-century reformist thought—the one perhaps best represented in France by Flaubert, in Germany by Nietzsche, and by Arnold or Ruskin or Pater in England; one that reacted to much of modern life with an essentially aesthetic repugnance raised, or anyway transported, to a moral level. Distaste transmogrified.

Just to show that this is a general theme in Lévi-Strauss, let me quote from his comments on Third World cities, describing them as a whole. (The passage, revamped and back-translated for Indian cities expressly, is in fact included in *Tristes Tropiques*, though it is one of the sections omitted in the Russell translation):

> Filth, promiscuity, disorder, physical contact; ruins, shacks, excrements, mud; body moisture, animal droppings, urine, purulence, secretions, suppuration—everything that [European] urban life is organized to defend us against, everything we loathe, everything we protect ourselves from at great cost—all these by-products of co-habitation never here [in the Third World] impose a limit on [urban life's] spread. On the contrary, these constitute the natural setting the town must have if it is to survive.[12]

And the crime, of course, is that it is we who have done this, whether out of greed and *pétulante activité* or mere fits of absentmindedness and callousness—we who have thrown, as he says somewhere in *Tristes Tropiques*, our filth in the faces of the rest of the world, which now proceeds to throw it back in ours.

As a reformist tract, *Tristes Tropiques* is an outburst, less of *moraliste* rage—which is one of the things that divides him from Sartre, who is rather more worried that people are dominated than that they are degraded—than of aesthetic repugnance. Like Swift's, Lévi-Strauss's deep social disgust seems to rise out of an even deeper disgust with the physical and the biological. His radicalism is not political. It is sensory.

Fifth, and finally, *Tristes Tropiques* is, quite deliberately, a kind of symbolist literary text (a fact James Boon, in his neglected study, *From Symbolism to Structuralism*, has alerted us to in Lévi-Strauss's work generally),[13] an application of *symboliste* views to primitive culture: Mallarmé in South America.

This is easier to see in the French text, where the prose as such mirrors the indebtedness. But it is emphatic enough at various points to survive translation as well.

> I see these predilections [to see space and time in qualitative terms, and so on] as a form of wisdom which primitive peoples put simultaneously into practice; the madness lies rather in our modern wish to go against them. Primitive peoples attained quickly and easily to a peace of mind which we strive for at the cost of innumerable rebuffs and irritations. We should do better to accept the true conditions of our human experience and realize that it is not within

our power to emancipate ourselves completely from either its structure or its natural rhythms. Space has values peculiar to itself, just as sounds and scents have their colours and feelings their weight. The search for correspondences of this sort is not a poet's game or a department of mystification, as people have dared to say of Rimbaud's *Sonnet des Voyelles*; that sonnet is now indispensable to the student of language who knows the basis, not of the colour of phenomena, for this varies with each individual, but of the relation which unites one phenomenon to another and comprises a limited gamut of possibilities. These correspondences offer the scholar an entirely new terrain, and one which may still have rich yields to offer. If fish can make an aesthetic distinction between smells in terms of light and dark, and bees classify the strength of light in terms of weight—darkness is heavy to them, and bright light light—just so should the work of the painter, the poet, and the composer and the myths and symbols of primitive Man appear to us: if not as a superior form of knowledge, at any rate as the most fundamental form of knowledge, and the only one that we all have in common.[14]

And he continues in the same vein, one which by *Mythologiques* will be a major theme. "Cities have often been likened to symphonies and poems; and this comparison seems to me a perfectly natural one: they are in fact objects of the same nature . . . something lived and something dreamed."[15] (Apparently these are different cities than the pestilent ones we just saw. And, in fact, this bit of lyricism is followed by a criticism of Brazilian towns, this time for being the results of "decisions of . . . engineers and financiers" rather than spontaneous growths, like poems or symphonies—unmelodic, out of tune, so to speak: mechanical cacophonies produced by tone-deaf "moderns.")

That Lévi-Strauss is concerned to place himself and his text in the literary tradition established by Baudelaire, Mallarmé, Rimbaud, and—though, as far as I can discover, he never mentions him in *Tristes Tropiques*—especially Proust, is clear from the way he writes, from what he writes, and from what he says he is concerned to do: decode, and, in decoding, recover the power to use the sensuous imagery of neolithic thought. *Tristes Tropiques* is, in one dimension, a record of a symbolist mentality, which Lévi-Strauss insists that not just his Indians but he himself has, at play in the forests and savannahs of the Amazon.

> Neither Brazil nor South America meant much to me at the time. But I can still see, in every detail, the images formed in my mind, in response to this unexpected suggestion [that is, that he go there]. Tropical countries, as it seemed to me, must be the exact opposite of our own, and the name of the antipodes has for me a sense at once richer and more ingenuous than its literal derivation. I should have been astonished to hear it said that any species, whether animal or vegetable, could have the same appearance on both sides of the globe. Every animal, every tree, every blade of grass, must be completely different and give immediate notice . . . of its tropical character. I imagined

Brazil as a tangled mass of palm-leaves, with glimpses of strange architecture in the middle distance, and an all-permeating sense of burning perfume. This latter olefactory detail I owe, I think, to an unconscious awareness of the assonance between the words *Brésil* ("Brazil") and *grésiller* ("sizzle"). No amount of later experience . . . can prevent me from still thinking of Brazil in terms of burning scent.

Now that I look back on them, these images no longer seem so arbitrary. I have learnt that the truth of any given situation does not yield so much to day-to-day observation as that patient and fractionated distillation which the equivocal notion of burning scent was perhaps already inviting me to put into practice. The scent brought with it, it may be, a symbolic lesson which I was not yet able to formulate clearly. Exploration is not so much a matter of covering ground as of digging beneath the surface: chance fragments of landscape, momentary snatches of life, reflections caught on the wing—such are the things that alone make it possible for us to understand and interpret horizons which would otherwise have nothing to offer us.[16]

The book is a record of a symbolist mentality (French) encountering other symbolist mentalities (Bororo, Caduveo, Nambikwara) and seeking to penetrate their wholly interior coherence in order to find in them the replication of itself—"the most fundamental form" of thought.

As I say, only even more extended quotation could bring this fully out: the stress on the affinity of memory, music, poetry, myth, and dream; the notion of a universal *sauvage* sense-language, half buried in each person (and more deeply buried in us, who have left the *société naissante,* than in primitives); and the closed-world view of meaning that results from it all. *Tristes Tropiques* is Lévi-Strauss's *A la recherche du temps perdu* and *Un Coup de dés* and insists on being read as such, as part of the symbolist effort to orchestrate immediate images into absolute signs—something your standard, average British or American anthropologist is not particularly well equipped, certainly not inclined, to do.

So: A travel book, even a tourist guide, if, like the tropics, out of date. An ethnographic report, founding yet one more *scienza nuova.* A philosophical discourse, attempting to rehabilitate Rousseau, the Social Contract, and the virtues of the unpetulant life. A reformist tract, attacking European expansionism on asethetic grounds. And a literary work, exemplifying and forwarding a literary cause. All of these set next to one another, juxtaposed like pictures from an exhibition, producing in their interaction precisely what? What is the moiré that emerges?

To my mind what emerges, not altogether surprisingly, I suppose, is a myth.[17] The encompassing form of the book that all this syntactic, metonymic jostling of text-types produces is a Quest Story: the departure from familiar, boring, oddly threatening shores; the journey, with adventures, into another, darker world, full of various phantasms and odd revelations; the culminating mystery, the absolute other, sequestered and opaque, confronted deep down in the *sertão;* the return home to tell tales, a bit wistfully, a bit wearily, to the uncomprehending who have stayed unadventurously behind.

This, too, of course, this Anthropologist-as-seeker myth, can be seen as just one more metonymically adjoined text, side by side with the others, the meaning of the whole lying in good structuralist style (thus with good structuralist elusiveness) in the conjunction rather than in the parts conjoined. What is clear, however, is that in the years since *Tristes Tropiques*—or, more exactly, after the experience that of course preceded *all* his writings—Lévi-Strauss has dedicated himself to the writing of a myth about myths that would do what the direct experiences related in *Tristes Tropiques* finally (and, in the nature of the case, inevitably) failed to do: bring together the multiple text-types into a single structure, a "mytho-logic," itself an example of its subject, and so reveal the foundations of social life and indeed, beyond that, the foundations of human existence as such.

Seen this way, the body of Lévi-Strauss's systematic work appears as a long utterance in which the separate texts of *Tristes Tropiques* are connected and reconnected and reconnected again to one another in a grand variety of syntactic relations. If the myth-text can in any sense be said to emerge from the congeries that is *Tristes Tropiques* to dominate the whole *oeuvre* that unfolds out of it, it is as, so to speak, the syntax of syntax, the enclosing form abstract enough to represent, or better, govern, the whole. *This* is why Lévi-Strauss regards myth, music, and mathematics as the most direct expressions of reality and their study the only true vocation. It all ends, to the extent that it can be said to end at all, in a formalist metaphysics of being, never stated but always insinuated, never written but always displayed.

But this takes us further toward interpreting Lévi-Strauss's doctrine, as opposed to investigating his discourse strategies, than it is possible to go here.[18] The critical issue, so far as concerns the anthropologist as author, works and lives, text-building, and so on, is the highly distinctive representation of "being there" that *Tristes Tropiques* develops and the equally distinctive representation, invertive actually, of the relationship between referring text and referred-to world that follows from it.

To put it brutally, but not inaccurately, Lévi-Strauss argues that the sort of immediate, in-person "being there" one associates with the bulk of recent American and British anthropology is essentially impossible: it is either outright fraud or fatuous self-deception. The notion of a continuity between experience and reality, he says early on in *Tristes Tropiques,* is false: "There is no continuity in the passage between the two. . . . To reach reality we must first repudiate experience, even though we may later reintegrate it into an objective synthesis in which sentimentality [i.e., *sentimentalité*—"consciousness," "sensibility," "subjectivity," "feeling"] plays no part. . . . [Our] mission . . . is to understand Being in relation to itself, and not in relation to oneself."[19]

But what is most interesting is that this conviction, amounting indeed to a proper faith, that "savages" are best known not by an attempt to get, somehow, personally so close to them that one can share in their life but by stitching their cultural expressions into abstract patterns of relationships is represented in *Tristes Tropiques* as arising out of a revelatory (or, perhaps better, antirevelatory) climactic experience: the barren, defeated end of his Quest. When, finally, he reaches the ultimate savages he has so long been looking for—the "untouched" Tupi-Kawahib—he finds them unreachable.

> I had wanted to reach extreme limits of the savage; it might be thought that my wish had been granted, now that I found myself among these charming Indians whom no other white man had ever seen before and who might never be seen again. After an enchanting trip up-river, I had certainly found my savages. Alas! they were only too savage. . . . There they were . . . as close to me as a reflection in a mirror; I could touch them, but I could not understand them. I was given, at one and the same time, my reward and my punishment. . . . I had only to succeed in guessing what they were like for them to be deprived of their strangeness: in which case, I might just as well have stayed in my [own] village. Or if, as was the case here, they retained their strangeness, I could make no use of it, since I was incapable of even grasping what it consisted of. Between these two extremes, what ambiguous instances provide us [anthropologists] with the excuses by which we live? Who . . . is the real dupe of the confusion created in the reader's mind by observations which are carried just far enough to be intelligible and then are stopped in mid-career, because they cause surprise in human beings [who are] similar to those who take such customs as a matter of course? Is it the reader who believes in us, or we ourselves . . . ?[20]

The answer to this rhetorical question is, of course, both: the reader because he or she credits the anthropologist with a kind of experience the anthropologist has not in fact had; the anthropologist because he (or she, of course) imagines he has had it and that his having had it is what gives him his authority to speak. Seeing through to the foundations of strange-looking lives—"being there" in the general sense—cannot be achieved by personal immersion in them. It can only be achieved by subjecting the cultural productions (myths, arts, rituals, or whatever), the things that give these lives their immediate look of strangeness, to a universalizing analysis that, in dissolving the immediacy, dissolves the strangeness. What is remote close up is, at a remove, near.[21]

And this brings us, at last and at length, to the marking characteristic of all Lévi-Strauss's work, one on which almost everyone who deals with it sooner or later remarks: its extraordinary air of abstracted self-containment. "Aloof," "closed," "cold," "airless," "cerebral"—all the epithets that collect around any sort of literary absolutism collect around it. Neither picturing lives nor evoking them, neither interpreting them nor explaining them, but rather arranging and rearranging the materials the lives have somehow left behind into formal systems of correspondences—his books seem to exist behind glass, self-sealing discourses into which jaguars, semen, and rotting meat are admitted to become oppositions, inversions, isomorphisms.

The final message of *Tristes Tropiques*, and of the *oeuvre* that unfolds from it, is that anthropological texts, like myths and memoirs, exist less for the world than the world exists for them.

NOTES

This essay was previously published in Clifford Geertz, *Works and Lives: The Anthropologist as Author* (Stanford: Stanford University Press, 1988), 25–48.

1. Susan Sontag, "The Anthropologist as Hero," in Sontag, *Against Interpretation* (New York: Farrar, Straus and Giroux, 1961): 69–81.

2. Roland Barthes, *Le Système de la mode* (Paris: Editions du Seuil, 1967); Howard Gardner, *The Quest for Mind: Piaget, Lévi-Strauss, and the Structuralist Movement* (New York: Knopf, 1973).

3. Alton Becker, "Text Building, Epistemology, and Aesthetics in Javanese Shadow Theatre," in A. Becker and A. Yengoyan, eds., *The Imagination of Reality* (Norwood, N.J.: ABLEX Pub. Corp., 1979): 211–243.

4. Roman Jakobson, "Closing Statements: Linguistics and Poetics," in Thomas Sebeok, ed., *Style in Language* (Cambridge: MIT Press, 1960): 350–377.

5. Claude Lévi-Strauss, *A World on the Wane*, trans. John Russell (London: Hutchinson, 1961): 31. Although Lévi-Strauss prefers the Weightmans' translation (*Tristes Tropiques*, trans. John and Doreen Weightman [Harmondsworth, Eng.: Pan: 1976]), and it is somewhat more accurate, I will for the most part use the Russell, because it seems to me to bring the tone of the French better into English. In any case, I shall also give at each citation both the Weightman reference (here, p. 32) and that in the original (*Tristes Tropiques* [Paris: Plon, 1955], here, p. 17).

6. Russell, 313 (Weightman, 419; original, 341).

7. Russell, 58 (Weightman, 66–67; original, 46–47).

8. Actually, in line with my argument that chronology of publication can be misleading as a guide to the development of Lévi-Strauss's ideas, the *Tristes Tropiques* formulation builds on papers published as early as 1942, passages from which are incorporated in it. It is as much a summa as it is a prolegomena, even if most of the classic texts postdate it.

9. Russell, 160 (Weightman, 229; original, 183).

10. Russell, 308 (Weightman, 313–314; original, 336). For more on this theme in Lévi-Strauss's work generally, see Clifford Geertz, "The Cerebral Savage" in Geertz, *The Interpretation of Cultures* (New York: Basic Books, 1973): 345–359.

11. Russell, 390 (Weightman, 315; original, 513).

12. I have been unable to recover the Lévi-Strauss passage in English. It appears in Weightman at p. 168; in the original, at p. 132.

13. James Boon, *From Symbolism to Structuralism: Lévi-Strauss and Literary Tradition* (Oxford: Blackwell, 1972).

14. Russell, 126–129 (Weightman, 153–154; original, 121).

15. Russell, 127 (Weightman, 154; original, 122).

16. Russell, 49–50 (Weightman, 55–56; original, 37–38).

17. Again, I have developed this point more fully in "The Cerebral Savage," and so merely reassert it here.

18. Though it is, of course, part of my argument (the heart of it, in fact) that the relation between the *ars intelligendi*, the art of understanding, and the *ars explicandi*, the art of presentation, is so intimate in anthropology as to render them at base inseparable. That is why to see *Tristes Tropiques* as an image of its argument is to revise our view of what that argument is.

19. Russell, 62 (Weightman, 71; original, 50).

20. Here I have used the Weightman translation (436–437), for it is a bit clearer than the Russell (327; original, 356–357).

21. For a vivid, and more recent, expression of his ambivalence about approaching other peoples too closely, see Claude Lévi-Strauss, *The View from Afar* (New York: Basic Books, 1985), especially the introduction and first chapter. For an examination of some of the moral implications of this stance, see Clifford Geertz, "The Uses of Diversity," in S. McMurrin, ed., *The Tanner Lectures on Human Values*, vol. 7 (Cambridge: Cambridge University Press, 1986): 253–275.

PART TWO

Identity Markings

Ethnic Selves/Ethnic Signs: Invention of Self, Space, and Genealogy in Immigrant Writing

Azade Seyhan

It may be that writers in my position, exiles or emigrants or expatriates, are haunted by some sense of loss, some urge to reclaim, to look back, even at the risk of being mutated into pillars of salt. But if we do look back, we must also do so in the knowledge—which gives rise to profound uncertainties—that our physical alienation from India almost inevitably means that we will not be capable of reclaiming precisely the thing that was lost; that we will, in short, create fictions, not actual cities or villages, but invisible ones, imaginary homelands, Indias of the mind.

—SALMAN RUSHDIE, *Imaginary Homelands*

Salman Rushdie's poignant observation describes in precise terms the conditions for the creation of a new frontier in modern literary study. This frontier marks the passage to writing in immigration, to accounts of lost, forgotten, fragmented, and re-membered histories that stake out a space of self-definition for the writing subject in foreign territory and idiom. The labors of memory transcribed in language reclaim the lost experience of another time and place. The discourse of dislocation and relocation often mirrors the reconfigured consciousness of postmodern culture itself. "Exile," writes the Polish émigré Eva Hoffman in her autobiography, *Lost in Translation: A Life in a New Language*, "is the archetypal condition of contemporary lives."[1]

The ruptured and resynthesized sign(ature) and portraiture of modern ethnicity is coeval with postcolonial, postindustrial, and postmodern experience. The postmodern is often defined as an awareness of the loss of the subject in representation, of the illusory essence of the authentic self in an endless series of reproductions and representations. Reality is experienced only as the "hyperreal" or the simulacra of the simulacrum.[2] The postmodern culture is highly conscious of the exacting role of language and image in creating reality as representation. In a twist to the traditional slogan of the American Revolution, "no taxation without representation," critic

W. J. T. Mitchell observes that there is "no representation without taxation. Every representation exacts some cost, in the form of lost immediacy, presence, or truth, in the form of a gap between intention and realization, original and copy."[3] This profound awareness of the representational status of language has also radically changed our perceptions of the experience of time. The postmodern perception of temporality is closely linked to the notion that time is recovered and understood only in terms of human narrative, which accounts for gaps in memory and history. "Modernism," writes Stephen A. Tyler in "Post-Modern Ethnography," "taught us to value postponement, to look ahead to scientific utopia, to devalue the past, and negate the present. In contrast, the postmodern world is in a sense timeless; past and present, and future coexist in all discourse."[4] The experience of modern exiles and immigrants reflects this coexistence of different times and particularly the dominant presence of their pasts as constitutive of their transplanted selves.

The last two decades have witnessed the widespread displacement and resettlement of a multiplicity of populations as a result of war, economic necessity, labor migration, brain drain from the countries of the Third World, search for political asylum, or the dissolution of onetime national borders, such as the unification of Germany and the demise of the Soviet state. The various ethnic, religious, and national groups that have left their traditional homelands voluntarily or under threat of death, torture, poverty, or imprisonment have arrived at the gates of more affluent and politically stable countries of the Western world in unprecedented numbers. The reception of these groups has often taken place in an arena of contestatory politics. For a long time, in the United States and more recently in Western Europe, the debate on the "melting pot" policies versus the preservation of cultural and ethnic heritages and diversity has maintained currency and a sense of urgency. However, the voice of the subject of this debate is rarely heard. Since most immigrant groups often have inadequate language skills, no rights of citizenship, and, thus, no political representation, and lack of consensus within their communities, their views on their own status and welfare are often obscured by the debate that takes place beyond their immediate lives. Although the economic, political, and sociological contexts of modern immigration have been widely discussed and written about from various ideological angles, the participation of the immigrant subject in the cultural life of the host country has not always received comprehensive treatment. The foreign soil has proved to be a fertile one for the transplanted writer's imagination. This is particularly true of American soil, which has been transformed into a cultural landscape of hybrid colors and contours as a result of immigration waves. This chapter is an attempt to articulate the critical dimensions of this landscape through a necessarily brief look at exemplary works of literary immigrants. These works have, in many ways, charted the complex course of a modern aesthetic sensibility that has redefined traditional notions of historical passages and geopolitical shifts, self-representation and identity formation, and the role of memory and invention in imposing an order on the chaotic dynamics of newly emerging "minor literatures" and border cultures.

Thus, this chapter is about reconfigurations that arise from unraveled historical and personal entanglements between subjects and their forebears, between the living and the ghosts, and between past, present, and future. It is about a kind of writing where language mediates between the dichotomies of loss and gain. It is about the reinvention of the displaced subject in language and memory. It is about the discourse of the other in all its metaphysical (in atemporal memory and imagination) and physical (in body, time, and geography) parameters. In short, it is about the constitution of selfhood as the interlinkage of personal experience and historical process and about the coextensivity between language and cultural space. In language, the immigrant subject experiences passages and re-members fragments of past lives. This remembrance may not correspond to the actual voyage, but it is the only available evidence for self-representation.

In a period when writing and reading ethnography is the object of much debate, the autobiographical writings of first- and second-generation immigrants of postindustrial societies suggest mulitperspectival ways of understanding cultural identity and difference. Modern anthropology's growing interest in the literary and allegorical dimensions of its writing has shifted the concern from the veracity and accuracy of personal narratives to an understanding of these as texts created in specific discursive conditions. The personal narrative is no longer seen as a mere record of a life but as the text of a life constituted in writing and interpretation. The interpretive strategies and protocols of a specific culture are inevitably deployed in personal narratives and determine the conditions and constraints of their articulation. In this context, autobiographies, memoirs, parents' biographies, and autobiographical and biographical fictions written by immigrants, exiles, displaced persons, and expatriates constitute a translation and representation of culture(s) in both theory and practice. They define culture not as a site of birthrights and blood rites but rather as one of translation and transfusion. In discussing the status of writers transported "across the world" into foreign soil and diction, Rushdie uses the term, "translated men." This translation, he insists, is an expansion of idiom rather than its loss: "It is normally supposed that something always gets lost in translation; I cling, obstinately, to the notion that something can also be gained."[5]

In "Ethnicity and the Post-Modern Arts of Memory," Michael M. J. Fischer writes that ethnic autobiography and modern theories of textuality "can revitalize our ways of thinking about how culture operates and refashions our practice of ethnography as a mode of cultural criticism." He suggests that,

> just as the travel account and the ethnography served as forms for the explo-
> ration of the "primitive" world . . . and the realist novel served as the form for
> explorations of bourgeois manners and the self in the early industrial
> society, so ethnic autobiography and autobiographical fiction can perhaps
> serve as key forms for explorations of pluralist, postindustrial, late twentieth-
> century society.[6]

However, Fischer argues that autobiographical texts that focus on the problematics of ethnicity cannot be adequately understood in terms of sociological categories such as group solidarity, family values, political mobilization, and enfranchisement. Similarly, the wealth and diversity of autobiographical acts by writers of many ethnic/immigrant groups cannot be reduced to neat, unambiguous models and boxed into generic categories such as documentary fiction, "autoethnography," ethnic novel, and the like. To initiate a critical discussion of the nature of immigrant writing, I shall attempt to delineate some common textual particulars operative in these "nongeneric" genres. It should also be mentioned that ethnic literatures of the United States have entered a critically transformative stage marked not only by literary innovation but also by theoretical self-reflexion. This investigation will focus on (a) the predominantly autobiographical nature of immigrant writing; (b) the celebration of the past and present languages of the writing subject in the reconstitution of a new self, history, and geography; and (c) the "collective" authorship of immigrant texts that reflect the conflicting politics and ideologies of the groups they represent. The naming of these features should not be read as quantitative or qualitative markers on any absolute scale. These markers constitute, at best, shorthand allegories subject to (re)vision. Ethnicity is generated, according to Fischer, by "transference, the return of the repressed in new forms."[7] It is characterized by multiple, ambiguous, and contestatory voices and by an impulse for redefinitions that, in turn, become instruments for a critique of self-representation.

The texts discussed here are productions of literary immigrants or their progeny who have left their native lands for various reasons. The site of departure is one perceived to be no longer hospitable. The site of arrival, the new land, in contrast, holds the promise of freedom, opportunity, wealth, and advancement. However, the state between expectation and realization is one marked by the panic of loss, the labor of salvaging what is lost to memory, and the struggle between what Werner Sollors has called descent and consent, that is, broadly speaking, preservation of inherited cultural identity and assimilation into the host culture. Recalling the development of the historical awareness of ethnicity in America, Sollors surmises that the tension between the rejection of hereditary old-world hierarchies (embodied by the European nobility) and the vision of a new people of diverse nativities in the fair pursuit of happiness marks the course that American ideology has steered between descent and consent. It is this conflict which is at the root of ambiguity surrounding the very terminology of American ethnic interaction.[8]

Sollors further states that the conflicts between consent and descent that inform American literature "can tell us much about the creation of an American culture out of diverse pre-American pasts."[9] Criticizing this conciliatory view of the conflicts in American culture, Ramón Saldívar counters that the construction of a "monolithic American 'ethnicity' within a single critical framework" threatens to move "beyond ethnicity toward the formation of a unitary American culture."[10] Saldívar correctly points out that Sollors's neat categorization of descent and consent only applies to "the ruling group or their educational, cultural, and political state apparatuses."[11] It is clear that the reference point of Sollors's model is the duality of descent and dissent (from ancestral tradition) among groups of Western European descent who claim a privileged cultural heritage. Saldívar's objections raise the very important question of how genuine differences represented by marginalized groups such as working-class people, people of color, and new immigrants whose cultures resist a seamless integration into a monolithic American ethnicity are to be accounted for in American literary history.

The modern immigrant tales, which are the focus of this investigation, are often accounts of transition from what is perceived to be an unprivileged existence in the homeland to a better life in the affluent host country. However, the account is rarely a tale of joy. It often barely masks the pain and anger inflicted by the high cost of the voyage. These transitions never entail an unproblematic integration. Most immigrant tales incorporate implicitly or explicitly a critique of the "mythology" of America as a land of opportunity and further debunk the myth that life in an affluent, industrialized, self-avowedly democratic society is liberating. Nevertheless, both the celebration and the discomfort of migration have unleashed a creative cultural force that has complemented and enriched the American literary traditions-in-the-making. "America, a nation of immigrants," observes Rushdie, "has created great literature out of the phenomenon of cultural transplantation, out of examining the ways in which people can cope with a new world."[12] Beyond and above defining strategies of coping, these works urge literary conventions and institutions to perform an act of critical self-examination. As Guillermo Gómez-Peña notes,

We practice the epistemology of multiplicity and a border semiotics. We share certain thematic interests, like the continual clash with cultural otherness, the crisis of identity, or, better said, access to trans- and multiculturalism, and the

destruction of borders therefrom; the creation of alternative cartographies, a
ferocious critique of the dominant culture of both countries, and, lastly, a proposal for new creative languages.[13]

The diversity of modern immigrant writing will not lend itself to abstract
categorization. The act of abstraction and theorizing presupposes the loss
of distinction and difference, as Nietzsche has so cogently argued in his
short essay, "Truth and Lie in an Extra-Moral Sense."[14] With that in mind,
the following reading of selected texts attempts to understand the operation
of oral, rhetorical, metaphorical, and reconstitutive impulses of immigrant
writing that lend it its intercultural and liberating force. This writing is often informed by critical vigilance, for it constantly negotiates between its
conflicting impulses of (past) genealogy and (present) geography and
memory and invention. The invisible presence of ancestral traditions controls the dichotomies of descent and consent and enforces interpretive negotiations during rites of cultural passage.

THE IMMIGRANT WRITES OF PASSAGE

Modern immigrant writing is almost exclusively autobiographical in nature.
It defies and redefines the boundaries of the genre. The long-standing critical debate about the status of autobiography as a genre and about the textual conventions that define autobiography has produced volumes on the
elusive act of self-portraiture. In *The Forms of Autobiography*, William C.
Spengemann names "historical self-explanation, philosophical self-scrutiny,
poetic self-expression, and poetic self-invention"[15] as the definitive formal
strategies of self-representation in the genealogy of autobiography. These
strategies are incorporated into immigrant writing in varying degrees and
are closely linked to the concepts of collective authorship and the dialogic
relationship of languages the subject inhabits. Many "novels" by first- or
second-generation immigrants are thinly veiled autobiographies or ancestral biographies. Such is Amy Tan's first novel, the runaway best-seller *The
Joy Luck Club* (1989), a tale of immigrant Chinese women and their Ameri-
canized daughters. This book defines itself as a work of fiction but is, in effect, the author's re-collection of the stories told by her mother and other
women of the storytelling club who meet regularly as a panacea to their
never-lessening isolation and alienation in a new culture. Another significant contribution to the repertoire of autobiographical fictions is Oscar
Hijuelos's *Our House in the Last World* (1983), an account of his family's
move to New York City from Cuba.[16] What makes *Our House* a fictionalized
account of what is obviously an autobiographical narration is the author's
rejection of an authorial narrator. Thus the referential dimension of
Hijuelos's story perpetually shifts. The narrating self is never the absolute
narrator here. The voice of the narrator constantly yields to that of his

mother whose "last world" is literally populated by ghosts. Every advance on
the path to her assimilation into the new culture turns to dissimilation by
the dictates of ghosts. For the mother, the family tree is not a mere representation in books, pictures, or records but a living presence. The narrator
lets the mother perform her ghost show, though not always suppressing the
ironic traces of his own limits of understanding her. Recounting his mother
Mercedes's youth in Holguín, the narrator mentions how the ghost of her
father, Teodoro, often appeared to her. She

> sometimes saw his ghost. Resting in bed, she would hear a noise and see on
> the wall a sprinkling of light, like the sun rippling on water, and her father
> would appear for a moment, shaking his head. Or she and Doña Maria would
> go to the cemetery, pray for his soul and come home to find him in the living
> room looking for something.[17]

These ghosts of her lost land accompany Mercedes all the way to the last
world to make her life there bearable. They embody, like memories, the lost
presence that can no longer be re-collected as concrete evidence of a life.

What is designated as fiction in *Our House* has "the status of remembered
fact."[18] Of course, autobiographical features in works of fiction have always
been a part of literary convention and do not subvert our expectations of
the genre of fiction. And, conversely, life stories of modern immigrants have
radically transformed reader expectations of autobiography. These writers
do not see the presence of fictionalized experience in their accounts as a
threat to the validity of autobiography. Paul de Man has rigorously investi-
gated the intricate negotiations between autobiography and fiction to thematize the sense of undecidability that challenges the assumed unity of the
autobiographical subject. The genre of autobiography has traditionally
been a form of an account of a life actually lived and factually experienced.
It "seems to depend on actual and potentially verifiable events in a less am-
bivalent fashion than fiction does. It seems to belong to a simpler mode of
referentiality, of representation and of diegesis." Although autobiographical elements contain dreams, fantasies, and illusions, such fabulations,
nevertheless, "remain rooted in a single subject whose identity is defined by
the uncontestable readability of his proper name." But the weight of this
proper name does not necessarily ensure an unambiguous referentiality.
We may assume that the facts of one's life produce autobiography, but is it
not equally possible "that the autobiographical project may itself produce
and determine the life and whatever the writer *does* is in fact governed by
the technical demands of self-portraiture and thus determined, in all its aspects, by the resources of his medium"?[19]

A notable case in point is Nicholas Gage's international best-seller, *Eleni,*
a thinly veiled autobiography presented as the tragic and courageous life
story of his mother, who was killed by Communist guerrillas during the

Greek civil war, and as the history of the Greek civil war as experienced by the peasants of the Greek village of Lia near the Albanian border. Is Gage's life produced by his relentless search for the murderers of his mother and his consuming desire for revenge and justice? In explicit negation of this question, Gage reiterates at every turn that his account is scrupulously researched, recorded, and verified and that his credentials as a top *New York Times* investigative reporter will not allow anything less than totally accurate record to go into print. "Every incident described in this book that I did not witness personally [that is almost everything in the book], writes Gage in an afternote,

> was described to me by at least two people who were interviewed independently of each other. All the interviews were recorded—secretly in the case of uncooperative witnesses—and translated into English by me. . . . All the skills learned and sharpened during my two decades as an investigative reporter were put to use in this most difficult and important investigation of my life; the reason I became a journalist in the first place.[20]

Ironically, this last statement subverts Gage's insistence on the absolute reliability of his account and the certainty that his and his mother's interlinked destinies have produced this joint biography-autobiography. Because he writes this passionate account as an obsession to right a wrong and because of his persuasive and artful prose, we are convinced of the guilt of the villagers apparently responsible for his mother's death and of his own sense of sacrifice, valor, and justice. However, there is no acknowledgment in this text that its narrative voice is not merely recounting the so-called facts of his and his mother's lives but rather represents Gage's elaborate speculative investigations about his mother's fate. The latter case, of course, transforms the referent(s) of this biography-autobiography into a fiction in the sense de Man has argued. Without a trace of self-reflective irony, the mother's reconstituted life becomes the pre-text of a Greek-American journalist's success as an investigative reporter.

Gage's book is masterfully written with raw emotion and rage and draws amply on suspense, mystery, and revelation, all staples of the detective story genre. Gage then produced a film based on his book. True to Hollywood expectations and ethos, the elements of suspense, horror, and the recurring dichotomous metaphor of bad guys/good guys (in this case, also highly politically colored) combined to make a watchable film. However, there is not a moment's worth of critical reflection and self-consciousness of fictiveness in Gage's book. In other words, Gage never stops to ponder the highly interpretive nature of the witness accounts, the role of hearsay, superstition, or failed or repressed memory that have shaped his own narrative. A sequel to this book, *A Place for Us: Eleni's Children in America* (1989), is also a nostalgic, idealized, and ideologically and patriotically colored account of growing up in America. This account is disarmingly personal but also, like *Eleni*, disturbingly unacknowledging of its own constitution as an act of story-telling. Again Gage writes as a "reporter," and although every chapter is pref-aced by quotations from well-known literary figures, he will not allow the literary to threaten the solidity of his-story.

Most autobiographies by immigrant writers, however, are celebrations of storytelling and a ready acknowledgment of the deconstructive effect of time and the reconstructive role of imagination. In *Lost in Translation*, Hoffman writes,

> The reference points in my head are beginning to do a flickering dance. I sup-pose this is the most palpable meaning of displacement. I have been dislo-cated from my own center of the world, and that world has been shifted away from my center. There is no longer a straight axis anchoring my imagination; it begins to oscillate, and I rotate around it unsteadily.[21]

Perhaps the absolute contrast to Gage's account is Maxine Hong Kingston's highly acclaimed *Woman Warrior: Memoirs of a Girlhood among Ghosts*. Here Kingston purposefully recasts her mother's accounts of their family history in alternative, fablelike, dreamlike settings in order to reclaim a forgotten past as an infinitely renewable and only re-presentable present. In this representation, she is freed from her double bind (and hyphenation) as a Chinese-American girl-child, marginalized not only by the American cul-ture but also by her own, which considers raising geese more profitable than raising daughters[22] and is much too fond of aphorisms like "when fishing for treasures in the flood, be careful not to pull in girls."[23] "There is a Chi-nese word for the female *I* which is 'slave,'" observes Kingston. "Break the women with their own tongues!"[24]

Kingston, thus, sets out with a vengeance to reclaim in a powerful lan-guage a life of honor, valor, and accomplishment that she feels has been de-nied her by cultural dictates. In this case, it is clearly the autobiography that re-produces the life. The reinvention of Maxine is facilitated by the talk-stories her mother, Brave Orchid, relates. In one such story, Brave Orchid narrates the tale of Fa-Mu-Lan, the woman warrior. In the person of this leg-endary figure, Maxine finds the context that links her both to her native cul-ture and to America. Like Fa-Mu-Lan, Maxine too has words on her back that need to be avenged. However, unlike Fa-Mu-Lan, Maxine's revenge in-volves "not the beheading, not the gutting, but the words."[25] In an interview, Kingston said that we all had the burden to figure out the reconfigurations of so-called facts in poetic imagination, to understand how "raw human event" is put through "the process of art."[26] Her poetic pilgrimage starts with the objective of restoring to language and memory a disgraced aunt who killed herself and her illegitimate child after giving birth. The family erased any trace of this aunt from memory and history by denying her a story and

a name. Kingston rewrites the story of the No Name Woman not in terms of
what has been said about her in her mother's narrative but as a tale that provides alternative scripts of her life. Through these imagined scripts, Maxine
reestablishes her familial links with her aunt in an attempt to reclaim her
cultural past: "Unless I see her life branching into mine, she gives me no ancestral help."[27] This configuration of biography-autobiography remembers
a life and events. The actual life and events may have been very different.
The reconfigured past is all that matters. "We can change the past by figuring out new meanings of events that took place,"[28] observes Kingston, and
this is precisely what happens in *The Woman Warrior*, where the oppressed
and forgotten women are resurrected and given a new history through the
legend of Fu-Mu-Lan.

LANGUAGE AS RECOVERY AND CELEBRATION

Just as Kingston's *Warrior* rewrites the past in the code of poetic imagination, Eva Hoffman's *Lost in Translation* reinvents self, geography, and genealogy in the mastery of a new language. Hoffman's autobiography is
written in the form of a reflection on language as the construct of mediation between the lost culture and the found one, helplessness and mastery,
and memory and anticipation. By remembering, reappropriating, and alle-
gorizing in language, the ethnic immigrant subject invents a new cultural
space for her personal and communal self. In *Fictions in Autobiography*, Paul
John Eakin correctly observes that "the writing of autobiography emerges
as the second acquisition of language, a second coming into being of self, a
self-conscious self-consciousness."[29] Thus, the autobiographical act duplicates the gestures of all metafictional texts that reflect on their own construction to suggest that our experience of reality is similarly constructed.
For the immigrant writer, the writing of autobiography goes beyond the
second acquisition of language. It represents a metadiscourse that accounts
for the acquisition of the second language in which the autobiography
itself is written. Often the mastery of this second language is the immigrant child's dream of grandeur. Kingston, Gage, Hoffman, and Richard
Rodriguez, in *The Hunger of Memory*, recount with relish and nostalgia their
obsession with acquiring language and nourishing their souls with the substance of words. Kingston comes to terms with her marginalized status in
both cultures by transforming the tradition of the talk-story and recharging
it with new meanings. She creates a new identity for herself and her forgotten aunt by translating her mother's talk-stories into written stories and re-
situating them in her hyphenated culture.

Rodriguez calls his autobiography "a book about language." "I write
about poetry," he reflects, "the new Roman Catholic liturgy; learning to
read; writing; political terminology. Language has been the great subject of

my life. In college and graduate school, I was registered as an 'English major.' But well before then, from my first day of school, I was a student of language. Obsessed with the way it determined my public identity."[30] The new language is the most distinct marker of the cherished public identity in the new culture. For all these writers it is also a compensation for the loss or absence of a supporting native culture, a very concrete experience of the acquisition of power and of the resolution of the outsider's resentment and rage. The possession of this acquired language makes them often aware of their privileged status with regard to those who are voiceless in their own language. Hoffman often reminisces about filling herself "with the material of language"[31] and is constantly reminded of how the proper mastery of language fortifies the subject against a hostile world. In a telling account, she reflects on the rage bottled up in the lame four-letter words brandished by ghetto youths.

> In my New York apartment, I listen almost nightly to fights that erupt like brushfire on the street below—and in their escalating fury of repetitious phrases ("Don't do this to me, man, you fucking bastard, I'll fucking kill you"). I hear not the pleasures of macho toughness but an infuriated beating against wordlessness, against the incapacity to make oneself understood, seen.[32]

Language is not only an empowering but also a redeeming practice. "Anger can be borne—it can be satisfying—if it can gather into words and explode in a storm," continues Hoffman, "but without this means of ventilation, it only turns back inward, building and swirling like a head of steam—building to an impotent, murderous rage. If all therapy is speaking therapy—a talking cure—then perhaps all neurosis is a speech dis-ease." Thus, mastery of the language of the "native speaker" reclaims with a healthy vengeance the social and cultural space from which the immigrant subject was banned as a result of exclusionary discursive practices. The pride of mastering the second language better than the native speaker is its own utmost reward. In this vein, Rushdie, discussing the reasons for British Indian writers' choice of English as their medium of literary expression, states, "To conquer English may be to complete the process of making ourselves free."[33]

These autobiographical texts explore in their themes, tropes, and representations and reconfigurations of experience the conceptual dimension of the act of writing itself as a political, emancipatory practice and investigate the tensions and conflicts traversing literary discourse in marginalized societies. Positioned in the treacherous shifts from the slippage of the past self to the claim of the present one, the immigrant writes in a language born of crisis and change, of translation and transplantation, a language that creates the symbols of a new reality. The writer salvages from a lost time, space, and culture symbolic fragments and reconfigures these as markers of a recharged personal and collective history. In the final analysis, finding words for spacelessness becomes an invention of a different space or the creation of a different concept of space. This is an internal rather than external space, a space that does not mimic that of the native but one that re-presents a reflected sense of being—a being that incorporates having been. In this sense, "ethnic discourse is finally free to become a sober instrument of cultural construction without regrets over a lost world of mimetic reproduction. . . . In fact, ethnocultural construction is itself a possible world among others, a different strategy for creating a world of referents."[34]

The dialogic and self-reflexive tone of immigrant writing marks a space of intervention in the cultural contexts in which it moves. This writing registers its distance from social and cultural norms by questioning the logic of the traditions it has inherited as well as those it is subjected to in the new world. As a presentation of a pastiche of conversations, of parable and allegory, it further defies any form of controlled narrative. "A given space (text) will support more life (generate more meanings)," writes François Lionnet, "if occupied by diverse forms of life (languages)."[35] These diverse languages manifest themselves as a conversation between opposing voices or as conflicting self-perceptions of ethnic groups. The immigrant's text of self represents a desire both for liberation and for transgression and danger. It is also another form of self-exclusion. Rodriguez was criticized for opposing bilingual education. He argued that it only led to a perpetuation of the failure to acquire English whose mastery is the immigrant's only access to relative success. His public display of the privacy of his family proved to be a blow to their traditional sensibilities and generated hurt feelings and reproachful responses. Thus, the narrator is caught in an ambiguous, self-ironic discourse of guilt, doubt, conflicting loyalties or preferences. This discourse legitimizes its own ambivalence by deploying tropes of double meaning, such as metaphor, allegory, and irony.

Kingston uses the allegories of the fantastic to subvert the order and logic of her family stories. The ghosts that populate her own versions are "the bizarre fragments of past, tradition, and familial self-overprotectiveness that must be externalized and tamed."[36] In Hijuelos's *Our House,* dreams and ghosts are metaphors of understanding and explanation. These nebulous figures set off a process in language that engages meaning with indeterminacy and leads to displacement of the self in the larger cultural context. The subject becomes an intertextual agency, positioned between texts of the new world and the old. This subject reaches beyond the cultural text of parents and ancestors and looks for ruptures in the dominant text in which to inscribe itself. As in the old storytelling tradition, interweaving of fable, dream, memory, and cold, hard facts of daily life becomes a blueprint for a reinvented reality. The last chapter of Hijuelos's *Our House,* "Voices from the Last World," is a narrative reconciliation of the realities of the lost and last worlds. After their father Alejo's death, Mercedes's two sons, Horacio and Hector, who had been alienated from their mother, mimic her never-ending indulgence in dreams and memories. Horacio tells of a dream about their father come back to life. Hector goes back in memories that stubbornly fade but that he always writes "down in a black-and-white notebook, the kind my mother writes poetry in."[37] But it is Mercedes, the mad poetess, whose visions defy reason and logic, who has the last word. Mercedes goes back in time, in a time machine of her own construction, which she calls rein-carnation, beyond the history of her known ancestors to the history of their primordial Spanish homeland. The novel ends on Mercedes's story of her previous life as a maid in Queen Isabella's castle during the time of Christopher Columbus. In Mercedes's voice, the voice of the storyteller-medium, the occluded histories of the oral cultures of several centuries are revalorized and reclaimed and, finally, reconciled with the present. The poetic voice becomes the reincarnated body of the lost culture.

In the construction of ethnic or intercultural identity, the subject rewrites the past. On revisiting her native Cracow, Hoffmann observes that

one has to rewrite the past in order to understand it. I have to see Cracow in the dimensions it has to my adult eye in order to perceive that my story has been only a story, that none of its events has been so big or so scary. It is the price of emigration, as of any radical discontinuity, that it makes such reviews and rereadings difficult; being cut off from one part of one's own story is apt to veil it in the haze of nostalgia, which is an ineffectual relationship to the past, and the haze of alienation, which is an ineffectual relationship to the present.[38]

This irony toward one's own memory is the essence of an ongoing critique—of self, past, community—in the records of immigrant experience. Because a past time cannot be restored except in image, that image is interlinked with the present. The site of this interlinkage houses a reinvented self that can no longer "offer a faithful and unmediated reconstruction of a histori-cally verifiable past; instead, it expresses the play of the autobiographical act itself, in which the materials of the past are shaped by memory and imagi-nation to serve the needs of present consciousness."[39] By reclaiming in memory and imagination a lost genealogy and geography and subjecting it to interrogation, the ethnic subject "opens a new inferencing field in which he can re-present the crisis of cultural foundations in a critical light."[40]

DISPERSED AUTHORSHIP

The autobiographical self in immigrant writing is not a unified subject. The possibility of self-representation is intricately linked to a collective memory and represents explicitly or implicitly conflicts with past and present contexts. The struggle against language (of oppression and exclusion) goes on in language (of affirmation, self-assertion, and critical response). Rodriguez, for example, is very explicit about the confused and confusing ideology of affirmative action that excludes many forms of difference. While writing his dissertation, he was deluged by lucrative academic job offers. Aware of the bitter irony of his privileged status, he questions the inherent exclusivity of affirmative action.

> The policy of affirmative action, however, was never able to distinguish some-one like me (a graduate student of English, ambitious for a college teaching career) from a slightly educated Mexican-American who lived in a barrio and worked as a menial laborer, never expecting a future improved. Worse, affirmative action made me the beneficiary of this condition. Such was the foolish logic of this program of social reform: Because many Hispanics were absent from higher education, I became with my matriculation an exception, a numerical minority.[41]

Obviously, these opinions did not gain Rodriguez many admirers either among the well-meaning American supporters of affirmative action or among his fellow Chicanos. He became the object of bitter criticism in both camps. However, among immigrant writers he is not alone in his sentiments. Their writing often becomes an instrument of criticism, directed at both the homefront and the host front. To find their own critical voice, these writers distance themselves from the practices of the dominant culture as well as from those of their own families and ethnic groups and strike out alone. Both Hoffman and Rodriguez chose the path of writing rather than that of academe, though both hold advanced degrees from top research universities. They and countless others, in their pursuit of creative and critical writing, reinvest the knowledge gained in language back in language and keep vigil at the boundaries of social, cultural, and political consciousness. Rodriguez's decision not to accept any one of the numerous offers of professorship from prestigious universities, a conscious protest against academic pretenses and false expectations, has led to the bitter disappointment of his family, who expected him to have a steady profession and hoped against hope that he would someday teach "at some Catholic college." Furthermore, the very act of autobiographical writing was seen as a violation of family privacy. After publishing his first autobiographical essay, Rodriguez received a letter from his mother, pleading with him never to write about the family again and reproaching him for telling the "gringos" how "divided" he feels from his own family. The price of self-reflexion, of subjection to the scrutiny of critical language, is often the disappointment and disapproval of one's own community. The alienation from all collective selves and the lonely vigil on the margins of two societies is the price of the success of writing, of the victory of language.

The precarious existence of the immigrant, the ethnic subject inside and outside communities, creates an unsettled and unsettling border culture. Gloria Anzaldúa begins her autobiography, *Borderlands/ La Frontera: The New Mestiza*, with the following observation:

> The U.S. Mexican border *es una herida abierta* where the Third World grates against the first and bleeds. And before a scab forms it hemorrhages again, the lifeblood of the two worlds merging to form a third country—a border culture. Borders are set up to define the places that are safe and unsafe, to distinguish *us* from *them*. A border is a dividing line, a narrow strip along a steep edge. A borderland is a vague and undetermined place created by the emotional residue of an unnatural boundary. It is in a constant state of transition.[42]

However, there is an exhilarating sense of rejuvenation and dynamism that is generated by being a new *mestiza*, as Anzaldúa states in the preface to her book. The book speaks of the preoccupations of the ethnic subject "amidst adversity and violation; with the confluence of primordial images; with the unique positionings consciousness takes at these confluent streams." This confluence of times and images urges the subject "to communicate, to speak, to write about life on the borders."[43] This communication often takes the form of a dialogic encounter with parents and ancestors, which helps the subject to reinvent an empowering identity. Through an identification with or rejection, reconsideration, reacceptance, borrowing, and extension of others' stories, the subject inherits a history. In both of Nicholas Gage's books, his mother, Eleni, is the memory that shapes the material destinies of the family. Through thick and thin, the financially struggling family pulls together, jolted into action and solidarity by the memory of the mother who died so that her children could be in America. Gage himself goes on to professional success motivated by the desire to revenge his mother's executors. Hijuelos and Kingston come to terms with their histories through the stories of their families as told by their mothers. In their tales of affiliation and disaffiliation, these narrators necessarily inhabit more than a single position of the speaking subject. In these (hi)stories, alterity assumes the form of dialogic imagination where the constitution of plural selves is seen as an enabling and liberating force that rejects polarizing notions of identity, race, and culture.

The act of rewriting is also an act of reflective repositioning, since it entails rethinking and resorting. In this act, the languages and discourses of the lost world and the "last world" engage in an investigative dialogue. In "Campus Forum on Multiculturalism," published in the *New York Times* of December 9, 1990, Renato Rosaldo, professor of anthropology at Stanford University, views multiculturalism "as a tool for grappling with vexed issues." He states that "educational democracy will not come easily" and involves what he calls "questions of cultural citizenship." Rosaldo, then, poses the fol-

lowing questions: "How can diverse groups retain their diversity and participate in a democratic community? Can they be full and equal citizens who
enjoy the privilege of shaping their destiny? Can they do so without having
to surrender their heritages?"[44] Multicultural citizenship unfortunately often comes under attack by those who are addicted to prescriptions and formulaic cures for the tired canon. Lest we cherish the illusion that we have
come a long way in our understanding and appreciation of ethnicity and
cultural diversity, I would like to quote a few remarks by distinguished pro-
fessors of *humanities* (emphasis mine) who resist the critical discourse that a
diversity of cultural perspectives has the chance of establishing. Their anger
is freely vented in the above mentioned "Campus Forum on Multiculturalism." "Consider the endless possibilities political correctness holds out for
research and publication, especially in the field of literature," writes John E.
Becker, director of the Core Curriculum at Fairleigh Dickenson University
in New Jersey, with not-so-subtle sarcasm. "Each new critical weapon opens
the whole Western textual tradition to a new campaign of slash and burn."
Sandra Stotsky, director of the Summer Institute on Writing, Reading, and
Civic Education at Harvard University's Graduate School of Education is
deeply perturbed by the "Europhobia" in high schools. "Most pre-college
students are too naïve to understand how university-trained teachers or
curriculum developers are manipulating them," she claims, "and school
committees and parents are usually totally unaware of what is going on because the Europhobia, national self-hatred and inter-ethnic hostilities that
these orthodoxies are promoting have been cleverly disguised by current
buzz words like multiculturalism, critical thinking, and diversity." And
Frederic T. Sommers, professor of philosophy at Brandeis University,
chimes in: "When the intellectual is political, the light of reason goes out."[45]
    These outbursts reflect the by now familiar sentiment against the so-
called political correctness issue on campuses. Clearly, these distinguished
educators are threatened by the possibility that other languages, cultures,
and texts that they obviously do not consider worth studying may make
claims on the curriculum. What is to become of their privileged status as
Knights of the High Order of Western Civilization? Obviously, they are prepared to go to great lengths to preserve the sanctity and legitimacy of what
they perceive to be their own superior intellectual training. The new bar-
barians are at the gates and must be stopped, or else the high culture as we
know it will cease to be. There is, of course, at work here a willed misinter-
pretation of diversity as the destruction of the so-called canon for the sake
of dubious curricular innovations that promote literary works of even more
dubious merit. What these critics, afflicted by a bad case of tunnel vision,
can or will not see is that literary cultural study is historically, socially, geographically conditioned, and a call for the inclusion of the underrepre-
sented literatures of minorities and immigrants is not an act of canon

bashing but one of critical engagement with the cultural (*mestizo*) mosaic that America has come to represent. Furthermore, at a time of overwhelming demographic shifts, when vast numbers of Middle Easterners and North Africans have permanently settled in Europe and the question of European identity has become the focus of an ongoing critical debate, it is rather naive, if not outright moronic, to talk of "Europhobia." The issue is clearly one of fear and mistrust of unfamiliar intellectual heritages that claim to be such. The problem is not "Europhobia"—let us get rid of this *buzzword* while we are at it, since it is not to be found in any respectable dictionary—but xenophobia. Granted, phobias may be less deadly in expression than they are in repression. Nevertheless, these phobias are clear testimony to Henry Louis Gates, Jr.'s observation that such self-serving ethnocentrism is "an attempt to deprive the black human being [and I might add, any person of color or representative of minority groups] of even the potential to create art, to imagine a world and figure it."[46]

Antidiversity sentiments and explicit and implicit institutional practices and exclusionary discourses terrorize and traumatize every citizen of the "Borderlands" where "two or more cultures edge each other, where people of different races occupy the same territory, where under, lower, middle, and upper classes touch."[47] The merger of times, memories, and images in the experience of migration and displacement moves the notion of borderlands from its traditional semantic domain, which designates a certain geographic location, to a domain of political, historical, and cultural experiences. Not only the border but also the foreign (land) beyond the border can no longer be mere drawings on a map. They can no longer be geographically defined but rather need to be understood in their temporal, sociocultural, and emotive contexts. Gino Chiellino, an Italian poet living and writing in Germany, defines the untranslatable word "die Fremde"[48] as "nicht mehr geographisch, sondern als Ort der Geschichte . . . wo Vergangenheit und Zukunft gleicher maßen zu entwerfen sind" (no longer geographically but as the place of history where the past and the future are equally projected).[49]

Against the odds and in the face of resistance, oppression, and disregard, border residents transform the social spaces they inhabit by turning the challenges they face into a resource for cultural reinvigoration. The self-recorded life stories of many Chicano authors, for example, represent a "preeminently political act seeking to fulfill the potentialities of contemporary life." In the final analysis, these textual productions are also "an attempt to recall the originary myths of life on the borders of power in order to fashion triumphantly a new, heterogeneous American consciousness, within the dialectics of difference."[50] Along these lines, in a very insightful article about the literary production of the new minorities in Germany, Ülker Gökberk states that the emerging literatures of these groups fulfill an important task by providing German readers with a guide for coexistence with minorities.

They do this by reorganizing "the German language, a language of a homogeneous society, toward one including the experience of diversity."[51] This experience challenges cultural isolationism and promotes a new consciousness of participation in a genuinely democratic process in which not merely the will of majority rules but where each group is granted self-expression and representation. Anzaldúa, Rodriguez, Hoffman, Hijuelos, Kingston, and numerous others aspire to responsible "cultural citizenship," while celebrating in the power of word, memory, and imagination the reclaimed legacy of cultures whose emotional and intellectual force had too long been eclipsed by the monolingual and monocultural parochialism that misrepresented itself as successful assimilation and acculturation.

NOTES

1. Eva Hoffman. *Lost in Translation: A Life in a New Language* (London and New York: Penguin, 1989):197.

2. See, for example, Jean Baudrillard's "The Precession of Simulacra," in his *Simulations,* trans. Paul Foss, Paul Patton, and Philip Beitchman (New York: Semiotext[e], 1983):1–79.

3. W. J. T. Mitchell, "Representation," in *Critical Terms in Literary Study,* ed. Frank Lentricchia and Thomas McLaughlin (Chicago and London: University of Chicago Press, 1990). 11–22, 21.

4. Stephen A. Tyler, "Post-Modern Ethnography: From Document of the Occult to Occult Document," in *Writing Culture: The Politics and Poetics of Ethnography,* ed. James Clifford and George E. Marcus (Berkeley, Los Angeles, and London: University of California Press 1986): 122–140, 138–139.

5. Salman Rushdie, "Imaginary Homelands," in his *Imaginary Homelands* (New York and London: Penguin):9–21, 17.

6. Michael M. J. Fischer, "Ethnicity and the Post-Modern Arts of Memory," in *Writing Culture,* 194–233, 195.

7. Ibid., 207.

8. Werner Sollors, *Beyond Ethnicity: Consent and Descent in American Culture* (New York and Oxford: Oxford University Press 1986): 4–5.

9. Ibid., 6.

10. Ramón Saldívar, *Chicano Narrative: The Dialectics of Difference* (Madison: University of Wisconsin Press, 1990): 217.

11. Ibid., 216.

12. Rushdie, "Imaginary Homelands," 20.

13. Guillermo Gómez-Peña, "Documented/Undocumented," trans. Rubén Martínez, in *The Graywolf Annual Five, Multi-Cultural Literacy,* ed. Rick Simonson and Scott Walter (Saint Paul: Graywolf Press, 1988): 127–134, 130.

14. Friedrich Nietzsche, "On Truth and Lying in an Extra-Moral Sense," in *Friedrich Nietzsche on Rhetoric and Language,* ed. and trans. with a critical introduction by Sander L. Gilman, Carole Blair, and David J. Parent (Oxford and New York: Oxford University Press, 1989): 246–257.

15. William C. Spengemann, *The Forms of Autobiography: Episodes in the History of a Literary Genre* (New Haven and London: Yale University Press, 1980): xvi.

16. Hijuelos's second book, a fictionalized biography of an uncle. *The Mambo Kings Play Songs of Love*, won the Pulitzer Prize.

17. Oscar Hijuelos. *Our House in the Last World* (1983; rpt. New York, London, Toronto, Sydney, Tokyo, and Singapore: Washington Square Press, 1990): 18.

18. Paul John Eakin, *Fictions in Autobiography: Studies in the Act of Self-Invention* (Princeton: Princeton University Press, 1985): 7.

19. Paul de Man, "Autobiography as De-facement," *Modern Language Notes* 94 (1979): 919–930, 920.

20. Nicholas Gage, "A Note from the Author," in *Eleni* (1983; rpt. New York: Ballantine Books, 1985): 624–625.

21. Hoffman, *Lost in Translation*, 132.

22. Maxine Hong Kingston, *The Woman Warrior: Memoirs of a Girlhood Among Ghosts* (1975; rpt. New York: Vintage Books, 1989): 46.

23. Ibid., 52.

24. Ibid., 47.

25. Ibid., 53.

26. Kingston, *Bill Moyers: A World of Ideas II: Public Opinions from Private Citizens*, ed. Andie Tucher (New York, London, Toronto, Sydney, and Auckland, 1990): 11–18, 11.

27. Kingston, *Warrior*, 8.

28. Kingston, *Bill Moyers*, 17.

29. Eakin, *Fictions in Autobiography*, 9.

30. Richard Rodriguez, *The Hunger of Memory, The Education of Richard Rodriguez: An Autobiography* (1982; rpt. Boston: Bantam, 1988): 7.

31. Hoffman, *Lost in Translation*, 191.

32. Ibid., 124.

33. Rushdie, "Imaginary Homelands," 17.

34. William Boelhower, *Through a Glass Darkly: Ethnic Semiosis in American Literature* (New York and Oxford: Oxford University Press, 1987): 132–133.

35. François Lionnet, *Autobiographical Voices: Race, Gender, Self-Portraiture* (Ithaca and London: Cornell University Press, 1989): 18.

36. Fischer, "Ethnicity," 210.

37. Hijuelos, *Our House*, 244.

38. Hoffman, *Lost in Translation*, 242.

39. Eakin, *Fictions in Autobiography*, 5.

40. Boelhower, *Through a Glass Darkly*, 140.

41. Rodriguez, *Hunger of Memory*, 150–151.

42. Gloria Anzaldúa, *Borderlands/La Frontera: The New Mestiza* (San Francisco: Aunt Lute Books, 1987): 3.

43. Anzaldúa, preface to *Borderlands*.

44. Renato Rosaldo, "Educational Democracy," *New York Times*, 9 December 1990, E5.

45. Ibid.

46. Henry Louis Gates, Jr., *Black Literature and Literary Theory* (London: Methuen, 1984): 7.

47. Anzaldúa, preface to *Borderlands*.

48. Roughly translated as foreign land. The word also denotes isolation and alienation.

49. Gino Chiellino, "Die Fremde als Ort der Geschichte," in *Eine nicht nur deutsche Literatur*, ed. Irmgard Ackermann and Harald Weinrich (Munich and Zurich: Piper): 13–15, 15.

50. Saldívar, *Chicano Narrative*, 218.

51. Ülker Gökberk, "Understanding Alterity: *Ausländerliteratur* between Relativism and Universalism," in *Theoretical Issues in Literary History*, ed. David Perkins (Cambridge and London: Harvard University Press, 1991): 143–172, 171.

EIGHT

Turks as Subjects:
The Ethnographic Novels of
Paul Geiersbach

Arlene A. Teraoka

Picture the arrival of the German sociologist at his field site, the Turkish ghetto of a large German industrial city in the Ruhr valley.[1] Already at six in the morning the street is filled with countless children and adolescents who witness the strange event. Driving up in his aging but still respectable Ford Granada pulling a trailer filled with furniture, an older, well-dressed man with glasses and graying hair emerges stiff-legged from his car to begin unpacking in full view of his unwanted audience. Paul Geiersbach, painfully aware of the damage being done to his status as German and as intellectual, is embarrassed to be seen.

> Anyone and everyone who passed by stopped to take a look at this strange bird, half in amusement, half critically. In the end there must have been twenty or thirty people gawking, whispering, giggling, or quietly marveling to themselves, at close range or from a distance. . . . No, this was not good! An educated man, not quite young anymore, who was moving his things himself and on top of it all, like this! I should have used INTERRENT or better yet, hired a real moving company.

> Alles und jeder, der vorbeikam, blieb stehen, um halb belustigt, halb kritisch diesen komischen Vogel in Augenschein zu nehmen. Zwanzig Leute waren es am Ende bestimmt oder dreißig, die da von Nahem oder von Ferne glotzten, tuschelten, kicherten oder sich still vor sich hinwunderten. . . . Nein, das war nicht gut! Ein studierter, nicht mehr ganz junger Mann, der seinen Umzug selbst macht und noch dazu so! Ich hätte doch INTERRENT nehmen oder besser noch, eine richtige Umzugsfirma beauftragen sollen.[2]

Once safely ensconced in his apartment, with mixed feelings of anxiety and self-satisfaction, Geiersbach can turn his attention to the chores of cleaning. His first days will be spent washing the floors, putting up wallpaper, and lay-

195

ing down carpet, all to ensure himself a necessary degree of comfort and personal security. "Within my own four walls I want to feel comfortable. Here I want to continue to be Paul Geiersbach, to have a bit of luxury, to feel at home, to be able to shut the door so I can be alone" (In meinen eigenen vier Wänden will ich mich wohlfühlen. Hier will ich weiterhin Paul Geiersbach sein, ein bißchen Komfort haben, mich zu Hause fühlen, die Tür schließen können, um allein zu sein) (W, 15).

After a week of intense scrubbing, painting, plastering, and patching up the apartment and his ego, Geiersbach retrieves his remaining furniture from Hamburg. This time the status-conscious academic plans to arrive in the middle of the night when the streets are deserted and when he can lug sofa and stove into his building unseen. Yet the noisy and intricate maneuvering of the trailer into the courtyard awakens the entire neighborhood, and again, Geiersbach perceives countless Turkish heads in dark windows shaking in disbelief and disapproval as the "Alman" carries the rest of his possessions—and those not of the finest quality, either!—up the stairs to his apartment. The fear that now no one will even believe that he is a "Dr. Geiersbach" sends him into another frenzy of home improvement. Geiersbach pays for a professional carpet layer; he polishes his old furniture, hangs pictures on his walls to enhance the character of each room, and relaxes to the sounds of Brahms on his stereo. For several weeks the precious and private apartment will be the safe haven in which his identity is secure, the fortress from which Geiersbach will watch, from the superior distance of his third-story window, the goings-on in the community that he wants to study and in which he is embarrassed to show his face.

One year and many adventures later, Geiersbach is ready to leave. He is now a well-established face in the community, someone his Turkish and Kurdish neighbors have grown to know, the guest they have invited countless times into their homes, the friend who has shared with them everything from birth, marriage, and family feuds to holy holidays, political rallies, and mystic Sufi trances. But once again, we find Geiersbach trying to hide. With a suitcase full of notes, tapes, and documents, the rich "harvest" of his field research in the ghetto, he feels like a thief leaving the scene of his crime. "As a thief you take your leave inconspicuously. Yes, I saw myself as a thief sneaking away from there" (Als Dieb empfiehlt man sich unauffällig. Ja, als Dieb sah ich mich davonschleichen).[3] The material will result in two volumes about the community that Geiersbach knows will irritate, if not enrage, his Turkish friends and acquaintances, should they even be able to, and want to, read them. The product of his research, Geiersbach knows, will be an irreparable act of betrayal. He chooses a Sunday morning for his departure, expecting that everyone will be asleep. Naturally, the community is up early. Friends and even enemies show up to wish the German researcher farewell, and Geiersbach is forced one last time to face, with guilty conscience, the people who have accepted him into their lives.

> It was therefore a shameless lie when I promised everyone who warmly embraced me once more in farewell that I would see them again soon. I already knew at that point that once the books were finished, I would not be able to look anyone from the colony in the eye again.

> Es war deshalb auch schamlos gelogen, wenn ich jedem, der mich zum Abschied noch einmal herzlich umarmte, ein baldiges Wiedersehen versprach. Ich wußte schon zu dem Zeitpunkt, daß ich, wenn die Bücher einmal fertig wären, niemandem mehr in der Kolonie gerade in die Augen schauen könnte. (G, 428)

The two scenes are more than just amusing; they display a telling twist in the usual encounter between the "subject," the "Self," and its "object," the "Other." At least a part of the irony does not escape Geiersbach himself, who notes in his journal soon after his awkward arrival, "You wanted to slip in here as a voyeur, unrecognized, to observe and sound out the people, and now you are the one being displayed on a platter, observed by everyone" (Du wolltest dich hier unerkannt als Voyeur einschleichen, die Leute beobachten und aushorchen, und jetzt bist du es, der da auf dem Präsentierteller sitzt und von jedermann beobachtet wird) (W, 37). On the basis of his middle-class background, his graduate education, his German nationality, and his Western European culture, Geiersbach stands worlds away from, and above, the Turkish guest workers and Muslim believers of the urban ghetto. As author and social scientist who will record their life for his fellow Germans, Geiersbach wields tremendous discursive power over his Turkish subjects. And yet what we witness in two key scenes is the German intellectual fearing at his arrival the loss of an image of superiority and at his departure, the full recognition of his less than honorable intentions. In one scene, worried about the damage done to his status, Geiersbach hides from view; in the other, he cannot face his Turkish friends, unable to withstand their looks of hurt and anger. In both scenes, it is the "Other" that is perceived as threatening, as the source of social approbation and moral authority, while the "Self" is forced to retreat and to hide its face from view. It is the "Other" that is powerful; the "Self" that is weak and shaken, fearful of being scrutinized, ridiculed, judged, or dismissed. The Turks here are subjects in two interconnected ways: as research subjects, they are open and exposed to the gaze of the ethnographic author; but they also meet that gaze of the Self as other selves. I wish here to explore this resistance of the Other in the subject's own text.[4]

The four ethnographic novels of Paul Geiersbach are rich and instructive for us, both for what they attempt to do and for what happens inadvertently in them. The first two volumes, published in 1982 and 1983, bear the idiomatic and anecdotal titles *Brother, Must Eat Onions and Water Together!* (Bruder, muß zusammen Zwiebel und Wasser essen!) and *How Mutlu Öztürk Must Learn to Swim* (Wie Mutlu Öztürk schwimmen lernen muß).[5] Abandoning the quantitative methods and research models of traditional sociology, Geiersbach explores a form of writing that attempts to record the actual speeches of the Turks just as they occurred, with minimal authorial interference.[6] Drawn as a "confidant" into the personal conflicts and problems of two families, Geiersbach is the object of intimate outpourings of trust, desperate pleas for help, impassioned arguments from all sides, each meaning to win his support—all of which is reproduced for us in various shades of broken German or in indirect discourse. The author is, at least in intention, only the medium through which the Turks will tell us their own stories in their own words. "The author appears essentially only as a witness and chronicler for the reader," Geiersbach states; "in my work I comment on and interpret the events hardly at all" (Ich kommentiere und interpretiere das Geschehen in meiner Arbeit so gut wie gar nicht. . . . Der Autor tritt im wesentlichen nur als Zeuge und Chronist für den Leser in Erscheinung) (B, 11).

The impulse behind such an attempt, which would make the ethnographer/author an attentive and compassionate listener rather than an authoritative expert, is praiseworthy and, to my knowledge, unique in German academic writing on the Turkish population of the Federal Republic.[7] Yet while Geiersbach promises to keep his interpretive categories and commentaries out of his novels and to let his Turks speak for themselves, their stories are nonetheless embedded within a narrative framework that is distinctly foreign to them. *Bruder, muß zusammen Zwiebel und Wasser essen!* records the crisis of a Turkish family, recounted in conflicting ways by its various members, occurring between May and October of an unspecified year and centering around a foolish daughter who has left her upstanding husband for an equally foolish and irresponsible man who is married to someone else and, furthermore, unemployed. *Wie Mutlu Öztürk schwimmen lernen muß* follows the adventures of an eighteen-year-old Turkish youth who has, at least initially, broken all ties to his family and community and struck out entirely on his own in an unhospitable German world. While the two works tell essentially separate and different stories, they share many of the same characters and take place concurrently. More important, they share a German narrative of maturation and enlightenment imposed as an authorial super-text on the stories told by the Turks.[8]

Not coincidentally, both novels deal with generational conflicts. As Geiersbach puts it succinctly in one introduction,

> The foreign youths, who for the most part, in contrast to their parents, have grown up or come of age in the Federal Republic, are striving first of all for

more emancipation than is traditionally granted to them. In addition this emancipation is directed toward the realization of ways of life that are incompatible with the traditional ways of life of their parents.

Die ausländischen Jugendlichen, die im Gegensatz zu ihren Eltern meistenteils bereits in der Bundesrepublik auf- oder herangewachsen sind, streben zum einen nach mehr Emanzipation, als ihnen traditionell zugestanden wird. Zum anderen zielt die Emanzipation auf die Realisierung von Lebenskonzepten ab, die mit den hergebrachten Lebenskonzepten der Eltern unvereinbar sind. (B, 9)

In Geiersbach's vision, emancipation is set against tradition, youth against parents, modernity against the preservation of older, now inappropriate, ways of life. Thus when the foolish daughter of the one novel is thrown out of her family home, we see Geiersbach responding to her appeal for help, securing temporary quarters for her in a *Wohngemeinschaft,* supporting her feelings of righteous anger, advocating her rights against the demands of her parents, and later encouraging her not to return to the parental fold, although ironically she wants to.

Geiersbach's sympathies come even more strongly to the fore in the narrative of Mutlu Öztürk, where again he goes to tremendous efforts to help maintain the son's financial and cultural independence from the traditional demands placed on him by his father.[9] The battle there is fought over the recognition of the son's sovereignty and maturity—between Mutlu's "I want" ("ich will") and his father's "he must" ("er muß"), verbs repeated throughout and characterizing the rebellion of the son and the absolute obedience demanded by the father. Furthermore, Geiersbach grants himself in this struggle the role of the enlightened educator who will aid Mutlu in his process of social maturation. As he makes amply clear in the introduction to the novel, Geiersbach helps where Mutlu cannot help himself, while taking care not to become simply another figure of authority: explicitly rejecting the roles of father, older brother, therapist, watchdog, or superego, Geiersbach claims instead to approach Mutlu "in an unbiased and friendly way" (vorurteilsfrei und freundlich) (M, 12). A benevolent rather than patriarchal father figure who rescues Mutlu from the threat of imminent deportation, Geiersbach is the metaphorical and enlightened parent of the "social rebirth" (soziale Wiedergeburt) that begins the novel (see M, 37, 82, 90).

We are offered the image of a liberal and sympathetic German researcher who seeks, both in his actions and in the manner of his writing, to support the autonomy of his subjects. Just as Geiersbach will help Mutlu to establish a new life independent of his domineering father, so too does he strive in his narrative to allow Mutlu to tell his own story. Crucial to the conception and execution of both novels is Geiersbach's ability accurately to transmit (transcribe) for us the assertions, explanations, and oral histories of his

Turks. Indeed, that ability—if we take the novels at face value—is phenomenal, as entire chapters and sequences of chapters in both works bear the titles "Mutlu speaks," "Param speaks," "Alda and Hoppa speak" (Mutlu erzählt, Param erzählt, Alda und Hoppa erzählen). Not only does Geiersbach open his text to these other voices; he thereby creates for himself the image of an unbiased, friendly listener, a positive model for gaining access to the Other without repressing it in the process.

Yet, as I indicated earlier, Geiersbach's noteworthy project is important both for what it does and for what happens inadvertently, and, I would add, contrarily, in it. The key scene is the disastrous conclusion of the *Mutlu Öztürk* novel. Mutlu has been tricked into returning home, supposedly to protect his sister while her husband completes his tour of duty in the Turkish army; once home, he is then convinced by his family to marry. Mutlu's bride has been arranged by his parents: although somewhat older than one would want, and a Kurd, the bride offers an advantageous match for Mutlu's family who seeks to reinstate their renegade son in the larger Turkish community. After the wedding Mutlu and his family discover that his bride is partly disabled; Mutlu runs away, and the bride is rudely sent back to her own family. The entire situation is unspeakably shameful, and Mutlu's father, Boga, receives an enraged and insulting letter from the bride's mother, who lays her curse on the entire Öztürk household. The letter claims that Boga's daughters are hunchbacks, that an ape would have made a better son than Mutlu, that the Öztürks are animals who grew up in a forest. But most important, it begins by casting a serious shadow on the reputation of Boga's wife.

> Boga, I shit in your beard. I cannot shit on the floor. The godless one slept with your wife. You can throw her out, you pimp. You should have your blond wife's ass and cunt examined. . . . It's better if you do your fucking with a donkey. To hell with your manliness. After the godless one fucked your wife, she became sweet to you.

> Boga, ich scheiße in Deinen Bart. Ich kann nicht auf den Boden scheißen. Der Gottlose hat mit Deiner Frau geschlafen. Du kannst sie fortjagen, Du Kuppler. Du solltest den Arsch und die Fotze Deiner blonden Frau untersuchen lassen. . . . Es ist besser, wenn Du mit einem Esel ficken übst. Pfui mit Deiner Männlichkeit. Nachdem der Gottlose Deine Frau gefickt hat, ist sie Dir süß geworden. (M, 227)

Boga, in a terrible state, contemplates taking the bride's mother to court, yet what he really wants to do is shoot her entire family dead. When Geiersbach tries to "reason" with him ("to bring Boga back to reason" [Boga . . . wieder zur Vernunft zu bringen] M, 230), something totally unexpected occurs. Boga pulls out a Bible, makes Geiersbach swear to tell the truth, and then demands to know what Boga's wife said to Geiersbach out on the balcony of their home on the eve of Mutlu's wedding. Geiersbach cannot remember a single thing.

> I become embarrassed: after some thought I do vaguely recollect that I was indeed on the balcony looking for my shoes on the evening in question, and that I also exchanged a few insignificant words there with Frau Öztürk, but I'm unable to remember one word of the specific content of this exchange.

> Ich gerate in Verlegenheit: Mir kommt zwar nach einigem Nachdenken dunkel in Erinnerung, daß ich an dem fraglichen Abend tatsächlich auf dem Balkon nach meinen Schuhen gesucht habe und daß ich dort auch mit Frau Öztürk ein paar belanglose Worte gewechselt habe, vermag mich aber mit keiner Silbe mehr an den genauen Inhalt dieser Worte zu erinnern. (M, 231)

Geiersbach finally understands when Boga taps the slanderous letter in his jacket pocket that Boga suspects him of being the heathen who has slept with his wife. Boga, Geiersbach knows, is "deadly serious" (blutiger Ernst) (M, 231) in his investigation, yet all Geiersbach can do is try to laugh off the accusation. Despite Boga's repeated attempts to jog Geiersbach's memory, the researcher can remember absolutely nothing. Boga, whose only remaining alternative, he says, is to have his wife killed, becomes increasingly desperate. The last words of the scene and the novel are his final, unanswered plea, "Please! *What* my wife say to you? . . ." ("Bitte! *Was* meine Frau dir sagen? . . .") (M, 232; ellipses in original).

The incident may be incorporated easily into Geiersbach's enlightenment project as the final say of "unenlightened" Turkish customs; indeed, the afterword to the volume offers Geiersbach's apology for Boga Öztürk whom we should try to understand, and thus not condemn, from the perspective of his own culture. Geiersbach explains,

> Boga is not a pedagogically enlightened person, capable of differentiated thought. Boga doesn't understand much. . . . He can't comprehend. . . . He is not able to reflect with sociological or social-psychological understanding on the peculiarities of his relationship to Mutlu that are conditioned by emigration. In his narrow understanding of human beings he finds only one explanation for Mutlu's defiance of him: Satan himself has entered Mutlu's head and heart, and he has to be driven out—through beatings; if necessary, through brutal beatings.

> Boga ist kein pädagogisch aufgeklärter und differenziert denkender Mensch. Boga versteht nicht viel. . . . Er kann nicht begreifen. . . . Er vermag auch nicht die durch die Emigration bedingten Besonderheiten seiner Beziehungen zu Mutlu soziologisch oder sozialpsychologisch zu reflektieren. Aus seinem engen Menschenverständnis heraus findet er für die Verweigerung, die Mutlu gegen ihn betreibt, nur die eine Erklärung: In Mutlus Kopf und Herz ist der leibhaftige Satan gefahren, und den muß man austreiben—durch Schläge, wenn's not tut auch durch brutale Schläge. (M, 236–237)

Boga, who belongs literally in another world and who has mistreated his son and made a shambles of his family's life in an unsupportive German setting, accordingly deserves the sympathy and solidarity of those who, like ourselves, have a deeper and social-scientific understanding of his problems.

I would argue, however, for another way of reading the scene, one that takes Geiersbach's dumbfounded silence to Boga's questions seriously. For in a novel based on the German's seemingly unlimited talent for listening attentively to the Turks, the tables are finally turned: now it is Geiersbach who is called on to speak and, furthermore, to fill in the gaps in a narrative of Boga's design. Ironically, when the ultimate listener/transcriber Geiersbach is asked to recount a key conversation in a story of adultery and tainted family honor, he is caught, so to speak, with his pants down. Significantly, Geiersbach's novel ends abruptly when he is confronted with the emergence of a surprising and incompatible Turkish narrative that places different emphases and vastly different values on the same events and conversations that Geiersbach has transcribed.[10] The two narratives, both steeped in their respective cultures, are in fact so separate at this point that the unmemorable "insignificant words" in one are literally a matter of life and death in the other. The German Self and the German narrative come face to face with a Turkish narrative and a Turkish Self with its own set of questions and demands.[11]

The appearance in 1990 of Geiersbach's two-volume study of a Turkish ghetto, *Waiting Until the Trains Leave Again* (Warten bis die Züge wieder fahren) and *Serving God Even in a Foreign Land* (Gott auch in der Fremde dienen), marks a new beginning. The research focus is no longer limited to a single individual or to a single Turkish family but takes as its object an entire community. With the shift from individual stories to scenes of community life comes the abandonment of long first-person Turkish narratives; here, Geiersbach is not the medium for the Turks to tell us their stories but the vehicle through which we are allowed to observe their lives. Living and wandering among the people of his community, Geiersbach, like an epic narrator, opens the life of the ghetto to our scrutiny. While earlier he had presented himself purely as listener, with a nonauthoritative stance toward his Turkish acquaintances who were ostensibly speaking for themselves, here Geiersbach is explicitly in charge of his text as he aggressively pursues various aspects of community life to present to us a complete ethnographic record of a social world.[12]

Yet despite the important difference between Geiersbach's texts, the narrative of emancipation versus dogmatic tradition survives in clear form. Volume 1 ends notably in failure and frustration when Geiersbach, with his liberal social conscience, runs up against the apparently rigid limitations of

Turkish culture. Geiersbach has occupied himself for much of the first six months of his fieldwork with a small group of Kurdish children whom he tutors every day after school. The low cultural value placed on German education, manifested in part in the lack of quiet space in the family home for doing school assignments, leads, according to Geiersbach, to poor achievement and to inadequate preparation for employment and thus to the perpetuation of ghettoization. Geiersbach's plan for a community child care and learning center should demonstrate to German readers and Turkish and Kurdish neighbors his understanding of, and solidarity with, the basic problems of ghetto life. But the plan dies on the drawing board when the Hoca, the Islamic leader of the community, insists that Muslim students and Kurdish heathens be instructed at different times, that Muslim boys and Muslim girls be taught in different rooms, that the girls be taught by a woman, and that no one be taught by non-Muslims or by Communists (W, 399). Geiersbach simply gives up at that point; confronted by such unyielding (and supposedly ignorant) views, he abandons his too progressive ideas and leaves the scene in near-disgust for a much-needed vacation.

Geiersbach's clear frustration with the Turkish community is in fact the typical experience of his fieldwork. Nothing, but nothing, seems to live up to his expectation, and Geiersbach seems to be chronically disgruntled. He is taken aback and sobered by the Hoca's aggressive stance regarding the proper (orthodox) dress and behavior of Muslim girls; the religious leader, whom Geiersbach had hoped to be able to present as different, that is, less dogmatic, from other Hocas, proves himself to be disappointingly typical (W, 310–311). The spiritual and deeply religious experience Geiersbach expects to find in the Ramazan services is made into something of a joke when two teenaged boys cause an entire row of praying Muslims to keel over like dominoes in the middle of a bow (W, 313). The long days of fasting required in observation of the holy holiday are exposed as a hypocritical game in which one Muslim after another offers his creative interpretation of the religious law to justify its nonobservance. The authentic Muslim wedding Geiersbach hopes to observe turns out to be "a completely ordinary Turkish wedding as I had experienced them five or six times before" (eine ganz gewöhnliche türkische Hochzeit, wie ich sie schon fünf- oder sechsmal vorher erlebt habe) (G, 164). The Turks are either too Turkish for the liberal Geiersbach or not Turkish enough for the sociologist in search of authentic ethnic culture.

There are two ways to view this recurring experience of frustrated desire. Geiersbach, who wants to present himself as open-minded and sympathetic in a project aimed at combating German prejudices and preconceptions, is clearly burdened by his own set of expectations and his own liberal but rigid agenda. But this familiar critique of the matter focuses too heavily or one-

sidedly on the activity and identity of the Germans. An alternative view
would accord a degree of subjectivity to the Turks as well and suggest that
Geiersbach's frustration has as much to do with their resistance, implicit or
otherwise, to his preconceptions. It is not that Geiersbach's expectations are
simply inappropriate; they are actively resisted by his object.

This distinction, which seeks to acknowledge the agency of the Turks,
is more than just a matter of words. For indeed the Turks of Geiersbach's
ghetto are more than just the objects (or subjects) of his research, there for
him to observe and record: they, in turn, exert their considerable collective
force on the new and foreign member of their community. Not only do they
fail to live up to Geiersbach's expectations of them but they, in turn, attempt
to force Geiersbach to live up to theirs. The Turks too have their own project, one that makes itself felt from the very beginning: they must teach this
German to conform as quickly as possible to the established life of their community. Almost immediately on his arrival Geiersbach perceives the tremendous and unexpected constraints placed on him by his new environment.

> It is not I who take possession of my new neighborhood by asking questions
> and observing, but rather the other way around. Of course I too ask questions
> and observe, but even more I am questioned, observed, sized up. It is not *I*
> who establish connections with *them,* but *they* with *me.* . . . It's just awkward that
> I thus become the target of expectations, that I am thus subjected to a social
> pressure to conform. No, no one forces me to do anything, of course! But I
> am threatened with gossip, isolation, disregard, being shut out of conversa-
> tions if I were to try to evade this pressure.

> Nicht ich ergreife fragend und beobachtend Besitz von meiner neuen Nach-
> barschaft, sondern diese von mir. Sicher, ich frage und beobachte ebenfalls,
> aber noch mehr werde ich befragt, beobachtet, abgetastet. Nicht *ich* setze
> mich zu *ihnen,* sondern *sie* setzen sich zu *mir* in Beziehung . . . . Mißlich nur,
> daß ich damit auch zum Adressaten von Erwartungen werde, einem sozialen
> Anpassungsdruck ausgesetzt bin. Nein, zwingen tut mich hier natürlich nie-
> mand zu was! Mir droht jedoch Klatsch, Isolierung, Nichtbeachtung,
> Gesprächsverweigerung, wenn ich mich diesem Druck entziehen wollte.
> (W, 32)[13]

Such statements reflect not just an abstract sense of cultural displacement
but a specific and exact behavioral code. A friendly Turkish teenager takes
Geiersbach under his wing and lays out the basic rules of neighborhood life;
Geiersbach ruefully summarizes the early lesson: "no Kurds, no women, no
cutlets, no beer" (keine Kurden, keine Frauen, keine Koteletts, kein Bier)
(W, 31). With curious schoolchildren rummaging through his refrigerator
and closets, it is clear that any transgressions will be found out. It is clear,
too, that the collective project to civilize the German in his Turkish environment is immensely difficult, if not impossible. Even some seven hundred
pages into his life in the community, Geiersbach, blundering badly, casts an

unintentional curse on a friend's newborn son: "You already know so much about us," he is told, "but you still make mistakes" ("Du weißt jetzt schon so viel über uns," . . . "aber du machst immer noch Fehler") (G, 311). And two days before his departure he innocently touches the shoulder of a married woman; "If you weren't a German," her husband tells him, "I would have beaten you up just now. My wife is no whore!" ("Wenn du kein Deutscher wärst," . . . "dann hätte ich jetzt zugeschlagen. Meine Frau ist keine Hure!") (G, 429). It seems that the Turks (and Kurds) are at least as frustrated by Geiersbach's behavior as he is by theirs.

Just as Geiersbach interacts with his neighbors with explicit expectations of their Turkishness, so too do they, in turn, make implicit and sometimes explicit demands on him as a German. Because the Germans are seen as the cause of the unsightly mountain of trash that fills one of the courtyards of the ghetto, Geiersbach, as a German, is held accountable and is expected to do something to get rid of it (W, 228). Because he is German and therefore wealthy, he is the one who must buy something from a traveling cookware salesman who has presented his high-priced merchandise to an embarrassed audience of Turks (G, 277). The examples seem trivial only to us; for Geiersbach such incidents are invasive and confining.

For our researcher is not simply German, he is unalienably German, and it is this core that is increasingly threatened as he pursues his friendly research project. It is not Geiersbach who intrudes into the community, so much as the community that makes itself felt as an intrusion into Geiersbach's life. As the Kurdish schoolchildren come to accept their foreign tutor, for example, Geiersbach must pay a price for the trust and confidence he has won: the children behave in his apartment the way they do in their own homes, and literally nothing is left unturned, unopened, or unexamined. This irritates the German to no end. "Even such precious things as my electric typewriter, my most important means of production, or my beloved record collection were not spared" (Davon blieben auch so schützenswerte Dinge, wie meine elektrische Schreibmaschine, mein wichtigstes Produktionsmittel, oder meine geliebte Schallplattensammlung nicht ausgenommen) (W, 144). Here the holiest of holies is violated by heathen hands: symbols of Geiersbach's research project and his cultural identity. Fittingly, Geiersbach will decide to end the project at a point when he is simply no longer able to put up with the demands placed on him by his research subjects: "the lack of privacy and the all-encompassing demands of neighbors or friends" (der Mangel an Privatheit und die totale Inanspruchnahme durch Nachbarn oder Freunde), necessary conditions of life in the close quarters of the community, become too much to bear (G, 398); Geiersbach's apartment is a local institution open to any and all who care to drop in; his car has become community transportation, with Geiersbach often the chauffeur. "A private sphere or private control over leisure time and property, these are things that are unknown in the colony, and so they are not perceived and respected as needs in others" (Privatsphäre oder private Verfügungsgewalt über Freizeit und Besitz, das kennt man in der Kolonie nicht und vermag es so auch nicht an anderen als Bedürfnis wahrzunehmen und zu respektieren) (G, 398). Geiersbach, insisting on his private life and a private sphere, defends the boundaries of his bourgeois cultural and personal identity in the face of a demanding and all-invasive Turkish community.[14]

We need to appreciate the full significance of the cultural encounter in which the power of the so-called Other makes itself felt, insistently and unexpectedly. For Geiersbach is in fact lucky to get away with his identity intact. Again we need to look at the manner in which his narrative ends—at the moment in which Geiersbach falls finally silent. Ironically, he is paralyzed and impossibly constrained by his own success: because he has asked so many questions and learned so much about Islamic teachings and customs during his time in the Turkish community, more than one of his informant-friends conclude that Geiersbach must be interested in converting. The Hoca for one makes it his personal mission to win Geiersbach over to Islam. The issue of conversion is not an arbitrary one, for it places the German's cultural identity directly on the line. The research project in which the Self gains access to the Other inspires a Frankensteinian counterproject in which the Other threatens to take over completely! The situation reaches crisis proportions when Geiersbach begins his exploration of the phenomenon of Sufi mysticism, that most "other" of the Other.

Geiersbach is invited by one of his most loyal informants to accompany him to a Sufi center near Mönchengladbach. Not surprisingly, he is disappointed by the appearance of the lauded temple, a decrepit factory building whose rooms smell of rotten wood, sweat, urine, and sweet perfume (G, 333–335). Geiersbach's account, filled with sarcasm, makes no effort to hide (from us, not from them) his disdain and disbelief. The scene deteriorates rapidly into absurdity when, as a result of an error in translation, the Sufis are told by their leader that "the ego is the cow in us, and we must kill this cow" (das Ego ist die Kuh in uns, und diese Kuh müssen wir töten) (G, 356). Whirling dervishes appear; Sufis shake, quiver, howl, and launch into gymnastic floor exercises—all signs of supposed "trance." Geiersbach, as the intellectual and rational Westerner, can take none of it seriously; indeed he contemplates a lawsuit (the resort of the bourgeois liberal) against the Sufi leader for what he considers to be child abuse when he witnesses even young children in apparent trance. But his only response at the time is to extricate himself from the situation without revealing his true feelings.

Two months later, in the scene that concludes the book, Geiersbach is after the Sufis again. Or rather, they are after him. Letting his unsatisfied curiosity about Sufi trance get the better of him, Geiersbach agrees to visit the regional Sufi center. Again, the place is disappointingly dilapidated, and the Hoca is introduced to us without delay as a phony. But this time Geiersbach is not allowed the privacy and protection of his sarcasm and irony as he penetrates the holy Sufi ground; it soon becomes clear that this Hoca, too, is aggressively intent on converting him right then and there. Geiersbach describes the turn of events as an "attack" (Angriff) (G, 390), and he obviously has little with which he can defend himself. Geiersbach is "anxious," "speechless," "helpless" (beklommen, sprachlos, hilflos) (G, 391–393); his adversary, in contrast, "a cunning fox" (ein ausgekochter Fuchs) (G, 393) who has an answer for every one of the German's weak protestations. Again our researcher is caught and bound in the situation, unable to speak his true mind.

> Alas, instead of finally telling this guy what I think, I resort to maneuvering again. But how do you free yourself from a trap that gives itself a veneer of such good intentions. You can do it only with a resounding slap in the face, something along the lines of: "Damn it, now just kiss my ass!"
>
> Fine, Tamer Hoca would have understood this language, but in front of the large number of onlookers gathered there, among whom I counted four faces I knew from the colony, I would have put myself flagrantly in the wrong. Such a reaction would have seemed to them like the rudeness of an arrogant German and obstinate unbeliever.

> Ach, anstatt nun aber dem Burschen endlich die Meinung zu sagen, verlege ich mich wieder auf's Taktieren. Aber wie löst man sich aus einer Umklammerung, die sich den Anstrich von soviel Wohlgesonnenheit gibt. Das geht nur mit einer schallenden Ohrfeige, etwa im Ton von: "Verdammt, jetzt leck mich doch am Arsch!"
>
> Gut, Tamer Hoca hätte diese Sprache wohl verstanden, aber vor den so zahlreich versammelten Zuschauern, unter denen ich auch vier mir aus der Kolonie bekannte Gesichter zählte, hätte ich mich damit eklatant ins Unrecht gesetzt. Eine solche Reaktion hätte ihnen als die Grobheit eines arroganten Deutschen und hartgesottenen Ungläubigen erscheinen müssen. (G, 392)

Unable to respond as Paul Geiersbach the private person would like, forced to behave as their familiar sympathetic "German" before his research subjects, Geiersbach is socially paralyzed. Unable to deal with the situation, he can only retreat from it; when the Hoca takes his hand once more in a passionate kiss, he rips himself away and brusquely announces his desire to leave. The scene, and with it the long account of life in the Turkish ghetto, ends with Geiersbach's abrupt withdrawal: "the fat fish broke free of the line and stayed that way" (der dicke Fisch war von der Leine und blieb es auch) (G, 395).[15]

Once again the tables have been turned. Here the sociologist, who entered the scene initially as a kind of epic narrator moving freely and sovereignly among his subjects, shows himself in the end to be an object himself, indeed, a prized one, to be manipulated, trapped, or otherwise won by the

Turks. Once again, the German in pursuit of his research project is confronted by Turks with their own agenda. The German, dangerously on their turf, falls silent and withdraws in self-defense; face-to-face with a powerful Turkish subject, his narrative comes to an abrupt, slightly outraged, and slightly embarrassed end.

It is not that Geiersbach is without critical self-reflection; indeed, he is often—though not always—aware of the impact of his presence on the events he observes. But he is not aware of, or if he is, he nowhere acknowledges, the impact of the *Turks* on what he sees. The methodological reflections offered in his afterword identify an expanded notion of participant observation as Geiersbach's manner of approach, one in which Geiersbach's own identity plays a constituent part: "To be involved or take part . . . inevitably means also to take an interest, that is to say, to make oneself recognizable as a *person* and to approach people as a *person*" (Mit dabei sein oder teilnehmen heißt aber unvermeidlich auch anteilnehmen, will sagen, sich als *Person* erkennbar machen und als *Person* auf die Leute zugehen) (W, 403). Geiersbach as a person, "so in my case as a man, as a German, as an 'educated' person, and finally also as Paul Geiersbach" (in meinem Fall also als Mann, als Deutscher, als "gebildeter" Mensch und schließlich auch als Paul Geiersbach) (W, 403), takes full part in the life of his community, that is, he becomes involved in the affairs of his neighbors, is drawn into their conflicts, takes sides, and creates new conflicts of his own; in the process, he knows that he has through his presence permanently changed the community he studies. But while he speaks of *his* participating activity, his sympathies, and the relevant aspects of his identity, the constitutive activity of his Turkish subjects goes largely unacknowledged.

Throughout his narrative Geiersbach claims for himself the authoritative and authorizing role in the experiences he relates. If his Turkish acquaintances reveal information to him, the reason for their new confidence—if Geiersbach offers one—can be only the friendship and trust growing between them. That the Turks may have their own motives, or any motives at all, does not seem readily to occur to him.[16] The circle is complete when, in a particularly exciting chapter describing a meeting of a nationalistic political organization, Geiersbach responds in a footnote to the possible criticism that he has been taken in by propaganda. The possibility of an intervening Turkish project is met with the claim of authority based on Geiersbach's presence on the scene: "However, to this I would object that I had my ear fairly close to the 'milieu' " (Dem ist jedoch entgegenzuhalten, daß ich mein Ohr ziemlich nahe am "Milieu" hatte) (G, 82). The argument is that he has seen and heard with his own eyes and ears; thus the possibility of a Turkish motive is nullified, or at least counteracted. Geiersbach does not reflect on the fact that his eyes and ears were there, "close to the 'milieu,' " only by invitation of the Turks. The researcher presents himself as penetrating into circles of Turkish culture hitherto unseen, to offer us privileged information. The truth is that for one reason or another—and there are reasons—the Turks have allowed him in.

It is clear to us, as it becomes finally clear to Geiersbach who must fend off the attempts to make a Muslim out of him, that the Turks have their own project—or projects—in mind. They seek to teach, to indoctrinate, to present the best side of themselves to Geiersbach; his books are their opportunity to tell their side to a German audience. But where Geiersbach does seem aware of a Turkish agenda, he presents it to us simply as unwanted influence (which he can effectively ward off); holds it at bay with a show of irony, bemusement, or outrage; retreats to what he considers a safe distance; or rationalizes the Turkish pressure as the exigencies of his research. In the process, the Turks are depicted affectionately as simpleminded (the figure of Kamil "Simplicius"), dogmatic (the local Hoca), superstitious and duped (the case of the Sufi followers), often self-contradictory—as everything but powerful.

But powerful they are indeed. In all the forewords and afterwords of his books, much is made of Geiersbach's role as listener, of the authenticity of the conversations and experiences he recounts. Nothing is made of the roles of the Turks who speak, or do not speak, with him. Geiersbach is "involved," "close to the 'milieu,' " recording a "reality he has himself experienced and lived" (selbst er- und gelebte Wirklichkeit) (G, iv)—yet such formulations conceal the fact that he sees only what the Turks allow him to see. Geiersbach's research is never simply a matter of looking and listening sympathetically; he experiences by invitation and with permission only. As we are reminded when Geiersbach tells us that he has never been allowed into the kitchen of a Turkish home (although he attempts to write about the life of women in the community!), the German researcher is on "their" turf, subject to their rules. His field site, the ghetto, is not open territory waiting to be penetrated by a long-awaited sympathetic, progressive foreigner who can arrive in his Ford Granada and slip smoothly and unnoticeably, without disruption, into the flow of community life. Rather, even the most sympathetic of Germans will meet with powerful attempts to confine and to convert and will feel his cultural and personal identity under attack.

I have told the story of Paul Geiersbach whose praiseworthy and unique project to record the social world of the Turks in Germany falls into silence and who retreats when confronted by the Turks with an agenda of their own. Boga Öztürk's demanding interrogation leaves Geiersbach in embarrassed and flustered silence, unable to recall what are for him "insignificant words" but for the Turk, a matter of life and death. Faced with Turks who try to convert him for their own purposes to their religion, Geiersbach can do nothing more than withdraw, declaring an arbitrary but at the same time logical end to his project and his ethnographic novel. As I have argued, these incidents are more than just amusing. They have *paradigmatic* value for the encounter with that entity labeled the "Other." Not only does the German subject represent and thereby constrict the Turkish Other; more important, we see here how the Turks manipulate, restrain, threaten, and finally silence the German in turn, even in his own texts. The Other, in short, is not simply a construction of the German subject but also potentially the site of resistance against it. Clearly the power of the Self in its creation of Others and otherness is more than just a matter of rhetoric, epistemology, or psychology. Real political, social, and economic oppression lies behind the manipulation of words. But the accompanying concept of the Other as constructed, manipulated, controlled, and thus inevitably weak, is a one-sided vision. We need to learn, too, to speak about the power of the Other, as an other Self, to constrain and constrict—and to resist—the Self.

NOTES

1. There were approximately two million Turks, predominantly "guest workers" and their families, living in the Federal Republic of Germany prior to reunification. On the history and politics of the immigrant workers in Western Europe, particularly West Germany, see Stephen Castles, *Here for Good: Western Europe's New Ethnic Minorities* (London: Pluto Press, 1984).

2. Paul Geiersbach, *Waiting Until the Trains Leave Again: A Turkish Ghetto in Germany*. Vol. 1 (Warten bis die Züge wieder fahren: Ein Türkenghetto in Deutschland. Band I) (Berlin: Mink, 1990): 24. Further references to this work, designated as "W," will be cited in the text. All translations from the German were provided by Karen Storz. Throughout this chapter I use the terms "German," "the Turks," and "Turkish" to refer to the cultural identities projected by the texts. I do not mean to imply any essentialist notions of Germanness or Turkishness.

3. Paul Geiersbach, *Serving God Even in a Foreign Land: A Turkish Ghetto in Germany*. Vol. 2 (Gott auch in der Fremde dienen: Ein Türkenghetto in Deutschland. Band II) (Berlin: Mink 1990): 428. Further references to this volume, designated as "G," will be given in the text.

4. For an epistemological analysis of the ethnographic subject being put at stake in its encounter with the Other, see Kevin Dwyer, "The Dialogic of Ethnology," *Dialectical Anthropology* 4 (1979): 205–224. My analysis is influenced by the critical reflection in the field of American anthropology on the constructed nature of ethnographic texts. Key contributions to this discussion are George E. Marcus and Dick Cushman, "Ethnographies as Texts," *Annual Review of Anthropology* 11 (1982): 25–69; James Clifford, "On Ethnographic Authority," *Representations* 1 (1983): 118–146, also in *The Predicament of Culture: Twentieth-Century Ethnography, Literature, and Art* (Cambridge: Harvard University Press, 1988): 21–54; and the essays in *Writing Culture: The Poetics and Politics of Ethnography*, ed. James Clifford and George E. Marcus (Berkeley, Los Angeles, and London: University of California Press, 1986). See also Steven Webster, "Dialogue and Fiction in Ethnography," *Dialectical Anthro-*

pology 7 (1982): 91–114; Paul Rabinow, "Discourse and Power: On the Limits of Ethnographic Texts," *Dialectical Anthropology* 10 (1985): 1–13; James W. Fernandez, "Exploded Worlds: Text as a Metaphor for Ethnography (and Vice Versa)," *Dialectical Anthropology* 10 (1985): 15–26; and Mary Louise Pratt, "Scratches on the Face of the Country; or, What Mr. Barrow Saw in the Land of the Bushmen," *Critical Inquiry* 12, no. 1 (Autumn 1985): 119–143, rpt. in *"Race," Writing, and Difference,* ed. Henry Louis Gates, Jr. (Chicago: University of Chicago Press, 1986): 138–162. On the relevance of the anthropological discussion for a redefinition of German literary studies as culture studies, see my "Is Culture to Us What Text Is to Anthropology?: A Response to Jeffrey M. Peck's Paper," *German Quarterly* 62 (1989): 188–191.

5. Paul Geiersbach, *Brother, Must Eat Onions and Water Together!: A Turkish Family in Germany* (Bruder, muß zusammen Zwiebel und Wasser essen!: Eine türkische Familie in Deutschland) (Berlin: J. H. W. Dietz Nachf., 1982); *How Mutlu Öztürk Must Learn to Swim: A Life Story* (Wie Mutlu Öztürk schwimmen lernen muß: Ein Lebenslauf) (Berlin: J. H. W. Dietz Nachf., 1983). Further references to these works, designated as "B" and "M," will be given in the text.

6. I discuss the virtues and problems of Geiersbach's experiment and compare his work to two other sympathetic and "ethnographic" accounts of Turks in West Germany, in "Talking 'Turk': On Narrative Strategies and Cultural Stereotypes," *New German Critique* 46 (Winter 1989): 104–128. Claudia Schöning-Kalender, in her review of the two works, raises questions about the methods and manner of Geiersbach's research; see *Zeitschrift für Volkskunde* 81 (1985): 116–117.

7. In his foreword to *Bruder, muß zusammen Zwiebel und Wasser essen!* Geiersbach discusses how he has broken away from the traditional and standard research model, based on questionnaires and statistical sampling, in which he was trained (B, 9–10). According to Geiersbach, his text, which he describes as something like a reportage, something like a case study, and something like a novel (B, 11–12), departs completely from usual sociological research practices in Germany. He claims to find parallels in American sociology and social anthropology, citing Oscar Lewis as a model; see *The Children of Sanchez: Autobiography of a Mexican Family* (New York: Vintage Books, 1963). There is no indication here or in his later novels that Geiersbach is influenced by—or even aware of—the theoretical discussion in American anthropology on the rhetoric of ethnographic texts and ethnographic authority. On the nonexistence of a tradition of participant observation in German anthropology, see Sabine Jell-Bahlsen, "Ethnology and Fascism in Germany," *Dialectical Anthropology* 9 (1985): 313–335; and Fritz W. Kramer, "Empathy—Reflections on the History of Ethnology in Pre-Fascist Germany: Herder, Creuzer, Bastian, Bachofen, and Frobenius," *Dialectical Anthropology* 9 (1985): 337–347.

8. At root here is Kant's famous definition of Enlightenment from 1784: "Enlightenment is man's release from his self-incurred tutelage. Tutelage is man's inability to make use of his understanding without direction from another" (Aufklärung ist der Ausgang des Menschen aus seiner selbst verschuldeten Unmündigkeit. Unmündigkeit ist das Unvermögen, sich seines Verstandes ohne Leitung eines anderen zu bedienen). Immanuel Kant, "Beantwortung der Frage: Was ist Aufklärung?" in *Werke,* ed. Wilhelm Weischedel, vol. 11 (Frankfurt am Main: Insel, 1964): 53–61, here p. 53; trans. Lewis White Beck, in Immanuel Kant, *On History,* ed. Lewis White Beck (Indianapolis: Bobbs-Merrill, 1963): 3. As Geiersbach's

project demonstrates, Kant's definition, emphasizing the automony of reason and the critical examination of previously held assumptions and prejudices, enjoys a powerful legacy in German intellectual and cultural life through the present day.

9. For Geiersbach, Mutlu's story illustrates the general situation of Turkish youths: his father "is first completely absent in the village in Turkey (patriarchal village society), and . . . then here in Germany suddenly pounces on his son and tries to stifle all independent thinking and action" (zunächst im Dorf in der Türkei [patriarchalische Dorfgesellschaft] ganz fehlt, und . . . sich hier in Deutschland dann plötzlich über [den Sohn] wirft und jedes selbständige Denken und Handeln zu ersticken sucht) (M, 10).

10. Ultimately the two narratives seek, in Boga's case, to preserve a sense of cultural difference of and Turkish cultural identity in Germany and, in Geiersbach's case, to recognize individual autonomy as a rigid universal value. Boga makes his position clear in a key conversation with Geiersbach at M, 201–203: "(From) person (to) person is all the same, (whether) German or Turk. Important is character! (whether) good character or bad character. But listen! Culture, German culture and Turkish culture different! . . . I live Germany, but I not German. I Turk! . . . I not want my children go (adopt) the same as German character" ("[Von] Mensch [zu] Mensch ist doch egal, [ob] Deutscher oder Türke. Wichtig ist Charakter!, [ob] gute Charakter oder schlechte Charakter. Aber, höre! Kultur, deutsche Kultur und türkische Kultur anders! . . . Ich Deutschland leben, aber ich nichts Deutscher. Ich Türke! . . . [I]ch will nicht, meine Kinder dasselbe wie deutsche Charakter gehen [annehmen]").

11. In fact Geiersbach has met with the Turkish subject dramatically engaged in the process of its self-construction and self-affirmation before, when Hoppa and Alda recast (with major changes) their romance for him as a feature film (B, 172–173), or when Mutlu creates his new identity, based on American comic books and other cultural cliches, as Bill Blad. These projects are presented by Geiersbach as quaint and amusing, as signs of irresponsibility or as evidence of a lack of a sense of reality. The Other is not recognized as being seriously engaged in a project of Self-construction. This is the blind spot of the Self that takes its own constructions too seriously and the constructions of the Other not at all seriously.

12. Thus while cultural, political, economic, and historical information is offered only in authorial footnotes to clarify various statements by Geiersbach's Turkish interlocutors in the earlier two novels, in the later works they occupy whole chapters of the main text. Compare, for example, the treatment of the radical right-wing Grey Wolves at B, 41 (fn. 1) and G, 47–83, 182–200, 208–226; or the explanation of Ramazen at B, 166 (fn. 39) and W, 273–323, 340–352.

13. Dorinne K. Kondo offers an illuminating analysis of the agency of informants in controlling the ethnographer and her or his experiences, in "Dissolution and Reconstitution of Self: Implications for Anthropological Epistemology," Cultural Anthropology 1, no. 1 (February 1986): 74–88.

14. As for Kondo in the context of her research into Japanese society, the demands placed on Geiersbach by the various members of the Turkish community reflect a different cultural understanding of the self in its relationships to others. I am unable here to pursue this point further; I limit my present analysis to the Western or European notion of bourgeois subjectivity that Geiersbach defends for himself.

15. Of course, Geiersbach reestablishes his authority and dignity through the act of writing his account for us, thus enjoying the final say against Tamer Hoca. See Kondo on the process of writing as a retrospective means of controlling the threat of the Other; see also Vincent Crapanzano, "On the Writing of Ethnography," *Dialectical Anthropology* 2 (1977): 69–73.

16. It is very possible that the Turks are offering information in exchange for (or to reward) Geiersbach's continued services as an advocate in dealing with the German bureaucracy and that "trust" and "friendship" are in part based on a mutually advantageous trade relationship. In all four novels, Geiersbach is called on on numerous occasions to perform bureaucratic tasks and errands for his Turkish acquaintances.

NINE

Narrative, Genealogy, and the Historical Consciousness: Selfhood in a Disintegrating State

John Borneman

INTRODUCTION

In response to the general loss of confidence in the truth-value of representations by social scientists, anthropologists have increasingly turned to narrative analysis, a subfield of literary studies long involved in understanding textual representations and the concomitant processes of authorship, writing, and reading. At this time of increased doubt and reflexivity, judicious borrowings from literary theory are now, more than ever before, attractive to anthropologists (e.g., Clifford 1988; Marcus and Fischer 1986; Clifford and Marcus 1986; Herzfeld 1985).[1] While literary critics offer anthropologists no dominant paradigms by which to decide exactly what to study in the field, or new techniques that might improve how to go about such work, they have developed a rather sophisticated understanding of how data—utterances, actions, events, and happenings—are made assimilable to structures of meaning by assuming narrative form (see the essays in Mitchell 1981). The key to representational form, we are told, is never merely a neutral evaluation and recitation of facts but also a narrativization of them (Mink 1978: 129–149; White 1978, 1973). By making stories out of fieldwork data, we are, then, not involved in deception or distortion but availing ourselves of the only means we have of making the facts comprehensible (Borneman 1993: 1–24; Bruner 1986: 139–158; Ricoeur 1984).

In this chapter, I wish to focus not so much on the ethnographer[2] and text as on the processes of narrativization during the telling, that is, the act of authorship or inscription.[3] I hope to show that the relationship between anthropology and literary studies is not merely one of convenience but necessary and indispensable. In fact, the two disciplines, interrelated through the process of narrativity, the method of genealogy, and the condition of historical consciousness, presuppose one another in a mutual practice centered around the production and interpretation of narrative texts.[4] I shall demonstrate this by investigating how narrative form is put to work and made to act during narration. How, in other words, is form (per)formed?

First, I will examine the autobiography of East Berliner Susan R., an ethnographic text about the struggle for self-articulation and definition told at a moment in time when Susan's self and the world around her—in particular, her citizenship and nationality—is rapidly losing coherence.[5] Her autobiographical life history typifies many of the properties of narrative—a reconstruction where the end writes the beginning and shapes the middle, told in temporally sequenced clauses, always anticipating her own retrospection—and of genealogy—an account related from present to past as a series of disjunctive and accidental events, with no universal History in mind, selectively fashioned into a relative coherence concerned more with descent (*Herkunft*) than origin (*Ursprung*).[6] Second, I will be situating this story in the fieldwork context of its narration. I do not separate Susan's story from my own analysis; instead, I bring both the fieldwork context and my analytic voice to bear on her text when it illuminates the relationship of genealogy to narrativity. Thereby I hope to address a theoretical issue central to the social sciences and humanities: how to reconcile Hans-Georg Gadamer's understanding of *historical consciousness* (taking into account the presentness of historical reconstruction) with Michel Foucault's notion of history as *genealogy* (a history of the present), which I take to be different but essentially complementary aspects of any project in the human sciences.

Before presenting Susan's narrative, let me define more precisely the analytical terms I will be employing. A genealogical approach is fundamental not only to ethnology but also to self-understanding. All memory, in fact, proceeds via genealogy, even though the result of memories, their final representations, may be made to appear like constructions of an original movement from past to present rather than reconstructions done in reverse. Ethnographers have long derived their authority from fieldwork situations in which they assemble knowledge genealogically told or performed. Even observed live performances, before they can take textual form, must be reconstructed at a point in time after the event. The particular genealogies for which the discipline of anthropology has become renowned have been accounts of kinship, often represented as affines and consanguines fanning out in ordered rows beneath an "ego." Kinship genealogies resemble all other reconstructions (of, e.g., objects, life stages, group memberships) in that their historical nature "does not consist in the restoration of the past, but in thoughtful mediation with contemporary life" (Gadamer 1979: 150). In other words, all genealogies share the fact that from a position in the present, someone imaginatively reconstructs the forms that preceded the current one.

What links the genealogical method to narrativity is that the ethnographer's method produces texts, some of which will invariably take narrative form, that is, sequentially ordered with a beginning, middle, and end. In short, narrative and genealogy, much like literature and anthropology, predicate each other: narration always proceeds via a genealogical ordering, but a genealogical mode of inquiry requires narrative for its representation. The study of this form of representation, and the process whereby it translates something told into something known, is precisely the shared object of literature and anthropology.

Finally, historical consciousness, which I take to be a condition to which one strives and not a state of being, involves the recognition and knowledge of one's own historicity. Following Gadamer, we are unable to confront the Other except through our own cultural prejudices. This, of course, implicates the present in any narration, or understanding, of the past. When anthropologists do fieldwork, they are doing precisely such histories of the present. They are engaged in a genealogy of forms that assumes no necessary movement from the past to the present but instead concedes that the present is an arbitrary result of past forms arrived at often willy-nilly and often through unintended consequences of past actions having little to do with the motivations at the original time of action. Though anthropologists always invert the usual historical method and proceed from the present to the past, they usually understand this inversion as a constraint and rarely see it as productive of a particular form of knowledge. Indeed, if we become conscious of what follows from our method, might we not better understand our own historicity and integrate that into the questions we ask? Might this consciousness make us less liable to read the past as teleologically unfolding according to some prior plan? Might we not gain from a recognition that, in the words of Edward Said, we are not "commanded by [some silent past] to speak in the present" but rather we describe the present "in the course of its articulation, [in] its struggles for definition" (1983: 51)? What, then, can we learn about narrative, genealogy, and historical consciousness by concentrating on the act of inscription itself, on Susan R.'s genealogical narrative at the moment of telling?

Susan R. told her life story to Jeffrey Peck and me on 10 September 1989, exactly two months before the opening of the Berlin wall. Like many anthropological documents, hers is a narrative primarily about kinship construction, genealogically told. Yet, while she was telling us the details of personal history, other events forced an awareness of the present moment and thus knowledge of historicity, which then threatened to undermine her narrative voice and change her story. During the late summer of 1989, other East Germans vacationing in Prague and Budapest had begun taking refuge in West German embassies in those cities, choosing to exit their own society and state. Just one month after we met with Susan, on 8 October 1989, about five hundred East German citizens took advantage of a local fair, where Hungarians and Austrians were celebrating the dismantling of their border, to flee to Austria. The trickle turned into a flood; thousands poured over daily. The Austrian government then sent them on by bus to automatic citizenship and social welfare payments in West Germany (see Borneman 1991). This flight destabilized the political and domestic situation in which Susan lived; her world was being transformed without her approval, resistance, or complicity. At the very moment when Susan was being asked to construct a coherent narrative about her identity, her social context—the state and forms of belonging in which she lived—was disintegrating.

Paradoxically, what most intruded and disturbed her account was the loss of a form of membership that she had never shared. She had never taken on citizenship of the German Democratic Republic (GDR) but merely maintained residence within its protective and confining borders. Yet she was embedded in a kinship network that included members of that state—parents, siblings, husband, children. It ultimately also contained her through her own lived experience. Despite being formally an outsider in the GDR, she could not escape a confrontation with its position in the international order of things. Both the construction and the disintegration of the East German state, along with its system of memberships, affected her equally. Hence kinship and the state provide the central tropes for her story.

We might begin with a formal representation of her late summer 1989 genealogy of kin and state membership, what I call, to borrow a term from Nietzsche, "effective historical" kin:

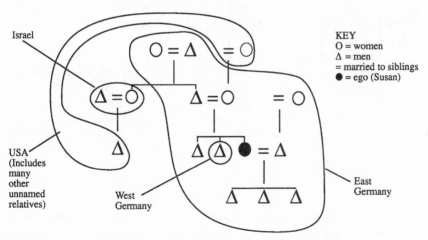

Figure 9.1.   Susan R.'s "effective historical kin," late summer 1989

I have included only those kin specifically mentioned by Susan. Her omissions were not a result of a bout of "genealogical amnesia," nor is her failure to distinguish between "fictive" and "real" kin, as anthropological accounts have been prone to do, a result of category error. Rather, she began by focusing on what was near to her, meaning significant for or memorable to her. At another point in time, she might have even narrated a different genealogy. An abstract lineage model, which, had I insisted, she certainly could have constructed, would have had little relation to the structures of her history. Illumination of these structures, represented by her "effective historical kin," was, after all, the point of her narrative. Note that of the four states in which her kin resided at the time of the interview, only three exist as of this writing (East and West Germany have since been reunited).

SUSAN R.'S GENEALOGY OF KIN AND STATE MEMBERSHIP

Susan was born in 1949 in the United States but fled with her parents to Austria in 1950, to the GDR the following year. "They had to leave," says Susan. "My father was very active politically, a member of the American Communist party, and because my mother was with him and then also had become a member of the Communist party, she too had problems because of this at that time." While attending an international medical conference in Switzerland, her father suspected a return to the United States would result in his arrest. He allowed the party to decide for him whether to return; they told him to stay in Europe. "Therefore my mother had to arrange everything, which wasn't so easy . . . because getting passports"—Susan introduces the word that tropes so much of her experience: "pass-ports," implying state borders, citizenship, freedom of movement—"for the children was problematical." In particular, she explains, it was a problem for her second-oldest brother, who was three years old at the time. He never was told that he had an American passport, "but he found out about it later. [While in the GDR] he had been forced to swear that he never did have a passport and never was an American." But on his last visit to the United States, the computers found him registered as a citizen, much to his surprise. After his return to the GDR, his no longer secret membership was a source of considerable tension between him and his parents.

Nearly half of Susan's two-hour-long narrative is about resisting and resigning oneself to the boundaries imposed by states. She tells this plot genealogically, both in the sense of a history of familial descent and of an archaeology of past events that anticipate her present. Reconstructing the history of interactions between legally inscribed memberships and the movements and motivations of her kin, she "effectuates a mediation between the once and the now" by describing, as Gadamer writes of historical consciousness, "a continual series of perspectives through which the past presents and addresses itself to [her]" (Gadamer 1979: 159).

"My father was born in 1912 in the Soviet Union," she began, immediately adding, "in the territory of Ukraine." Since then, of course, the Ukraine was absorbed into the Soviet Union; in 1912, it was a sovereign territory. And two years after this interview, the Ukraine again became a sovereign state. His personal diaspora began in 1920, when a pogrom directed against the Jews drove his parents—who, like his other relatives, were primarily orthodox Jews—to Austria. The rest of the kin group resettled in the United States. Although subject to anti-Semitism in Austria, Susan's father nonetheless succeeded in going to a private school and later the university, studying medicine and chemistry. Meanwhile, he joined the Communist party in 1930, at the age of eighteen, something about which "he doesn't speak too much," and "insofar as [she] knows, also was imprisoned [for his activities] twice." He lived in Austria until 1937, when he left to accept an offer to study and do research in the United States. To Susan, and, I suspect, to her father, it is unclear whether he had to leave Germany because of his Communist activities or because he was a Jew, the two identities being entwined. He was identified by the authorities as an enemy of the state not on racial grounds but because of his political activities. It is clear, however, that his Jewish background would have eventually also placed him in danger and forced him to leave.

Susan's mother, born in 1912 to a German father and Jewish mother who converted to Christianity, traces her natal home to Africa, where her maternal grandfather did business. This African part of the Jewish family's participation in German colonial history is left unelaborated. Her parents divorced, "not because of the Jewish thing, although it was in 1934, but because of another woman who my grandfather wanted to marry—who then also left him sitting alone."

"My grandmother," Susan explains, "had to earn money herself then, in 1934, [even though] she came from a wealthy family. My grandfather controlled her money and squandered her entire inheritance." Susan lowered her voice and said softly, "She didn't speak too well of him."

Susan's mother grew up in Hamburg, Germany, also studied medicine there, and "first through the National Socialists became interested in Jewishness. She definitely knew nothing about it before." German Jews were perhaps the most assimilated of the European Jewry around the turn of the century. Hitler's racial programs forced many fully "assimilated" Jews to reconstruct an identity that had been partly or wholly superseded by others. Susan is careful not to impute an identity to her mother which was not part of her mother's own subjectivity. In the period before the Nazis came to power, Jewishness, for her mother as well as for many German Jews, was not part of a universal History to be recovered but rather one identity, among others, to be *selected* and reconstructed. After 1934, however, German Jews had little or no "choice" about determining their own selfhood: their Germanness was denied to them; their Jewishness was elevated to a primordial category of being.

"[Sometime later]," she continues, [my mother's] belief in God was broken, and since then she's been [an] atheist." Though her mother had not been politically or religiously active, living with a Jewish mother classified her as "full Jew." On this basis she was denied her doctorate in medicine. In 1938, she emigrated to the United States, with her mother following shortly after. Susan's uncle from this side of the family managed to survive the Nazi period living in Germany and emigrated to the United States in 1950. "Since my parents had already returned [to Germany]," adds Susan, "they never even met [each other] here." Like ships without a compass crossing in the night, Susan's kin in this century were in constant motion but never sure about direction, fleeing from and escaping to territorial units that themselves had shifting residents and boundaries, recovering old identities and shedding new ones, often with no plan or design for life other than survival.

According to Susan, her parents remember the twelve-year period in the United States as "the happiest years of [their] lives. But why they were so happy is because they met there and it was the first love [for them]; my father had his work. They had most of their friends there, either old comrades [from the party] or friends from youth who live in the GDR or Austria now." The great master narratives of the American experience—freedom, liberty, wealth—were not central to her parents' experience. It was something more parochial and concrete—love and friendship—that imprinted itself as America on the memory of her parents.

In this act of recalling the remembrance of her parents, Susan is in effect doing a Nietzschean or Foucaultian genealogy, and she is reaching for a mode of historical understanding of the sort explicated by Gadamer. She seeks out "the singularity of events outside of any monotonous finality" and finds them "in the most unpromising places, in what we tend to feel is without history—in sentiments, love, conscience" (Foucault 1977: 139). Her story is not the progressive realization of an ideal, such as choice or freedom. Genealogical analysis, argued Nietzsche (1964: 9), shows that the concept of liberty is an "invention of the ruling classes," neither fundamental to nature nor connected to being and truth. Susan cannot reconstruct her life with reference to a tale about freedom being realized. Rather, as she descends into the past, she talks of disrupture, dispersion, discontinuity. Yet for Susan this historical knowledge is not part of a nihilistic project, as is often the case when employing the genealogical approach of Nietzsche or Foucault. For her, it "does not necessarily lead to the dissolution of the tradition in which [she] live[s]" but, as Gadamer (1979: 107) has maintained, enables her to discover her own identity by enriching this tradition, either by "confirm[ing] or alter[ing] it."[7]

Exactly why her father had to leave the United States remains unclear. He was sent to Japan by the American government for six months in 1947 to deal with the outbreak of an epidemic. While there, the army discovered that he was a member of the Communist party and called him back. Meanwhile, in America, her mother "distributed leaflets in some apartment area, arguing that blacks should be able to live there. She had her children [especially the oldest son] help her. People shot at her with rifles to terrify her into giving up." This story trails off into micro-events, episodes of what, in retrospect, seem minor political fights but that undoubtedly formed the basis for, as Susan argues, "getting the entire family put on the Black List." Susan's dispersed narrative parallels the uncertainty at the moment of her telling. The trope of disintegration figures both her text and context. Her search through descent in time for the beginning of her family's persecution in America does not settle and provide solace but rather "disturbs what was previously considered immobile," as Foucault characterizes genealogy more generally. "It fragments what was thought unified; it shows the heterogeneity of what was imagined consistent with itself" (Foucault 1977: 147). Accompanying her recognition of the fragmentation around her, Susan is confirmed in her sense of self as relative and incomplete. By not forcing events into a coherent plot that would allow a single interpretation—which, in any case, appears unavailable to her—Susan finds herself able to narrativize her past. She concludes simply that something happened to make her parents enemies of the United States. They left America before she had reached her first year; they ended up in East Germany.

From the United States, the family first fled to Austria. Her father then applied for work: in Austria, France, Israel, and the Soviet Union. Despite his international preeminence in the field of medicine, he found no takers. After nearly a year, he received and accepted an offer from the GDR to found a research institute. Since her parents took the pursuit of science to be central to their identities, their work made them integral to East Germany. And they integrated rather quickly, but they did not assimilate. Even during the height of division in the cold war, they enjoyed a cosmopolitan identity, moving freely from East to West and West to East. In the early 1970s, her father was invited back to the United States to receive an award from the American army for an invention still in use which improves blood conservation. Not until 1978 did they take on GDR citizenship—for what reasons Susan is still unsure. During family dinners possibilities to go elsewhere were discussed constantly. "My mother raised us as if this was a way station," exclaims Susan, "that we'd eventually leave, that we weren't German."

Her mother, also a medical doctor, found the adjustment to life in Germany more difficult than did her father, precisely because she had once felt fully assimilated and then was branded as a foreigner during the Third Reich. "My mother hated the Germans; my father was actually not so nationalistic as my mother. He hadn't actually lived here. He had other things for which he fought, which he had already dealt with personally. He was in the Communist party and fought for other things, while my mother, for her it was as if the whole thing came from another galaxy." Susan is pointing to the apolitical stance of many German Jews before the war, a depoliticization that, on the one hand, enabled them to assimilate into German cultural life (perhaps even a precondition for the assimilation) around the turn of the century and to rise to the top in many fields but, on the other hand, blinded them to the precariousness of their position, to the actual racism around them. The outsider status of her father—coming from an orthodox Jewish family in the Ukraine and then growing up in Austria—enabled him to see the Germans more dispassionately, neither bitterly remembering a rejection nor anticipating full acceptance.

When the Nazis finally achieved power in 1932, their radical anti-Semitic program still seemed unbelievable to many assimilated Jews. Yet inscribed on the body of Susan's grandmother was a history of difference that her mother inherited, though no longer as a physical difference but a historical-psychological perception. "She wasn't big, blond, and blue-eyed, nor a brunette," Susan describes her grandmother, "[but] a classical Jewish type, with black hair. And because of that [my mother] felt herself to be different; she always felt inferior." A physical distinction, though not shared in her mother's body, nonetheless formed the basis for an exclusion, a historical inheritance to be carried around. "My mother can develop an incredible hate. And she developed this hate for the Germans, directing it against West Germany: there is that state that never stopped, never broke [with the Nazis]." In this she shared a sentiment with many leftists, especially Communists, who returned to the GDR after the war. For them, West Germany, which incorporated many leading Nazis into its administrative ranks and judicial system and was tied to the same capitalist structure as the Third Reich, was the bastard child of Hitler. East Germany, in contrast, did not identify itself with German tradition (at least not until the 1980s); additionally, a clean sweep was made of the bureaucracy and judicial system, with, for example, 85 percent of all Nazi judges being fired.[8]

For Susan's parents, this distrust, or hate, in the case of her mother, of all things German extended even to a refusal to identify as victims of the Germans. They wanted nothing more to do with official German systems of classification; in fact, they delayed for twenty-eight years the decision to become GDR citizens. And her mother hesitated for years before applying for *Wiedergutmachung*, recognition as a victim of fascism. To obtain that recognition, one had to offer proof of persecution, something many actual victims viewed as humiliation before old German authorities. Her father, Austrian by birth, had to file his claims in Austria. He also refused to apply, but eventually a friend did it for him—not for reasons of conscience or historical reckoning, emphasizes Susan, but because it was available and he needed the money. "Western currency is short here," he reportedly said. Succumbing to his needs and the pressures of a friend, he obtained official status as a victim of fascism from the Austrian government.

The process of obtaining and maintaining citizenship had a perverse meaning for the "R." family, because, Susan stressed, they were "vagabond types, who never were interested in having a fixed home and a position. I was always for that. I always wanted to leave and experience something else. [When we discussed moving] it was mostly to countries where they had to build something." Yet this building—termed the *Aufbau* in the GDR—was finished by the time Susan reached adulthood. By the mid-1970s, the economy had stagnated, and the leadership sought merely to protect its past accomplishments rather than risk proposing new changes. Indeed Susan had the paradoxical *Schicksal* of being exiled in a country that presented itself as future oriented but romanticized its past (see Borneman 1992*b:* 74–82). She enjoyed neither the protections of East German citizenship nor a sense of belonging there, although she did share with its residents the experience of being contained.

Entering into Susan's homelessness is another dimension of experience and membership from which she was estranged but which, paradoxically, also had a hold on her: religion. Much like in the case of her citizenship and loyalty to a state, Susan was estranged from religion, having only formal ties through her genealogy. Her subjectivity was elsewhere: she identified herself as an atheist. Yet even this belief, seemingly in agreement with official state doctrine, did not facilitate finding a home in the officially called "worker and farmer state," for that state practiced a particular interpretation of Marxism as religion. Atheism functioned as dogma and creed within a holistic system of state-mandated rites and rituals. Therefore, with respect to belief, Susan felt very much on her own.

SUSAN'S JEWISHNESS

"In my family there was constant discussion over Christianity and Judaism, about which is better. My mother," says Susan, "was very much taken by Christianity, my father by Judaism. We [children] were only spectators." In recalling her spectator role in the past, Susan is merely finding earlier forms of the activity that, as she was talking to us, so dramatically characterized her present situation. It seems as if she is always watching and listening but never able to arrive at a final standpoint; she assumes positions that are constantly relativized by changing contexts. Her radical reflexivity and readiness "to understand the possibility of a multiplicity of relative viewpoints" (Gadamer 1979: 110) decenters her narrative, enabling her to place herself in the perspective of others, including, as we will see, non-Jewish Germans. This recognition is in fact a precondition of historical consciousness. "Today no one can shield himself from this reflexivity characteristic of the modern spirit," writes Gadamer (1979: 110). As soon as Susan finds a fact or event or story located in her past to which she might cling and which might be used to frame and interpret her self, it seems to escape from its time sequence and reenter her consciousness as part of a different sequence of events.

How does she deal with the radical indeterminacy of her position? She oscillates between different frames. "But it somehow really made an impression on me that I was living as a German but felt myself to be Jewish, in the sense that I wasn't somehow guilty of the *Taten* [deeds, implying complicity with the Nazis], that I was one of the persecuted peoples." And then she switches frames. "I somehow had the proud feeling of belonging [to the Jews], but at the same time [that produces] insecurity, because I know so little about it. . . . It's quite the vogue now to live as a Jew in the GDR, and there again I'm a little different." According to Susan, the desire of so many contemporary Germans to meet a Jew or their interest in Jewish things "is like observing foreign, exotic animals. . . . I also always see it from the other side"—she emphasizes her relativity, her Jewish and German positions, but then takes a stand, at least on this issue—"I'm not a religious person, and I'll never be. It's simply too late for that." Susan is only too aware of how "late" it is, as she talks to us in the waning months of the cold war, on the abyss of a new, unimaginable era that she suspects will totally destroy the old. The descent into herstory painfully deconstructs the illusions and myths that might make her life seem linear and coherent. However, this descent is also a way to finding a voice, an enabling predicate for narrativity and historical consciousness. It makes more transparent the coming devastation of her parent's political ideology and the collapse of the state, as well as her own situatedness in the present contexts framed by this ideology and this state.

Unable to find a fixed frame located either in the past or in the future, Susan expresses a basic ambivalence about commitment and hesitance about moving out of her present. Nietzsche, in his essay "On the Advantage and Disadvantage of History for Life," characterized positions of radical historicality, like Susan's, as lacking "the strength of being able to *forget* and enclose oneself in a limited *horizon*" (1980: 62). Indeed her stark honesty in remembering opens, instead of delimiting, her horizon, making her vulnerable, as Nietzsche says, in "an endless-unlimited light-wave-sea of known becoming" (ibid.). Moreover, her ambivalence about claiming an essential otherness is prefigured by an unabridgeable sense of apartness from any group. "I always see some danger there," she avers, referring to practicing Judaism in Germany, which "holds [her] back" from entering the Jewish community as a member. Where precisely does she locate this danger?

Susan points to an answer in response to our question as to whether she was raising her children to be conscious of their Jewish background. "They don't even know it. There's always the question: Is it a religion or a race? When it's a religion, then it's really the case that it doesn't make sense, because I'm not religious. Thomas [her husband] also actually is somewhat afraid, because there's always some anti-Semitism. And why should you put this burden on the children? Otherwise," she repeats, "they don't even know about it," stressing the obvious fact that no identity is out there to be found, but, rather, all identities are constructed by seeking them out and learning the rites and behaviors that go with group membership. For Susan, Jewishness is not an essential identity waiting to be confirmed but a learned story that would frame her experience in a particular way. Furthermore, it is a dangerous identity when affirmed in Germany. She addresses this question choosing not to affirm a Jewish identity: her decision is not a matter of finding the really real, a truth outside of history. It is not, Nietzsche would say, like art or religion, which reaches for a truth independent of context. Her Jewishness is contingent on and inseparable from her present situation.

One might ask if her rejection of Judaism is not derived from a fear of anti-Semitism. She can recall only one incident in her past: "I was with my school class in a village, and we were quite loud. Someone said, 'That's just like a Jewish school.' Otherwise, I never experienced anything of the sort." Vastly unlike the conditions under which her parents constructed their identities, Susan's own experience of anti-Semitism is limited to one retold as humor: Jewish children are less disciplined than German children—certainly not a pernicious comparison.

This is not to say, however, that Susan is wholly unconcerned about the resurfacing of anti-Semitism in the virulent forms experienced by her parents. She has reservations and fears, as stated above, about informing her children about Jewishness. Regarding her marriage to Thomas, who is not Jewish, her parents were unconcerned about his ethnic or religious background, only "they were quite relieved that Thomas's family didn't do anything in the Third Reich. My stepmother was an opponent of the regime." Yet Thomas resists her constructing any Jewish identity for herself. "I do not decide alone; the decision rests with my husband. I myself would go to the Jewish community, I think, I would, if it were up to me. But I know exactly that he wouldn't like it, because he doesn't even accept [it]; he would ask what kind of sense it made [to go there]." And she concludes forcefully, "I think that anti-Semitism is still there."

"In the school I always had problems because I was raised to be so critical," she continues. "I always spoke up about what I found unfair. Thomas [whom she met at age 17] saw the problems I had. He thinks that I'm naive. I am naive, but I'm not so political that I'd . . . " And Susan reverses gears, imputing to herself more agency. She did go to the Jewish community once but says, "I can't say that I felt comfortable there. I rationalize my time: I am studying English; I exercise to keep a bit fit. That's already two days. And [as a medical doctor] I often have to work nights. To be an atheist takes a lot of energy, even in Germany." Whatever Jewishness means for Susan, it is not religion and it is not race. Her connection to Jewishness is historical, one that can be traced genealogically, that can be experienced in the present but affirmed only in a particular social space, specifically, in Israel and America.

SUSAN, AMERICA, AND ISRAEL

Susan's personal relationship to America parallels, in an extreme form, her relationship to Austria and the GDR. All three are partial, truncated, subject-object relations, with seemingly overdetermined histories that permit little dialogue and no agency for herself. With respect to America, she has, in fact, no history of her own. "In any case, I have had absolutely no connection to America. We fled while I was still small." The United States took her father's citizenship away, and her mother "gave her [passport] back, on moral grounds." Her father then reassumed his Austrian citizenship, through which her mother, as wife, and the three children automatically obtained citizenship also. (It is striking how her mother's identity is taken completely out of her hands by states and men: first, by the Nazi state, then by her legal marriage to a man disliked by his state [the U.S.A.] and to whom she is bound.) The family entered the GDR with Austrian citizenship, which set them apart from other East Germans. "We were somewhat different," explains Susan about her family status in East Germany. "Anyway, [this fact] certainly made an impression on me."

Her parents "were completely into the rituals of the GDR, . . . immediately joined the ruling Socialist Unity party (SED), [though] they weren't GDR citizens." European socialist parties had traditionally defined membership in nonnational terms, but following the end of World War II, most of these parties became more national focused and based. The SED, in particular, was selective about its foreign national members, given the cold war context and its fear of spies in the ranks. For Susan, even though she "felt [herself] somewhat different" from other GDR citizens, there was "no confrontation in the political domain," because her parents, being in basic agreement with the regime, were strong supporters of the state at home.

"Back then that was all no problem; I don't know," she hesitates, "how that is today." She joined the Young Pioneers, for children up to the age of twelve, and later the Free German Youth, for those aged twelve to thirty, even though, she emphasizes, "I do not have GDR citizenship."

And then Susan reflects, "I can only say that I've lived my conscious life [*bewuβtes Leben*] here"—emphasizing that she is constituted by those personal experiences of which she is conscious. "My conscious life has taken place only in the GDR. For that reason, I am bound to the GDR. In upbringing, we [in the family] were not raised as Germans. We had Austrian citizenship; therefore we traveled on vacation to Austria or England. My parents never allowed these limits to subjugate them after 1961" (she elliptically refers to the building of the wall).

For Susan, whose conscious life is intimately "bound to the GDR," being Jewish is not part of living there but rather only possible for her in two other territories: Israel and the United States. She begins answering a question about her own relation to Jewishness as follows: "About the topic of Jewishness. I basically did not know that I was American"—she slides from identity to topography, bringing in America and Israel—"not until I visited a cousin of mine, whose father lives in Israel." Her father's sister had resettled in Israel in 1934, married, and had two sons, one of whom resettled in New York. This son, Susan's cousin, got married in 1971 and invited Susan to his wedding. She went to the American embassy in West Berlin to get a visa on her Austrian passport. But she needed no visa, the embassy officials explained, since she was already an American citizen. She need only apply for a passport, which would take six weeks to obtain. Since the wedding was in four weeks and a visa took only three, she applied for the visa instead. When she returned to pick it up, the embassy surprised her, however, with a passport. "I needed only a pass photo and I would get a passport!"

Susan did actually attend that Jewish wedding in the United States, traveling on an American passport, making her relatives "insufferably proud" of her—a Jew from East Germany with an American passport. But she found it all somewhat embarrassing. "Since I wasn't really raised a Jew, it presented me with certain problems. On the other hand," she turns back on herself again, "I didn't make the attempt to know about it definitely." Therefore, during the trip, she "always felt uncertain," which did not detract from her most important memory, of "a fantastic belonging, what you don't at all know here [in the GDR]. Naturally," says Susan about the Americans, "I told them only [about] their merits." Much as the size and wealth of America impressed her, so did the "fear of the Americans, the [general] fear of blacks," the racism, and the fact "that I was forbidden to travel alone in the subway in New York." Moreover, she found it odd that later, when she decided to marry Thomas, she had to justify to her American relatives her decision not to have a Jewish marriage.

In narrating her life, Susan counterbalanced her genealogy of kin, along with its entire affective and experiential import, with genealogies of other memberships, particularly those of citizen and nation. Her perspective is informed by cross-cutting and overlapping genealogies, each of which positions her differently with respect to culture, nation, and state. Through a process that selects, foregrounds, highlights, sequences, and periodizes, she creatively narrativized each descent out of heterodox events and happenings. No single membership necessarily takes priority over the others. "It's quite clear," she asserts about the relativity of citizenship and political membership, "that you don't feel yourself bound to a country just because you have a passport from there."

Susan even goes so far as to maintain that she feels bound to countries from which she has no passport. Like many German Jews who still live in some part of Germany, Susan shares a special relationship with the state of Israel. "I did go alone to Israel once. I happened onto the idea that I'd go and see how things are there. My parents agreed." She could stay with her father's sister, who had settled in Palestine in the early 1930s. "Then came the war," meaning the 1967 war, "and my parents thought it was too dangerous and uncertain." Several years later, the opportunity presented itself again. She finds most memorable about the trip an event that marked her sense of Jewishness: the experience on the airplane from Bucharest to Israel. "That was like a big family. You had the feeling that it wasn't important where you came from. Talking with one another, somehow I was taken by that." The trip seemed more meaningful than either the departure or arrival. Susan was "taken by" the unconcern for "where you came from," the disregard for ultimate kin and citizen origins. Israel was a topos on which she could place her dreams of belonging to a community of vagabonds (see the interviews in Ostow 1989).

SUSAN AND HISTORICAL CONSCIOUSNESS

With no fixed tradition—neither Jewish nor German, Communist nor capitalist—to which she could claim any primordial belonging, Susan felt stranded in an ethereal, disintegrating present. The mass exodus to West Germany of her fellow GDR residents—all citizens, unlike her—left her feeling, she tells us, even more like a beached whale. The formal documents—Austrian and American passports, East German visa—granting her freedom to go where she wanted meant very little to her. "Now even more [of the people] with whom I work are gone, more [of those] from my circle of friends have gone over there [to West Germany]. I have a permanent visa, so I have the possibility to travel to West Berlin, and I've kept contact with those who have left. But it's like this: I don't make myself an exception from the other GDR citizens. In this respect, I feel as if I am fully GDR. It's a fact that I could always travel. It's a fact that other citizens of the GDR could also travel when they have relatives. But it's somewhat different to travel alone and not with a partner or with your family. Since I married, I've nearly quit traveling."

"I can still travel to West Berlin, and I go shopping and visit someone, but it's different. Basically, I'm just as imprisoned as the other GDR citizens. I feel pretty much identical to them in this respect." Susan is, then, technically free to move around as she wishes. The restrictive laws of GDR do not apply to her, an Austrian citizen. Yet she feels "just as imprisoned as other GDR citizens." Why? Because, for Susan, reaching adulthood entailed finding "a partner," marriage, and having children. It is her commitment to these individuals, to domestic life, that positions her in their world and hence imprisons her.

Though technically registered as an American citizen, her American passport has since lapsed, and Susan laments her failure to get it renewed in 1976. By that time, the Americans had an embassy representative in East Berlin. She went in and applied, but the man behind the counter couldn't give her any direct answers. "Later I found out that he was a GDR citizen working there, not an American. I found that unfair." American embassies in Eastern Europe, which were forced to hire a certain number of native personnel, were notorious for their lax security. Susan asks herself, "Why [didn't I get it renewed]? I guess out of laziness. I would have had to go someplace, and . . . " Anyone with experience in Eastern Europe before 1989 knows what a labyrinth the bureaucracy presented when one sought to obtain things that the state did not want to distribute but that the state reserved for itself to distribute. Rather than complain about these obstacles, Susan criticizes herself for laziness. In her struggle to find a voice to articulate her own needs, she always returns to self-critique— in a fashion that became the norm in the waning months of the existence of East Germany—about her own shortcomings, her own lack of initiative, her own inability to stand alone. Paradoxically, her search for belonging is compounded, not facilitated, by the fact that she is a full member of no group and therefore not bound formally to, or privileged by, the rules and traditions of any particular group.

She sees her self as a mediator between sets of interests and constraints: her German husband and Jewish descent, East and West, career and children. Though she is a very capable doctor, as capable as her two brothers, whom she views as geniuses, she cannot commit herself to her work and career at the cost of others. Her parents exhort her to study for an advanced degree and become a head doctor at the Charitee. But she is torn between the "huge responsibilities [of the head doctor], responsibilities that you can't push onto others, that you have to decide for yourself," and being a "simple doctor." Susan equivocates: "Actually, whether that is what I want, I don't know." She has three children, one of whom is "somewhat handicapped," requiring special daily attention. The service shifts for head doctors "are so long. These are all things that you have to consider. Either you do this, or you do that." Indeterminacy tropes Susan's story, as she searches for a definition of "what [I] want to do, what [I] want to be." Her past, reconstructed genealogically, has imprisoned her in one corner of the present, yet an awareness of this present swings her back to a reflection on beginnings. Reflection on beginnings, in turn, presents the past as arbitrary, as possible paths taken and not taken. Hence it opens up a painfully indeterminate future, not fixed by history but nonetheless articulated through it.

Here we might quote Gadamer as our witness on the nature of experience. He states that "the truth of experience always contains an orientation towards new experience. That is why a person who is called 'experienced' has become such not only through experiences, but is also open to new experiences. The perfection of experience . . . does not consist in the fact that someone already knows everything and knows better than anyone else. Rather, the experienced person proves to be, on the contrary, someone who is radically undogmatic; who, because of the many experiences he has had and the knowledge he has drawn from them is particularly well equipped to have new experiences and to learn from them" (1982: 319). Hence, rather than confuse Susan's basic indeterminacy with a lack of clarity or will, we should commend it as a result of knowledge obtained from experience properly reflected on.

CONCLUSION

Through this examination of Susan R.'s narrative autobiography, I hope to have demonstrated the necessary relationship among genealogy, narrative, and historical consciousness. If genealogy is an essential method of reconstruction and narrative the form by which that reconstruction obtains meaning, then historical consciousness is the way one situates and evaluates that meaning in time and space. Each performs a job that predicates the others in reaching the common goal of cultural understanding. Susan's story seems a perfect demonstration of Foucault's statement about genealogy: "The forces operating in history are not controlled by destiny or regulative mechanisms, but respond to haphazard conflict. They do not manifest the successive forms of a primordial intention and their attraction is not that of a conclusion, for they always appear through the singular randomness of events" (Foucault 1977: 154–155). Indeed, Susan's narration of her story in the waning days of the cold war dramatized the "single randomness of events," making her often painful choices more sober, more reasoned. Her acceptance of indeterminacy in culture, nationality, and citizenship, of ambiguity and conflict within identity, bespeaks a contemporary heroism, one less of the ritual leader than the everyday survivor.

Drawing on Susan's genealogy of "effective historical kin," we uncovered what Nietzsche called an "effective history," meaning one that inverts the relationship that traditional history establishes between proximity and distance. We began by focusing on things nearest to us, on personal events rather than political history and theoretical models of how Susan's kin should be represented. Her telling was perspectival, inseparable from and indeed informed by the moment of its inscription. Despite his equivocations about hermeneutics, Foucault supports Gadamer's conception of historical consciousness when he writes that a "final trait of effective history is its affirmation of knowledge as perspective" (1977: 156).

Anthropologists have often evaded acknowledging the historicity of their own productions. While priding themselves on knowledge of place, they often deny their special grounding in time (see Fabian 1983). By striving toward a fuller historical consciousness, we anthropologists are doing much more than merely acknowledging the historicity of our productions. For method and context are not merely constraints that might be bracketed or overcome, or in some way understood as dependent variables. They might also be seen as the necessary and enabling space in which narrative is made to work. Our understanding of historical space is more than a prelude to knowledge of the objective world; it is also a form of knowledge about events of cultural significance necessary for a self-articulation and definition in the present.

This articulation proceeds genealogically and is given form by narrative. But narratives do not contain within them a measure for their truth-value. They are fictions of events, representations of what happened, one no more true than the other. It is historical consciousness that redeems this endeavor by "affirming knowledge as perspective," by restoring truth-value to the articulation of form. A mature narrative obtains truth-value only and insofar as it is conscious of the conditions of its production, aware of and capable of learning from its own beginnings. In much the same way that Susan's telling though genealogy is tied to a presentness that she cannot—and should not try to—mask, that, in fact, situates her knowledge, we anthropologists are also, if we remain faithful to our method of intensive fieldwork, bound to a present that we cannot—and should not try to—flee from. Indeed, it is in this space where form is (per)formed that one finds the articulation of narrativity, genealogy, and historical consciousness. Hence the inescapable embeddedness of the fieldwork situation in the present should not be seen as a problem to overcome but as a fundamental and specifically anthropological source of knowledge.

NOTES

1. In an article, Scott Long and I (1991: 285–314) were interested in demonstrating how a dialogue between practitioners in the disciplines of literary study and anthropology could generate a mutual practice of textual criticism. My project here is to demonstrate a *necessary* conceptual relationship between anthropology and literature. I wish to thank Andy Wallace and Jeannette Mageo for their insightful comments in helping me clarify the relationships discussed in this chapter.

2. The usual distinction made between ethnographer and anthropologist is that the former merely engaged in fieldwork, that is, in data collection at the site where "the native" or subject studied lives, whereas the latter goes beyond fieldwork to fit data into forms that facilitate comparison cross-culturally. In this chapter, I compare anthropologists to literary critics who deal with narrative, both of whom depend on some sort of ethnographer or kind of ethnographic activity to construct the texts to be analyzed.

3. Paul Ricoeur (1981: 197–221), in a foundational essay on social action as a text, argued for the autonomy of text from author after its initial inscription in writing. I would maintain, following Edward Said, that this distinction is overdrawn, for the initial event of production is "incorporated in the text, an infrangible part of its capacity for conveying and producing meaning" (1983: 39). The understanding of texts has already commenced on reading, argues Said, and "is already constrained by, and constraining, their interpretation" (ibid.). Indeed, many anthropologists have experienced the situation of inscription itself—that means the fieldwork setting and the moment of authorship—as a revealing source of anthropological knowledge.

4. I am aware that anthropologists and literary critics also concern themselves with texts that do not take narrative form, such as some fragments, poems, and chronicles. However, I would argue for the cultural primacy of the narrative document. As "a primary and irreducible form of human comprehension, an article in the constitution of common sense" (Mink 1978: 132), which fashions diverse experiences into a form assimilable to structures of meaning that are generally human rather than culture-specific (White 1984), narrative is central to the disciplines of anthropology and literature. "Narrative in fact seems to hold a special place among literary forms," maintains Peter Brooks, "because of its potential for summary and retransmission: the fact that we can still recognize 'the story' even when its medium has been considerably changed" (1984: 4).

5. Susan R. is one of 23 German Jews whom Jeffrey Peck and I interviewed during the summer of 1989. We interviewed 11 in West Berlin and 12 in East Berlin; 12 who reached adulthood before World War II, 11 who reached adulthood after. All participants in our project had been in exile (or their parents had been in exile) in one of the countries of the Allied forces, and all had returned to either East or West Berlin. Our criteria of selection was not random but was designed to illustrate a range of comparative historical contexts. We have also completed a book, entitled *Soujourners: The Return of German Jews and the Question of Identity in Germany* (Lincoln: University of Nebraska Press, 1995), as well as a film of the same name on those who returned to East Germany. This interview with Susan R. was conducted in German; the translation and interpretation are mine.

6. See the discussion of Nietzsche's use of these terms by Foucault (1977: 140–142).

7. Foucault and Nietzsche nearly always used the genealogical approach to take apart and destruct some putative unitary whole. Although I am not problematizing my differences with them here, I would, in fact, insist—and a reading of both authors consistent with mine is also possible—that in addition to its deconstructive role, genealogy also provides the possibility for a reconstruction, though less authoritative and more fragile and, of course, historically contingent.

8. On denazification, see Weber (1985: 107–109) and Niethammer (1988: 115–131). For a comparative discussion of the meaning of postwar reform in East and West Germany, see Borneman (1992*a*, 1992*b*).

REFERENCES

Borneman, John.
    1991.   *After the Wall: East Meets West in the New Berlin*. New York: Basic Books.
    ———. 1993. "Uniting the German Nation: Law, Narrative, and Historicity." *American Ethnologist* 20 (2): 218–311.
    ———. 1992*a*. "State, Territory, and Identity Formation in the Postwar Berlins, 1945–1989." *Cultural Anthropology* 7(1): 44–61.
    ———. 1992*b*. *Belonging in the Two Berlins: Kin, State, Nation*. Cambridge: Cambridge University Press.
Brooks, Peter.
    1984.   *Reading for the Plot: Design and Intention in Narrative*. New York: Alfred A. Knopf.
Bruner, Edward, ed.
    1984.   *Text, Play and Story: The Construction and Reconstruction of Self and Society*. Washington, D.C.: American Ethnological Society.
    ———. 1986. "Ethnography as Narrative." In *The Anthropology of Experience*, ed. E. Bruner and V. Turner, 139–158. Urbana: University of Illinois Press.
Clifford, James.
    1988.   The Predicament of Culture. Cambridge: Harvard University Press.
Clifford, James, and George Marcus, eds.
    1986.   *Writing Culture*. Berkeley, Los Angeles, and London: University of California Press.
Fabian, Johannes.
    1983.   *Time and the Other: How Anthropology Makes Its Object*. New York: Columbia University Press.
Foucault, Michel.
    1977.   *Language, Counter-Memory, Practice*. Ed. and intro. by Donald F. Bouchard. Ithaca: Cornell University Press.
Gadamer, Hans-Georg.
    1979.   "The Problem of Historical Consciousness." In *A Social Science Reader*, ed. Paul Rabinow and William Sullivan, 103–160. Berkeley, Los Angeles, and London: University of California Press.
    ———. 1982. *Truth and Method*. New York: Crossroad Publishing Company.

Henke, Klaus-Dieter, and Hans Woller,
 1991. Politische Säuderung in Europe: Die Abrechnung mit Faschismus und Kollaboration nach dem Zweiten Weltkrieg. Munich: Deutscher Taschenbuch.
Herzfeld, Michael.
 1985. *The Poetics of Manhood: Contest and Identity in a Cretan Mountain Village.* Princeton: Princeton University Press.
Long, Scott, and John Borneman.
 1991. "Power, Objectivity, and the Other: Studies in the Creation of Sexual Species in Anglo-American Discourse." *Dialectical Anthropology* 15 (4): 285–314.
Marcus, George, and Michael Fischer.
 1986. *Anthropology as Cultural Critique.* Chicago: University of Chicago Press.
Mink, Louis O.
 1978. Narrative Form as Cognitive Instrument." In *The Writing of History: Literary Form and Historical Understanding,* ed. Robert H. Canary and Henry Kozicki, 129–149. Madison: University of Wisconsin Press.
Mitchell, W. J. T., ed.
 1981. *On Narrative.* Chicago: University of Chicago Press.
Niethammer, Lutz.
 1988. "Entnazifizierung: Nachfragen eines Historikers." In *Von der Gnade der geschenkten Nation,* ed. Hago Funke and W.-D. Narr, 115–131. Berlin: Rotbuch Verlag.
Nietzsche, Friedrich.
 1964. "The Wanderer and His Shadow." In *Human, All Too Human.* II. *The Complete Works of Friedrich Nietzsche,* Vol. VII. Ed. Oscar Levy. New York: Russell and Russell.
 1980. *On the Advantage and Disadvantage of History for Life.* Trans with intro. by Peter Preuss. Indianapolis: Hackett Publishing Company.
Ostow, Robin.
 1989. *Jews in Contemporary East Germany: The Children of Moses in the Land of Marx.* New York: St. Martin's Press.
Ricoeur, Paul.
 1981. *Hermeneutics and the Human Sciences.* Cambridge: Cambridge University Press.
———. 1984. *Time and Narrative.* Vol. 1. Chicago: University of Chicago Press.
Said, Edward.
 1983. *The World, the Text, and the Critic.* Cambridge: Harvard University Press.
Weber, Hermann.
 1985. *Geschichte der DDR.* München: C. H. Beck.
White, Hayden.
 1973. *Metahistory: The Historical Imagination in Nineteenth-Century Europe.* Baltimore: John Hopkins University Press.
———. 1978. "The Historical Text as Literary Artifact." In *The Writing of History: Literary Form and Historical Understanding,* ed. Robert Canary and Henry Kozicki, 41–62. Madison: University of Wisconsin Press.
———. 1984. "The Question of Narrative in Contemporary Historical Theory." *History Theory* 23 (1): 1–33.

TEN

Race and Ruins

Zita Nunes

Pouca saúde e muita saúva Os males do Brasil são.

With fewer ants and better health Brazil will lead the world in wealth.[1]
—MARIO DE ANDRADE, *Macunaéma*

The question, What is Brazil(ian)? has informed much of Brazilian writing—political, sociological, or historical. For literary critics and theorists, however, defining this identity has become, according to the critic Angel Rama, a patriotic mission, making out of literature the appropriate instrument for forging a national identity.[2] Literature, then, is central not only to the reflection but also to the formation of a national identity. Most nationalisms base themselves on a return to a pure, homogeneous origin involving the repression of all that troubles the integrity and purity of that origin. This logic, which informed Brazil's discourse on race through the beginning of this century and which also inhered in the quest to come up with a fixed identity, was threatened by the reality of miscegenation. I maintain that much of Brazilian literature relating to the question of national identity is an attempt to resolve the "problem" of miscegenation.

During the course of the slave trade, Brazil received 37 percent of the total number of Africans brought by force to the Americas (as compared to North America's 5 percent).[3] By the mid-nineteenth century, according to Emilia Viotti da Costa, the population of Brazil consisted of 1,347,000 whites and 3,993,000 blacks and mulattoes.[4] Throughout the nineteenth century, debate centered on the necessity of creating the conditions that would allow Brazil to emerge not only as a nation but also as a participant in the movement of modernization, progress, and development taking place in Europe and the United States.[5] After the abolition of slavery in 1888 did away with an institution that many abolitionists argued was an impediment to integration with the West, the increasing popularity of theories of biological and social determinism appeared to confirm the elite's anxiety about the inherent inferiority of the nation's largely black and mulatto population. The question became one of citizenship and the creation of a national

235

myth. Any notion of a universal (white) subject became difficult to sustain; blacks, no longer Africans but subjects of the republic of Brazil (established in 1889), were perceived to be threats to stability of the "self," the family, and the nation by an elite anxious to reproduce itself as "Brazilian."[6]

Euclides da Cunha expressed this anxiety very clearly in *Os Sertões,* a work widely acknowledged to be one of the masterpieces of Brazilian letters. Early in the work, which chronicles the battle between government troops and followers of a charismatic leader in the interior of the northeast of Brazil, da Cunha inserts a chapter entitled "An Irritating Parenthesis" (Um parêntesis irritante). The mixture of races is harmful, he claims, because the resulting brief individual existence undermines centuries of natural selection and consolidation of a race. Mestizos are by nature unstable and incapable of reproducing themselves as they are but only as approximations of one or the other of the component races. In da Cunha's conception, Brazil cannot claim a unity of race and, therefore, violates what he calls natural laws: instead of the nation originating from a race (as in the guiding myths of Europe), the nation must be constructed as a unity to allow the formation of what da Cunha calls a "historic" race.[7] In this formulation the nation is a narrative of becoming fraught with ambivalence[8] and race a construct always in danger of coming undone. As will become clear, there is conflict between the elite's post-abolition desire to reproduce itself within a context of a modern notion of the nation based on citizenship (where whites could continue to dominate) and the necessity to create a national unity based on a concept of mixture. The conflict was addressed through the elaboration of a myth of racial democracy.

It has become almost cliché to call attention to the need of separating "race" from "biology" when addressing Brazilian thinking on issues of race. I am referring here to the habit of claiming that in Brazil race is not defined solely, if at all, in terms of biology. This tenet of racial democracy could appear to lend support to recent theoretical debates that rightly reveal race as a construct.[9] Many have been misled, however, into thinking that Brazil has achieved a deconstruction of race; the irony is that race in this case is being disavowed in the interest of protecting and ensuring this continuation of a highly racialized system. Paul Gilroy reminds us that while races "are not simple expressions of . . . biological and cultural sameness," "the brain-teasing perplexities of theorizing about race cannot be allowed to obscure the fact that the play of difference in which racial taxonomy appears has extradiscursive referents."[10] In Brazil the very appearance of a deconstruction of race has permitted the obscuring of the fact that the statistical gap between whites and "browns" (*pardos*) in terms of infant mortality, life expectancy, and household income is consistently wide, while the statistical gap between "browns" and blacks is consistently narrow.[11]

The issues that occupied the attention of politicians and intellectuals during the early decades of the republic continue to engage Brazilians. This is clear from debates that took place in 1989 during the campaign preceding the first direct presidential election in three decades. Soon after the election of Fernando Collor, the *Folha de São Paulo,* one of Brazil's most prestigious newspapers, published a response by a widely known journalist to a complaint of racism received from a reader. In an earlier article, the journalist had described the new president as "tall, handsome, white—white in the Western mold" (Ele é alto, bonito, branco, branco ocidental). The journalist defended himself against the charge of racism by claiming that in attaching a value of Collor's whiteness, he does nothing different from the vast majority of Brazilians[12] and that if this is sick, there are not enough doctors in Brazil to provide treatment. He wrote that people of color are as "palatable" to him as any other but to consider Brazil a Third World country and to seek to forge links with Africa (as the other candidate, Luis Ignacio da Silva, had proposed) would require that "we [Brazilians] distance ourselves from our cultural heritage which is the West . . . [and] the United States" (Nós nos afastamos da nossa herança cultural que é o Ocidente, os EUA).[13]

In addition to demonstrating the continuity of a concern with defining a Brazilian identity, particularly in relation to the rest of the world, and with defining the representative Brazilian, this article calls attention to a metaphorics of the body that has been a constant in discussions of race in Brazil and that received its clearest and most organized expression during the modernist movement of the 1920s.

It would be impossible to overstate the impact of the modernist movement or its importance as a point of reference for subsequent generations. The Semana de Arte Moderna (Week of Modern Art) is generally acknowledged to be the inaugural event of the modernist movement, an event that one of the organizers called "o primeiro sintoma espiritual da transmutação de nossa consciência" (the first intellectual symptom of the transformation of our consciousness).[14] Of the many events leading up to the Semana de Arte Moderna, one of the most important was a 1917 exhibit of art by the Brazilian painter Anita Malfatti, who had just returned from a trip to Europe and the United States where she had been influenced by cubist and expressionist aesthetics and techniques. The exhibit drew together the writers, artists, journalists, and scholars who would organize the Semana de Arte Moderna.

From the 11th to the 18th of February 1922, the Municipal Theater in São Paulo was the site of art exhibitions, dance and music performances, lectures, and readings that explored or staged various aspects of modernism. The event launched a movement that proclaimed a rupture or a break with the past in order to subvert what were considered bourgeois methods of artistic expression. The modernists allied themselves with European vanguard movements such as surrealism and futurism. The writers published newspapers, journals, and manifestos in addition to works of fiction, poetry, and ethnography.

Although the speakers and performers were roundly jeered and heckled by the crowd that filled the theater, a contemporary observer of the events noted that the Semana de Arte Moderna had been financed by many of São Paulo's most established business and social figures and supported by the *Correio Paulistano,* the newspaper of the governing PRP (Partido Republicano Paulista, or Republican party of São Paulo) with the consent of Washington Luis, the republic's president.[15]

The decade of the 1920s in Brazil was marked by intense cultural and political unrest. The prevailing view is that during this decade the new generation of Brazilian artists who formed the modernist movement caused a profound intellectual upheaval by giving national values and themes precedence over foreign values and themes. One of the most prominent ideas to draw the attention of the modernists was that concerning the role and contribution of blacks to Brazilian society. By the 1930s, a parallel socioanthropological literature had appeared which emphasized (in ways that were paradoxical) that blacks were an integral element in Brazilian society as a result of their significant contributions to Brazil's history and development.

The most vibrant personality associated with this new socioanthropological school was Gilberto Freyre, who had returned to Brazil in 1925 after studying at Columbia University with the anthropologist Franz Boas. Many Brazilians, as well as Americans and Europeans, have accepted as valid Freyre's luso-tropical assertions of racial tolerance.[16] Many scholars, however, have criticized Freyre for dwelling on interracial liaisons while masking the basic economic and political realities of racial exploitation and oppression.

In an introduction to *The Masters and the Slaves* (Casa grande e senzala), a work that has greatly influenced the question of race and identity in Brazil, Freyre states that he based the method for his socioanthropological work on methods developed by Pablo Picasso in the realm of art, an approach that linked him (despite avowed differences) to the modernists in São Paulo. In addition, Freyre, like the paulista modernists, takes up the issues that had preoccupied Euclides da Cunha, particularly those related to perceived threats to Brazil's modernity.

In *Casa grande e senzala,* Freyre writes that there existed in the Northeast a superstition that the blood of blacks (rather than the usual whale oil) mixed into the mortar would increase the strength of the foundation. It was rumored that a plantation owner, anxious to guarantee the perpetuity of his domain, ordered that two blacks be killed and buried in the foundation of the Big House. "The irony, however, is that for lack of human potential this arrogant solidity of form and material was often useless: by the third or fourth generation, huge houses built to last centuries began to crumble, decayed by abandonment and lack of conservation. The inability of the great-grandchildren to save the ancestral heritage" (O irônico, porém, é que, por

falta de potencial humano, toda essa solidez arrogante de forma e material
foi muitas vezes inútil: na terceira ou quarta geração, casas enormes edifi-
cadas para atravessar séculos começaram a esfarelar-se de podres por aban-
dono e falta de conservação. Incapacidade dos bisnetos ou mesmo netos
para conservarem a herança ancestral). (lxvii–lxviii)

After recounting this anecdote which demonstrates how Brazil's foundation degenerates when the blood of Africans is (literally) mixed in, Freyre
addresses the "problem" of miscegenation. He states in the introduction,

> It was as if everything was dependent upon me and those of my generation,
> upon the manner in which we succeeded in solving age-old questions. And
> of all the problems confronting Brazil, there was none that gave me so much
> anxiety as that of miscegenation. (xxvii)

> Era como se tudo dependesse de mim e dos de minha geração; da nossa
> maneira de resolver questões seculares. E dos problemas brasileiros, nenhum
> que me inquietasse tanto como o da miscigenação. (lvii)

Freyre continues,

> Once upon a time, after three straight years of absence from my country, I
> caught sight of a group of Brazilian seamen—mulattoes and *cafusos* crossing
> the Brooklyn Bridge. I no longer remember if they were from São Paulo or
> from Minas, but they impressed me as being caricatures of men, and there
> came to mind a phrase from a book on Brazil by an American traveler:
> "The fearful mongrel aspect of the population." That was the sort of thing to
> which miscegenation led. I ought to have had someone to tell me then what
> Roquette Pinto had told the Aryanizers of the Brazilian Eugenics Congress in
> 1929: that these individuals whom I looked upon as representatives of Brazil
> were not simply mulattoes or *cafusos* but *sickly* ones. (xxvii)

> Vi uma vez, depois de mais de três anos maciços de ausência do Brasil, um
> bando de marinheiros nacionais—mulatos e cafusos— descendo não me lem-
> bro se de São Paulo ou do Minas pela neve mole de Brooklyn. E veio-me à lem-
> brança a frase de um livro de viajante americano que acabara de ler sobre o
> Brasil: "The fearfully mongrel aspect of most of the population." A miscigi-
> nação resultava naquilo. Faltou-me quem me dissesse então, como em 1929
> Roquette-Pinto aos arianistas do Congresso Brasileiro de Eugenia, que não
> eram simplesmente mulatos ou cafusos os indivíduos que eu julgava repre-
> sentarem o Brasil, mas cafusos e mulatos *doentes*. (lvii)

The discourse on race and miscegenation in Brazil is tied to a
metaphorics of the body and an economy of eating, incorporation, and sickness. The body politic has a sickness that it must rid itself of: The "problem"
with miscegenation is not miscegenation in and of itself but miscegenation
as the perpetuation of a sickness. In this assessment blacks maintain the status of a foreign body. A healthy body is one that overcomes the weakening

effects of an offending organism. Freyre's project of defining the relation of race to identity is grounded in this discourse: "Having considered these points [the ethnic groups to which Africans belong, physical characteristics, relative intelligence, etc.] which appear to me to be of basic importance in studying the African influence on Brazilian culture, character, and eugenics, I now feel more inclined to undertake the task of discovering the more intimate aspects of this contagious influence" (321). (Considerados esse pontos, que nos parecem de importância fundamental para o estudo da influência africana sobre a cultura, o caráter e a eugenia do brasileiro, sentimonos agora mais à vontade para o esforço de procurar surpreender aspectos mais íntimos dessa influência e desse contágio" [314].) The strategy for overcoming the contagious influence was so widely disseminated that even Roosevelt could summarize it: "In Brazil . . . the idea looked forward to is the disappearance of the Negro question through the disappearance of the Negro himself—that is through his gradual absorption into the white race."[17] Faced with miscegenation's threat to the superiority of whites, Freyre transforms miscegenation into a narrative of assimilation. Of course, the absurdity of this formulation cannot be overemphasized given Brazil's population.

Freyre was certainly not the only scholar to link the notions of race, health, and nation. Wilson Martins discusses at length how the athletics and robust health important to writers such as Graça Aranha and Marinetti "were themes directly and consciously connected with a concern for hygiene, public and private, and the problems of national defense."[18] Others who discussed the "disadvantages" of miscegenation in these terms were Silvio Romero, Euclides da Cunha, and Paulo Prado, whom Martins calls "a physician or a surgeon who wishes to effect a cure" (90). In *Retrato do Brasil,* Prado writes,

> The Brazilian mulatto has undoubtedly furnished notable examples of inteligence, breeding, and moral value to the community. On the other hand, this population shows such physical weakness, such organisms which cannot defend against disease and vices, that it is natural to ask if this state of things isn't the result of the intense crossing of races and subraces. . . . In Brazil, if there is harm in this, it has been done, irremediably. We wait in the slowness of the cosmic process for the uncoding of this enigma with the patience of laboratory researchers.[19]

> O mestiço brasileiro tem fornecido indubitavelmente à communidade exemplares notaveis de intelligencia, de cultura, de valor moral. Por outro lado, as populações offerecem tal fraqueza physica, organismos tão indefesos contra a doença e os vicios, que é uma interrogação natural indagar si esse estado de coisas nao provem do intenso cruzamento das raças e subraças. . . . No Brasil, si ha mal, elle esta feito, irremediavelmente: esperemos, na lentidao do

processo cosmico, a decifração do enigma com a serenidade dos experimentadores de laboratorio.

It is to Paulo Prado that Mário de Andrade, folklorist, poet, and theorist dedicates *Macunaíma*. Mário de Andrade states that one of his goals in *Macunaíma* was to deregionalize his creation while trying to "conceber literariamente o Brasil como entidade homogênea" (conceive Brazil literarily as a homogeneous entity).[20] Like Mário de Andrade, the modernists in general searched for a way to "Brazilianize" Brazil. For them, however, this "Brazilianizing" was to be accomplished through artistic and literary efforts whose aesthetics and techniques were almost entirely drawn from those of contemporary Europe. Let us remember that the cubists had already discovered the value of incorporating Africa.

The modernists' method was outlined by Oswald de Andrade in "O Manifesto Pau Brasil" (The Brazilwood Manifesto) and the "Manifesto Antropófago" (The Cannibalist Manifesto). This method consists of swallowing and absorbing what is useful in a culture and excreting what is not useful. The supposed cannibalism of the indigenous population served as a model for a different cultural relationship between Brazil and the outside world (defined largely as Europe)—a relationship wherein foreign influences would not be copied but digested and absorbed as a precondition to the creation of a new, more independent national civilization. *Macunaíma* is one practice of the modernist project and has been upheld as a celebration of Brazil's "indigenous past." In fact, we shall see that the indigenous past is merely a repository of possible paradigms and that *Macunaíma* is localized in a metaphorics of the body in which eating, incorporation, and disease are foregrounded.

The story, or *rapsódia,* to use Mário de Andrade's term, traces Macunaíma's origins in the Amazonian forest, his trip to São Paulo, and his return to the forest before ascending into the heavens to become the Big Dipper. In his letters and in the introductions to *Macunaíma,* Mário de Andrade describes how *Macunaíma* was composed mainly of found texts that he then exaggerated. In the epilogue, the narrator describes how Macunaíma's story comes to be told.

> There in the foliage the man discovered a green parrot with a golden beak looking at him. He said, "Come down, parrot, come down!"
> The parrot came down and perched on the man's head, and the two went along together. The parrot started to talk in a gentle tongue, something new, completely new! Some of it was song, some like cassiri sweetened with honey, some of it had the lovely fickle flavor of unknown forest fruits.
> The vanished tribe, the family turned into ghosts, the tumbledown hut undermined by termites, Macunaíma's ascent to heaven, how the parrots and

macaws formed a canopy in the far-off times when the hero was the Great Emperor, Macunaíma: in the silence of Uraricoera only the parrot had rescued from oblivion those happenings and the language which had disappeared. Only the parrot had preserved in that vast silence the words and deeds of the hero.

All this he related to the man, then spread his wings and set his course for Lisbon. And that man, dear reader, was myself, and I stayed on to tell you this story.[21]

Entaõ o homem descobriu na ramaria um papagaio verde de bico dourado espiando pra ele. Falou: / Da o pé, papagaio. / O papagaio veio pousar na cabeça do homem e os dois se acompanheiraram. Então o pássaro principiou falando numa fala mansa, muito nova, muito! que era canto e que era cachiri, com mel-de-pau, que era boa e possuía a traição das frutas desconhecidas do mato. / O tribo se acabara, a família virara sombras, a maloca ruíra minada pelas saúvas e Macunaíma subira pro céu, porém ficara o aruaí do séquito, daqueles tempos de dantes em que o herói fora o grande Macunaíma imperador. E só o papagaio no silêncio do Uraricoera preservava do esquecimento os casos e a fala desaparecida. Só o papagaio conservava no silêncio as frases e as feitas do herói. / Tudo ele contou pro homem e depois abriu asa rumo de Lisboa. E o homem sou eu, minha gente, e eu fiquei pra vos contar a história.[22]

Interestingly enough, this parrot is not a Brazilian parrot but a German one. Mário de Andrade came to his story of "Brazil's indigenous past" and Brazil's hero via Europe. Mário de Andrade was always clear that in writing *Macunaíma* he owed a great debt to Teodor Koch-Grünberg, a German anthropologist who traveled throughout Brazil between 1911 and 1913. Andrade relied particularly on volume 2 of *Von Roroima zum Orinoco*, which contained the myths and legends of the Taulipang and Arekuna people. According to Mário de Andrade, the debt was not only one of inspiration but also of whole passages: "Confesso que copiei, as vezes textualmente" (I confess that I copied, sometimes word for word).[23]

The name Macunaíma (Makunaima) was taken from Koch-Grünberg. According to Koch-Grunberg, Makunaima's name is made up of two words that join to mean the "Great Evil" (maku=evil, ima=great).[24] In the collection of myths and legends related to Koch-Grünberg, Makunaima is the hero of the tribe and the creator of the Taulipang people. He is the youngest of five brothers, two of whom, Maanape and Ziguê, appear most often with Makunaima.

The birth of Makunaima is not described in Koch-Grünberg's collection. In Mário de Andrade's book, Macunaíma is born in the middle of the forest to an old woman of the Tapanhuma tribe. In the text it is claimed that the name of the tribe signifies "black." It is significant that Mário did not take the name of Makunaima's people offered by Koch-Grünberg, preferring instead to find the name of another tribe which, correctly or incorrectly, signifies black. Macunaíma, unlike Koch-Grünberg's Makunaima, is dark black, "preto retinto" and an ugly child, "criança feia." As a result of an encounter with an animal/spirit in the forest. Macunaíma grows a man's body but keeps the head of a child. Mário de Andrade manipulates his ethnographic sources so that Makunaima becomes black, ugly, lazy, and an adult with a child's head.

After the death of their mother, the three brothers travel through the forest. They meet Ci Mãe do Mato, whom Macunaíma rapes with the help of his brothers. Macunaíma and Ci have a child, the only child of the inter-racial relations of the book. Ci has one shriveled breast, a sign that she belongs to the tribe of the *mulheres sozinhas* (solitary women). A Cobra Preta (the Black Snake) bites Ci's other breast, and her child is poisoned while nursing. In a letter to Manuel Bandeira, Mário claims that he chose the color black for the snake by chance as he very easily could have chosen green. The choice hardly seems a coincidence given that Mário adheres closely to superstitions associated with the color black. Maanape and Jiguê, for example, become sick with leprosy and die. Under their contagious influence, Macunaíma becomes sick but overcomes the disease by passing it to a mosquito, the seventh creature he bit. This is linked to a folk belief that a leper can be cured after biting seven children.[25]

I began this essay with an epigraph from *Macunaíma*. The sickness described in this couplet was associated with miscegenation at the time of the publication of *Macunaíma* (1928). Macunaíma's and Ci's child, Macunaíma's two brothers, Jiguê and Maanape, become sick and die. By the last third of the book, every black person, person of mixed race, and indigenous person has become sick or has died. Their illnesses must be seen in the context of the couplet that Macunaíma repeats throughout the book: "Pouca saúde e muita saúva, os males do Brazil são."

For all the celebration of racial mixing that the cannibalist approach to writing implies, and contrary to the usual readings of *Macunaíma,* there is no racial mixture in this book. The three brothers are of three separate races.

> The heat of the Sun had covered the three brothers with a scum of sweat, and Macunaíma was thinking of taking a bath. . . . Just then Macunaíma caught sight of an islet right in the middle of the stream in which there was a hollow the shape of a giant's footprint, full of water. They landed there. The hero, squealing because the water was so cold, washed himself all over. But this water was magic water, for the hollow was St. Thomas's footprint, a relic from the time when he went around preaching and bringing the teachings of Jesus to the Indians of Brazil. When the hero had finished his bath he was white-skinned, blue-eyed, and fair-haired; the holy water had washed away all his blackness; there was nothing left to show in any way that he was a son of the black tribe of Tapanhumas.

As soon as Jiguê saw this miracle he sprang into St. Thomas's footprint. But by this time the water was very dirty from the hero's ivory blackness, so although Jiguê mopped himself like mad, splashing the water in all directions, he was left the color of freshly minted bronze. Macunaíma was bothered by this and to comfort him said, "Look, brother Jiguê, you didn't become white, but at least the blackness has gone away. Half a loaf is better than no bread!"

Then Maanape went to wash, but Jiguê had splashed all the water out of the pool. There was only a cupful left at the bottom, so that Maanape could wet only the palms of his hands and the soles of his feet. That's why he remained black like a good son of the Tapanhuma tribe with only the palms of his hands and the soles of his feet pink after their washing in holy water. This grieved Macunaíma, who consoled him by saying, "Don't be vexed, brother Maanape, don't let it get you down! Worse things happen at sea!"

The three brothers made a superb picture standing erect and naked on the rock in the sun; one fair, one red-skinned, one black. (31–32)

Uma feita a Sol cobrira os três manos duma escaminha de suor e Macunaíma se lembrou de tomar banho. . . . Éntão Macunaíma enxergou numa lapa bem no meio do rio uma cova cheia d'água. E a cova era que nem a marca dum pé gigante. Abicaram. O herói depois de muitos gritos por causa do frio da água entrou na cova e se lavou inteirinho. Mas a água era encantada porque aquele buraco na lapa era marca do pezão do Sumé, do tempo em que andava pregando o evangelho de Jesus pra indiada brasileira. Quando o herói saiu do banho estava branco louro e de olhos azuizinhos, água lavara o pretume dele. E ninguém não seria capaz mais de indicar nele um filho da tribo retinta dos Tapanhumas. / Nem bem Jiguê percebeu o milagre, se atirou na marca do pezão do Sumé. Porém a água já estava muito suja da negrura do herói e por mais que Jiguê esfregasse feito maluco atirando água pra todos os lados só conseguiu ficar da cor do bronze novo. Macunaíma teve dó e consolou: / Olhe, mano Jiguê, branco você ficou não, porém pretume foi-se e antes fanhoso que sem nariz. / Maanape então é que foi se lavar, mas Jiquê esborifara toda a água encantada pra fora da cova. Tinha só um bocado láno fundo e Maanape conseguiu molhar só a palma dos pés e das mãos. Por isso ficou negro ben filho da tribo dos Tapanhumas. Só que as palmas das mãos e dos pés dele são vermelhas por terem se limpado na água santa. Macunaíma teve dó e consolou: / Não se avexe, mano Maanape, não se avexe não, mais sofreu o nosso tio Judas! / E estava lindíssima na Sol da lapa os três manos um louro um vermelho outro negro . . . (37–38)

In Legend 5, Koch-Grünberg relates how Makunaima created human beings but makes no allusion to race. J. W. Boddam-Whetham, writing in 1879, however, records in his ethnographic collection from the same region the following origin of races myth:

The Caribs in their account of creation say that the Great Spirit sat on a mora tree, and picking off pieces of the bark threw them in a stream and they became different animals. Then the Great Spirit—Makanaima—made a large mold and out of this fresh clean clay, the white man stepped. After it got a little dirty the Indian was formed, and the Spirit being called away on business for a long period the mold became black and unclean, and out of it walked the negro.[26]

John R. Swanton records two variants that follow the same pattern (white, Indian, black). He records a third variant in which the hierarchy is Indian, white, black.[27] All of the Native American tales begin with white people who are transformed into people of other races. In Mário's version, however, all the brothers are black before the bath. Once again Mário turned away from his Indianist sources on a point having to do with race, thereby producing an account consistent with the Brazilian elites' attitudes toward race and *en-braqueamento*. When we recall that with the advent of urban industrialization blacks (seen as inferior to whites in terms of working with technology) disappeared from the economic stage,[28] it is also interesting to note that Macunaíma turns white before entering the city of São Paulo.

Also important is the fact that Mário makes Macunaíma's enemy, the giant cannibal Piamã, an Italian immigrant. During the period in which *Macunaíma* was written, the Brazilian government had a policy of encouraging immigration from European countries so as to speed up the process of *embranqueamento* (whitening). In 1921, the statesmen Fidelis Reis and Cincinato Braga drafted legislation to halt the immigation of nonwhites to protect the ethnic (read racial) formation of the nation, which had already suffered from the introduction of blacks. This project had the support of the National Academy of Medicine.[29]

In her book, *Macunaíma: Ruptura e tradição,* Suzana Camargo maintains that Rabelais's *Gargantua* is an intertext of *Macunaíma.* Using Mikhail Bakhtin as a theoretical base, she analyzes the relationship of *Gargantua* and *Macunaíma* to each other and to the body.

One aspect that *Macunaíma* and *Gargantua* share is that the grotesque body and eating are inscribed in both narratives. According to Bakhtin,

> The most distinctive character of the [grotesque] body is its open, unfinished nature, most fully revealed in the act of eating where the body transgresses its limits. . . .
>
> The encounter of the man with the world, which takes place inside the open, biting, rending, chewing mouth, is one of the most ancient, and most important objects of human thought and imagery. Here man tastes world, introduces it into his own body, makes it part of himself. . . . Man's encounter with the world in the act of eating is joyful, triumphant; he triumphs over the world, devours it without being devoured himself. The limits between man and the world are erased, to man's advantage.[30]

If this incorporation works to man's advantage, it does not work to the advantage of all men—or women. What is seen as liberatory or subversive in Bakhtin becomes suspect, even oppressive, when race or indeed gender are factored in. The question becomes, *quem come quem* (who eats whom)? It is important to note that the mulatta plays a very significant role in the linking of race and nation, for it is through her body that embranqueamento takes place. In other words, *o branco comeu a mulata* (the white man ate the mulatta—in Brazilian slang, *comer* [eat] means to have sexual intercourse); the couple is rarely a white woman and a black man. One implication of this is that the patrimony is European. Much is made in Brazilian sociological literature of the father giving his name, education, and historical and genealogical continuity to his children. This is in contrast with the representation of blacks in general and mulattas in particular, who are identified with nature, sensuality, and lack of family ties. The following citation from an essay by Gilberto Freyre is only one example of this among many.

> In the Orient, in Africa, in America, his [the Portuguese] vigorous male body is multiplied in red, yellow, and brown bodies; in new colors and new shapes of the human form, and these bodies communicate the qualities of the Portuguese or the Christian soul. . . . The African, Asian, and Amerindian mothers also are rendered Portuguese [*aportuguesadas*] by him most often in their souls and even, to a certain point, in the way they dress, adorn themselves, and care for their bodies. This is reflected in the arts and literature of these people who through the Portuguese are in this way integrated into European civilization.[31]

It should be noted that Macunaíma engages in his anthropophagist activities after having been miraculously transformed into a white man and that the giant cannibal Piamã is white.

According to Camargo, the theme of anthropophagy and its images of ingestion and absorption that so occupied Rabelais were taken up by Mário de Andrade to support the modernist maxim. Just as Rabelais manipulated *Le grandes croniques* simply to structure his story, Mário de Andrade similarly manipulated the Indian legend.[32] Once again the African and the Indian have been incorporated into a (digestive) system. It appears that blacks and indigenous peoples are exploited for their transgressive shock value, which derives from the modernists' ideas about the "primitivism" of Africans and indigenous peoples. What is useful is extracted; the rest is excreted.

Although the philosophical trappings of anthropophagism would seem to imply a political vision of a democratic society, this is not the case. In fact, blacks have not been equal participants in a Brazilian "mixture." This is not the result of vulgar or individual prejudice; it lies at the heart of a notion of citizenship and is an enabling condition of a construction of a national identity. In the anthropophagist model, however, we discover that assimilation is unthinkable without the excretion. The law of assimilation is that there must always be a remainder, a residue, something (someone) that has re-

sisted or escaped incorporation, even when the nation produces narratives
of racial democracy to mask this tradition of resistance.

NOTES

1. A more literal translation would be: Little (or poor) health and many ants /
are the problems of Brazil.

2. Angel Rama, *Transculturación narrative en America Latina* (Mexico: Siglo
Veintiuno Editores, 1982): 13.

3. Philip D. Curtin, *The Atlantic Slave Trade: A Census* (Madison: University of
Wisconsin Press, 1969): 47–49.

4. Emilia Viotti da Costa, *Da Senzala a Colónia* (São Paulo: Brasiliense, 1989): 18.

5. See Roderick J. Barman, *Brazil: The Forging of a Nation* (Stanford: Stanford
University Press, 1988).

6. See, for example, José de Alencar's play, *O demónio familiar.*

7. Euclides da Cunha, *Os Sertões,* Obra Completa, Vol. II, org. Afrânio Coutinho
(Rio de Janeiro: José Aguiar, 1966): 166–168. See also Dante Moreira Leite, *O caráter
nacional brasileiro* (Sáo Paulo: Pioneira, 1983).

8. See Homi K. Bhabha, *Nation and Narration* (New York: Routledge, 1990),
particularly the introduction.

9. See, for example, Carl Degler, *Neither Black nor White* (New York: Macmillan
1971).

10. Paul Gilroy, "One Nation under a Groove: The Cultural Politics of 'Race' and
Racism in Britain," in *Anatomy of Racism,* ed. David Theo Goldberg (Minneapolis: University of Minnesota Press, 1990): 264.

11. See Charles H. Wood and José Alberto Magno de Carvalho, *The Demography
of Inequality in Brazil* (New York: Cambridge University Press, 1988).

12. This is an accurate assertion. When requested as part of an opinion poll to
describe the ideal president, 89 percent of the respondents agreed that he should
be white. Roger Atwood, "Brazil Marks 100 Years of Abolition but Blacks Are Still
Bitter," *Reuters,* May 11, 1988, cited in Peter R. Eccles, "Culpados ate prova em con-
trario," *Estudos Afro-Asiaticos,* no. 20 (June 1991).

13. Paulo Francis, "Lamurias da galeria e glasnost," *Folha de São Paulo,* February
3, 1990. E-10 (my translation).

14. Menotti del Picchia, cited by Daniel Pécault, *Os intelectuais e a política no Brasil*
(São Paulo: Atica, 1990): 27.

15. Mário da Silva Brito, "A Revolução modernista," *A literatura no Brasil,* Vol. III,
ed. Afrânio Coutinho (Rio de Janeiro: São José, 1970): 455. For analysis of the ways
in which the modernists contributed to and advanced conservative agendas, see
Daniel Pécault, *Os intelectuais e a política no Brasil,* trans. Maria Julia Goldwasser (São
Paulo: Atica, 1990); Sérgio Miceli, *Intelectuais e classe dirigente no Brasil: 1920–1945*
(São Paulo: DIFEL, 1979); and *Estado e culture no Brasil* (São Paulo: Difel, 1984);
James Holston, *The Modernist City.* (Chicago: University of Chicago Press, 1989).

16. "The fact should be stressed that among the Portuguese of the continent theo-
logical hatreds and violent racial antipathies or prejudices were rarely manifested.

The same is true of the relations between whites and blacks: those hatreds due to class or caste extended and at times disguised, in the form of race hatred such as marked the history of other slave-holding areas in the Americas, were seldom carried to any such extreme in Brazil. The absence of violent rancors due to race constitutes one of the particularities of the feudal system in the tropics, a system that, in a manner of speaking, had been softened by the hot climate and by the effects of a miscegenation that tended to dissolve such prejudices." Gilberto Freyre, *The Masters and the Slaves,* trans. Samuel Putnam (New York: Knopf, 1946): xii–xiii.

17. Theodore Roosevelt, cited by Thomas E. Skidmore, *Black into White* (New York: Oxford University Press, 1974): 68.

18. Wilson Martins, *The Modernist Idea* (New York: New York University Press, 1970): 90.

19. Paulo Prado, *Retrato do Brasil* (Rio de Janeiro: F. Briguiet, 1931): 196–197.

20. Mário de Andrade, cited by Heloisa Buarque de Hollanda, *Macunaíma: Da literatura ao cinema* (Rio de Janeiro: Empresa Brasileira de Filmes, 1978): 100.

21. Mário de Andrade, *Macunaíma,* trans. E. A. Goodland (New York: Random House, 1984).

22. Mário de Andrade, *Macunaíma: O herói sem nenhum caráter. Coleção Arquivos,* ed. Telê Porto Ancona Lopez (Brasilia, D.F.: CNPq, 1988): 168.

23. Mário de Andrade, cited by João Etienne Filho, "Introduction," *Macunaíma: O heroi sem nenhum caráter* (Belo Horizonte: Itatiaia, 1986).

24. Teodor Koch-Grünberg, *Del Roraima al Orinoco,* Tomo II, trans. Frederica de Ritter (Caracas: Ernesto Armitano Editor, 1981).

25. M. Cavalcanti Proença, *Roteiro de Macunaíma* (São Paulo: Civilização Brasileira, 1987): 224.

26. J. W. Boddam-Whetham, *Roraima and British Guiana* (London: Hurst and Blackett, 1879): 172.

27. John R. Swanton, *Myths and Tales of the Southeastern Indians* (Washington, D.C.: Government Printing Office): 75.

28. Celia Maria Marinho de Azevedo, *Onda Negra, Medo Branco: O Negro no Imáginario das Elites Século XIX* (Rio de Janeiro: Paz e Terra, 1987): 20. My Translation.

29. Fidelis Reis, *Pais a organizar* (Rio de Janeiro: Coelho Branco, 1931). The document from the Academia Nacional de Medicina is appended to the book.

30. Mikhail Bakhtin, *Rabelais and His World,* trans. Helen Iswolsky (Cambridge: MIT Press, 1968): 281.

31 Gilberto Freyre, "A estetica da miscigenação," in *Vida, forma e cor* (Rio de Janeiro: Record, 1987): 239.

32. Suzana Camargo, *Macunaíma: Ruptura e tradição* (São Paulo: Massoa Ohno/João Farkas/Editores, 1977): 100.

ELEVEN

Race under Representation

David Lloyd

This racism that aspires to be rational, individual, genotypically and phenotypically determined, becomes transformed into cultural racism. The object of racism is no longer the individual man but a certain form of existing.
—FRANTZ FANON, "RACISM AND CULTURE"

Far from having to ask whether culture is or is not a function of race, we are discovering that race—or what is generally meant by the term—is one function among others of culture.
—CLAUDE LÉVI-STRAUSS, "RACE AND CULTURE"

In the main, the experience and the analysis of racism or race relations have been and continue to be cast in *spatial* terms. On the one hand, the concept of race has throughout its history been articulated in terms of the geographic distribution of peoples or, as the discreteness of geographic location gradually dissolves, as if there were a spectrum of races in contiguity with one another. On the other hand, in the politics of racism it is the *confrontation* of races in opposition to one another and the literally and figuratively spatial disposition of inequitable power relations between them that is most striking. Unquestionably, neither the history nor the theory of racism can be thought without reference to spatial categories, whether we attend to the global geographies of imperial expansion and international capital or to the more intimate geographies of the inner city, ghettoization, or the displacement of peoples. The human experiences recorded in these terms are the material substrate of other, equally spatial terms in which the antiracist cultural politics of the last decade has been expressed: euro- or ethnocentrism, marginalization, exclusion, not to mention those now critical categories, orientalism and the West.

It is not my intention here to critique those categories, without which neither the analysis of nor the political struggle against racism could have been articulated but rather to argue that these spatial terms need to be supplemented by an analysis of the temporal axis that is equally constitutive of racist discourse. Recent critiques of development and modernization theories have drawn attention to the manner in which racist and ethnocentric

discourses in economic and political spheres deploy a normative temporality of human development that is applied at once to the individual, to individual nations or cultures, and to the human race in general.[1] But beyond
even such critiques, the discourse on culture that emerges in the "modern
era" of the West is itself structured at every level by this normative developmental schema: the racism of culture is not a question of certain contingent
racist observations by its major theoreticians nor of the still incomplete dis-
semination of its goods but an ineradicable effect of its fundamental structures. These structures, indeed, determine the forms, casual and
institutional, that racism has taken in the post-Enlightenment era and account for the generally racist disposition of the "West," understood not as a
bounded geographic domain but as a global complex of economic, political, and cultural institutions that represent, in a universal *temporal* schema,
the locus of the modern in any society. The discourse of culture is not
merely descriptive but crucially productive, in that it directs the formation
of the modern subject both in the geographic west and wherever the West
has imposed its institutions.

In their recent study, *Racial Formation in the United States,* Michael Omi
and Howard Winant discuss the manner in which racial formations operate
on both the micro- and macro-levels of society.

> The racial order is organized and enforced by the continuity and reciprocity
> between these two "levels" of social relations. The micro- and macro-levels,
> however, are only analytically distinct. In our lived experience, in politics, in
> culture, in economic life, they are continuous and reciprocal.[2]

Part of the intention of this chapter is to indicate how the meshing of racial
formations can take place between various levels and spheres of social practice, as, for example, between political and cultural spheres or between the
individual and the national level. In doing so, I will be restoring to the concept of "formation," properly used here in its current sociocultural sense,
the equally important sense that it has traditionally had in aesthetic pedagogy, the sense of self-formation or *Bildung.* Culture will have here not, in
the first place, its generalized sense of the totality of life-forms of a particular society or group but quite strictly the sense of *aesthetic culture.*[3] It will be
my contention that the terms developed for aesthetic culture in the late
eighteenth century, as constituting the definition of human identity, continue to regulate racial formations through the various sites of contemporary practice.[4] Crucial to this function of aesthetic culture is its formulation
and development of a *narrative of representation,* by which is meant not only
the representative narratives of canonical culture but also the narrative
form taken by the concept of representation itself. As we shall see, within
this narrative the same processes of formalization occur at every level, al-

lowing a series of transferred identifications to take place from individual to nation and from the nation to the idea of a universal humanity. By the same token, the fissures and contradictions that trouble this narrative are replicated equally at every level or in every site that it informs.[5]

What I will attempt here, then, is to sketch a phenomenology of racism as it is embedded in the "disposition of the subject" produced and maintained by Western culture. Though I will use the term "culture" throughout to imply first of all "aesthetic culture," it will become clear that the idea of aesthetic culture governs not only what is loosely referred to as "high culture" but also, if less evidently, most other subsequent usages of the term. For the theoretical construction of a domain of aesthetic judgment in late eighteenth- and early nineteenth-century cultural theory provides the constitutive forms of the "public sphere" itself. Grounding the idea of a common or public sense, the subject of aesthetic judgment supplies the very possibility of a disinterested domain of culture and prescribes the development of that domain through history as the ethical end of humanity itself.

For this reason, I wish to start with a moment from one of the founding texts of cultural theory, namely, Immanuel Kant's third critique, *The Critique of Judgement*. As is well known, Kant's deduction of the universality of the aesthetic judgment relies on the disinterest of the subject of judgment, on what I shall call the "Subject without properties." This abstract Subject is merely regulative in the case of pure aesthetic judgments: it is the measure of the disinterest of the judge by which he conforms ideally to the condition of universality. In the case of the *social* faculty of taste, however, to judge as if one were the Subject without properties is constitutive of the possibility of such a universal validity, actualizing that common sense which is otherwise assumed only as a latent condition of disinterested judgment in all humans.

Kant makes this positive or constitutive function of taste clear in number 40 of the *Third Critique*, "Taste as a kind of *sensus communis*." Here, a movement within the judgment itself, from the material particularity of the object to its formal universality as a disposition of the subject, doubles an identical movement from the peculiarity of a singular judgment to its representative universality. What is universal, and therefore constitutive of the domain of common or public sense, is the *form* of the judgment rather than its object or matter.

> However, by the name *sensus communis* is to be understood the idea of a *public* sense, i.e., a critical faculty which in its reflective act takes account (*a priori*) of the mode of representation of every one else, in order, *as it were,* to weigh its judgements with the collective reason of mankind, and thereby avoid the illusion arising from subjective and personal conditions which could readily be taken for objective, an illusion that would exert a prejudicial influence upon its judgement. This is accomplished by weighing the judgement, not so

much with actual, as rather with the merely possible, judgements of others, and by putting ourselves in the position of every one else, as the result of a mere abstraction from the limitations which contingently affect our own estimate. This, in turn, is effected by so far as possible letting go of the element of matter, i.e., sensation, in our general state of representative activity, and confining attention to the formal peculiarities of our representation or general state of representative activity. (*CJ*, 151)

In this prescription for the aesthetic judgment, the movement from matter to form in the representation of the object corresponds to a less immediately evident formalization internal to the subject, a formalization that becomes the condition for the existence of a public sense. Only a subject formalized, if momentarily, into identity with "every one else," that is, with the Subject in general, can provide the conditions for the universal accord of a common or public sense. In turn, it is the idea, not necessarily always actualized but nonetheless operative, of this common sense that underlies the concept of a public sphere.[6] As we shall see, what is at first the merely logical temporality of the aesthetic judgment becomes prescriptive for the narrative of representation through which this actualization of common sense in the modern public sphere is to be realized.

That process can be summarized in the following propositions:

1. the ordering of "our general state of representative activity" is such as to imply a narrative organization of the senses that moves from sensation to form;
2. this narrative of the senses within the individual human subject finds a correspondent form in the development of the human race;
3. this narrative can be expressed as or, alternatively, depends on a movement from contiguity to identity, or from metonymy to metaphor.

Each of these formally correspondent narratives, yet to be analyzed, gives in its way the condition for the emergence of the public sphere.

1. As the simultaneously literal and metaphoric usages of both the terms "common sense" and "taste" might suggest, what these concepts describe is the very movement they require from the immediate particularity of sensation to the formal generality of the social. For "sense" to become "common," its conditions must be formalized as a disposition of the Subject in each of us; for "taste" to emerge as a social phenomenon, the cultivation of the senses must proceed from the pleasure derived from the existence of the object that is characteristic of literal "taste" to the contemplative relation to the object, which is the capacity of sight. This narrative of the organization of the senses toward an increasing distance from the object and an increasing formalization of its representation is parallel for Kant to the movement from the merely agreeable, which is private and entirely singular, to the beautiful, which is to be universally communicable. In the discourse of aes-

thetic culture, which itself emerges in the increasing abstraction of *aesthetics* itself from the science of pain and pleasure to that of fine art, this narrative organization of the senses in a crucially *developmental* hierarchy is fundamental. Indeed, in the most minimal moment of perception, such a development is already present within any judgment as the move from *Darstellung* (presentation), in which the senses are merely passive recipients, to *Vorstellung* (representation), in which the object is constituted as a possible object for the reflective or the logical judgment. A process of formalization, the initial abstraction of a form from a manifold of sensations as an object assimilable to other such objects, is inseparable from any completed act of perception.

As Friedrich Schiller puts it with characteristic clarity,

> It is nature herself which raises man from reality to semblance, by furnishing him with two senses which lead him to knowledge of the real world though semblance alone. In the case of the eye and the ear, she herself has driven importunate matter back from the organs of sense, and the object, with which in the case of our more animal senses we have direct contact, is set at a distance from us. What we actually see with the eye is something different from the sensation we receive; for the mind leaps out across light to objects. The object of touch is a force to which we are subjected; the object of eye and ear a form that we engender. As long as man is still a savage he enjoys by means of these tactile senses alone, and at this stage the senses of semblance are merely the servants of these. Either he does not rise to the level of seeing at all, or he is at all events not satisfied with it. Once he does begin to enjoy through the eye, and seeing acquires for him a value of its own, he is already aesthetically free and the play-drive has started to develop.[7]

2. As Schiller's remarks suggest, the developmental narrative of sensual organization is required by the developmental history of the race of which, at every stage of that development, it is the index. In a version of the thesis that "ontogeny recapitulates phylogeny," the movement, as Kant puts it, from "the charm of sense to habitual moral interest" that taste makes possible (*CJ*, 225; see also 65) is at once an affair of the individual and of the human "race." The same development that produces in each individual a capacity for subjectively universal judgments of taste produces in human societies the civilized form of the public sphere. Kant thus describes the movement from a primitive interest in the "charms of sense" to "universal communicability."

> Further, a regard to universal communicability is a thing which every one expects and requires from every one else, just as if it were part of an original compact dictated by humanity itself. And thus, no doubt, at first only charms, e.g., colours for painting oneself (roucou among the Caribs and cinnabar among the Iroquois), or flowers, sea-shells, beautifully coloured feathers, then, in the course of time, also beautiful forms (as in canoes, wearing-apparel, &c.) which

convey no gratification, i.e., delight of enjoyment, become of moment in society and attract a considerable interest. Eventually, when civilization has
reached its height it makes this work of communication almost the main business of refined inclination, and the entire value of sensations is placed in the
degree to which they permit of universal communication. (*CJ*, 155–156)

The narrative of sensual development is thus directed toward the emergence of the public sphere and depends clearly on an ever-increasing degree of formalization. On the face of it, then, the relegation of the Iroquois
or the "Carib" to a correspondingly low stage of development could be taken
as merely incidentally "racist" (parenthetically, to be precise), especially
given that the interest in universal communicability is already conceived as
"an original compact dictated by humanity itself." It would indeed be incidental in the case that the interest in immediate gratification or in universal communication were seen as merely among the accidental cultural
characteristics of the American and the European, respectively. On the contrary, however, it is in a very real sense the capacity for "universal communicability" that *defines* civilization, with the Europeanness of that civilization
being, strictly speaking, merely incidental.

Despite its articulation through the ascription to particular races of "essential" characteristics, racism is structured in the first place by the cultural
determination of a public sphere and of the subject formation that is its condition of existence. Though this proposition finds some empirical corrobo-
ration in the constant appeal of white racism to ethical categories, its
justification is to be found rather in the (albeit contradictory) logic of racist
thought and culture, the fuller analysis of which follows. Suffice it to say at
this point that it is not the claim of an ethical disposition as a racial characteristic but the establishment of a peculiar and historically specific social
form, the public sphere as defined in aesthetic theory, as the end of humanity
that defines the logical structure of racist discourses. For this reason, it is possible for an interchangeably ethical, political, and aesthetic judgment as to
the inferiority of the "savage races" to saturate post-Enlightenment discourses on race from liberals such as John Stuart Mill or Matthew Arnold to
extreme conservatives such as Arthur Gobineau, Louis Klemm, Josiah Nott,
or Charles Hunt.[8] The inadequacy of the native to self-government is demonstrated by "his" lack of aesthetic productions or by "his" subordination to immediate sensual gratification: the capacity for autonomy is either as yet
undeveloped or absent in the savage and requires to be developed or supplied by external force.

Though both arguments continue even now to be presented, it is the developmental model rather than that of irredeemable lack that tends eventually to dominate. Sound material grounds for this gradual transition can
be traced. As Colette Guillaumin has argued, the discourse on race (as on

other categories of heterogeneity) undergoes a crucial shift in the late eighteenth century from a system of arbitrary marks to the ascription of natural
signs. We can, as Fanon does, attribute such a shift to the necessity to legitimate, within the context of appeals to universal humanity, the intensified
and systematic domination of subordinated peoples: in this case, any discourse on difference must cease to be contingent and casual and establish
instead a regular scheme of discriminations that at once preserves and legitimates domination. Initially there may be no absolute correlation between racist and imperialist discourses, since fear of contamination and
environmental derivations of racial variation can offer strong arguments for
not encouraging interracial encounters or even the colonization of alien
climes. Gradually, however, through the intersection of liberal humanism
with the necessities of imperial polity, the developmental discourse on race
comes to dominate, precisely because it allows for the assimilation of a frac-
tion of the colonized population to the imperial culture in order that they
may function as administrators and professionals.[9]

We will return to this last point. It is important here, however, to note
that Guillaumin's formulation allows us to grasp how racist discourse maintains its capacity to replicate and circulate in several spheres. For what she
indicates, in describing the transition from *allegorical* marks, which retain
the arbitrariness of their social constitution, to *symbolic* "natural signs,"
which represent externally the inner, organic constitution of the object, is
the regulatory force of the narrative of representation across the social
field. For even where a representation is at first a representation of difference, it conforms formally to the general demand for any representation to
maintain the structure of identity within which the part can stand for the
whole. Across differences, identity is formally preserved; across cultures, human nature is essentially the same and can therefore be developed along
identical lines.[10]

As Guillaumin points out, to the "natural mark" (color, gender, facial appearance) that inscribes the dominated correspond the absence of marks
attributed to the dominator.

> It inscribes the system of domination on the body of the individual, assign-
> ing to the individual his/her place as a dominated person: but it does not
> assign any place to the dominator. Membership in the dominant group, on
> the contrary, is legally marked by a convenient lack of interdiction, by unlim-
> ited possibilities.[11]

We can reformulate this as indicating that the position occupied by the
dominant individual is that of the Subject without properties. This Subject
with "unlimited possibilities" is precisely the undetermined subject,
Schiller's Person as yet abstracted from Condition, whose infinite potential

is a function of a purely formal identity with humanity in general.[12] Its universality is attained by virtue of literal indifference: this Subject becomes representative in consequence of being able to take anyone's place, of occupying any place, of a pure exchangeability. Universal where all others are particular, partial, this Subject is the perfect, disinterested judge formed for and by the public sphere.

The Subject without properties is the philosophical figure for what becomes, with increasing literalness through the nineteenth century, the global ubiquity of the white European. His domination is virtually self-legitimating since the capacity to be everywhere present becomes a historical manifestation of the white man's gradual approximation to the universality he everywhere represents. It is still not uncommon to hear it remarked that the human race (as opposed, implicitly, to the Eskimo or Nuer, for example) is singular in its capacity to occupy any habitat. By the same token, in the postcolonial era, immigration from former colonies is a source of especial ideological scandal, not least because it upsets the asymmetrical distribution of humanity into the local (native) and the universal. What governs this distribution, as, perhaps until quite recently, it governed the discipline of anthropology, is the regulative idea of Culture against which the multiplicity of local cultures is defined. Like Kant's Saussure, the anthropologist and the colonial administrator occupy the place of disinterest as representatives of that Culture, with the critical consequence that every racial judgment is simultaneously an aesthetic, an ethical, and a political one.[13]

3. To reformulate the foregoing, it is not in the first instance the antagonistic recognition of difference that constitutes the discourse of racism but the subordination of difference to the demand for identity. This identity principle governs racism in both its exclusive and its assimilative modes, the former narrowing the domain of identity, the other apparently expanding it but, as we shall see, only at the cost of a dissimulated but logically necessary exclusion. As the very expression "assimilation" might suggest, racism elevates a principle of likening above that of differentiation such that its rhetorical structure is that of metaphorization.

Paul Ricoeur observes that the tension between likeness and difference constitutes the metaphoric process.

> The insight into likeness is the perception of the conflict between the previous incompatibility and the new compatibility. "Remoteness" is preserved within "proximity." To see *the like* is to see the same in spite of, and through, the different. This tension between sameness and difference characterizes the logical structure of likeness.[14]

Such a description accounts quite adequately for the pleasurable shock of novel metaphors. What it is unable to do, however, is to grasp the finally normative function of metaphor that makes it so central a figure both for an organic poetics and for postromantic literary pedagogy. The point can be made most succinctly by remarking that Ricoeur's description would allow no distinction between metaphor and those poetic figures that a pre-romantic poetics terms "conceit" or "wit." Unlike metaphor, which Etienne Bonnot de Condillac more succinctly and classically describes as "thinking of the properties in which things agree," wit and conceit derive their effects from the salience of difference.[15] Accordingly, both Ricoeur's definition and, among others, Paul de Man's even more radical reading, which sees metaphor as rhetorically subversive of the identity principle of philosophy by virtue of its catachrestic foundations, require supplementation. What both arguments omit is the narrative subordination within metaphor of difference by identity, a narrative entirely coherent with the philosophical as with the literary critical tradition. Metaphor is not merely the oscillation between sameness and difference but the process of subordinating difference to identity, and it is precisely that narrative that makes metaphor ultimately compatible with philosophical projects in general and with aesthetic projects in particular.

Ricoeur virtually acknowledges the narrative aspect of metaphor in another essay when he remarks on the conjunction in Aristotle's *Poetics* of metaphor and plot. Metaphor functions structurally and mimetically at a minimal stylistic level, as does plot at the largest organizational level. Both are directed toward the uncovering of concealed identities, to moments of *anagnorisis*.[16] In the last instance, even the most jarring of metaphors, if it is to be accepted as tasteful, must allow the *recognition* of an identity that was already there. It is re-creative, not transformative. The question with regard to metaphor becomes not what it signifies but how it signifies within the larger matrix of cultural elements. What this allows us to perceive is the function of metaphoric processes, as minimal narratives of identity, within the larger plot of self-formation: both are directed toward the gradual overcoming of difference by identity.

But, as Ricoeur's own argument implies, it is not merely that a happy analogy exists between metaphor and the plot of self-formation. More pertinently, metaphor operates at the most fundamental levels of feeling to produce effects of identification or "assimilation" in the subject.

> If the process [of metaphor] can be called, as I have called it, predicative *assimilation*, it is true that *we* are assimilated, that is, made similar, to what is seen as similar. This self-assimilation is a part of the commitment proper to the "illocutionary" force of the metaphor as speech act. We feel *like* what we see *like*.[17]

This being the case, we can locate in metaphor a minimal element of the processes of cultural formation which is replicated at larger and larger levels of identity and identification. Culture can be understood as a learning to be like what we should like to like;[18] that is, as assimilation.

Like the expressions "taste" and "common sense," "assimilation" is a concept that is at once a metaphor and structured like a metaphor. But unlike taste and common sense, which embody the narrative of a movement from immediate sensation to universality, the very logic of assimilation betrays an inverse movement equally intrinsic to the process of metaphorization in general but accentuated by its status as a material practice. The constitution of any metaphor involves the bringing together of two elements into identity in such a manner that their differences are suppressed. Just so, the process of assimilation, whether in bringing two distinct but equivalent elements into identity or in absorbing a lower into a higher element as by metastasis, requires that which defines the difference between the elements to remain as a residue. Hence, although it is possible to conceive formally of an equable process of assimilation in which the original elements are entirely equivalent, the product of assimilation will always necessarily be in a hierarchical relation to the residual, whether this is defined as, variously, the primitive, the local, or the merely contingent.[19] The process of identification, therefore, whether instanced in metaphorization, assimilation, or subject formation, not only produces difference but simultaneously gives that difference a determinate sense that is to be resistant to sense. Differences that in the first instance have no meaning and no law come to signify negatively under the law of identity that produces them. Racial discriminations, accordingly, "make sense" and achieve their self-evidence only in relation to the law of identity that governs equally assimilation and exclusion.

A contradictory logic thus structures equally the abstract, identical Subject and the public sphere that it subtends. Since the production of difference as negative identity is inherent to that logic, the Subject that results may be conceived as obsessionally anxious, since its very formation produces what might undo that formation. It would be proper in this, if not all, instances to speak of the insistence rather than the return of the repressed, since the repressed is here produced in every moment of the Subject's formation. What is true for the Subject is, on account of the logic of doubling analyzed above, true on other levels for the public sphere and for aesthetic culture. In the following section, the consequences of the insistence of the repressed will be examined in terms of the resistance it poses to the assimilative drive and developmental claims of a universalizing culture. Since the emphasis here will be on the logic of individual self-formation, and since I have been stressing until now how cultural formation *works* rather than how it breaks down, it is worth making the remark that it is racism itself, as a social phenomenon, that brings to light the contradictory nature of the powerful and remarkably effective institutional logic of culture. At a later point, we will return to this issue through the work of two Third World writers.

It is a frequent characteristic of racism that where the apparently neutral ascriptions of difference depend on relations of contiguity and therefore on metonymic usages (e.g., skin color for race—black, yellow, white), the racist epithet that asserts relations of superiority is generally metaphoric: black boy, savage, baboon. The metaphoric structure of the epithet here legitimates a violent assertion of superiority by way of the appeal to developmental categories: against the achieved identity of the white man, the black appears as being in greater proximity to childhood or animality. Yet at the same time, racism constantly makes appeal to the *immediacy* of its discriminations, to their self-evidence: "You only have to look at them."

The argument of the foregoing section establishes, however, that the appeal to visual immediacy is always illusory, not insofar as there is no difference to be seen but insofar as the significant difference that is registered depends already on the transfer from metonymy to metaphor or on the acculturation of the subject that sees. These processes transform the recognition of differences into a positing of lack of identity in the object. Indeed, the very emergence of the subject that sees, or, more properly, the Subject that *judges,* is already predicated on a prior development of the senses that is ethically structured. What is seen by the racist vision is an underdeveloped human animal whose underdevelopment becomes the index of the judging subject's own superior stage of development.

The visual structure of racism can, accordingly, better be compared with what psychoanalysis supposes to take place in the castration complex than, as some have argued, with the processes of fetishism.[20] For while fetishism is produced out of a *disavowal* of anatomical difference, the fetishist refusing "to take cognizance of the fact of his having perceived that a woman does not possess a penis" (*OS,* 352), the castration complex emerges in the recognition of difference and its interpretation as a mutilation of identity.[21] On the one hand, the castration complex is the primary agency of the formation of the little boy as at once male and ethical, initiating the internalization of the father in the form of the superego. In a phrase highly significant for the meaning of identity formation, Freud remarks that this process constitutes "the victory of the race over the individual" (ADS, 341). On the other hand, it achieves this only at the cost of producing an ineradicable anxiety in the subject as to the possibility of itself undergoing a mutilation that would undo that identity. In an associated move, woman is seen, by virtue of her mutilated identity, as incapable of ethical development: the impossibility of a castration complex prevents the internalization of the father as superego and the identity formation of the woman remains incomplete (ADS, 342). Freud's interpretation at this juncture nicely recapitulates the little boy's. Where the little boy reinterprets the girl's or woman's "lack of a penis" at first as the sign of an underdeveloped organ and then as a mutilation, Freud reads the "lack of a penis" as the grounds of an underdeveloped ethical sense only then to confront female sexuality as something gapped and interrupted.

That Freud's interpretation should thus appear to recapitulate that of the little boy whom it seeks to interpret is not surprising once we reflect that the boy's judgment is in any case not as immediate as the phrase "first catches sight of" implies but is predicated on a prior development of the organs and of the ethical sense of which the castration complex is only the final stage. In the first instance, Freud is quite clear that the castration complex depends on what he had long before identified as "the Phases of Development of the Sexual Organization."[22] It depends on the movement of the organization of sexual pleasure away from the "polymorphous perversity" of infancy toward the "phallic stage." Once again, the narrative of development moves from a moment of contiguity and substitution to one organized around a single term that, like a metaphor, comes to effect the distribution of phenomena into identity and difference. (For this reason, regression to the point prior to the castration complex in psychosis produces the effects of verbal non-sense and physical disintegration.) The development of the organs, like that of the senses in Schiller, is already directed toward an ethical end. Accordingly, in the second instance, the apparent visual immediacy of the little boy's judgment is in fact prepared for by an ethical formation of however rudimentary a kind. Freud's revision of his understanding of the process between "The Dissolution of the Oedipus Complex" (1924) and "Some Psychical Consequences of the Anatomical Sex Distinction" (1925) makes this clearer. Where in the first essay, it is the "first sight" of the female genitals that induces the castration complex, in the second essay, the first sight may be attended by disavowal and "irresolution," and it is only "later, when some threat of castration has obtained a hold upon him, that the observation becomes important to him" (ADS, 336). The visual index, in other words, only gains sense in relation to moral development.[23] In turn, it is the sense given to the visual as a mark of identity and of difference reinterpreted as the mutilation of identity that structures the Subject in its very identity as always subject to the ineradicable threat of a difference on which it depends. The identity of the subject is not only structured against difference, its own possibility depends on producing precisely the internal difference that threatens it.

In the field of racism as of sexuality, the appeal to visual immediacy in any judgment of difference may be seen as a disavowal of the contradictory logic of the subject's identity formation.[24] The anxiety of the racist is that what is constantly represented as an immediately visible, self-evident difference is in fact internal to the subject. The racist shares with the obsessional neurotic the anxiety of being found out. But while it is doubtless the case that the psychic structure of racism depends, as some have argued, in large degree on projection, the critical point that needs to be stressed is that it is the *insistence* of a difference internal to the constitution of identity which underlies the cultural logic of racism rather than either the return or the projection of repressed material.[25]

Instances of racism in which the visual index of difference is by any measure minimal, if not absent, throw the cultural logic of racism into relief with peculiar force. In such instances of white on white racism, the phantasmic projection of differences appears as a wishful resolution of a disturbance in the visual field. In what has become a celebrated passage, Charles Kingsley wrote to his wife of the poor Irish in 1860,

> But I am haunted by the human chimpanzees I saw along that hundred miles of horrible country. I don't believe they are our fault. I believe there are not only many more of them than of old, but that they are happier, better, more comfortably fed and lodged under our rule than they ever were. But to see white chimpanzees is dreadful; if they were black, one would not feel it so much, but their skins, except where tanned by exposure, are as white as ours.

In such perceptions, what is disturbed is the law of verisimilitude that governs the metaphorical system of racism. For this law, the identity between ape and black is self-evident, and it is scandalized by the possibility of a conjunction between whiteness, as the outward sign of human identity, and the simian, which, as a metaphor, becomes a metaphor of nonidentity in the very structure of the human. The same scandal to the order of identity is registered in Thomas Carlyle's phrase for the Irish, "the white negroes," an impossible, catachrestic conjunction that persists as an anomaly in English racist discourse: "If only they were black."[26]

The point here is not to underestimate the importance of external marks of difference to racist practices but rather to emphasize how the apparent visual anomaly of white on white racism is the index of a prior constitution of the racist Subject-who-judges by which alone the appeal to visual immediacy of discrimination is legitimated. Whiteness is the metaphor for the metaphorical production of the Subject as one devoid of properties rather than the natural sign of difference to which the attributes of civilization and culture are in turn attached. Where whiteness is suddenly, forcibly conjoined with the metaphors of difference, the order of development is radically disrupted. And insofar, as we have seen, as the metaphoric logic of culture works always through the production of a residual order of difference, what Kingsley or Carlyle discover in the form of an anomaly constantly troubles the discursive and institutional practices of assimilation.[27]

As is well known, different colonial regimes have had quite various policies with regard to the assimilation or exclusion of dominated populations. It is often remarked, for example, that French colonialism differs from British in that French policy tended to emphasize the process of acculturation while British policy instituted virtual apartheid, especially in its African do-

mains. Though such distinctions may be accurate with regard to the regulatory tendencies of each imperial state, it is nonetheless the case that any
imperial apparatus, once the initial period of conquest and domination by
force is over, requires a greater or lesser number of native administrators
and professionals to mediate its hegemony. Even if, as in many British
colonies, this caste is relatively small numerically, its political function is crucial both for the colonial administration and for the development of national resistance movements.[28]

Many writers have noted and analyzed the regularity with which nationalist movements are formed among the most assimilated elements of the colonized population.[29] One constant and critical factor in this process is the
confrontation with racism precisely as a contradiction in the logic of assimilation itself. Unlike the "subaltern" population, whose oppression and resistance alike remain largely outside the domain of state institutions for
which the subaltern has no subjective existence at all, the colonial intellectual confronts racism as a limit to the line of development that cultural assimilation appears to propose to him *as Subject*. Racism exposes the residual
elements required by the logic of assimilation in constituting the colonial
subject as a divided self, one part constituted by acculturation as "modern,"
the other identified by the racist judgment as permanently lodged in a primitive moment incapable of development. Nationalism offers to suture this
division by relocating the institutions of the modern state on the very terrain that the colonizer regards as primitive. It restores continuity to the interrupted narrative of representation by reterritorializing it within the newly
conceived nation. Nationalism, in other words, accepts the *verisimilitude* of
imperial culture while redefining its purview.

Fanon's *Black Skin, White Masks* is deeply informed by the experience of
assimilation as a cultural practice with a dense and contradictory history
both at the level of colonial institutions and for each particular subject of
colonialism. It is also a work deeply informed by the realization that not only
is race a cultural construct but racism is the structure of culture. From the
very opening pages, Fanon is quite clear that the analysis of racism can only
proceed in relation to the discourse on man and on "his" development to
which culture itself gives the structure.

> What does a man want?
> What does the black man want?
> At the risk of arousing the resentment of my colored brothers, I will say that
> the black is not a man. . . .
> The black man wants to be white. The white man slaves to reach a human
> level. (*BSWM*, 10–11)

The identity of the black man is to be a difference always suspended in the
developmental trajectory of a humanity figured in terms of whiteness. Only

in terms of this trajectory can what Fanon names in the title of one chapter of the work "The Fact of Blackness" be understood in the full network of the social relations that constitute that "fact." If, in the course of this chapter, Fanon makes clear that the appeal to "negritude" has, for him, no longer any sense, it is because the larger trajectory of *Black Skin, White Masks* shows in detail that the appeal to essences is of no account where racist social relations constitute the black in a merely negative relation to an other defined as human. The enormous task that this work proposes is the transformation of the nonidentity of the black into the means to a dismantling of the discourse of racism on several axes: that of the formation of the individual subject, that of the metaphoric structure of culture, and that of the social institutions in which the former are sedimented.

This task involves what at the outset Fanon describes as the attempt "to penetrate to a level where the categories of sense and non-sense are not yet invoked" (*BSWM*, 11). That is to say, it entails a decomposition of the subject akin to what would be required to break with the effects of the "castration complex" and a collapsing of the metaphoric organization of identity and nonidentity that structures the Subject as such. Fanon is constantly aware of how closely his analysis must skirt psychosis, yet it is only in the light of this task that we can grasp the process of transfiguration involved in the remark, late in the work, that "the Negro is comparison" (*BSWM*, 211). This remark is, in the first place, an analytic description of the neurotic condition of Antillean society.

> We have just seen that the feeling of inferiority is an Antillean characteristic. It is not just this or that Antillean who embodies the neurotic formation, but all Antilleans. Antillean society is a neurotic society, a society of "comparison." (*BSWM*, 213)

But these remarks make quite clear that "we are driven from the individual back to the social structure" (*BSWM*, 213). This suspension in perpetual comparison of self and other is not an individual aberration but is to be seen as the very social condition of being black in racist culture. This recognition transforms an analytic description of a malformation of the black subject into a culturally critical concept that opens up the inherently contradictory metaphoric logic of identity. For if the "Adlerian comparison" of the *individual* neurotic consists only of two terms "polarized by the ego" and is expressed as "Ego greater than The Other," the social neurosis of "Antillean comparison" is "surmounted by a third term: Its governing fiction is not personal but social" (*BSWM*, 215). The comparison is expressed thus:

$$\frac{\text{White}}{\text{Ego different from The Other}}$$

The formula is of exceptional analytical force. The surmounting term consists of one, self-identical word, the metaphor of metaphorical identity: white. As the citation from Fanon at the beginning of this section indicates, the possibility of placing "White" in this position derives from positing the white man as standing closer to the identity of the human that is the telos of history. The white occupies the position of universally representative man within a narrative that we can describe as the narrative of representation itself. But what its elevation produces, in relation to the Adlerian comparison, is a dissolution of the previous axis of superiority (Ego greater than The Other) into a relation of pure difference. What this implies, finally, is that there can be no therapeutic adjustment of the neurotic *individual,* not only because racist society continually reproduces the conditions of the neurosis but also because that adjustment would necessitate the impossible, a total crossing of the line that demarcates superior from inferior, identity from difference.

This is, nonetheless, the demand imposed by imperial culture on its colonized subjects and of which *Black Skin, White Masks* is an extended analysis.[30] Its larger narrative, schematized in the formula above, is that of a process of Bildung that falters in the workings of its own logic. Imperial culture, in Fanon's case, French culture, holds out the promise of citizenship to all its subjects but at the cost of the abandonment of "local cultural originality."

> Every colonized people—in other words, every people in whose soul an inferiority complex has been created by the death and burial of its local cultural originality—finds itself face to face with the language of the civilizing nation; that is, with the culture of the mother country. The colonized is elevated above his jungle status in proportion to his adoption of the mother country's cultural standards. He becomes whiter as he renounces his blackness, his jungle. (*BSWM*, 18)

It is perhaps worth stressing again that the question of race and color is secondary to and produced by the question of culture and to culture seen as a process of development. This developmental narrative absorbs the geographic narrative that is that of the move to and return from the metropolis, allowing the trajectory of displacement to be conceived as a cycle of completion, a *Bildungsroman.*

> By that I mean that Negroes who return to their original environments convey the impression that they have completed a cycle, that they have added to themselves something that was lacking. They return literally full of themselves. (*BSWM*, 19n)

But *Black Skin, White Masks* is a bildungsroman against itself and demonstrates over and again that the taking on of the imperial culture, whose first embodiment is the language, "is evidence of a dislocation, a separation"

(25) rather than a fulfillment. If greater mastery of the language is the index of a greater approximation to whiteness (38), it is always precisely as approximation that development takes place, producing in the assimilative process of "likening" the one who can never be more than "just like a white man," "l'homme pareil aux autres." The process of assimilation for the colonized is one that discovers within the identity that is to be formed the difference on which assimilation's very logic depends. The process of likening produces a residue of difference that insists on the ineradicable blackness of the culturally racialized subject. For this reason, for the colonized, who had never conceived of themselves as black while "at home," the trajectory of Bildung must be inverted.

> More especially, they should become aware that the line of self-esteem that they have chosen should be inverted. We have seen that in fact the Antillean who goes to France pictures this journey as the final stage of his personality. Quite literally I can say without any risk of error that the Antillean who goes to France in order to convince himself that he is white will find his real face there. (*BSWM*, 153n)

The end of Bildung is not identity but the discovery of the culturally *constitutive* function of racism; it reveals the insistence of a splitting rather than the fulfillment of a developed subject. Racism appears at once as the product and the disabling limit of the cultural formation of that Subject which subtends and gives the possibility of the "public sphere." At that limit, the racialized individual splits between what assimilation absorbs and what it necessarily produces as its residue. That impossible predicament issues perforce in madness or resistance as the subjective correlative of the process by which the colonizer's attempt to assimilate produces the national consciousness that revolts. Fanon's subsequent writings accordingly become increasingly concerned with the necessity of violence as the only means to the overthrow of imperial domination.

I have argued throughout this chapter that culture itself constitutes the formal principles of racist discourse, that the indexes of difference on which racism relies gain their meaning from a distribution of values determined by that culture which founds the idea of common sense and its space of articulation, the public sphere. This implies that there can be no simply cultural solution to the problem of racism and that all the measures taken by liberal cultural institutions in the name of assimilation are at best half measures, at worst misrecognized means to the reproduction of a singular cultural form that will continue to produce racialized residues. For the demand for representation within existent institutions will be self-defeating so long as it is not accompanied by the demand for the transformation of those institutions, since every partial instance of representation of difference succumbs to the larger narrative of representation that absorbs it.

Current debates on cultural education have helped to highlight the pivotal role played by educational institutions in the interpellation of individuals as subjects for the state. Fanon's work, in highlighting the cultural and, more important, hegemonic dimensions of racism, brings out the necessity to conduct the analysis of racist discourse and practices in relation to the *form* of the state. The persistence of racism is then to be understood, in keeping with the foregoing arguments, as an effect of ideological interpellation: approximation to the position of the Subject, theoretically available to all regardless of "race or creed," in fact requires the impossible negation of racial or cultural differences. To Fanon's diagram we can add the formula of "race under representation":

$$\frac{\text{Representation}}{\text{Race}}$$

Just as it is impossible for the colonized individual to escape the social neurosis of colonialism by passing over into identity or "whiteness," so it is impossible for the racialized individual to enter the domain of representation except as that Subject which negates difference.

One consequence of this argument is that the concept of the "racial state" developed by Omi and Winant stands in need of supplementation by the *idea* of the state that regulates the formation of citizen-Subjects fit to participate in what is effectively state culture. For the state is not merely a contingent ensemble of institutions but is ultimately determined by the desire to unify the public sphere. What the Subject is to individuals, the state represents for civil society, the site of its formal identity. Obscured as the idea of the state generally is by the contradictions that in practice seem to frustrate it, its unifying ends become quite apparent at moments of pressure. Such has been one effect of recent educational debates in the United States in which appeal is made explicitly to the need to adhere to a common, central culture as a means to preserving loyalty to the state's institutions. At the same time, "ethnic" cultures are relegated increasingly to the re-creationary and preaesthetic domain of private cultural consumption. If race is, as Omi and Winant argue, "a *central axis* of social relations," this is because it is continually, and necessarily, constructed and reproduced as the constitutive negation of the identity that the state represents.[31] No more than are class or gender, race is no ontological or essential quality but is constructed in differential relation to the normative culture of the state.

These remarks indicate how the elements of that vexed triad—race, gender, class—can be articulated with one another without collapsing them into false identity or allowing one or another to "be subsumed under or reduced to some broader category or conception."[32] Indeed, the analysis of the formation of these categories in relation to the Subject of ideology ultimately *requires* an unrelenting specificity that we have scarcely even begun to produce here. Both moments are indispensable: on the one hand, the formal analysis of the ideological Subject, precisely because its effectiveness is inseparable from its very formality; on the other, material histories of the specific transformations that take place through the dialectic between the state and what it perforce negates as a condition of its existence. This implies, of course, that the theoretical model of the ideological Subject to which I have been alluding, Althusser's "Ideology and Ideological State Apparatuses," stands in need of correction insofar as it claims a transhistorical existence for ideology and the impossibility of standing outside it. The analysis of racist discourse is instructive in this respect, precisely because one can show the history of its transformation in relation to specific political or economic demands and, more important, because many of its contradictions derive from the capacity for any individual to be at once inside and outside, subject and object of the discourse.

The insistence of contradiction in racial formations, their inability to totalize the domain of the Subject, is politically as well as historically instructive. It suggests at once a theoretical agenda and a practical purpose for that agenda. For if the public sphere or culture furnishes a crucial ideological, and racist, regulative site, its critique is guided by what Walter Benjamin designated as the task of the materialist historian—"to brush history against the grain." This entails, in Gramscian terms, the reconstruction of histories of subaltern classes, of those social groups, that is, whose practices fall outside the terms of official culture.[33] To do so is, in effect, to decipher the history of the possible and to trace the contours of numerous alternatives to dominant modes of social formation. Without such a history, not only is the universal history of cultural development—the narrative of representation—all the more difficult to displace but radical politics becomes all the more confined to issues of civil rights, that is, to the extension of representation and the implicit affirmation of assimilation.

ACKNOWLEDGMENTS

This chapter has benefited to a more than usual extent from others' criticisms and comments. It originated as a paper given at the conferences "The Formation of Culture" at the University of Ljubljana, June 1989 and "Colonialism Now" at the University of Southampton, June 1989. Subsequent versions were delivered to the Conference on Race and Difference, Centro Interdisciplinar por Estudos Contemporaneos, Rio de Janeiro, in October 1989 and to the seminar on "The Function of Cultural Criticism" at the University of California Humanities Research Institute, December 1989. I am grateful to the organizers of these sessions for the opportunity to present this work and to the participants for their comments. I am especially indebted to Rastko Mocnik, John Higgins, Zita Nunes, Robert Young, Homi Bhabha, Carlos Alberto Pereira, Abdul JanMohamed, Paul Rabinow, Martin Jay, and Dipesh Chakrabarty for their attentive criticisms. I am also greatly indebted to Michel Chaouli for his detailed critical reading of the chapter and for his invaluable research assistance.

NOTES

1. Among many such critiques, see Johannes Fabian, *Time and the Other: How Anthropology Makes Its Object* (New York: Columbia University Press, 1983); Andre Gunder Frank, *On Capitalist Underdevelopment* (Bombay: Oxford University Press, 1975); Arturo Escobar, "Discourse and Power in Development: Michel Foucault and the Relevance of His Work to the Third World," *Alternatives* 10 (Winter 1984–85): 377–400; Majid Rahnema, "Under the Banner of Development," *Seeds of Change* 1–2 (1986): 37–46.

2. See Michael Omi and Howard Winant, *Racial Formation in the United States: From the 1960s to the 1980s* (1986; repr. New York: Routledge, 1989): 67.

3. For an elaboration of the concept of "aesthetic culture," see the introduction to David Lloyd, *Nationalism and Minor Literature: James Clarence Mangan and the Emergence of Irish Cultural Nationalism* (Berkeley, Los Angeles, and London: University of California Press, 1987): 6, 14–19.

4. I follow Omi and Winant in deriving this concept of sites from Herbert Gintis and Samuel Bowles: "A site is defined not by what is *done* there, but by what imparts *regularity* to what is done there, its characteristic 'rules of the game,' " cited from "Structure and Practice in the Labor Theory of Value," *Review of Radical Political Economics* 12, no. 4 (Winter 1981): 4, in *Racial Formation,* 166. As may be apparent from what follows, I would annex the notion of a *regularity* within sites to a quite Kantian concept of the "regulative idea" to indicate that it is the implicit teleology, not merely the contingent practices, of social institutions that structures those institutions as reproducible at all levels, including that of the subjects formed by them.

5. I have developed the concept of a narrative of representation further in "The Narrative of Representation: Culture, the State and the Canon," in *Rethinking Germanistik: Canon and Culture,* ed. Robert Bledsoe et al. (New York: Peter Lang, 1991): 125–138.

6. See Immanuel Kant. *Critique of Judgement,* trans. James Creed Meredith (Oxford: Clarendon Press, 1982): 151. I discuss this passage and the process of Subject-formation further in "Analogies of the Aesthetic: The Politics of Culture and the Limits of Materialist Aesthetics," *New Formations* 10 (Spring 1990): 109–126.

7. Friedrich Schiller, *On the Aesthetic Education of Man, in a Series of Letters,* ed. and trans. Elizabeth M. Wilkinson and L. A. Willoughby (Oxford: Clarendon, 1967): 195. In an interesting extension of this narrative of the senses, the German philosopher and racial theorist Lorenz Oken would divide the races of man according to whichever of the five senses dominated a race. Cited in Michael Banton, *Racial Theories* (Cambridge: Cambridge University Press, 1987): 18–19.

8. Cf. Frantz Fanon's remarks on this aspect of colonial self-legitimation in "Concerning Violence," in *The Wretched of the Earth,* preface by Jean-Paul Sartre, trans.

Constance Farrington (New York: Grove Press, 1968): 41: "The native is declared insensible to ethics; he represents not only the absence of values, but also the negation of values." I have discussed the cases of Arnold and Mill more extensively in *Nationalism and Minor Literature*, 6–13, and in "Genet's Genealogy: European Minorities and the Ends of the Canon," *Cultural Critique* 6 (Spring 1987): 162–170. On the conservative figures mentioned here, and others, see Michael Banton, *Racial Theories*, 19–60.

9. See Colette Guillaumin, "Race and Nature: The System of Marks, the Idea of a Natural Group and Social Relationships," *Feminist Issues* 8, no. 2 (Fall 1988): 25–43; Fanon, "Concerning Violence," 41. On the misfit between racism and imperialism, see Banton, *Racial Theories*, 62.

10. Guillaumin, "Race and Nature," 32–33. Guillaumin uses the expression "symbol" to describe arbitrary marks. We would prefer to keep the term "symbol" for those signs that, in principle, "participate in what they represent," that have, that is, "an organic relationship" to the signified. It is a commonplace of literary critical history that the devaluation of allegory in favor of the symbol takes place in the late eighteenth century and early nineteenth century. A shift in aesthetics accordingly corresponds to a shift in racist discourse, confirming one's sense of a certain congruence between relatively discrete spheres of cultural practice.

11. Guillaumin, "Race and Nature," 41.

12. On Person and Condition, see Schiller, *On the Aesthetic Education of Man*, 73–77. I discuss these concepts further in *Nationalism and Minor Literature*.

13. On the botanist Saussure, see Kant, *Critique of Judgement*, 115–116. Jacques Derrida discusses the complicity between a moral discourse and an empirical culturalism in relation to the Third Critique in "Le Parergon," in *La verité en peinture* (Paris: Flammarion, 1978): 42. The anthropological subject is, as Gregory Schrempp has put it in a very valuable article, "boundless." See Schrempp, "Aristotle's Other Self: On the Boundless Subject of Anthropological Discourse," in *Romantic Motives: Essays on Anthropological Sensibility*, ed. George W. Stocking, Jr. (Madison: University of Wisconsin Press, 1989): 10–43. In tracing anthropology's founding terms to Aristotle and, more immediately, Kant, Schrempp most valuably demonstrates its indebtedness to the "principle of identity," a point that has interesting implications for this discussion. For an eloquent defense of the value of anthropology's encounter with other cultures, though still ultimately oriented to the understanding of modern society, see Louis Dumont, *Homo Hierarchicus: An Essay on the Caste System*, trans. Mark Sainsbury (Chicago: University of Chicago Press, 1970): 2.

> Anthropology, by the understanding it *gradually* affords of the most widely differing societies and cultures, gives proof of the unity of mankind. In doing so, it obviously reflects at least some light on our own sort of society. But this is not quite enough, and anthropology has the inherent and occasionally avowed aim of achieving this in a more systematic and radical way, that is, of putting modern society in perspective in relation to the societies which have preceded it or which co-exist with it, and of making in this way a direct and central contribution to our general education.

It is perhaps unnecessary to remark that the tendency of this remark is to place the achievement of that unity finally in modern societies, that is, in the West. On the relation between scientific rationality, Western cultural hegemony, and anthropology, see Partha Chatterjee, *Nationalist Thought and the Colonial World: A Derivative*

Discourse? (London: Zed Books, 1986): 14–17. Zita Nunes's work on modernism and anthropology in Brazil shows powerfully how the unity of the national culture is constructed through a racializing discourse and how anthropology contributes to this process. See her essay, "Os males do Brasil: Antropofagia e a questão da raça," Papeis Avulsos do CIEC, 22. For a valuable study of the formation of the white colonial self as "ubiquitous," as "abstract, unspecifiable in its contents," see S. P. Mohanty, "Kipling's Children and the Colour Line," *Race and Class* 31, no. 1 (July/September 1989): 36.

14. Paul Ricoeur, "The Metaphorical Process as Cognition, Imagination, and Feeling," in *On Metaphor,* ed. Sheldon Sacks (Chicago: University of Chicago Press, 1979): 146.

15. Condillac quoted by Paul de Man, "The Epistemology of Metaphor," *On Metaphor,* 20.

16. See Paul Ricoeur, "Metaphor and the Main Problem of Hermeneutics," *New Literary History* 6, no. 1 (Autumn 1974): 108–110. Cyrus Hamlin draws attention to this moment in Ricoeur's essay in order to develop his argument concerning the place of metaphor in the Romantic construction of selfhood. See "The Temporality of Selfhood: Metaphor and Romantic Poetry, *New Literary History* 6, no. 1 (Autumn 1974): 172. His argument has been very valuable for some of the contentions of this chapter. See also, on the relation between metaphor and implicit narrative, de Man, "Epistemology of Metaphor," 21–22: "From the recogniton of language as trope, one is led to the telling of a tale, to the narrative sequence I have just described. The temporal deployment of an initial complication, of a structural knot, indicates the close, though not necessarily complementary, relationship between trope and narrative, knot and plot."

17. Ricoeur, "Metaphorical Process," 154. Emphasis in original.

18. If a little playful, this formulation is close, for example, to the insistent terminology of Matthew Arnold's *Culture and Anarchy.* In light of Ricoeur's argument as developed here, Donald Davidson is perhaps saying more than he means concerning the intimate relation between aesthetic culture and metaphor when he remarks that "there is no test for metaphor that does not call for taste"; "What Metaphors Mean," in *On Metaphor,* 29. Rastko Mocnik has remarked very cogently on the crucial ideological function of a certain teleology in the reception and interpretation of metaphorical utterances. See Mocnik, "A Theory of Metaphor," typescript, 17: "We may call it a teleological trope—or, as Lacan conceptualizes it, as a subjectifying trope: a metaphor does autonomize a signifier in its meaninglessness, but only in view of producing a sense-effect."

19. Michael Banton notes how the term "assimilation" transforms in meaning from "any process by which peoples became more similar" to a process by which one people "was expected to absorb another . . . without itself undergoing any significant change," in *Racial Theories,* ix. Fanon's comment, in "Racism and Culture," 38, is a fittingly acerbic comment on the ideological bent of *both* understandings: "This event, which is commonly designated as alienation, is naturally very important. It is found in the official texts under the name of assimilation."

20. I think here especially of Homi K. Bhabha's "The Other Question," *Screen* 24 (November/December 1983): 18–36. I might remark here that the "four-term strategy" of colonial discourse that Bhabha posits (circulating between metaphor and

metonymy, narcissism and aggression) seems to restore to the stereotype the fixity that his analysis critiques, only in the form of an anxious oscillation between lack and the masking function of the fetish. I would contend that the transfer from metonymy to metaphor in the process of assimilation is both irreversible and determinant for the form that resistance to assimilation takes—a dialectic succinctly analyzed by Fanon in "Racism and Culture."

21. Sigmund Freud, "On Fetishism," in *On Sexuality: Three Essays on the Theory of Sexuality* (Harmondsworth: Penguin, 1977): 352. For the theory of castration, see the essays "The Dissolution of the Oedipus Complex" (1924) and "Some Psychic Consequences of the Anatomical Distinction between the Sexes" (1925), in *On Sexuality*, 313–322 and 323–344, respectively. The latter is cited hereafter as ADS in the text.

22. In Freud, "Infantile Sexuality" (1905), *On Sexuality*, 116–119.

23. The subject of psychoanalysis, which is produced, as Lacan's Schema L illustrates, in suspension between the ego and the superego, that is, between the I formed in the mirror stage and the Other or "Name-of-the-Father," is not identical to the Kantian aesthetic Subject but is similarly structured in a process of formalization. For Schema L, see Jacques Lacan, "D'une question preliminaire a tout traitemaent possible de la psychose," *Ecrits 2* (Paris: Seuil, 1971): 63. Louis Althusser begins to sketch the relation between this subject, the ethical subject, and the ideological subject in "Ideology and Ideological State Apparatuses (Notes Towards an Investigation)," in *Lenin and Philosophy and Other Essays*, trans. Ben Brewster (New York: Monthly Review Press, 1971): 127–186.

24. The considerable anxiety aroused in many racist societies by miscegenation is a mark of the loss of verisimilitude in appeals to immediate visual discrimination. Miscegenation, as a metaphor for different possible cultural formations, is in turn troublesome precisely insofar as it raises the question of the versimilitude or canonicity of dominant cultural narratives and suggests the possibility of a limitless transformation of cultures. Unlike assimilation, it cannot be organized in terms of a developmental hierarchy and in relation to the formation of national culture must always be recast in the form of an *embranqueamento*, which restores both the developmental narrative and, at a quite literal level, its "residual" logic. I am indebted for these observations and for much of the thinking on assimilation in this chapter to Zita Nunes's work on Brazilian modernism and anthropology in relation to the formation of national culture. See her "Os males do Brasil," esp. 1–2. See also Jean Bernabe, Patrick Chamoiseau, Raphael Confiant, *Eloge de la creolite* (Paris: Gallimard, 1989): 27–28: "Du fait de sa mosaique constitutive, la Creolite est une specificite ouverte. . . . L'exprimer c'est exprimer non une synthese, pas simplement un metissage, ou n'importe qu'elle autre unicite. C'est exprimer une totalite kaleidoscopique, c'est a dire la conscience non totalitaire d'une diversite preservee."

25. Though in most respects this chapter is profoundly indebted to Frantz Fanon's analysis of racism in *Black Skin, White Masks*, trans. Charles Lam Markmann, foreword by Homi K. Bhabha (London: Pluto Press, 1986), at this point I would depart somewhat from the emphasis he places on projection as the psychic mechanism of racism. See chapter 6, "The Negro and Psychopathology," esp. 190–194. As I shall argue below, Fanon very rapidly moves beyond and complicates the notion of projection, not least by invoking what he terms "cultural imposition" (193). Cited in the text hereafter as BSWM.

26. Kingsley, cited in L. P. Curtis, *Anglo-Saxons and Celts: A Study of Anti-Irish Prejudice in Victorian England* (Bridgeport, Conn.: University of Bridgeport, 1968): 84. Thomas Carlyle's oxymoron is to be found in *Sartor Resartus;* I discuss its implications for understanding the ascription of inauthenticity to the colonized in *Nationalism and Minor Literature,* 206–207.

27. On the relation between "whiteness" as a metaphor and the identitarian structure of metaphor, for which it is a metaphor, see Jacques Derrida's "White Mythology: Metaphor in the Text of Philosophy," *New Literary History* 6, no. 1 (Autumn 1974): 5–74. In a longer work, it would be necessary to supply here some account of the history and contradictory logic of imperial practices of assimilation. Suffice it to say here that racism is at once the structure and limit to assimilation insofar as it is predicated on a hierarchy of cultural differences yet universal in its claims and aims. Nunes's work, cited above, is very suggestive in this respect.

28. For some comments on the differences between British and French colonialism, see Renate Zahar, *Colonialism and Alienation: Concerning Frantz Fanon's Political Theory* (Benin City: Ethiope Publishing Co., 1974): xxi–xxii. Though differences of intensity may appear, the structure of assimilation remains largely the same where applied by either regime.

29. See, for example, Benedict Anderson, *Imagined Communities: Reflections on the Origin and Spread of Nationalism* (London: Verso, 1983): esp. 106–107. This phenomenon is crucial to the dialectic of decolonization outlined throughout Fanon's writings, especially in "Concerning Violence" and "The Pitfalls of National Consciousness" in *The Wretched of the Earth.*

30. Zahar comments that "there can be no doubt that by the very fact of idealizing assimilation, while at the same time brutally preventing its realization, the officially proclaimed policy of French colonialism contributed in no small measure to the specific phenomena of alienation and frustration analysed [in her study]." *Colonialism and Alienation,* xxii.

31. See Omi and Winant, *Racial Formation,* 61; on the "racial state," see 76–77.

32. Omi and Winant, *Racial Formations,* 62.

33. Walter Benjamin, "Theses on the Philosophy of History," in *Illuminations,* ed. Hannah Arendt, trans. Harry Zohn (London: Fontana, 1973): 259; Antonio Gramsci, *Selections from the Prison Notebooks,* ed. and trans. Quintin Hoare and Geoffrey Nowell Smith (New York: International Publishers, 1971): 52–55. The concept of "Subaltern Studies" has been most consciously put into practice by the Indian Subaltern scholars. See, for a selection of their work, *Selected Subaltern Studies,* ed. Ranajit Guha and Gayatri Chakravorty Spivak, foreword by Edward Said (Oxford: Oxford University Press, 1988).

PART THREE

Unsettling Texts

TWELVE

Reading Culture:
Anthropology and the Textualization
of India

Nicholas B. Dirks

"And this also," said Marlow suddenly, "has been one of the dark places of the earth."—Joseph Conrad

For all of anthropology's emphasis on its ordinary encounters, ethnographic presents/presence, and fieldwork, anthropological knowledge has always been heavily dependent on texts. The textual field that is the pretext for fieldwork has been erased for some obvious and other less obvious reasons, but the erasure has further fetishized the anthropological field in relation not only to an earlier disinterest in ethnographic writing (until recently; see Clifford 1983; Clifford and Marcus 1986; Geertz 1988) but also to a systematic inattention to ethnographic reading. The resistance of anthropologists to footnotes is more than a stylistic conceit, for it still conceals a lack of serious concern for the reading behind (before and after) the writing of culture.

Recent interest in the writing of culture has focused some attention on the way earlier anthropologists have inscribed stylistic aspirations and professional investments in the anthropological canon we have inherited as "the literature" of ethnography. For the most part, the invocation of the new commitment to "textuality" has been used to argue for the literary "reading" of the great texts of anthropology, or to focus attention on the anthropologist's keyboard, our own writing of culture. While this has led to an extraordinarily important recognition of the power of writing and the extent to which textual virtuosity conceals the specific conditions of possibility of anthropological knowledge, much of anthropology has been plunged in positivist despair. The backlash to the debate has rehearsed the tired question of whether anthropology is a science and if so (or for that matter, if not), whether it is about "us" or "them," all leading to desperate deliberation about whether anthropology is any longer possible. If anthropology is just a text, it simply can no longer claim to be real, or true. And, ironically, the debate has worked in a peculiar way to make fieldwork (for all the contestants in the debate) all the more an originary moment, the origins of writing as the origins of interpretation. Arguments about textuality thus frequently serve to displace anthropological desire into the past, before writing, before encounter.

The focus on writing works to emphasize the individual in the text; as Clifford Geertz made clear in his analysis of anthropological writing, anthropology, now more than ever, cannot concede the death of the author. And the critiques of the author in *Writing Culture* (Clifford and Marcus 1986) resurrect the modernist moment in anthropology even despite the incongruous musings of Stephen Tylor's postmodernist position. My argument in this chapter is not that culture is not constituted by writing, for indeed I focus on historical examples of anthropological writing, on moments and processes through which culture is inscribed textually, but rather that we would do well to focus on the textual and contextual field that produces culture, on the reading practices that make writing possible. Although individuals do the reading, reading is self-evidently a social and historical practice and works to focus attention on how certain texts are created and made available as knowledge, on the production and circulation of the assumption, data, and knowledge necessary for fieldwork itself, on the inchoate accumulation of the preconditions for anthropological writing and interpretation, as well, of course, as subsequent reading. And this focus on reading should remind us that there is really very little difference between what we call text and what we call context: there seems as little good reason today to think of contexts as outside texts as there is to think of texts solely within the discrete covers of autonomous textual fields.

In literary studies, the shift in emphasis from writing to reading was propelled by the move from new criticism to hermeneutics. The realization that each reading of a text produced a different kind of text was the methodical pretext for Paul de Man's elegiac reading of the impossibility of textual fixity or closure. In a canonical statement, de Man wrote, "Prior to any generalization about literature, literary texts have to be read, and the possibility of reading can never be taken for granted. It is an act of understanding that can never be observed, nor in any way prescribed or verified. A literary text is not a phenomenal event that can be granted any form of positive existence, whether as a fact of nature or as an act of the mind" (1983: 107). The written text dissolved into the multiple readings that critics like de Man could perform so powerfully, persuasion the proleptic product of skilled textual play. And the contexts into which texts folded were fragments of particular kinds of readings; the more disturbing, the more powerful they seemed. But as Jerome McGann has observed, the textual model was in many ways little changed: "It is a model in which there is only one agent, the solitary 'reader,' whose pursuit of meaning involves an activity of ceaseless metaphoric production" (1991: 6). McGann goes on to suggest that the great gulf between the empiricists and the interpreters in de Man's rhetorical self-presentation was in fact bridged by a similar notion of reading, in which the text continued to be the ideal referent, ineffable yet self-enclosed in its intractable—whether empirical or interpretive—unknowability.

McGann proposes a different way of thinking about texts, one that begins with readings that "like the texts which stand before them—are materially and socially structured" (8). McGann's own interest is in textual histories that encompass the concrete production histories, with all the entangled institutional and individual interests and moments, of texts as well as the historical conditions that govern—and are governed by—the reading of texts. His historical method works best when trained on the specific histories of post-eighteenth-century Western texts, debunking our certainties about the stability of actual texts, the inalienability of the final intentions of authors, the separability of abstract texts from their multiple material conditions. Because he works within the heart of literary studies, on romantic and modernist poetry, those of us who read and write anthropological texts can only take general inspiration from his approach, however much we benefit from his inspired critique of underlying continuities in contemporary literary studies.[1] But we can certainly learn from his insistence that context does not exist outside of texts but rather at the core of their materiality and historicity.

Indeed, in invoking a historical method, I do not mean to suggest that texts can be inserted into, or simply read in terms of, historical contexts that themselves are any more readily "readable" than the texts that recent critics have placed under such relentless hermeneutic suspicion. Writers as various as Stephen Greenblatt (1988) and Hayden White (1973), Michel de Certeau (1986), and Slavoj Zizek (1991) have shown how heterological history itself is, how the past dissolves into its textual mediations at the same time that our discourses about the past secure their rhetorical power by reference to the unknowable. Not only does history have multiple narratives; it is itself a function of historicity, of culturally distinctive ways of marking, remembering, realizing, and retelling the "past." Anthropology may be slow to historicize its own practice, but it has provided compelling examples of how historical knowledge is constructed through cultural form (see Dirks 1993).

If the historicizing move seems always to refer ultimately to the real, it is also the case that the real is frequently coded by unspoken certainties about the material conditions that constitute the real. But Marjorie Levinson has suggested that this other great peg of context, materiality, offers no easy solutions either. Indeed, Levinson suggests that the material at one level is precisely the unreadable, the referent that resists all familiar forms of access; by its very nature, the " 'material' describes an event neither reflecting nor yielding to a human interest" (1992). The material exists, therefore, less as a fixed "thing" than as a relentless challenge, a reflexively grounded call to critique the "forces and relations that accomplish the ceaseless reproduction of physical and social life." But since the text can never be made to acknowledge its determinations, the critical function engages the materiality of texts at the level of the "political unconscious," a level invariably at odds with the work's own self-representation.

Michael Taussig has recently questioned the conceit of context that drives much of history and anthropology. "I believe that for a long time now the notion of contextualization has been mystified, turned into some sort of talisman such that by 'contextualizing' social relationships and history, as the common appeal would have it, significant mastery over society and history is guaranteed—as if our understandings of social relations and history, understandings which constitute the fabric of such context, were not themselves fragile intellectual constructs posing as robust realities obvious to our contextualizing gaze" (1992: 44–45). Taussig's distrust of context reflects his own disquiet about the uses of materiality in social science discourses by Marxists and non-Marxists alike, his insistence on the "flip-flop from spirit to thing and back again—the decided undecidability that could so clearly, so mistily, be seen in Marx's statement regarding the fetish quality of commodities" (5). The commodity form exceeds its materiality by concealing itself through the effects of desire and displacement. The boundary between text and context secures itself by the same logic of reification that Marx so powerfully attacks in his thinking about commodity fetishism. It is imperative to read contexts as texts, even as we set out to read texts in terms of contexts.

When the influential and much debated volume of essays *Writing Culture* was published in 1986, it focused the attention of anthropologists on the textual character of their practice in ways that many found disconcerting, even shocking. Anthropology was portrayed neither as unproblematic science nor as unmediated experience but rather as the product of textual strategies and moments. Much useful debate was stimulated by these essays, in addition to the kind of backlash that mistook textual discussion for the denial of anthropology's truth. Wherever anthropologists have stood in the debate, it is fair to say that few of us any longer think of "writing up" as the kind of neutral, incidental activity it used to be when it was seen as the straightforward transcription of "analysis." Nevertheless, despite all the penetrating analyses of Conrad's literary influence on Bronislaw Malinowski, and of Geertz's stylistic invocation of his authorial/authoritative presence in his classic essay on the cockfight, we have still for the most part limited our textual analyses to specific texts and balanced our textual preoccupations with inchoate calls to recontextualize. We have also not come to terms with the fact that much of the new reflexivity works to refetishize fieldwork, to fashion the ethnographic encounter as the true originary moment for anthropology's new historicism.

In this chapter I propose that we think of context as pretext, that is to say, as both the texts that are read before and the conditions of the production, circulation, and consumption of these texts. I try to take texts and contexts as, at best, supplements to each other, those destabilizing additives that mark the original referent as always already inadequate. By extension, the same must be true for history, which will not be located outside of texts but rather in an intertextual field, constructed out of the genealogical relations between histories of prior texts and the reflexive conditions that construct—and are constructed by—successive readings of these texts. I try to show what happens to culture when we focus on reading rather than writing and what happens to fieldwork when we locate it in larger historical fields than can be encompassed by reference to our own ethnography.

ANTHROPOLOGY AND COLONIALISM

All the same, I begin with a (pre)fieldwork story. Before I went to the field, I had decided to do a historical anthropological study of a small South Indian kingdom, concentrating on the relationship between political authority and social relations at the local level. To gain some preliminary sense of the structure and meaning of caste in areas where these kingdoms had survived well into the colonial period, I turned to a seven-volume work entitled *The Castes and Tribes of Southern India,* by Edgar Thurston (1907). The volumes were thick and authoritative, arranged like an encyclopedia, with entries for more than three hundred caste groups listed in alphabetical order. The entries on each caste ranged in length from one sentence to seventy-five pages, and they included such salient ethnographic facts as origin stories, occupational profiles, descriptions of kinship structure, marriage and funerary rituals, and manner of dress and decoration, as well as assorted stories, observations, and accounts about each group. The text was designed as an easy reference work for colonial administrators, for the police as well as revenue agents, district magistrates, and army recruiters. But years later the text still seemed useful and has provided the ethnographic baseline for most anthropologists who have worked in southern India. If the information was inevitably flawed by the colonial character of its compilation, it still provided fundamental ethnographic data and a rough sense of the hierarchical position and geographic distribution of the core components of South Indian society, organized appropriately by caste.

I looked up the caste entries for those warrior castes that had spawned the most long-lived chiefly families in the early modern period of South In-

dia's past and was pleased to find extensive ethnographic detail for these
Kallars, Maravars, and Tottiyars. I was somewhat surprised, however, to discover that the very castes that attained the reputation of kingship had also,
by the late nineteenth century, been most consistently branded as criminal
castes: tribes habitually given over to feckless lives of plunder, disorder, and
violence. As my studies proceeded, it became clear that it was precisely the
kingly virtues of these castes in the eighteenth century that had been transformed into the incriminating signs of imperial ethnography, the military
prowess of royal retinues and armies now disaffiliated from the structures of
power, unemployed martial clans cast out into the delegitimated spaces of
resistance and disruption under the new colonial regime. Colonial ethnography seemed suspicious; but it has only been years later that I have been
able to track the whiff of suspicion through the historical genealogies of
these colonial texts, texts that still populate the footnotes of contemporary
ethnography, texts that are still important among the pretexts for most anthropological practice that is conducted even today. This chapter is about
the implication of colonial ethnography in the criminalizing not just of
these once royal caste groups but of the study of Indian society itself.

Zizek writes, "At the beginning of the law, there is a certain 'outlaw,' a
certain Real of violence which coincides with the act itself of the establishment of the reign of law: the ultimate truth about the reign of law is that of
an usurpation, and all classical politico-philosophical thought rests on the
disavowal of this violent act of foundation" (1991: 204). Zizek is examining
here not only the problem of origins but the fact that this search for origins
leads to a recognition of the horror that lies just below the surface of civility, the realization that the law, indeed lawfulness itself, is predicated on its
originary establishment in violence. The horror never disappears entirely;
paraphrasing Kant, Zizek writes, "From the standpoint of Nature, 'Spirit'
itself is a 'crime which can never be effaced' " (209). As anthropologists, we
should perhaps read *culture* here instead of spirit. And when we think about
the origins of anthropology in colonialism, it is not difficult to see that the
originary/absolute crime has folded into ethnology in a way that confirms
Zizek's suggestion about the relationship between violence and the law.
Zizek writes, "The absolute, self-relating crime is thus 'uncanny' [*unheimlich*] in the strict Freudian sense: what is so horrifying about it is not its
strangeness but rather its absolute *proximity* to the reign of law" (204). Here,
too, we can recognize that we cannot efface the original crime and still do
anthropology; in this chapter, I seek to show the perversity of colonial anthropology, but I seek also to suggest that this perversity is familiar, that however much we invoke the tropes of irony or parody we can never totally
rupture the colonial genealogy of our enterprise. Indeed, I would suggest
that we need to hold onto the uncanny character of the relationship, for fear
that we might forget the crime and then repeat it all over again.

ANTHROPOLOGY AND THE POLICE

Crime and anthropology are related in more than Zizek's metaphorical sense. In 1893, Frederick S. Mullaly, a senior official in the Madras police, was appointed the first honorary superintendent of ethnography for Madras Presidency.[2] Mullaly's principal qualification for the job was his publication the year before of a book entitled *Notes on Criminal Classes of the Madras Presidency*. This book, which borrowed heavily from standard mid-nineteenth-century texts on such subjects as caste in India, as also from various district manuals that were being compiled from the 1860s on, was written first and foremost for his fellow policemen. As he states in the preface, "These notes on the habits and customs of some of the criminal classes of the Madras Presidency have been collected at the suggestion of Colonel Porteous, Inspector-General of Police, and put in the present form in the hope that they may prove of some value to Police Officers who are continually brought in contact with the Predatory classes, and of some slight interest to such of the public who may wish to know something of their less favoured brethren." Mullaly went on to suggest his personal authority in terms that sound highly anthropological: "The facts given here have, for the most part, been verified by personal association with the people themselves."

The construction of entire castes by the British in colonial India as "criminal castes" was part of a larger discourse in which caste determined the occupational and social character of all its constituent members, though criminal castes were seen simultaneously as typical and deviant (Yang 1985). The colonial notion of caste was that each group had an essential quality that was expressed in its occupational profile, its position in the social hierarchy, and in a whole set of moral and cultural characteristics that adhered to each group qua group. The British labeled some castes as martial and recruited them for the army (under the Raj, the appellation "martial" implied both physical prowess and political loyalty). Some castes were seen as specifically agricultural, others as merchant, and the British government attempted to keep these categories from getting mixed up when merchants began assuming land that had been mortgaged for loans in large quantities in the nineteenth century. Although the designation of particular qualities in relation to caste changed over time, often in response to the political evaluation of such factors as loyalty, the notion that each caste had an essence was predicted on a belief in the changelessness of caste. The theories about criminal castes also partook of a set of late-nineteenth-century notions about the genetic and racial character of criminality, characteristics in the Indian case that were always seen to apply to entire caste groups and not, as was often the case in the West, to particular individuals.

Mullaly's book consists of a series of chapters on different criminal castes, each chapter including a large range of ethnographic detail with special attention to the kinds of crimes the group committed. Two of the most conspicuous criminal castes in his book—castes that were subsequently included in the Criminal Tribes Act when it was extended to Madras Presidency in 1911—were Kallars and Maravars. The very word *Kallar* has generally been translated as "thief," and there is little debate that many Kallars and Maravars had engaged in forms of predation (as well as of protection) that were part of a highly volatile political system in eighteenth-century southern India (see Dirks 1987). Mullaly begins his remarks by being reasonably descriptive. He writes about Maravars, that they "furnish nearly the whole of the village police (kavilgars, watchmen), and are at the same time the principal burglars, robbers and thieves of the Tinnevelly District. Very often the thief and the watchman are one and the same individual." About Kallars, he notes, "The word 'kallan' means thief or robber in many of the languages of Southern India, and is supposed to have applied to them as indicative of their peculiar mode of earning a livelihood—their violent and lawless habits. Their profession is that of stealing with or without violence as opportunities offer." Agency here is completely subordinated to the normative principles—the traditions and customs—of Indian society. In the essentialist language of the colonizer, Mullaly refers to the "profession" of these caste groups as lawlessness.

Mullaly, however, does not stop with these perfunctory statements about the historical basis of the criminal castes. He uses ethnographic material not just to exemplify certain assertions but to condemn an entire caste group. For example, he writes as follows:

> The savage disposition of the Kallars appears from the following description of a custom which exceeds in atrocity almost every crime of violence of which history affords an example. The Survey Account states that—The women have all the ill qualities and evil dispositions of the men; in most of their actions they are inflexibly vindictive and furious on the least injury, even on suspicion, which prompts the most violent revenge without any regard to consequences. A horrible custom exists among the females on the class; when a quarrel or dissension arises between them, the insulted woman brings her child to the house of the aggressor and kills it at her door to avenge herself, although her vengeance is attended with the most cruel barbarity.

He goes on to note that if the crime is shown to be true, the offending husband must kill his child in public in return. "Such is the inhuman barbarity in avenging outrage which proves the innate cruelty of the people and the unrestrained barbarity of their manners and morals." Mullaly concludes this gripping atrocity story by noting casually that these customs are unknown in the present day, and he does nothing to evaluate the evidence or context of the report.

The report serves its purpose, by naturalizing the assertion that criminality and cruelty are innate to Kallars as a whole and providing irrefutable evidence for their inclusion in the general provisions of police surveillance that consigned certain subcastes to periodic long-term imprisonment (well before the Criminal Tribes Act was officially used). Mullaly also includes within his consideration of these two "criminal" castes the royal genealogies of the ruling families of Pudukkottai and Ramanathapuram, the first the only princely state in the Tamil area of Madras Presidency, the other the largest zamindari in the same area. Although it seems extraordinary to come across a royal genealogy in a book on criminal castes, Mullaly admits neither embarrassment nor contradiction. At best, Mullaly is trivializing the kingship of these groups, implying that local kings in India ruled principally by force, though he goes further and charges that the kings themselves were brigands and thieves who ruled by terror and extortion. Here colonial anthropology has displaced Indian history with a vengeance!

The post of honorary superintendent of ethnography had been instituted at the request of H. H. Risley, who in the early 1890s was the secretary to the government of Bengal and the acknowledged expert in matters concerning Indian ethnology. In 1890, he had addressed the government of Bengal advocating the extension throughout India of the ethnographic project he had begun in Bengal.[3] He wrote at the time that anthropological research is conducted by two methods: first, by inquiry into customs; second, by examination and record of physical characteristics. His first concern in Madras was that the appropriate castes and tribes for this kind of study be selected, and thus he was pleased with Mullaly's appointment. However, Risley still felt that the government had not allocated enough importance, and money, for a comprehensive scheme to collect ethnographic information throughout India. In 1901, the government of India resolved its support for a scheme to carry out an ethnographic survey of India. At that time, Risley was appointed director of ethnography for India; and Edgar Thurston, superintendent of the Madras Museum between 1885 and 1908, was appointed the superintendent of ethnography for Madras Presidency.[4] The replacement of Mullaly by Thurston signified the grander scale and scientific status of the ethnographic project in Madras; ethnography was now to be a general science rather than an applied form of colonial knowledge.

Thurston was the obvious and ideal choice for this position. By training a medical man, Thurston lectured in anatomy at the Medical College in Madras in addition to directing the activities of the Madras Museum. He began his extensive Indian research with work in numismatics and geology and began his anthropological research in 1894.[5] His first ethnographic writings were on the Todas, which though superseding in "scientific importance" the earlier writings of missionaries, was itself superseded by W. H. R. Rivers's publication of *The Todas* in 1901. But by that year his "ethnographic researchers in the South of India" were already "well known," and Risley in particular was delighted with Thurston's availability because of their common enthusiasm about anthropometry as the principal means for collecting physical data about the castes and tribes of India. Thurston's obsession with anthropometry was so marked that before he delivered a lecture to the Royal Society of the Arts in London in 1909, Lord Ampthill introduced him with the following story: "A visit to the Government Museum at Madras was always a very pleasant experience, although at first alarming. Such was the author's zeal for anthropometry, that he seized every man, woman, or child in order to measure them."

In the proposal for the ethnographic survey of India, the secretary to the government of India wrote, "It has often been observed that anthropometry yields peculiarly good results in India by reason of the caste system which prevails among Hindus, and of the divisions, often closely resembling castes, which are recognized by Muhammadans. Marriage takes place only within a limited circle; the disturbing element of crossing is to a great extent excluded; and the differences of physical type, which measurement is intended to establish, are more marked and more persistent than anywhere else in the world."[6] Thus the government justified its project—and its choice of Risley and Thurston—for a survey that was specifically directed "to collect the physical measurements of selected castes and tribes." Risley's advocacy of anthropometry and his theories about the relation of race and caste were clearly fundamental to the definition of the ethnographic project in turn-of-the-century colonial India. The scientific claim about caste reflects Risley's justification for the ethnographic survey in terms that make India into an imperial laboratory, for he is confident that he can actually test in India the various theories about race and the human species that had been merely proposed on speculative grounds in Europe. At the same time, these claims concealed the continuities between the assumptions that castes were biologically discrete and earlier statements, made, for example, in the context of explaining the difference between phrenology in Europe and in India, that consistently treated caste groups in India as equivalent to individuals in Europe (Marshall 1873).

During the 1890s, Thurston lectured on the methods and claims of "practical anthropology" to Madras University students, as well as on occasion to members of the Madras police. In the 1899 issue of the Madras Museum *Bulletin*, Thurston published the syllabus of his course in practical anthropology, in which he stated that anthropology, which he saw as a "branch of natural history," was broken into two main divisions. First, ethnography deals with "man as a social and intellectual being, his manners and customs, knowledge of arts and industries, tradition, language, religion, etc." Second, anthropograhy deals with "man and the varieties or species of the human family from an animal point of view, his structure and the functions of his body." According to Thurston, the most important division of anthropography was anthropometry, which he defined as the "measurement and estimation of physical data relating to people belonging to different races, castes and tribes."

Anthropometry included the determination of everything from average height and weight (and average weight relative to stature) to detailed measurements of the shape and size of the skull, the face and the nasal index (breadth × 100/height), the relation of head size to body size, and the relative sizes of different body parts. For example, Thurston measured the relative length of the upper extremities, the arm span and the distance between middle finger and kneecap, for English, Brahmans, Pariahs, Paniyans, and Negroes. As part of his lecture he compared the skeleton of a Negro with that of an orangutan, "in which hands reach far below knees." He complained about the difficulty in measuring the heads of Todas, "whose dense locks offer [an] obstacle to [the] shifting of callipers in search for [the] right spot." Elsewhere he had noted that "the measuring appliances sometimes frighten the subjects, especially [the] goniometer for determining facial angle, which is mistaken for an instrument of torture." He encouraged the offering of a two-anna piece for conciliation, "supplemented by cheroots for men, cigarettes for children, and, as a last resource, alcohol." He discussed the relative merits of gunshot or seed when measuring skull capacities. He also noted, displaying a rather perverse sense of humor, that "European inhabitants of a hill station objected to my weighing local tribesmen in [the] meat scales of [the] butcher's shop." His best results, he thought, were in scientifically demonstrating that the nasal index was lowest in Aryans and highest in jungle tribes and that the index increased as body height diminished.[7]

Thurston also noted the importance of anthropometry for criminal identification, which had been the reason for his lectures to the police. In the early 1890s, the Bertillon system of using anthropometric measurements had been adopted first in Bengal and then in Madras. The idea was to identify habitual criminals who moved from place to place and shifted their identities. In India, the Bertillon system was applied according to conventions set out by the colonial sociology of criminal castes. The basic operational principle was that "only members of criminal tribes and persons convicted of certain definite crimes" should be so measured.[8] Since most crime was committed by circumscribed groups of people, anthropometry seemed to be the perfect means to apprehend the principal suspects. As E. R. Henry, the inspector-general of police in Bengal put it, "With anthropometry on a sound basis professional criminals of this type will cease to flourish, as under the rules all persons not identified must be measured, and reference concerning them made to the Central Bureau."[9]

In the early years of the 1890s, the police in both Bengal and Madras became increasingly confident that they were accumulating a central file of measurements that would help them apprehend criminals in a systematic and scientific manner. The major problem was that the measurement process turned out to be rather subjective and required extensive training and great care. In 1893, it was announced that "no officers fit for court duties will be promoted until they hold certificates of proficiency as measurers."[10] Col. C. A. Porteous, inspector-general of police in Madras, wrote in 1894 that he had earlier "expressed the opinion that the anthropometrical system for the identification of habitual offenders was too Scientific and too dependent on extreme nicety of measurement and mathematical accuracy to be suited for universal adoption in this country; a more practical acquaintance with this subject has led me to modify my views."[11] Thus experts such as Thurston were called in to train police throughout the Presidency and to devise means to make the measurements as standard as possible. By 1895, police officers regularly underwent courses of training in anthropometry. And by 1897, Henry could write that the experience of the previous three years had "shown that success achieved has been progressive, and that the figures compare favorably with those submitted for Provincial France by Mons. A. Bertillon, to the Fourth International Congress of Criminal Anthropology held at Geneva in August 1896." Henry went on to note that "this outturn justifies the opinion that the anthropometric system is being worked on sound lines and effectively since, by means of it, four out of every possible ten cases were identified."[12]

Nevertheless, there was residual concern that measurements varied not only from measurer to measurer but from measurement to measurement. The instruments were costly, the course of instruction was lengthy, the statistics were hard to classify, and the measurement process itself was time consuming. In the last years of the decade anthropometry began to yield to fingerprinting, which was initially developed in Bengal, as a means of criminal identification that had all the advantages of anthropometry, with none of its difficulties. Fingerprinting was considered error-free, cheap, quick, and simple, and the results were more easily classified. By 1898, Henry wrote, "It may now be claimed that the great value of finger impressions as a means of fixing identity has been fully established."[13] Fingerprinting quickly established itself as the universal system of criminal identification (see Ginzburg 1989). In the technologies of policing, as in many other areas, empire served as an important laboratory for the metropole.

The replacement of anthropometry by fingerprinting did not lessen Thurston's commitment to the physical measuring of Indian subjects. During the first decade of the twentieth century, he worked systematically on his ethnographic survey along the lines set down by Risley, collecting myriad ethnographic details and extensive archives of measurements, all arranged according to the different castes and tribes in the Presidency. As suggested throughout this chapter, Indian subjects were not only organized by but contained in their castes or tribes, which determined the cultural, economic, social, and moral characteristics of their constituent members. Individuals only existed as empirical objects and exemplary subjects. The ethnographic survey ended in Madras with the completion of Thurston's seven-volume work, *The Castes and Tribes of Southern India* (1907). Thurston was assisted by K. Rangachari, a lecturer in botany at Presidency College in Madras,[14] and together they solicited the comments and observations of fellow officers and scholars throughout the Presidency. Naturally, Thurston also included the results of his anthropometric research, which he said were "all the result of measurements taken by myself, in order to eliminate the varying error resulting from the employment of a plurality of observers."

Within the caste entries, the material is mostly made up of quotations from a wide variety of sources. The citations are reported cumulatively and used comparatively, but there is no critical evaluation of the sources, even at the level of noting the particularity of each report. Quotation marks are meant solely for attribution and do not in any way set anything within them off from the authorial narration, at the same time that they accumulate an encyclopedia sense of authority through the citation of so many authorities. For the Kallars, as indeed for the other "criminal castes," we find citations from Mullaly's work as well as some of the same citations used by him. For example, Thurston reports without comment the remarks of one T. Turnbull, who in 1817 wrote that the Kallars "still possess one common character, and in general are such thieves that the name is very justly applied to them." Turnbull goes on, "The women are inflexibly vindictive and furious on the least injury, even on suspicion, which prompts them to the most violent revenge without any regard to consequences" (III:54). And then the same stories of revenge told by Mullaly, the same generalized indictment of Kallar character, through these reports of the viciousness of their women and the remorselessness of their revenge. One citation leads to the next, the writing of Mr. Nelson, a noted jurist and onetime collector of Madura District, promiscuously mixed in with articles from the "Illustrated Criminal Investigation and Law Digest" (III:69). Curiously, Mullaly's disclaimer that the most horrifying of practices had not actually been known to have taken place in living memory is absent here, despite the enhanced scientific status of the account. The ultimate confirmation of Kallar criminality is the statistic that 40 percent of the people jailed in Madura were Kallars, though there is no critical reflection that the obvious reason behind this was the self-fulfilling character of criminality, the fact that whenever there was a crime a Kallar would be accused and arrested. But again, as with Mullaly's text, the ultimate charge was that the Kallars had traditionally been thieves: "The Kallans had until recently a regular system of blackmail, called kudikaval, under which each village paid certain fees to be exempt from theft" (III:64). In fact, this criminal system had been, through the eighteenth century, a form of local rule articulated through the institution of protection, a local politics that had proved particularly resistant to British colonization at the turn of the century. A precolonial system of authority was taken to be the primordial sign of colonial criminality (see Dirks 1987).

Moreover, if one turns to the rest of Thurston's ethnographic writing, we see that the relationship of colonial anthropology to criminality continues to be significant in other respects as well. Criminality under colonialism was about both classification and control; thus criminal castes occasioned some of the first ethnological monographs, and thus anthropology collaborated with policing to provide a scientific means to measure—and by measurement, to contain the subjectivity of—criminals whose identities were otherwise fluid within caste boundaries. Science worked on society at the level of the body; caste was defined as the genetic boundary of the Indian body, which was measured and explained in relation to a displaced Victorian enthusiasm for the colonized body. It is perhaps no accident that Sir Francis Galton purportedly invented regression analysis when surveying— for the greater glory of science—the naked bodies of Hottentot women in southern Africa.

THE COLONIAL BODY AS ETHNOGRAPHIC TEXT

The colonial anthropological obsession with colonized bodies is revealed through Thurston's anthropometric enthusiasm; it is also an important component of his general ethnographic writings. In 1906, Thurston published a long ethnographic work while he was in the middle of his labors for the ethnographic survey. This work, *Ethnographic Notes in Southern India,* consisted of a series of essays, some previously published in the Government Museum *Bulletin,* on a variety of ethnographic subjects that Thurston thought held intrinsic interest. Perhaps also Thurston realized that these essays could not be readily contained by the format of the ethnographic survey.

The book begins with two long essays, the first on marriage customs, the second on death ceremonies, that look like compilations of material that had been collected on a caste-by-caste basis. Caste seems slightly less important in the third essay, on "omens, evil eye, charms, animal superstitions, sorcery, etc.," since the ethnographic material is presented as instances of a general set of beliefs and practices. But in the subsequent chapters, the organizing principle is no longer the conventional frame of caste, and the subjects seem no longer to be standard anthropological fare. The fourth chapter is entitled "Deformity and Mutilation," the next "Torture in Bygone Days," followed by such other chapters as "Slavery," "Firewalking," "Hookswinging," "Infanticide," and "Meriah Sacrifice." If the caste-by-caste entries of Thurston's ethnographic survey volumes focus on the social (which in India was for the British caste), these essays instead focus on the body.

These essays can be seen as the critical link in the genealogy between official anthropology and the kinds of investigative inquiries and reports that the British collected in their routine administration of Indian society. These chapters are in large part encyclopedic collections of official material that was generated by the colonial interest in suppressing practices such as hookswinging, slavery, and torture. In Thurston's introduction to his *Castes and Tribes of Southern India,* he had written that he had followed the scheme for the ethnographic survey which had recommended that he "supplement the information obtained from representative men and by their own enquiries by 'researches into the considerable mass of information which lies buried in official reports, in the journals of learned Societies, and in various books.' Of this injunction full advantage has been taken, as will be evident from the abundant crop of references in foot-notes." But it is in the *Ethnographic Notes* that we can see the extraordinary extent of the connection between official colonial reports and official colonial ethnography.

The article on hookswinging is in fact little more than a compilation of the kinds of writings on the custom that were used to recommend the abolition of what was seen as a barbaric rite. The essay begins (487–501) by quoting a government report of 1854 and notes that in 1852 two men had been killed during the celebration of the festival in Salem District because the pole from which they were suspended had snapped. The unstated motivation for this observation was that the only provision under colonial law that could be used to suppress this rite was one that necessitated the documentation of actual physical harm. Thurston does not always moderate his language, for like earlier missionary and colonial reports, he refers to the ritual as a "barbarous ceremony" and quotes indiscriminately from commentators as various (and as contemptuous of Indian customs) as Abbe Dubois and Sonnerat. Aside from the general narrative style and the lack of any specific argument about suppression, there is little to distinguish this ethnographic chapter from the accounts produced by government officials themselves. What is different, of course, is that although there is no moral or legal argument about the suppression of hookswinging, virtually all of the material had in fact been generated out of this concern and was initially narrativized as part of an argument in the context of governmental debate. The absence of argument in Thurston's account has the effect of representing the account as scientific (as do all of Thurston's credentials and the entire framework of the book), when it can be seen that this representation works to conceal the nature of the genealogical connection between the work and its sources. In ethnography, the once-compelling stakes of official debate seem to disappear altogether.

I am not arguing that Thurston attempts to conceal his sources; he is far better than many colonial authors in providing footnotes and references. Furthermore, he is in total agreement with Risley that one of the tasks of the ethnographer is to digest the massive accumulation of material in governmental reports and then to present it in clear and systematic form. Thurston was himself a government servant and saw no contradiction between science and government in the task of accumulating anthropological knowledge about India. The relation of knowledge and rule is not simply a colonial fact; it is a fact that was actively celebrated in such colonial projects as the ethnographic survey. But it is easy in retrospect to lose sight of the genealogies of the relations between knowledge and rule, and readers of Thurston's treatise on hookswinging need never know the historical context in which his footnotes were produced.

Thurston's essay on torture (407–432) is similarly based almost entirely on the report of a commission that was appointed by the government of Madras in 1854 to investigate various forms of torture employed in the Madras Presidency. Thurston notes that the commission used a broad definition of torture, construing it as "pain by which guilt is punished, or confession [and we may add, money] extorted." Although Thurston is clear about his use of this source, he tells us nothing about the nature of the commission's task or the historical provenance of the many examples of torture. The inclusion of a series of graphic descriptions of torture under the general title, "Torture in Bygone Days" suggests that torture had been a constant feature of southern Indian life, and Thurston shares with the members of the commission the belief that the examples of torture they uncovered were traditional practices of native revenue and police officers. As the commission's report states, "Knowing, as we do, the historical fact, that under the Governments immediately preceding our own, torture was a recognized method of obtaining both revenue and confessions" (4). The report also asserts that "there are many circumstances in the peculiar condition of this country which may well account for the prevalence of even a systematic and general practice of personal violence, used for the purpose of extortion among the native population," and notes the "whole of this mass of testimony emanates from parties intimately acquainted with the country, its administration, the people and their character. It cannot but afford a deep and clear insight into the actual position of matters" (15). But the report also admits, "In point of fact our investigation starts from a recent definite point" (4–5), and provides no evidence other than assertion and assumption that torture, like caste and custom, is an essential component of Indian society.

Even as I do not argue that caste or custom are invented ex nihilo by colonialism, I am not suggesting here that torture only arrived on Indian soil with the British. However, the torture report is silent about the fact that the revenue demand in the Indian countryside escalated exponentially under British rule. If torture in revenue and police matters was prevalent in the middle of the nineteenth century, as the report convincingly argues, the new level of revenue demand, the suddenly dire consequences of non-compliance (loss of jobs and land), as also the new legal contexts that gave new powers to policemen (see Arnold 1986), were factors that were deeply implicated in the social fact of torture. But these were not part of the commission's brief and were totally factored out of the commission's explanations, which as we saw depended on a multitude of expert understandings of the Indian "country, its administration, its people and their character." And these factors were even more critically not included in Thurston's ethnographic account, which gave even less contextual information than the actual report about the nature of the material it provided.

Indian anthropology was thus born directly out of the colonial project of ruling India. On the basis of the writings of Mullaly and Thurston, the latter author undoubtedly the most important official ethnographer in Madras during colonial times, we can see the key texts of early anthropology as not simply being produced in the context of colonial projects but as culminating what had been a long series of colonial projects (and colonial texts written) to rule and reform India.

One final note. Thurston's *Ethnographic Notes* attracted considerable attention, within official and scholarly circles as well as from general readers. G. H. Forbes, the secretary to the Madras government, noted, "It is evident that the book, from its title and contents, is being bought up by the tourist, male and female; and there is certainly some matter which, though quite unobjectionable for scientific readers, is scarcely what we should put in the hands of young people who read merely from curiosity or to acquire a general knowledge of out of the way tribes."[15] Forbes did not object to the book as a scientific work, but he was deeply concerned about the ready availability of scientific detail, particularly in matters sexual. He recommended that a "bowdlerized edition . . . would be of value and use to the general public and priced low" and that a new edition of the complete work "with full scientific detail" be released at a higher price. In recommending bowdlerization, Forbes highlighted such explicit phrases as "pendulous testes" and "protuberant breasts," as also many of the most graphic examples of torture. Although most concerned about the sexual detail in the chapter on marriage, he also noted that "the subjects of hookswinging, infanticide, and meriah sacrifice are revolting though not prurient." Thus the distillation of ethnography out of government reports led not only to the advance of science but to the production of what outside of its proper domain was seen as pornography. There was little danger that either scientists or ordinary citizens were going to sift through the mass of material that had been accu-

mulated during British rule. This, of course, is my point; and it is important
to realize that Thurston's work was generally read without any sense of the
multiple readings I have provided. Instead, Thurston was read in decon-
textualized reference to other ethnographic notes for other areas and to
other compendia on castes and tribes, sometimes even as travel literature.
Although I have provided a set of readings of genealogies to make my case,
my argument also depends on the fact that these genealogies were obscured
by the very project of ethnographic writing engaged in by the new generation of official anthropologists at the turn of the century.

For colonial ethnography, the colonized subject was first and foremost a
body, to be known and controlled through the measurement and interpretation of physical subjects organized in caste and gender categories. In
all this attention to the body, there was little interest in the subjectivity,
will, or agency of colonial subjects. When colonial officials debated the nature or presence of colonized agency, the debate was focused on the denial
or suppression of this agency, in contexts in which the colonial state sought
to regulate or abolish such barbaric practices as sati, child marriage, and
hookswinging. Agency was an absence, only there when it could be seen as
precisely not there. On all other occasions, agency was neither relevant nor
significant, expressed as it was in the social body of custom and tradition.
Even crime was performed without agency; crime was a function of habit, a
social occupation, an effect of caste rather than an act of will. And with the
prevalence of anthropometry and ethnographic interest in bodily practices,
the materiality of the text of custom, for colonial ethnographers, was the colonized body itself.

ANTHROPOLOGICAL GENEALOGIES

Only when we begin to unravel the genealogies of colonial encyclopedias
of ethnographic knowledge does it become fully clear how problematic
is the knowledge we perforce take to the field with us. Now that colonial
texts have been put under ironic question, it is perhaps too easy to think
that we have charted a clear postcolonial passage for anthropology, but
colonial epistemologies fade most slowly in the categories and frames we
still use when we refurnish our anthropological practice. We must remember that the refurnishing has been done before; in the twentieth century
the study of caste shifted the site of its inquiry from the body to the mind
(see Dirks 1992), from British anthropometry to French and American culturalism,[16] writing caste on the mind of India itself rather than on its corporate bodies. At the same time, the biological basis of caste, and the
importance of the bodily frame for cultural hermeneutics, continues to
dominate contemporary anthropologies of India, both academic and political. And writing caste on the mind rather than the body still has the effect

of removing social formations from historical processes, reessentializing the body politic of India through the reiteration of this key metaphor of social difference.

By establishing the colonial context for the production of the first official ethnographies of southern India, particularly in Thurston's work, we are led back to a succession of other texts that could be produced and cited only because of a complex colonial history in which texts secured the status of context itself. The history of the nineteenth century in India is the history of desperate attempts to fix an inchoate and uncolonizable place in textual form: texts of proprietary title, legal procedure, customary tradition, ultimately of claims to political sovereignty itself. Ethnographic citation produced colonial conviction, the reality effect of context. It is through reading the texts that constitute the pretexts of fieldwork that we learn how the conditions of anthropological knowledge really were constituted historically; our exploration of the quotidian features of this history takes us to the heart of darkness, the crime at the beginning of anthropology, the horror that undermines but also undergirds the heterological task of reading culture.

NOTES

1. This has partly to do with the distinctive character of literary texts, despite the extent to which textual theory need not apply specifically to literary genres of writing. I take Edward Said's definition here as helpful: "that literature, unlike other forms of writing, is essentially mimetic, essentially moral, and essentially humanistic (1983: 227)."

2. G.O. 6/6A/Public/10-1-93, Tamil Nadu Archives (TNA).

3. G.O. 86/25-1-93/Financial (TNA).

4. G.O. 647/26 June 1901/Public (TNA).

5. Madras Museum *Centennial Bulletin;* also see preface to Thurston (1907).

6. *Man* I (1901).

7. See Gould (1981) for an insightful analysis of the relation between statistics and prejudice in this kind of research.

8. G.O. 1838/9-9-93/Judicial (TNA).

9. Ibid.

10. Ibid.

11. G.O. 2454/Judicial/9-10-94 (TNA).

12. G.O. 1472/Judicial/9-10-97 (TNA).

13. G.O. 1014/Judicial/1-7-98 (TNA).

14. G.O. 792/Public/5-9-03 (TNA).

15. G.O. 787/Public/2 November 1906 (TNA).

16. I refer here to the American school of ethnosociology (see Marriott 1990), which, as Dennis McGilvray (1982) has pointed out, mistook medical for social knowledge; and to the work of Louis Dumont in his important writing on caste in *Homo Hierarchicus* ([1966]/1980).

REFERENCES

Arnold, David.
   1986.   *Police Power and Colonial Rule in Madras.* Delhi: Oxford University Press.
de Certeau, Michel.
   1986.   *Heterologies: Discourse on the Other.* Minneapolis: University of Minnesota Press.
Clifford, James.
   1983.   "On Ethnographic Authority." *Representations* 1: 118–146.
Clifford, James, and George Marcus, eds.
   1986.   *Writing Culture: The Poetics and Politics of Ethnography.* Berkeley, Los Angeles, and London: University of California Press.
de Man, Paul.
   1983.   "The Rhetoric of Blindness." In *Blindness and Insight: Essays in the Rhetoric of Contemporary Criticism.* Minneapolis: University of Minnesota Press.
Dirks, Nicholas B.
   1987.   *The Hollow Crown: Ethnohistory of an Indian Kingdom.* Cambridge: University Press. Reprinted 1993, Ann Arbor: University of Michigan Press.
———. 1992. "Castes of Mind." *Representations* 37 (Winter): 56–78.
———. In press. "Is Vice Versa? Historical Anthropologies and Anthropological Histories." In *The Historic Turn in the Human Sciences,* ed. T. McDonald. Ann Arbor: University of Michigan Press.
Dumont, Louis.
   [1966] 1980.   *Homo Hierarchicus: An Essay on the Caste System and Its Implications.* Chicago: University of Chicago Press.
Geertz, Clifford.
   1988.   *Works and Lives: The Anthropologist as Author.* Stanford: Stanford University Press.
Ginzburg, Carlo.
   1989.   *Clues, Myth, and the Historical Method.* Baltimore: Johns Hopkins University Press.
Gould, Stephen J.
   1981.   *The Mismeasure of Man.* New York: W. W. Norton.
Greenblatt, Stephen.
   1988.   *Shakespearean Negotiations.* Berkeley, Los Angeles, and London: University of California Press.
Levinson, Marjorie.
   1992.   "After the New Historicism: Posthumous Critique." Unpublished manuscript (quoted with permission).
McGann, Jerome J.
   1991.   *The Textual Condition.* Princeton: Princeton University Press.
McGilvray, Dennis.
   1982.   "Mukkuvar Vannimai: Tamil Caste and Matriclan Ideology in Batticaloa, Sri Lanka." In *Caste, Ideology and Interaction,* ed. D. McGilvray, 22-41. Cambridge: Cambridge University Press.
Marriott, McKim, ed.
   1990.   *India through Hindu Categories.* New Delhi: Sage Publications.

Marshall, William E.
    1873.   *A Phrenologist amongst the Todas.* London: Longmans, Green, and Co.
Mullaly, Frederick S.
    1892.   *Notes on Criminal Classes of the Madras Presidency. Report of the Commission-ers for the Investigation of Alleged Cases of Torture in the Madras Presidency.* 1855. Madras: Government Press.
Said, Edward.
    1983.   *The World, the Text, and the Critic.* London: Faber and Faber.
Taussig, Michael.
    1991.   *The Nervous System.* New York: Routledge.
Thurston, Edgar.
    1906.   *Ethnographic Notes in Southern India.* Madras: Government Press.
    ———. 1907. *The Castes and Tribes of Southern India.* 7 vols. Madras: Govern-ment Press.
White, Hayden.
    1983.   *Metahistory.* Baltimore: Johns Hopkins University Press.
Yang, Anand, ed.
    1985.   *Crime and Criminality in British India.* Tucson: University of Arizona Press.
Zizek, Slavoj.
    1991.   *For They Know Not What They Do: Enjoyment as a Political Factor.* London: Verso.

THIRTEEN

Ghostlier Demarcations:
Textual Phantasm and the Origins of
Japanese Nativist Ethnology

Marilyn Ivy

Words of the fragrant portals, dimly-starred
And of ourselves and of our origins,
In ghostlier demarcations, keener sounds.
— WALLACE STEVENS, "THE IDEA OF ORDER IN KEY WEST"

The most scandalous literary figure in twentieth-century Japan, Mishima Yukio, once wrote a short contribution for a newspaper column in which writers and critics commented on the prose masterpiece of their choice for the weekly edification of the reading public. Mishima chose a small text called *The Tales of Tōno* (Tōno monogatari), a work published in 1910 that had come to be recognized as the founding work of Japanese folklore studies as well as a literary classic.[1] He says this: "*The Tales of Tōno* speaks, coldly, of innumerable deaths. Taking those deaths as its place of origin, Japanese folklore studies is a discipline in which the smell of corpses drifts."[2] This essay finds its own point of origin in Mishima's lurid assertion, unraveling its implications in an attempt to rethink the relationship of ethnography and literature within Japanese modernity. What kind of discipline is founded on death and its after-effect, the smell of corpses, a linked image both horrifically concrete and ungraspable? Indeed, Mishima's trope plays out in its very form the general contradiction of an ethnographic impulse that would want to document the punctual event, the unwritable ("death"), but which must always displace that impulse through the vagaries of the figuratively written—what some would call the literary. *The Tales of Tōno* emerged in the early twentieth century both to embody and to allegorize that particular contradiction of modernity—that is, the difference between "science" and "literature"—with its literary rewritings of oral tales of ghosts and gruesome goings-on in the Japanese rural remote. What is at the specific origin of Japanese folklore studies as a science (*gakumon*), as a field of scholarship, is not simply death but a text that speaks, figurally, of deaths. To anticipate my own end(s) here, literature and ethnography (in Japan, in modernity) are always in a deathly—and thus ghostly—complicity with one another. Even when one would most like to disavow that complicity (or conversely, to insist on a sheer identity without distinction), the figure of the other returns to reinstitute the distinction, now made unstable and tenuous. And this complicity is unthinkable outside the interlinked struggles about literary authority, speech and writing, and the status of representable "reality" in twentieth-century Japan.

The textual birth of Japanese nativist ethnology is thus a strange one: a birth that is deathly, an appearance that is at the same time a disappearance. That doubleness is the necessary condition of folklore studies (and that necessity extends to a more generalized anthropology). "In the Beginning, a Death" reads a subheading in "The Beauty of the Dead: Nisard," Michel de Certeau's subtle reflections on the discursive birth of popular culture in nineteenth-century France and the internal exoticism it presumes.[3] For, as he shows, the disappearance of the object—whether newly imagined as the folk, the community, authentic voice, or tradition itself—is necessary for its ghostly reappearance in an authoritatively rendered text. The object does not exist outside its own disappearance. If its coming-to-be is never simply punctual, a sheer event, neither is its death. There is always a temporal structure of deferral, of loss and recovery, across which the fantasy of folklore, of ethnography, stretches; thus, the spectral status of the ethnographic object. It is only in the difference between those moments that the object of the fantasy can be said to exist. Susan Stewart has spoken of those genres that fantastically detemporalize the difference between loss and recovery as "distressed."

> Thus distressed forms show us the gap between past and present as a structure of desire, a structure in which authority seeks legitimation by recontextualizing its object and thereby recontextualizing itself. If distressed forms involve a negation of the contingencies of their immediate history, they also involve an invention of a version of the past that could only arise from such contingencies. We see this structure of desire as the structure of nostalgia—that is, the desire for desire in which objects are the means of generation and not the ends.[4]

The generalization of that structure is, of course, inseparable from the claims of modernity itself. Why Mishima, some six months before his own death, would choose to write about *The Tales of Tōno* is not insignificant. For the scandal of Mishima lies not so much in his writing, however much his interlinking of eros and ultra-nationalism shocks bourgeois sensibilities.[5] The public scandal resides rather in his own spectacular death in November 1970, in which Mishima—at the head of his own little army—briefly took over the Self-Defense Forces Headquarters in Tokyo and ritually disemboweled himself in front of a crowd of spectators. What Mishima opposed with his desperate, dangerously fascist, finally suicidal attempt to recover the spiritual core of Japanese culture (exemplified by the fallen symbol of the Japanese emperor) was modernity itself. In short, his was an attempt to regain the lost object of modernity at the post-'60s moment when there was no question that the Japanese economic miracle, the postwar civil society, and things American were here (there) to stay. It seems, then, retrospectively fitting that Mishima would have been attracted to *The Tales of Tōno*. For that text also demarcated a certain crisis of Japanese modernity in the early twentieth century.

In 1910, the *Tales'* date of publication, Japan had existed as a nation-state only some forty years. To grasp the implications of that statement is to imagine the severity of the epistemological break that occurred with the Meiji Restoration of 1868 and the ending of the Tokugawa *bakufu*'s 250-year rule and its elaborate system of "feudal" governance.[6] During that time (and during Japan's long history before the Tokugawa period) there had developed enormously complex worlds of philosophy, aesthetics, and sociality—worlds largely independent of concurrent developments in the West. Japan had many of the ideal-typical marks of the European early modern, including a wealthy merchant class, a professional literati (and a vast publishing industry), and hugely populated cities (including the largest city in the world in the eighteenth century—Edo, the city now known as Tokyo). Yet its "forced opening" (as it is often called) by the United States in 1854 operated as perhaps the primary efficient cause in the decline of the Tokugawa order and the precipitate scramble for modern nationhood and its accouterments. In the interests of state power and development, not only the technologies and institutions of Western capitalism but hundreds of years' worth of aesthetic theories, literary forms, and modes of representation were imported within an extraordinarily compressed span of time: not only railroads but Descartes; not only finance capital but Renaissance perspective; not only Prussian-style militarism but also Ibsen and the form of the novel. Within the unequal relationship of power between Japan and the Western nations transpired countless moments of intrusion and resistance, seduction and assimilation, but what Japan's postrestoration meant in the largest sense was the construction of a modern nation-state at the same time that entire worlds of representation and thought were grafted onto existing indigenous ones, activating what one Japanese critic has called a veritable "overturning of the semiotic constellation" of pre-Meiji Japan.[7]

The Tales of Tōno was written at a time when the specificities of local beliefs and practices had long been threatened by the comprehensive, central state ideology of "civilization and enlightenment" (*bunmei kaika*); this ideology was backed by fiercely ambitious policies and programs for inculcating modern habits and ideas into the populace. The widespread importation of Western knowledge into Japan during the Meiji period led to a questioning and reassessment of native forms. The goal of parity with the West led to the single-minded incorporation of Western structures and institutions and a bureaucratization of power based on norms of objective rationality; the formation of national compulsory education and conscription incorporated the newly emergent Meiji "citizen" (*kokumin*) into ever-widening circles of standardized participation and cooptation in establishing the body politic (*kokutai;* literally, the "national body").[8] The building of railroads and nationwide communication and transportation facilities, banking and finance, foreign trade—the infrastructure of the modern state—advanced at a stunning pace, safely enclosed within civilization and its associated enlightenment.

Modernizing rhetoric and policies were not uniformly received, however, and new kinds of political associations and groups arose in response to the state's claims at determining legitimate interests. The state became increasingly aware of the destabilizing social forces that modernization could unleash and came to temper its calls for advancement with appeals to time-honored "tradition." In a nation composed primarily of peasants (80 percent at the start of the Meiji period),[9] yet with capital and political power concentrated in the cities, an increasingly valorized "tradition" (*dentō*) signified rural "custom."

It is important to recall that there was a trajectory to this process of extolling "tradition." The two decades immediately following the Restoration of 1868 produced a dominant rhetoric more explicitly modernizing and renovationist in tone than traditionalist. In keeping with the reformist mood and with the attempts to civilize and enlighten the masses in Western ways, numerous "custom reform associations," for example, arose. In this phase, a concern with custom served essentially as the precondition for locating regressive aspects in need of reform and modernization. Yet as the more pragmatic and decisive nation-building years progressed and the welter of contending and contentious groups advanced their own particular interests, the government began to revalorize rural customs as a means of stabilizing the nation. A preoccupation with custom developed as the pretext for definitively locating the traditional. Although works describing peasant beliefs and the customs of remote regions can be found in "nativist scholarship" (*kokugaku*) of the Tokugawa period (1603–1868), the earliest modern attempts to record folkloric data were the Ministry of Justice's surveys of customary precedents in 1877 and 1880 (*minji kanrei ruishū*), compiled prior to the first attempts to formulate a civil code. These bureaucratic, legalistic codifications of custom as the basis of law were not far removed from the interest in custom emerging in the private sphere. In 1884, the Ethnological Society (*jinruigaku gakkai*) was formed with ten members; in 1886, it changed its name to the Tokyo Ethnological Society and began publishing reports on manners and mores (*fūzoku*). Reports of 1888, for example, detail regional variations in New Year's activities. The popular magazine *Fūzoku gahō*, published from 1889 to 1916, satisfied a larger public interest for descriptions and depictions of annual events and popular practices. The Tokyo

Ethnological Society continued publishing reports, examining such topics as "taboo words" (*imi kotoba*), "five-man groups" (*gonin gumi*) as a basic unit of social organization, and Okinawan beliefs.[10]

Written at a moment (1909–1910) when it had become inescapably clear that the apparatuses of Western industrial capitalism meant not only civilization and enlightenment but the effacing of much of an older Japanese world, the *Tales* thematized this effacement in its descriptions of an obscure region of northeastern Japan, the region of Tōno. Presented as an unmediated transcription of oral tales and lore told to its "author" (the father-to-be of the nascent discipline of folklore studies, Yanagita Kunio) by a local storyteller, the *Tales* enscripted the uncanny remainder of capitalist modernity, that which could not be contained within the nationalist, rationalist discourse of the maturing state system of the Meiji period. *The Tales of Tōno* also took its place as a text signifying the rediscovery of the rural countryside; in time, it would come to be one of the most famous of these late Meiji texts. The content of the tales—or, rather, the sequence of information that the storyteller Sasaki Kizen gave to Yanagita—speaks of the same degradation and poverty that infused the ascendant form of the Meiji "naturalist" (*shizen-shugiteki*) "novel" (*shōsetsu*). Murder, incest, grotesque births, and famine are presented as commonplaces in the tales. This revelation of rural misery was in itself later seen as exposing an immense, hidden underside of Meiji Japan, one completely at odds with the official discourse of civilization and enlightenment. Yet not only murders and incest occurred but ghosts, mountain apparitions, deities, and monsters inhabited the world surrounding Tōno. Sasaki's stories revealed a universe of fear, of splits in appearance, of the irrational and fantastic. It was this aspect of the *Tales* that indicated the frightening seductions of an older world that had seemingly escaped the intrusions of the central state. The surviving numinous became the romantic object of those caught up in the disenchantment of the world.

So far we have a story not entirely unfamiliar. Anxieties about cultural transmission, valorizations of the unwritten, discoveries of the marginal, and textual constructions of the "folk" are the replicable constituents of modern cultural nationalisms throughout the world.[11] Japan strikes us, however, with the lateness of its condensed absorption within the global problematic of national modernity and by the extremity of its differences from the Euro-American context—differences that were obsessively remarked within the writings of Japanese nativist ethnology. For not only was the discipline concerned with preserving the traces of a folkic world representing the unwritten essence of ethnic Japaneseness. That world also indicated the non-West that could never be subsumed under the dominant signs of Western modernity.[12]

That difference and the fear of its subsumption was imagined, above all else, as a difference in language. With new forms of literary representation (primarily, realism and naturalism) and techniques of description came a particular anxiety about language and its powers. It is not as if objectifying, rationalist, even positivist, forms of discourse were unknown to pre-Meiji Japan. The intricacies of neo-Confucian, Buddhist, and nativist philosophy incorporated many of the problematics of representation that Western philosophies took to be uniquely their own. But these discourses had not been systematized into the particular, and the particularly powerful, ensemble of practices, technologies, apparatuses, and institutions that constituted Western science. Both for state politics and for literature, the linkage of writing, speech, and external "reality" emerged as one of the core issues of the Meiji period, constituting what can be truly called a crisis in representation. One dimension of this crisis appeared as a series of debates about the difference between speech and writing, truth and fiction, literature and its other in early twentieth-century Japan. *The Tales of Tōno* enacted these differences within a hybrid text that would come to be read as a mysterious suturing of the fissures between forms of representation.

Meiji Japan's strong milieu of state-sponsored reform and standardization extended directly into the realm of language. Intense debates on the formation of a standard national language (*kokugo*) accompanied debates on the formation of the national polity. For the Japanese of pre-Meiji Japan spanned an awesome range of written styles—many of them quite distant from the world of everyday speech, with their plethora of purely literary verb endings, formal conventions, Sinified compounds, and difficult Chinese characters. A hierarchy of delicate gradations separates different forms of literary Japanese: *kanbun,* written entirely in Chinese characters but read in Japanese word order; *sōrōbun,* the so-called epistolary style, with its mixed use of Chinese characters and the Japanese syllabary (*kana*); *wabun,* a revival of classical Japanese style that used the syllabary as much as possible; and *wakankonkōbun,* primarily kanbun with an admixture of classical wabun style.[13] What we might think of as the ideographic principle in Japanese writing determined that people speaking vastly different dialects could still read the same texts, because the Chinese characters used to write Japanese were graphic signs relatively independent of voicing: to those who were sufficiently literate their meaning was graphically apparent to the eye without the mediation of the voice.[14] This principle lent itself to the tendency to create written worlds sharply distinct from everyday enunciations, particularly apparent in the kanbun style written entirely in Chinese. Although certain forms of popular fiction and sermons and tracts transcribed for the common listener faithfully reproduced colloquial dialogue, much literary writing distanced itself from the direct reproduction of speech. One of the primary tasks of the new state was to codify and align the written language more closely with the contours of the colloquial, an endeavor the Meiji ideologies grasped as essential for creating a unified national polity.

In this the phonetic scripts of the West served as models of efficiency, ease, and transparency.

But what was to serve as the standard colloquial language that the written language was to reflect without mediation? Hundreds of dialects extended throughout the country: spoken Japanese was fragmented, various, and bore the marks of locale. This diversity had to be contained, to be molded into a singular national language. In language as in everything else, the power of the center determined the result: the dominant dialect of Edo (the pre-Meiji name for Tokyo) gradually became the standard spoken language in Japan.

The state sought to regularize the language (one minister of education, Mori Arinori, even suggested replacing Japanese with English!) by establishing a standard spoken Japanese and by making written Japanese closer to this standardized colloquial Japanese. Meiji writers and intellectuals, newly fascinated with European fiction, poetry, and thought, were also absorbed by this problematic. Their object was not the creation of standard speech and colloquial writing as powerful instruments for the formation of a unified polity, however; they instead were concerned with the representation of reality in fiction. At the heart of these debates was the question of literature and verisimilitude: How does one represent "reality" in prose fiction?

These debates were encapsulated by the phrase *genbunitchi*, "the unification of spoken and written languages."[15] The considerable difference between the spoken and written languages was the starting point for modern Japanese fiction.[16] Although Tokugawa period writers had often reproduced dialogue in faithful fashion, they still couched the narrative portions in a formal, written style. This split between dialogue and narrative was one of the first areas of debate among them young Meiji writers influenced by Western prose fiction. Many of them sought to increase verisimilitude in fiction by reproducing dialogue more faithfully and by retaining the vernacular in the narrative portions as well. By reproducing everyday speech accurately in literature, it was argued, greater realism could be attained in the novel. Thus, many of these writers became associated with what is now called Japanese naturalism (*shizenshugi*) in their efforts to transcribe reality directly through a technique they termed *shasei*, or "sketching," a sketching from life. This visual metaphor sharply describes the attempt at an almost photographic reproduction of external reality, including speech itself, within prose narratives.

The debates over genbunitchi started in the later 1880s and continued throughout the Meiji period. Yanagita Kunio, then a young bureaucrat in the Ministry of Agriculture and Commerce and a productive poet as well (and founder of the Ibsen Society of Japan), took an active part in these de-

bates and was a friend of many of the luminaries of Meiji literary society: Ku-
nikida Doppo, Shimazaki Tōson, Tayama Katai, Izumi Kyōka. Coming from
a line of Shinto priests, Yanagita was involved with state agricultural policy,
traveling to villages and talking to farmers about rural uplift. His rural background and his continuing concern with nonurban Japan meshed with his
literary preoccupations through a set of circumstances that brought the
problematic of oral narratives to his attention.

In an essay published in 1907, " 'Sketching Technique' and the Essay"
(Shasei to ronbun), three years before the publication of *The Tales of Tōno*,
Yanagita came out in support of a colloquial literary style.[17] The essay is an
examination of the premises of *shaseibun*, the "direct description" technique
advocated by Masaoka Shiki. Yanagita states that previously he thought that
literature was something constructed with difficult characters and crafted
sentences; it was not something that was natural or easily achieved. But since
the advent of the technique of direct description, literature is conceivable
as something that "anyone can write," since it is written "just as one has seen
and heard, without any artifice."

"Direct description" destroys the notion that literature, as a means to express thought, cannot attain its object unless it is difficult. To write essays,
to write literature, merely cultivate your own sensibility, and write what you
see, hear, think, and feel just as it is, Yanagita admonishes his readers. In this
admonition, we hear clear echoes of his famous prefatory remarks to *The
Tales of Tōno*, where he would aver that he wrote down the tales "as they were
related to me without adding a word or phrase."[18] Yanagita continues in his
essay on "sketching technique":

> Heretofore, if an essay [*ronbun*] were not written in literary style [*bungotai*],
> it did not seem like a real essay, and it was said that its power was diminished.
> But that is a narrow view caught up in convention. It is natural to assume that
> since writing is a method for expressing thought, the style of that writing should
> be as close as possible to thought. . . . Both speech and writing [*gengo to bun-
> shō*] exist as means for expressing one's thoughts, *but at present writing is not as
> close to thought as speech is*. If speech is able to express eight thoughts out of ten,
> writing is only able to express six. . . . Just because colloquial style [*gen-
> bunitchitai*] is closer to speech than literary language is, I think it is able to ex-
> press thought more intimately than literary language.[19]

In this essay we find a theory of language couched primarily in terms of
expressing "thoughts" (*shisō*). Thoughts are placed on the same plane as ex-
ternals, as realities to be "expressed" via language; embodied speech, placed
in intimate proximity to thinking, naturally takes its place as the more de-
sirable mode of expression. A writing that mimetically traces the contours
of speech will thus accede as closely as possible to the transparent reflection

of the object—whether conceptual, visual, or aural. And the writing that makes the closest approach to speech is the genbunitchi style.[20]

Yet something happened to Yanagita's theories of literature and representation between 1907 and 1909, a period in which he was beginning to think more deeply about what he called the "invisible world."[21] This shift marked a series of returns to the formal and figural powers of a writing that no longer pretends to transcribe speech in all its transparency, a speech he now divested of its unique capacity to act as the most intimate metaphor of inner thought. While it is not clear what precisely prompted Yanagita's move to what has often been described as an "antinaturalist" stance, his essays from this period suggests that a growing familiarity with Japanese naturalist writings and his own attempts to write in genbunitchi style convinced him of its impoverishment, as his 1909 essay, "The Distance between Speech and Writing" (Genbun no kyori), reveals.[22] In this essay, Yanagita makes a full-blown attempt to discredit the techniques of direct description; he now argues instead for the unabashed rhetoricity of texts. For Yanagita, this rhetoricity consists in *not* giving all the facts, which paradoxically gives the work more verisimilitude, more of an *appearance* of truth. He upholds a form of withholding, a reticence within a rhetorical economy that—rather than attempting an impossible transcription—conveys the "real" all the more sharply through its constructed absences. Instead of recording the brute fact itself, the work of literature should "sound *as if* it were factual" (*jijitsu rashiku kikoeru*).[23]

Yanagita seeks to impress, to convey feelings, and to move the reader, who has now emerged as the object of literary writing. He insists on the paradoxical reversal of literary effects when writers attempt to imitate life too directly: the more one tries to imitate speech and thus "reality," the more "unnatural" the result. Yet Yanagita goes even further. Completely dismissing the claims of genbunitchi, he states that on the contrary, the spoken language should instead draw closer to the written. Instead of believing in a world of oral discourse that writing reflects by drawing closer to speech, Yanagita reverses the terms by advocating an improvement, through education, of spoken Japanese—an improvement that would then bring spoken discourse closer to bungotai, or "literary style."[24] Literature could only take its place as truly literary by keeping its distance from the chaos of (Japanese) speech as well as from the pretensions of a photographic/phonographic reproduction of the world (he even speaks of Japanese naturalist writers as bad amateur photographers). The anticipation and containment of many of the concerns of grammatology—of the philosophical prerogatives of speech and its relationship to truth, of the problem of writing as a subsidiary form of representation—are in striking evidence here, with an eventual reversal (the preeminence of writing over speech) that seems to double but of course historically differs (in its discursive effects and location) from

Jacques Derrida's deconstructions proper. Nowhere does Yanagita question the "distance" between speech and writing that Derrida would put into undecidability. That Yanagita as the future founder of folklore studies would advocate not only a distancing from the (oral) object of nostalgia but a disciplinary taming of vocal forms on the model of orderly writing reiterates the split in representation that the *Tales* would come to embody.[25]

Near the end of his 1909 essay on the distance between speech and writing, Yanagita states, "I would like to try and write some sort of strong, solid book using literary style."[26] That book would not be a fictional work but *The Tales of Tōno*, the one and only work of Yanagita's that is considered a masterpiece of prose literature, yet a work that Yanagita insisted was based on "present-day facts."[27] The book—the substitute for the novel he never wrote—would become, in time, the undisputed origin of the discipline of nativist ethnology, the science of the Japanese cultural unwritten.[28]

It was during this precise time, starting in November 1908, that Yanagita began to listen to the stories of Sasaki Kizen in Tokyo. From his notebooks from November 4 comes the following statement: "Sasaki is a person from Tōno in Iwate prefecture, and the mountain villages of that region are very interesting. I shall construct *Tōno monogatari* by writing down the stories of those villages just as they are." The entry for November 5 declares, "I shall write *Tōno monogatari*."[29] The very title of the collection—the rubric that would unify the real diversity of Sasaki's rumors, stories, and recollections under the name of "narrative" (*monogatari*)—had been fixed. The writing of the tales was not just a chance encounter with a rural storyteller (who was in fact a university student and an aspiring writer) and an equally casual and unmediated transcription of the facts, although Yanagita's "Preface" to the *Tales* and other writings create that sense. It was instead a coherent and deliberate project that went through a whole series of mediations.

It is entirely clear that there is a theoretic trajectory that culminates in the writing of the text of the tales, and the question is, why? Why does *The Tales of Tōno* provide the theoretic space that Yanagita needed at that time? We know that he was deeply interested in what he called the "concealed" world—a world of ancestors, of the monstrous, of the unseen, of death. The concealed world indicates a discursive space articulated in peasant practice and by Tokugawa nativist thinkers; by the late Meiji period, it doubly pointed to the marginalized obverse of Meiji civilization and enlightenment: the rural, the unwritten, the vanishing.[30] But was it sheerly Yanagita's interest in the concealed world—and his political concern to recover it—that attracted him to these tales that speak so obsessively of ghosts, deaths, and disappearances? That attraction would not account for the centrality of *these* stories in all their particularity. Nor would it fully account for their position as the book that crystallized Yanagita's thoughts on representation and literature. I would argue that part of Yanagita's interest lay in that which resists representation, that which is left out of any attempt at naturalized direct description. Thinking about that which evades representation—voices, dialects, margins, ghosts, deaths, monsters—was a way of thinking about literary writing: that writing which (for Yanagita) says more when it says less and thus writes what cannot be said.

Yet the *Tales* is not just a collection of "fictional" narratives. Yanagita takes great pains to distinguish his text from Tokugawa period "ghost stories" (*kaidan*) or collections of medieval "tale literature" (*setsuwa bungaku*). The difference? These tales are "present-day facts."[31] Yanagita purports to be directly transmitting tales he has heard from the voice of another, who in many cases is describing his own experience or those of someone he knows or someone he has heard of. The Preface tells the tale, usurping as prefaces often do, the authority of the narrative remainder. Indeed, when contemporary critics cite the *Tales* as one of the masterpieces of modern Japanese literature, they usually linger on the Preface as the most exquisite sample of prose in the entire text: the parasitic preface now significantly replaces the textual body. So in that peerless preface, Yanagita claims, "I have recorded the stories as they were related to me without adding a word or phrase."[32] He also claims, "Kyōseki [Sasaki Kizen] is not a good storyteller," and "I have been writing the stories down as they were told to me during his many evening visits since February 1909."[33] We know that Sasaki knew hundreds of tales—that by many measures he was, indeed, a "good storyteller"—and that he had been visiting Yanagita at least since November 1908 (not February 1909). We know as well that during the initial hearing of the tales, Mizuno Yōshū (the writer who had first introduced Sasaki to Yanagita) acted as the hidden interlocutor; he was present on all the occasions when Sasaki told Yanagita his tales. Mizuno took notes of the stories, which have provided a basis for the comparison of Yanagita's versions. But more important, Mizuno had already published variants of the same tales that Yanagita then later recorded in *Tōno monogatari*. As Iwamoto Yoshiteru has discovered, Mizuno published various ghost stories based on these notes before *Tōno monogatari* was published. At least eleven are identical with those found in *Tōno monogatari*.[34]

Japanese scholars have meticulously examined the various manuscripts of the text, and we thus know that Yanagita altered the tales enormously, rewriting and reworking them with great care.[35] The crucial line, "I have recorded the stories as they were related to me without adding a word or phrase," in Ronald Morse's translation, is more complex in the original Japanese, implying, "I have written them down *as I have felt* [*kanjitaru mama*] without *neglecting* [*kagen sezu*] one word or phrase."[36] With the addition of "feeling" to the naturalist sensual relay of hearing and seeing—an addition that appeared in Yanagita's 1907 essay on direct description and writing—the author enables himself to assert an unmediated transmission from voice to writing in a preface that strangely announces the contradictions (if not untruths) of the conditions of its production.[37]

In the guise of transparently recording someone else's tales, Yanagita maintained the ruse of direct transcription and description, while his prose announces its distance from all worldly referents (exemplified by the voice itself). At the same time, the terseness and brevity of his literary writing mimics the simplicity of naturalistic writing; he writes as if he has abandoned all figuration. Yanagita had to repress a writing that was too close to voice in order to constitute the unwritten as the proper object of what would become native ethnology. Yet he dissimulated that repression by the appearance of a direct transcription, a dissimulation that allowed Yanagita to establish himself as the doubled amanuensis and author of the tales.

Yanagita is enabled in this doubled ruse by an expanded notion of the "fact" (*jijitsu*, also translated as "truth" or "reality"), which by the 1909 essay had come to include an inner domain, a domain that in its complexity evokes an epistemological space akin to Freud's "psychical reality," whereby Freud renounced his insistence on the empirically real origins of (primal) fantasy in favor of the reality *effects* of fantasy. The empirical origin of fantasy was itself found to be ungraspable, sedimented within a structure of memory and retroactive desire not unlike the framework of nostalgia erected by distressed genres. It is not so much that the fact does not exist, nor is it the fact that only fantasy does. Rather, the two exist in an aporetic relationship to one another, ensuring that only across their difference can narratives of desire and loss find their way.[38]

What, then, constitutes these narratives of desire and loss? The book (published at Yanagita's own expense with only 350 copies) is a compendium of different sorts of narrative. Numbered and sequenced in Yanagita's text without comment or commentary, a description of the geography of Tōno lies next to a recounting of Tōno's feudal past as a castle town, which is juxtaposed to a local legend about the origins of a bird's name, which comes before a recounting of a local ax murder, which precedes the report of a ghost sighting in the mountain, and so on. There are no titles to the tales, only numbers in a serialization that indicates the possibility of infinite extension without resolution.[39] At the beginning of the text, however, is a table of "themes" (*daimoku*) that classify the tales: monkeys, bears, mountain gods, household gods, goddesses, apparitions, the destination of the dead, river sprites, folktales—some forty categories constructed along proto-anthropological lines. Not, then, a collection of fairy tales like the Grimms' (although Yanagita is often compared to the Grimms), the tales rarely accede to the kind of narrative development and closure or moral finality of fairy tales. They instead strike the reader with their episodic, fragmented, even flattened qualities—qualities that Mishima spoke of as an unexpected ghostliness [*fusoku no kiki*], like when someone

starts to talk and then suddenly stops speaking."[40] What is that unforeseen
ghastliness of which Mishima spoke?

> 33. Should you go and spend a night in the mountains of Shiromi, you would
> see that late at night it becomes somewhat light. People who have gone to
> gather mushrooms in the autumn and stay overnight in the mountains have
> seen this strange phenomenon. The crash of a big tree falling or the voice of
> someone singing can sometimes be heard in the valley. . . .

> 34. Along the mountainous area of Shiromi there is a spot called Hanare-mori
> [detached woods]. One small area called the "chōja's grounds" has no one liv-
> ing there. There is a man who sometimes goes there to make charcoal. One
> night someone raised the straw mat that hung over the entrance to his hut and
> peeped in. It was a woman with long trailing hair. In this area it is not unusual
> to hear the screams of women late at night.

> 35. Mr. Sasaki's grandfather's younger brother went to the Shiromi mountains
> to gather mushrooms and spent the night there. He saw a woman run across in
> front of a large wooded area on the other side of the valley. It seemed as though
> she were racing through the air. He heard her call out "just wait" two times.[41]

In this sequence of three "tales" we can begin to grasp Mishima's "unforeseen ghastliness." Mishima, in the same paragraph, had spoken of the
preponderance of "half-finished" (*shirikire tonbo*) "fragmentary episodes" in
the *Tales,* that with their "lack of completion" (*kanketsu shinaide*) can never
give the reader a "satisfactory explanation" (*manzokuna setsumei*). He links,
then, the "unforeseen ghastliness" of the text with its fragmentation, its essential incompleteness, its insufficiency. (And is it a mere coincidence that
a homonym of this *fusoku*—"unexpected" or "unforeseen"—translates as "insufficiency"?) Mishima puts the tales and abrupt ghastliness ("like when
someone starts to talk and then suddenly stops speaking") in the register of
what we could call "uncanny lack." And with that register, we can also sense
the dimensions of the tales that articulate them within a certain psychical
economy of the modern, elaborated most clearly by Freud and then Lacan.
Freud's classic conception of the uncanny refers most broadly to that class of
objects or experiences—initially very familiar—that return out of time and
place to trouble the stable boundaries between subject and object, interior
and exterior: ghosts, automata, doubles, animated objects, and the fantastic
of all species can fall into this class of the uncanny. In Lacanian terms, the
anxiety of the uncanny occurs when the part of oneself that was repressed in
order for one to be constituted as a subject (what Lacan calls *petit objet a,* one's
"self-being" before the necessary split introduced by the mirror stage) returns
in the guise of a double (probably the most powerful instance of this return),
a ghost, or an untoward repetition. To constitute oneself as a subject (who
can distinguish itself from an object) requires an initial lack; the very possibility of recognizing myself in a mirror, for example, implies that I have already lost some essential, unmediated self-being. Many theorists of the
uncanny or the fantastic (like Tzvetan Todorov) would argue that the un-

canny lies in some uncertainty about what is real or imaginary, self or other: it is an anxiety caused by an insufficiency (of knowledge, of certainty), not so different from the everyday anxiety that stems from the constitutive lack of the subject. But Lacan and others argue differently. The uncanny effect does not arise from a simple lack of knowledge, for example; it instead erupts from an *excess* of what was supposed to be kept hidden and repressed (what Lacan would call the "real"). That is, there is an "insufficiency of lack" and thus an excess of the "real" in his formulation: the repressed part of being that allows subjects to constitute themselves ("lack") has somehow reappeared in alienated form. Lack is thus no longer lacking, and it is the horror of being confronted with this excessive and terrible certainty (a certainty based on lack) that accounts for the anxiety of the uncanny.[42]

Although this story of the formation of the uncanny may seem to universalize, Freud was writing about a specific historical moment, although he did not explicitly thematize it. That is, the Freudian uncanny (exemplified by his analysis of Hoffman's tales, for example) emerges at a distinct moment: that of modernity and industrial capitalism.[43] It is, of course, not coincidental that Freud was theorizing the unconscious and the notion of the uncanny at the same time that Yanagita was reflecting on the invisible world, the question of the real and its relation to language, and the specificity of the Japanese uncanny. It marks a period when the uncanny becomes unplaceable, free-floating, part of a new, larger national-cultural imaginary. And the modern uncanny also arises as the double of the modern subject: the transcendental subject as the very subject of the natural sciences (and by extension, literary naturalism) that Yanagita wanted both to retain and reject.

The ghostly and grisly nature of many of these tales has led Japanese commentators (and there have been a great number of them) to note how limited the inroads of "civilization and enlightenment" had been in the Japanese outback. There is no doubt that Yanagita wanted to use these tales as evidence of a whole stratum of belief that persisted despite the increasing sway of the modern rational and that this persistence had a connection with what was enduringly Japanese. Yanagita and others later insisted that these stories pointed to a world "before history," to an essential, timeless Japan resisting the incursions of Western modernity.[44] But Yanagita equally considered the stories "present-day facts" (*genzai no jijitsu*), and it is the simultaneous insistence on timeless ahistority and factual contemporaneity that indicates precisely a structure of deferral and desire—of nostalgia— that shapes *The Tales of Tōno*. The spectral status of an object that is both factually present and yet absent, that is dead but lives, describes, in a doubled fashion, the tales of *The Tales of Tōno*—tales that themselves speak, through the deferred writing of the memories of a storyteller, of things spectral. These present-day facts indicated not so much a resistance to the modern but rather the product of Japanese modernity, its uncanny counterpart. Of the 119 episodes recorded by Yanagita, 85 of them took place in the early Meiji period or happened to people who were still alive.[45] Fully 70 percent

are Meiji occurrences. Far from sheerly indicating a timeless Japan somehow preserved intact within the space of modernity, the tales became,
through Yanagita's writing, modernity's uncanny other.

What Mishima finds most strikingly insufficient, I think, is Yanagita's language. Nothing is finished, nothing is completed. These narratives are almost antinarratives: they are like stacks of lumber, Mishima says, one
episode next to another, lacking the unifying gesture of the author as the
authoritative subject who is supposed to know and complete the circuit of
knowing for the reader. The necessary information that would supplement
the lack is never given; instead, there is speech that is silenced, stories in
abeyance, leading only to the next one. As such, then, there is absolutely no
logic of suspense in *The Tales of Tōno*. It is not as if the reader waits to find
out the resolution to a narrative conundrum but rather waits to see if the
terrible certainty of these "facts" could possibly be all there is.[46]

Yet what the privation of Yanagita's writing tried to convey are facts that
exceed the expected. The darkness of night is mysteriously illuminated;
screams occur where there should be none; women unexpectedly appear,
all framed within a restricted rhetorical economy. The lack of explanation
and of narrative suspense and resolution—written *as if* facts could speak for
themselves—is located at a far remove from the often excessive, fantastic nature of the events narrativized. What is left out (and here one is certainly reminded of Yanagita's 1909 essay in which he insists that literary effects are
increased by "not telling all") evokes what goes beyond representation. It is
that disjunction alongside the events retold that is ghastly: there is no attempt to reinscribe the original lack that institutes the clear division between the real and the fantastic in the first place. If Yanagita had sustained
the authorial role he displayed in his Preface, commenting on his collection, he would have placed it back into a normalized economy where lack
plays its part, where the fantastic properly exists but can be accounted for.
That normalization would in fact describe the future trajectory of Japanese
native ethnology, where its discursive construction as a bona fide discipline
and the stabilization of its object as the "everyday folk" (*jōmin*) coincided
with a diminution of its concern with the uncanny.[47]

Perhaps the most famous tale of the collection is number 22, one that
Yanagita himself compared to Maeterlinck's "The Intruder".

> 22. When the great grandmother of Mr. Sasaki died of old age the relatives as-
> sembled to put her into her coffin. . . . The daughter of the dead woman, who
> was insane and had been cut off from the family, was also in the group. Since
> it was the custom of the area to consider it taboo to let the fire die out during
> the period of mourning, the grandmother and the mother sat up alone on
> both sides of the large hearth. The mother put the charcoal basket beside her
> and from time to time added charcoal to the fire. Suddenly, hearing the sound
> of footsteps in the direction of the back door, she looked up and saw it was the

old woman who had died. She recognized how the bottom of the old woman's kimono, which dragged because she bent down a lot, was pulled up as usual into a triangle and sewed in front. Other things were also the same, and she even recognized the striped kimono cloth. Just as she cried "Oh!" the old woman passed by the hearth where the two women sat and brushed the charcoal basket with the bottom of her kimono. The round basket wobbled as it went round and round. The mother, who was a strong-nerved person, turned and watched where she went. Just as the old woman drew close to the parlor where the relatives were asleep, the shrill voice of the mad woman screamed out, "Here comes granny!" The others were awakened by the voice and it is said they were all shocked.[48]

Mishima was a great admirer of this tale, particularly of the moment when the old woman brushes the charcoal basket and sends it spinning: "When the scuttle spins, all efforts to sustain reality [*genjitsu*] are over."[49] The charcoal basket becomes, in that punctual instance, the point of division between the revealed world and the concealed, a wobbly mediator between life and death. But rather than sheerly marking their division, that detail allows the troubling of the separation, for what is truly uncanny is not the transgression of a difference that then remains unproblematically in place after the occurrence but the calling into question of the difference itself. Yanagita writes of the shock of the uncanny in a language that, in its restraint and narrative paucity, implies that there is no shock. That difference is once again left undecidable within the narrative economy of the tales.

The restrained writing by which Yanagita conveys the ghastliness of Tōno always maintains a distance from its source: the local storyteller and his voice. Sasaki spoke in dialect (Yanagita even stated in an interview that he could not understand him at first), and it is not surprising that all the nonstandard inflections of Tōno have been erased in the text. But Yanagita distanced himself from the transcription of even Tokyo-based everyday speech in his tales. Only in moments of direct quotation (like "Here comes granny!" [*Obāsan ga kita!*] in tale number 22) do spoken voices intrude. Throughout, Yanagita's elegant, terse, "old-fashioned" literary constructions displace themselves from originary voices, voices that remain suspended through a writing that asserts yet obscures its own rhetoricity.

The origins behind the tales almost always rest in the perceptual experience of one of Tōno's inhabitants; chains of hearsay culminate in narrative disclosures that, located within Sasaki's memory and his stories, speak the truth of Tōno. Tale number 22 ends by deferring the source of authority by saying "it is said," as do so many of the episodes. Yet the shifting of the ostensible narrator of the episodes continually leaves the authorial position in question. For example, tale number 87 begins with the first person.

87. I have forgotten the person's name, but he was the master of a wealthy family in the town of Tōno. He was seriously ill and on the brink of death, when

one day he suddenly visited his family temple. The priest entertained him
courteously and served tea. They chatted about things and then the priest,
somewhat suspicious when the man was about to leave, sent his younger dis-
ciple to follow him. The man went out the gate and headed in the direction
of home. Then he went around a corner in the town and disappeared. There
were also other people who met him on that street and he greeted everyone
as politely as ever.

He died that night and, of course, was in no condition to be going out at
that time. Later at the temple, the priest checked the spot where the tea cup
was, to see if the tea had been drunk or not. He found that the tea had all been
poured into the crack between the straw mats.[50]

Who has forgotten the name? If it is Yanagita, why has he inserted that
question (particularly since Yanagita concealed the actual names of people
that Sasaki told him, in good anthropological fashion)?[51] We assume that it
is Sasaki and that Yanagita has chosen to position his informant as the
speaker/narrator. In this tale of a ghostly double who classically prefigures
his own death, Sasaki stands in for the authorial voice of the folklorist. Indeed, the life of Sasaki and his failed attempts to become the double of the
famed folklorist Yanagita became the elements of Japanese intellectual
tragedy.[52] In tale number 22, however, Yanagita is the speaker, as he opens
by saying, "When the great grandmother of Mr. Sasaki died. . . . "

By shifting the narrator's position, by relaying the events within chains of
deferred experience and flattening differences between speakers, Yanagita
obscures the source of ethnographic authority, as it becomes repeatedly displaced through hearsay.[53] Yet the fact that most of the tales can be traced to
an experiencing subject—one who often has experienced something untoward—gives Yanagita's tales the aura of uncanny certainty. The displacement of narrators and the obvious (yet not too obvious) crafting of the tales
mark them as "literary"; the naming and placing of origins and the insistence on tracing back through remembered voices to improbable events
claimed to be true mark the text as (proto-)"ethnographic."

Yet that difference—to the extent that Yanagita was clearly aware of it—
was allowed to remain in haunting undecidability. What is strange, then, is
the way different orders of reality are juxtaposed and allowed to occupy the
same textual and epistemological space; no hierarchy is imposed on these
orders, no final demarcating of the factual from the fictional, the real from
the fantastic. The fact that an experience is said to have occurred and the
implausibility of the experience itself are placed on the same plane, enfolded within a larger (implicit) notion of psychical reality.

The Tales of Tōno is thus a peculiar hybrid, and it conformed to no law of
genre in 1910. Although only 350 copies were printed, Yanagita's connections with the Japanese literary world ensured that prominent Meiji authors
read and reviewed it. When it was first published, many readers did not

know what to make of it: it seemed to fit most comfortably within the varied collections of "strange tales." Its status as literature (*bungaku*) was not quite assured, and there was little or no conception of its status as a work of "folklore" at all.[54]

The novelist Tayama Katai, who is often credited with introducing the word *naturalism* into Japanese, stated,

> While Kunio maintains that I, a naturalist writer, cannot understand his feelings and am not really qualified to evaluate his work, I find the work infused with an extravagance of affected rusticity. I remain unmoved. His use of on-site observation to create the background in an essay is significant. The work's impressionistic and artistic qualities, however, derive more from the treatment of the data than the actual content.[55]

Another famous author and friend, Shimazaki Tōson (also an exponent of naturalism) wrote in an essay on *Tōno monogatari*,

> That work [*Tōno monogatari*] consists in its entirety of a collection of legends [*densetsu*] from a remote region. As the author states in his preface, after having heard these stories and seen their place of origin, he felt compelled to convey them to others, so fascinating were the realities contained therein. The concise and honest style of the stories—as well as the critical preface and thematic arrangement of the tales—immediately attracted me. The copy that Yanagita presented to me is here before me now, and I have just finished reading it. . . . After reading these kinds of story, I feel that I have come to know something, however faintly, about the wonder [*kyōi*] and terror [*kyōfu*] found within the midst of rural life [*rūraru raifu*]. These stories of mountain gods, goddesses, and strange men and women who live in the mountains—as well as stories of mysterious yet actual occurrences, like the tale that reminded Yanagita of Maeterlinck's "The Intruder"—have made me feel this way. . . .
>
> Even though this work was written out of a scholarly interest in ethnic development [*minzoku hattatsu*], I still felt as if I could hear something like the distant, distant voices of the fields in this work. . . . I would like to know more about the place where these stories were born and passed down. The reason I would like to know more is due, I think, to the fact that the author of *Tōno monogatari,* more than being just a collector of strange tales or a scholar of ethnic psychology, is a traveler with acute powers of perception. As far as I know, there are few travelers like Yanagita, and there are even fewer travelers with Yanagita's powers of observation.[56]

Shimazaki's critique astutely points out the "ethnic" dimension of Yanagita's tales, yet in 1910, there was no clear perception of folklore studies as a pursuit. Instead, "ethnology" was in its early stages of formation, preceded by the founding of ethnological societies and journals. Shimazaki may have been one of the few critics to point out this dimension of *Tōno monogatari,* a dimension to which Yanagita himself does not clearly allude.

The first person to recognize the value of *The Tales of Tōno* as *folklore,* not literature, was in fact a Chinese author and scholar of Japanese literature, Chou Tso-jen (Shūsakujin, in Japanese).⁵⁷ In 1933, twenty-three years after Yanagita had published the tales, Chou Tso-jen discovered the text and praised its peerless value for folklore studies.⁵⁸

The preceding ten years had witnessed the formation of nativist ethnology as a discipline. In 1925, Yanagita founded the journal *Minzoku,* which marked the beginning of all anthropological studies in Japan, according to the eminent ethnologist Aruga Kizaemon.⁵⁹ Not until the 1930s, however, did nativist ethnology attain widespread credibility. *The Tales of Tōno* only became a recognized classic on its republication in an expanded edition in 1935. Not coincidentally, 1935 marked in many ways the apogee of nativist ethnology as a discipline. It was the year of Yanagita's *kanreki* (sixtieth birthday celebration, always a landmark event in Japanese society); the year the journal *Minkan denshō* (Oral Tradition) was formed; and the year nativist ethnology as a discipline was finally established on a national scale.⁶⁰

It is significant that the republication of the *Tales* coincided with the moment of nativist ethnology's disciplinary consolidation, the moment of high fascism and militarism in the Japanese empire. It is possible to see the entire trajectory of nativist ethnology with its emphasis on the unwritten, the marginal, and the impoverished as a species of resistance to elite, documentary, modernist scholarship as such, providing an alternative to state-sponsored mainstream scholarship. Yet to the extent that it became disciplinarily constituted as the study of what was uniquely Japanese, that which was outside the corruptions of Western modernity, Yanagita and his folklore studies (there was no doubt it was his discipline) contributed to the chauvinism and cultural nationalism of the wartime period.⁶¹

It was with the expanded republication of the text in 1935 that *The Tales of Tōno* emerged as the founding text of native ethnology. It finally achieved the complex acclaim that did not—could not—greet it on its initial publication. Only the deferral of twenty-five years and the construction of a discipline allowed the retroactive recognition of the strange birth that the text commemorated. As Yanagita himself remarked in his comments to the second edition,

> In fact, when *Tōno monogatari* first came out, the public still had no knowledge of these matters, and it appears they judged the attitude of a "certain person" who was attempting to problematize them as that of a dilettante or curiosity seeker. But today, times have completely changed. These kinds of experience have now been repeated any number of times, and they have come to be recognized as the important object of one field of scholarly endeavor.⁶²

The Tales of Tōno must be grasped as two publications across which the "birth" of nativist ethnology took place. The import of the first event—the appearance of the *Tales*—could not be known except as it occurred again within a structure of repetition. Only through repetition could the text emerge as originary. The second edition contained a supplement to the first, a new collection of tales assembled with the help of Sasaki Kizen. These tales were primarily bona fide "folktales" and were *now* written in colloquial style. It is telling that one of the most influential commentators on the *Tales* after its celebrated second birth complained about the supplement, stating, "The tales of the newly expanded second part are written in colloquial language, but for me, the nostalgic flavor of the original edition's tales, left as they are in straightforward literary style, is stronger."[63]

Nostalgia can only emerge across a temporal lag, and the nostalgic flavor of a text is more potent the farther it is from the ostensible source and goal of nostalgic desire. The *Tales* and its readings not only encode that desire for a regressing world of orality (that in any case is more pleasurably known through its deadly enxtextualization) but expose the nostalgia of a discipline for its own origin, an origin that remains dislocated from itself. To the extent that the *Tales* remains the obsessively re-marked "memorial marker of the birth of Japanese folklore studies" (*Nihon minzokugaku no hasshō no kinentō*), it becomes precisely that: a *memorial* marker, a monument to an absence, to a loss that must be perpetually recovered through a discipline that ensures the disappearance of its origins as it produces them.

To return once more to Mishima, he reads the text as mysterious (*fushigina*), not only because of the deaths it writes but because it is "data as it is, but at the same time it is literature–and that's what's mysterious about this work."[64] The tales speak of ghastly matters that can never properly become the objects of a discipline as such, because they cannot be situated in an objective relation to positive knowledge.[65] Yet because literature intervenes as the sign of that discursive space where anything is possible, those deaths— already uncannily situated within the narratives—both thematize and exemplify an impossible knowledge, a knowledge enabled by the uncanny suspension of literature and science: nativist ethnology itself.[66]

Years later, Yanagita himself spoke of these matters.

Hori Ichirō: How did you come to write *Tōno monogatari?*
Yanagita: That was through Mizuno Yōshū, who died recently. He was a strange kind of poet, who had an interest in the village life of old. When we were talking about . . . our native places, the name of his friend Sasaki Kizen came up. Sasaki was, in fact, a naive, good person. He was stubborn about some things. He was a person who would oppose what we said—if we thought something was not so, he would believe it was, and would get angry. *It's probably correct to say that* Tōno monogatari *is mostly a literary work.*
Hori: But, *Tōno monogatari* has been very influential, hasn't it.

Yanagita: That's true. *The special feature of that work is that there's absolutely no at-tempt at interpreting or commenting upon its contents.* This seems to have ap-pealed to European scholars. In England there was talk at one time of having it translated into English.

Hori: That lack of interpretation was probably something that was different from the scholarly attitudes that had existed until then.

Yanagita: I think that stance [taken in the writing of Tōno monogatari*] was the same as the stance of the natural sciences or biological sciences.*[67]

Yanagita first offers the opinion that the text is mostly a "literary work," yet immediately afterward he maintains that there was no "interpretation" what-soever in the text; last, that its stance was "the same as the stance of the nat-ural sciences." One wonders at the serenity of his assertions, a serenity that has not been shared by a generation of Japanese critics struck by what they see as a founding contradiction in Yanagita's discipline. Yet without engag-ing the apparitions of the *The Tales of Tōno* itself, no criticism can confront the constitutive yet uncanny commingling of literature and science in that discipline. Nativist ethnology, institutionally born out of the haunted unde-cidability of literature and science, is devoted to preserving the distinctive-ness of the enduring Japanese customary, of cultural transmission itself. Yet the elaborate monstrosity of its textual origin—a monstrosity that really con-sists of nothing more than the impossibility of finally demarcating literature from science, the figural from the literal, the fantastic from the factual—re-turns to trouble the present. As a writing perpetually *between* literature and science, nativist ethnology must repeat the uncanny gestures of its origin, insisting on a transmission without remainder from a beginning that can only ever be—finally—memorialized.

NOTES

1. "Folklore studies" is the conventional translation for *minzokugaku.* I sometimes translate this term as "nativist ethnology" (a translation that H. D. Harootunian has used) because of its links with nativist scholarship (*kokugaku*) of the Tokugawa period (1603–1868) and its claims as a discipline of indigenous Japanese knowledge and practices. The connections of the discipline of folklore studies with the discipline of anthropology in Japan are multiple, not the least of which is the homophonic con-gruence of the two terms: *minzokugaku* is also a standard term for "anthropology." It differs from the "minzokugaku" of folklore studies, however, in its graphic constitu-tion (although both terms share the same Chinese character for "min," the charac-ters used for "zoku" in each word are different). I shall use both "folklore studies" and (Japanese) "nativist ethnology" to translate "minzokugaku" in this essay.

2. Mishima Yukio, "*Tōno monogatari,*" in *Yanagita Kunio kenkyū,* ed. Kamishima Jirō (Tokyo: Chikuma Shobō, 1973): 198. First published in the *Yomiuri shinbun,* June 12, 1970.

3. Michel de Certeau in collaboration with Dominique Julia and Jacques Revel, "The Beauty of the Dead: Nisard," in *Heterologies* (Minneapolis: The University of Minnesota Press, 1986): 119.

4. Susan Stewart, "Notes on Distressed Genres," in Stewart, *Crimes of Writing: Problems in the Containment of Representation* (New York: Oxford University Press, 1991): 74.

5. Masao Miyoshi has written of the Japanese rejection of Mishima's literature, declaring, "Much of Mishima Yukio's dazzling performance now looks merely flamboyant, or even kitschy. The list of his works is long, but the list of those that might as well remain unread is nearly as long." Mishima's short review of *The Tales of Tōno* remains a piece that bears reading. See Masao Miyoshi, *Off Center: Power and Culture Relations between Japan and the United States* (Cambridge: Harvard University Press, 1991): 149.

6. The Meiji Restoration aimed to "restore" the emperor to his rightful place of authority after centuries of merely titular kingship under the military government of Japan, which held de facto power. For an analysis of the Meiji Restoration as the complex culmination of intellectual debates about authority and representation, see H. D. Harootunian, *Toward Restoration: The Growth of Political Consciousness in Tokugawa Japan* (Berkeley, Los Angeles, and London: University of California Press, 1970).

7. The concept is Karatani Kōjin's, developed in his *Nihon kindai bungaku no kigen* (Tokyo: Kodansha, 1980). Karatani's book is an examination of the formation of modern Japanese literature, in which he emphasizes the discursive production of the category and institution of "literature" (*bungaku*) itself in the Meiji period. As Brett de Bary argues in an unpublished introduction to her translation of Karatani's first chapter, "The Discovery of Landscape" (Fūkei no hakken), "Karatani proposes that the fundamental rupture between Edo and Meiji literature is to be located, not in the discovery of a previously non-existent 'interiority' or individual self, but rather in the changed conception of writing implicit in the institutionalization of the *genbunitchi* system. For Karatani, the written word shifts from its status as rhetorical instrument and assumes new significance in the Meiji period as a tool for 'reflecting' reality." Karatani's book has been translated into English as *Origins of Modern Japanese Literature*, translation edited by Brett de Bary (Durham and London: Duke University Press, 1993).

8. For a sharp analysis of the process of rationalization at the state level, see Bernard Silberman, "The Bureaucratic State in Japan: The Problem of Authority and Legitimacy," in *Conflict in Modern Japanese History: The Neglected Tradition,* ed. Tetsuo Najita and J. Victor Koschmann (Princeton: Princeton University Press, 1982): 226–257.

9. Mikiso Hane, *Peasants, Rebels, and Outcasts: The Underside of Modern Japan* (New York: Pantheon, 1982): 11.

10. I have taken the above from a chronology of Japanese folklore studies prepared by the National Museum of Japanese History and Folklore. Fukuda Ajio, "Nihon minzoku kenkyūshi nenpyō," *Kokuritsu Rekishi Minzoku Hakubutsukan Hōkoku* 2 (March 1983): 41–81.

11. See Katherine Trumpener's masterful work, "The Voice of the Past: Anxieties of Cultural Transmission in Post-Enlightenment Europe" (Ph.D. dissertation, Stanford University, 1990).

12. The search to find a domain of pure ethnic Japaneseness merged with the nationalist project, culminating in the concerted effort to "overcome the modern" (*kindai no chōkoku*) in the 1940s.

13. See Nanette Twine, "The Genbunitchi Movement: A Study of the Development of the Modern Colloquial Style in Japan" (Ph.D. dissertation, University of Queensland, 1975): 4–43.

14. Of course, Chinese characters—contrary to what Derrida and others have proposed as a potentially nonlogocentric alternative to phonetic writing—*do* contain phonetic components that allow the reader to sound the character in many (if not all) instances. But the point still remains that ideographs allow the reader to read without voicing to a higher degree than phonetic writing would normally allow.

15. See Twine, "The Genbunitchi Movement." *Genbunitchi* was also the phrase for the state's move to bring literary Japanese into the realm of the spoken.

16. Masao Miyoshi, *Accomplices of Silence: The Modern Japanese Novel* (Berkeley, Los Angeles, and London: University of California Press, 1974): 3–37.

17. "Shasei to ronbun," *Bunshō no sekai* 2, no. 3 (February 1907). Extensive passages from this essay are analyzed in Iwamoto Yoshiteru, *Mō hitotsu no Tōno monogatari* (Tokyo: Tōsui shobô, 1983): 105–106. Iwamoto's title translates as *One More "Tales of Tōno,"* as he examines the contradictions surrounding the writing of *The Tales of Tōno*. All translations are mine unless otherwise noted.

18. This is Ronald Morse's translation of the famous passage. Kunio Yanagita, *The Legends of Tōno,* trans. Ronald Morse (Tokyo: Japan Foundation, 1975): 5.

19. Yanagita, "Shasei to ronbun": 31–32; emphasis added.

20. Speech here occupies (at least) two positions. One is externalized speech—speech-in-the-world, speech as natural object. People talk, one hears their voices, and thus the imperative for writers to record their speech as perfectly as possible in the objective mode of the natural scientist. But speech occupies a second position, one determined by what is *not* said. That is, speech is the sign of "thought"; it is a vehicle for "expressing" thoughts that are silent. Speech indicates something other than itself, something more originary that it carries forward. A relay is instituted, originating in thought, moving to speech, then to written colloquial style, then to literary styles, with their ascending degrees of distance from speech. Because writing is viewed here as the graphic analogue of speech, the dilemmas of direct description are more fraught when speech is the object, as opposed to the visual. That is, it is assumed that textually describing a scene in nature will of necessity be farther removed from that scene—moving across the mode of the visual to that of language—than a faithful phonographic textual recording of a dialogue, for example (which moves only across forms of language, from the spoken to the written). But as the term *shasei* (direct description) indicates with its provenance in art theory, similar debates took place about visual representation, where the continuum of arguments moved from the status of photography to Western-style realism (effected by live "direct description") to the rediscovery of Japanese-style "impressionism."

21. Gerald Figal has discussed this problem of the invisible world, the fantastic, and questions of representation in his "Yanagita Kunio Writing-in-Wonderland: The Limits of Representation and the Representation of Limits" (M.A. thesis, University of Chicago, 1987).

22. "Genbun no kyori," *Bunshō no sekai* 14, no. 4 (October 1909), 167–172.

23. Ibid., 169.

24. In this same essay, Yanagita asserts that spoken Japanese, unlike "Western languages," with their clearly delineated progression of clauses and connecting articles, is full of pauses, elisions, and repetitions. If one tries to write this confusion down, he states, the result is nothing but an incoherence that can hardly ascend to the "literary." Therefore, it is not possible to have a "true" (*shin*) genbunitchi at the present, he avers. To have a true colloquial written language, *spoken* Japanese must move closer to the written (literary) language with its regularity and refinement. Education, starting with primary school, is the means to attain this remolding of spoken Japanese into a simulacrum of the properly written. What this passage also discloses is an example of the inexhaustible binarism situating the "Japanese" language as opposed to "Western" ones, Japan vs. the West. It is implied that in the West, because the spoken language is rational and coherent, truly objective, scientific, "naturalist" colloquial writing (and literature) is a possibility. This is an impossibility in Japan with the irrationalities of its spoken discourse, and thus literature, above all, should not aspire to reproduce the spoken as is. We can see the implications for a theory of Japanese cultural essentialism emerging from these reflections on speech and writing. Ibid., 170–172.

25. See Jacques Derrida's *Of Grammatology* (Baltimore: John Hopkins University Press, 1974). This problematic—the relationship between speech, writing, and native Japaneseness—also reiterates many of the abiding concerns of Tokugawa nativist scholarship (kokugaku), as analyzed, for example, in the English-language works of H. D. Harootunian and the recent work of Naoki Sakai, *Voices of the Past: The Status of Language in Eighteenth-Century Japanese Discourse* (Ithaca: Cornell University Press, 1992).

26. Yanagita, "Genbun no kyori," 169.

27. *Tōno monogatari*, 57.

28. Yanagita had already started his proto-ethnographic project during the period between 1907 and 1909, culminating in his self-published *Nochi no karikotoba no ki*, a collection of hunters' terminology from the mountains of the southern island of Kyūshū and his *Dialogues of the Stone Gods* (Ishigami mondo) published in 1909.

29. Entries from Yanagita's diaries cited by Kamata Hisako, "*Tōno monogatari* no shitazome," *Iwate nippō,* 24 February 1975.

30. See H. D. Harootunian's work on the discursive construction of the invisible and visible worlds in Tokugawa nativist thought, *Things Seen and Unseen: Discourse and Ideology in Tokugawa Nativism* (Chicago: University of Chicago Press, 1988).

31. *The Legends of Tōno*, 8. Note that Ronald Morse translated *monogatari* as "legends," a translation that far exceeds the mandate implied by the Japanese term, which simply indicates a tale, story, or narrative. Unless otherwise noted, I have relied on Morse's translation of *Tōno monogatari*.

32. Ibid. 5. The original Japanese reads, "mata ichiji ikku o mo kagensezu kanjitaru mama o kakitari." Yanagita Kunio, *Tōno monogatari* (Tokyo: Yamata Shobō, 1972): 55.

33. Ibid., 5.

34. Iwamoto, *Mō hitotsu no Tōno monogatari*, 39.

35. See Oda Tomihime, "Shokōhon *Tōno monogatari* no mondai," *Kokubungaku* 27 (January 1982): 72–78. Oda's article is a painstaking analysis of the various manuscripts, drafts, and proofs of the first edition of *The Tales of Tōno*, an analysis that demonstrates how ornately crafted the finished text actually was. We also know that a number of the narratives included in the *Tales* had been previously published in different versions by Mizuno Yōshū.

36. Iwamoto Yoshiteru interprets *kagen sezu* this way, although literally the phrase does mean "without adding or subtracting." If the nuance of "neglecting" is accepted, it points even more clearly to Yanagita's crafting of the text. Emphasis mine.

37. The preface constitutes the real "ethnographic" moment of the text, including in it Yanagita's description of his travels to Tōno (undertaken *after* he had heard the stories from Sasaki in Tokyo). A classic arrival scene is interspersed with a compelling description of a festival on the hillside, seen from a distance. The importance of distance—which is also central to Yanagita's theories of literature—emerges to preserve the aura of the object in a way not totally alien from Walter Benjamin's writings on aura and the effects of distance.

38. Jean Laplanche and Jean-Bertrand Pontalis, "Fantasy and the Origins of Sexuality," in *Formations of Fantasy*, ed. Victor Burgin, James Donald, and Cora Kaplan (London: Methuen, 1986): 5–34. Note their discussion of "psychical reality" in Laplanche and Pontalis, *The Language of Psycho-Analysis*, trans. Donald Nicholson-Smith (New York: W. W. Norton, 1973): 363. See also Gerald Figal's discussion of Yanagita's analogue of "psychical reality" in his Ph.D. dissertation, "The Folk and the Fantastic in Japanese Modernity: Dialogues on Reason and Imagination in Late Nineteenth and Early Twentieth-Century Japan" (University of Chicago, 1992).

39. It is clear that Yanagita was deeply invested in the process of collection itself, indicated by his later mobilization of scores of disciples to gather data for his science. This investment is also clear from the relationship of rivalry that later developed with Sasaki Kizen over the publishing of future folktales.

40. Mishima, *Tōno monogatari*, 198. *Fusoku no kiki* might be literally translated as "unforeseen ghastliness." What I think is implied here, however, is the ghastliness of a certain insufficiency, "like when someone starts to talk and then suddenly stops speaking," and thus I also find the phrase "ghastly insufficiency" suggestive.

41. *The Legends of Tōno*, 31–32.

42. I am indebted to Mladen Dolar's explication of the modern uncanny (and the distinction between Todorov's and Lacan's readings) in his " 'I Shall Be with You on Your Wedding-Night': Lacan and the Uncanny," *October* 58 (Fall 1991): 5–23.

43. See the classic discussion of the uncanny in Sigmund Freud, "The 'Uncanny' " (1919), in *The Standard Edition of the Complete Psychological Works*, ed. James Strachey, Vol. XVIII (London: Hogarth Press, 1955).

44. Kuwabara Takeo, "*Tōno monogatari* kara," in *Yanagita Kunio kenkyū*, 128. Essay originally published in 1937. The original phrase is "rekishi izen no sekai."

45. Oda, "Shokōhon *Tōno monogatari* no mondai," 75.

46. Questioners at the conference "Imagining Japan: Narratives of Nationhood" at Stanford University in May 1993 reminded me that much of Japan's "tale literature" also has this fragmented, episodic quality. The *Nihonreiki* was mentioned as an example. My point is not to deny that Yanagita might have been relying on, alluding to, or citing earlier forms of Japanese literature. Even his use of *monogatari*

GHOSTLIER DEMARCATIONS *321*

(tale) points to an entire class of literature often classified by that term. The specific difference arises, however, with Yanagita's doubled insistence on factuality and fantasy within the debates about representation and modernity that arose in the Meiji period.

47. Many commentators have noted how Yanagita shifted from his earlier concerns with *yamabito* (mountain men), wanderers, and the fantastic of various forms to a central concern with the "everyday folk" and what was common to all Japanese, particularly Japanese peasants. Figal has discussed this shift across a number of levels in his "From *tengu* to *senzo:* The Hidden World in the Writing of Yanagita Kunio." Paper written for the 39th Annual Meeting of the Midwestern Conference on Asian Studies, Bloomington, November 1990.

48. *The Legends of Tōno*, 25–26.

49. Mishima Yukio, *Shōsetsu to wa nanika* (Tokyo: Shinchōsha, 1972): 133.

50. *The Legends of Tōno*, 60.

51. Oda, "Shokōhon *Tōno monogatari* no mondai," 76.

52. The tragedy of their relationship is analyzed in Iwamoto's book and also in a roundtable discussion among Nakazawa Shin'ichi, Kosaka Shūhei, and Kasai Kiyoshi entitled "Ima 'Nihon' to wa," in *Nyū Japanoroji*, ed. Kosaka Kiyoshi (Tokyo: Satsukisha, 1984): 18–76.

53. See James Clifford's essay "On Ethnographic Authority," in his *The Predicament of Culture: Twentieth-Century Ethnography, Literature, and Art* (Cambridge: Harvard University Press, 1988): 21–54.

54. Ōtō Tokihiko claims that most people just thought it was an unusual book with strange stories in it and were primarily attracted to it because of the beautiful writing. Ōtō Tokihiko in his "Kaisetsu" (Commentary) to *Tōno monogatari*, by Yanagita Kunio (Tokyo: Kadokawa Bunko, 1982): 206.

55. Translated by Ronald Morse and cited in Morse, "Yanagita Kunio and the Modern Japanese Consciousness," in *International Perspectives on Yanagita Kunio and Japanese Folklore Studies*, ed. J. Victor Koschmann et al. (Ithaca: Cornell University China-Japan Program, 1985): 23–24.

56. From Shimazaki Tōson, "Nochi no Shinkatamachi yori," in *Tōson Zenshū*, vol. 6 (Tokyo: Chikuma Shobō, 1967): 200–201. Translation mine.

57. Chou Tso-jen (1885–1966) was a professor at Peking University and leader of the "new literature movement." He was also a translator and pioneer in the study of children's literature and tales. *Kōjien*, 2d ed., s.v. "Shūsakujin."

58. Ōtō, "Kaisetsu," 201.

59. Yoneyama Toshinao, "Yanagita and His Work," in Koschmann et al., *International Perspectives*, 41.

60. Kurata Hisako, compiler, "Nenpyō" (Chronology) in Kadokawa Bunko edition of *Tōno monogatari*, 221.

61. Victor Koschmann disentangles the immensely complex ideological weave of Yanagita's folklorism—its "conservative antiestablishment" implications—in his "Folklore Studies and the Conservative Anti-Establishment in Modern Japan," in Koschmann et al., *International Perspectives*. Yet he also states that "Yanagita was basically receptive to state authority," an observation made, for example, by Kamishima Jirō (148).

62. Yanagita, "Saihan oboegaki" (1935), *Tōno monogatari* (Tokyo: Yamata Shobō, 1972): 60–61.

63. Kuwabara, "*Tōno monogatari* kara," 124.

64. Mishima, "*Tōno monogatari*," 198.

65. Mishima, in working through the implications of *Tōno monogatari*'s doubled status, said as much: "to the extent that something is factual [*fuakuto*] it's the object of scholarship" (fuakuto de aru kagiri de wa, gakumon no taishō de aru), 198. Of course, part of Mishima's point is that the strangeness of the tales—their very implausibility—attains the status of "fact" in Yanagita's rendering: the sheer factuality of language, if nothing else (*korera no genzairyō wa, ichimen kara mireba, kotoba igai no nanimono demo nai:* "these data, from one perspective, are nothing at all other than language").

66. "What is heralded and refused under the name of literature cannot be identified with any other discourse. It will never be scientific, philosophical, conversational. But if it did not open onto all these discourses, it would not be literature either. There is no literature without a *suspended* relation to meaning and reference. . . . In its suspended condition literature can only exceed itself." Jacques Derrida, " 'This Strange Institution Called Literature': An Interview with Jacques Derrida," in Derrida, *Acts of Literature,* ed. Derek Attridge (New York: Routledge, 1992): 47–48.

67. Hori Ichirō and Yanagita Kunio, "Watashi no ayunde kita michi," in *Denki* 1, no. 5–6. Cited by Iwamoto, *Mō hitotsu no Tōno monogatari,* 103–104; emphasis added.

FOURTEEN

The Construction of America:
The Anthropologist as Columbus

Michael Taussig

Over the long haul, he said, history is subjected to the conflict of writing.[1]
—THOMÁS ZAPATA

It will speak a secret language and leave behind documents not of edification but of paradox.
—HUGO BALL

In response to the quincentenary of the European invasion of America, the Colombian Anthropology Association has invited us to Bogota today to discuss "the construction of America." This is a good choice of topic, it seems to me, because it grasps the opportunity of the quincentennial ritual to stand aside from our usual practice and reflect on what we are doing and why we do it, to what degree and in what manner of ways we are constructing America, and to what degree America constructs us—our identities, in all their multifacetedness, as much as our ways of perceiving and interpreting the world and producing knowledge. Herein, of course, lies a fundamental quandary: how do we make sense of the construction that constructs us? In particular, bearing in mind the stuff of which the quincentennial event is made, what is the role in such construction of memory and of rituals of memorization?

As we see it, there are two great narrative forces in the construction of America, forces that have preoccupied us in our examination of the anthropology of the southwest of Colombia, from the Pacific coast over the *cordilleras* of the Andes to the eastern foothills of the Amazon basin. These are the narrational configurations centered on the Indian, on the one hand, and the Negro, on the other, configurations that owe much, of course, to the needs and fantasies of the European imagination as transplanted in America.

There are many threads to follow and sort out here, but there is one that is strikingly dominant. For while the Indian has been recruited to the task of carrying the originary America and thus the seed of the great American story and its authenticating seal (perhaps no time more than now, when

323

there are burgeoning Indian movements and worldwide concern for the rain forest), the *Negro* has been recruited as the carrier of disturbance and fragmentation in that great American story, even threatening it with destruction.

One has only to look at anthropology itself, the basic professional instrument for the fetishization of the Indian. With its aura of scientific expertise combined with the romance of fieldwork, anthropology has seized on the Indian to create a vision of society no less than of history as coherent intelligible structures—structures of so-called mythology, structures of so-called kinship, structures of ecology, structures of annihilation and nostalgia, a veritable structure of structure itself, the New World order and a master narrative if ever there was one.

By contrast, anthropology's interest in the Negro in the New World has been quite diminutive, and what anthropology there is has certainly provided discomfort for the claims of structure and structure's claims for the project of making sense of the world. Take the endless anthropological attempts at juggling an endless parade of statistics on household "structure" in the Caribbean, for instance, as an ever-intensifying obsession because of the lack of recognizable, ordered "kinship" and, in most places, the absence of a mythic or religious "order." We recall a French student of Claude Lévi-Strauss who had previously worked in West Africa setting out in 1970 or 1971 for the Pacific coast of Colombia returning to Bogotá complaining, "Those blacks have no myths!" So she returned to the coast not to study blacks but to study Indians. This story has the added virtue of reminding us of those studies and contemporary social movements devoted to the attempt to locate African vestiges and links with Negro communities in the New World because in that way the threat of dislocation, fragmentation, and ultimate senselessness can be mollified, if not thwarted, by the flow of narrativity.

For whatever complicated historical reasons, and by whatever complicated and always already stupendously politically saturated logics of representation, the fact is that the Negro in the New World acquired both the burden and the advantage of the power to persistently disturb the patterns of contrast to which white and Indian had been harnessed, to harass them, to overturn them, to make fun of them, whatever, but to never let those contrasts rest in peace. This we might call, then, the deconstruction of America, and it is surely no less American for so being.

THE PRAGUE ARCHIVE

In light of these remarks, and bearing in mind our being located in a scholarly ritual of memorialization by virtue of this quincentennializing project, I would like to draw your attention to the theory and practice of historiography of a very old, very black, blind man, Tomás Zapata, who appears in the diaries, papers, photographs, and tape recordings discovered in the belongings of an unidentified white man traveling from England and Australia whose name in the recordings appears simply as Miguel and who, so it appears, went to live in the small town of Puerto Tejada, Cauca, in the southwest of Colombia in late 1969, two years before Tomás Zapata died. From these papers it seems that although his initial impulse was to write a history of the *Violencia,* the reason this traveler stayed almost two years (and apparently visited frequently thereafter) was because he got interested in the local history of the abolition of slavery and its aftermath.

Although there are many unanswered questions about these papers, the bulk of which are typed with effusive energy and many typographical errors, they are of obvious anthropological interest and, in the right hands, the tape recordings would seem especially valuable, stretching back, as they do, some twenty-two years with the original voices of the town's inhabitants. They were discovered four years ago in an obscure archive of Latin American Studies in Prague and have been kindly made available by the director of the archive, despite financial and administrative difficulties hardly worth going into here.

THE TOWN

From government censuses and the traveler's records, it appears that in 1970 Puerto Tejada was a town largely of poor wage laborers working in the fields of the nearby sugar plantations that had taken over most of the peasant farms. A generation or so before, however, it is said to have been the center of a thriving economy of smallholders cultivating cacao, coffee, and plantains. As many as one-third of the peasant households were headed by women, who were no less capable of running the farms than men, and the farms were analogues of the rain forest with large red-flowering cachimbo trees shading the cacao trees, which, together with the broadleafed plantains, in turn shaded the coffee, which came later, in the early twentieth century. These "forest-farms" were created in the mid-nineteenth century when the former slaves took up independent farming in the *monte oscuro,* the dark forest, as it was called, along the Palo and Paila rivers running through the former slave estates. This rain forest type of agriculture was a kindly one, inhibiting weed growth, hence labor, and flattening out the cycles of heat and rain. The arboreal net diminished the harsh sun, while at the same time it conserved throughout the summers the water from the rainy season downpours. The plantains, which are self-reproducing, bore fruit every year after first planting, and the cash crops were harvested every two weeks throughout the year; when the coffee was abundant, the cacao was minimal, and vice versa, over a six-month cycle. Because there was always a little to gather and because the trees were in place, the farmers could avoid large labor, capital, or energy inputs, bank loans, or long waiting periods.

But with the arrival of what has come to be called "agribusiness," first with the sugarcane plantations in the 1950s and then with the state-sponsored U.S.-inspired "green revolution" of chemicals and machines in the late 1960s, the opposite occurred. In the Recorder's notes we see that the little red and white checkered logo of Ralston-Purina (St. Louis, Missouri), flagship of U.S. corporate farming, sprouted on mud walls of stores in the humblest villages. "They're going to get hens to lay square eggs," the *paisa* said after he and his portly brother won a free trip to the company's headquarters in St. Louis, having sold more fertilizer, hormones, and herbicides to peasant farmers than any other agent in the area that year. A few months later he was shot dead in his store in a dispute over a debt. "It could have happened to anyone," noted the Recorder, "but it seems somehow prophetic of a new type of violence, that of chemicals and an imported technology developed for rich farmers in a totally different climate and ecological setting." Meanwhile, a whole culture of agriculture was being demolished. Those peasant lands that did not fall into the hands of the sugar estates were denuded and exposed to sun and floods as the peasant men themselves felled the cacao and coffee trees on their own small farms. Weeds shot up within weeks of clearing, and expensive and dangerous pesticides and herbicides were used, contaminating water supplies and altering the insect and plant disease balance. Long periods of waiting and dependence on wage labor and banks took the place of harvesting the coffee, cacao, plantain, fruit trees, and leaves every two weeks throughout the year. In general, women peasants resisted the change, refusing to grant their sons permission to fell the trees. "It gives me little, but it gives," they would say about their farms. As the peasant farms were destroyed by plagues and inability to manage the new technoeconomy, so they were assumed by the sugar plantations. A new world came into being. A familiar story, perhaps more stark than usual, and just beginning when the Recorder first set foot in the town.

In 1970, Puerto Tejada had a population of around 11,000, and from the Prague archive it seems that most of the inhabitants—maybe 95 percent— were descendants of African slaves, many of whom, from the eighteenth century until the abolition of slavery in 1851, had worked in the alluvial gold mines and on the haciendas, Japio, La Bolsa, and Quintero, of the Arboleda family in that stunningly beautiful region of plains and woods bounded east and west by the ranges of the Andes, twenty five miles apart, rising dark blue to disappear in mysterious clouds. By 1970, many other people of African descent had recently migrated to the town from the far-off and isolated Pacific coast to find work in the cane fields or as servants in the city nearby.

THE RECORDER AND THE MADNESS OF HISTORY

We gather that the person who assiduously tape-recorded and noted things down, whom we have referred to as the Recorder, had been only two months in Latin America when he began his interviews with Tomás Zapata, that his ability to converse in Spanish was rudimentary, and that his knowledge of local life and history was negligible. His interviewing was impatient. Instead of letting his subjects speak at will, when they appeared to be meandering, he would interrupt and choke off what to us, many years later, sometimes seem like astonishing lines of thought. He seemed inclined to cancel out the woolly associations, stutterings of thought, and illogically organized reminiscences. Now while people, especially old people, do talk in meandering ways, we cannot but wonder how other recorders obtain texts concise and harmonious, and, beyond that, we feel impelled to ask what it implies for representation in general, and the writing of history in particular, if the texts of lived speech of reminiscence are strewn with leaps and swerves, let alone with the debris of false starts and detours?

We also want to ask if the Recorder was trying to have his cake and eat it too—have the spontaneity of conversation and the rolling weight of the human voice echoing the past, making it really real as salvaged material, while at the same time have the carefully wrought orderliness of a prepared text. As we shall see, this takes us to the heart of the problem of history—cleaning out the opaque density and minutiae of the past so as to get to its secret? its meaning? its power to unseat bad history? the lineaments of the well-told tale? Now look who's meandering! Perhaps the problem here lies in assuming that one can be sufficiently outside of history so as to ask the sorts of questions implied by these dubious answers, while a more accurate response would be to give history and not the recorder primacy of place, to see the historian as constructed by history, and to see ourselves no less than the professional historian as embodiments enslaved by past obsessions to which we usually succumb, other times struggle with, and from which, by and large, we rarely escape. The reason for doing history, then, would be because one can do naught else but try to breathe in this turmoil and, if possible, escape from it. Simply put, as we are driven to it, for the person *is* history and history is, if anything, an incessant demand, hauling in the past with the demands for expression, demands stretched into life's despair, life's promise.

What is today understood by History is the attempt to dignify this obsessive madness with fine-sounding goals such as the search for "meaning" or design, goals whose primary function is to ensure the empowering illusion of standing freely above History, now the object of study. To the contrary, the end point of the madness that is history would be that the patient is able to get off the psychoanalyst's couch for the final time because the transference with the present had achieved a functioning praxis.

Of course, we know how easy it is to be critical of the Recorder after the event. Indeed the director of the Prague archive has urged us to exercise restraint lest we merely repeat the Recorder's anxious impatience and lose sight of the history of the erasure of history.

THE PHILOSOPHER

Early on the Recorder found his way to the poorest section of that poor town where an elderly cigar maker, Eusebio Cambindo, introduced him to his neighbor, don Tomás Zapata, who, from the notes typed up that night, is said to have been a massive and gentle blind man of eighty years of age seated in the sun in the corner of a tiny patio, his trembling hands resting on a walking stick. He spoke in a high-pitched, quavering, singsong voice as his daughter and some great-grandchildren cleared a space for their unusual guest.

"He's a philosopher," Eusebio Cambindo is recorded as saying with admiration, although later there was exasperation, too—like when the Recorder was asking don Tomás about the legendary bandit, Cenecio Mina, who had been, he said, a colonel in the War of One Thousand Days and active in this area in the early twentieth century when the large landowners, rich, white men and women from Bogotá and Boyaca, returned after the Conservative party victory so as to force the black "squatters" off what the large landowners considered to be their land or else make them pay rent. These landowners belonged to the Conservative party and came from the families that had owned many slaves in these parts. But the blacks had long been supporters of the Liberal party. It was the Liberal party that had freed the slaves in 1851 and the blacks had at times shed blood for it, there being apprehension among them throughout the second half of the nineteenth century that the landowners intended to restore slavery. And if the blacks were worried, we should not forget that during much of the second half of the nineteenth century, travelers recorded that whites feared that, as in Haiti, the black horde would sweep out of the dark woods to engulf the towns and haciendas of the Cauca valley.

"This was in one sense a super-man, in one sense, and in another sense was . . . a reproductor because he had the capacity to make his writing, to send his writings all over, and being a super-man he was thus able to outwit the law, he juggled the law, and this man had everything, had everything, because amongst the people of our time and further back, all have contained people of different measure and capacities, as you can see in the work of. . . . [and he paused a while], Pythagoras."

"Good! But, pardon, pardon me a small intervention," broke in Eusebio. "Let's not put in Plato or Pythagoras or other great sages that history tells us about. . . . Let's work with nothing more than the facts involving this man, what sort of a person he was, his intelligence, his cunning, . . . and his political deliberations that you knew."

Swerve and Flow

But at least on that day don Tomás's mind was elsewhere as he pondered the differences between common men, supermen, and God. He would swerve between sources such as Pythagoras plucked from the heart of the Western canon, on the one hand, and complicated accounts of local history, on the other. That is how the Recorder saw this, as an unpredictable back-and-forth between these poles of cultural reckoning. Yet in the process those poles dissolved. Mix and motion became stronger than boundary. In his notes the Recorder seems to have been confused at this process of what he called "flow and mix," "flow and swerve." The Director, known for his heavy-handed humor, pointed out that when you look at the Recorder's own writing, however, it is also prone to this process of flow and mix, swerve and flow. At this point we, too, became somewhat confused.

As the discussion lingered for a moment on the bandit's magical capacity to transform himself, don Tomás went on, "An example . . . to study the word of God one has to go back, to the beginning . . . and Greek apology tells us that gallant Zeus, in love with Leda, being on the other side of the lake, converted himself into a swan. . . . Zeus is the sun, Leda, the earth, space is . . . how can I explain this? Eventually in this sacred euphoria he lay with Leda and from this came many gods." His voice trailed off. "For instance," he went on, "I was having a conversation with a man who just wouldn't believe anything. Nothing! Sometimes he'd understand but other times he'd just close up saying there was only one heaven. And I told him No! Just one heaven! No!"

"Pardon, don Tomás, are you speaking of Greek mythology?" asked Eusebio Cambindo.

"Sí, señor. Sí, señor," replied Tomás.

"Well! It's clear that Greek mythology can never be anything but myth, and that myth is nothing but farce," said Eusebio, and he went on to rebuke Tomas for his failure to talk of what he had been personally acquainted with. "Just try to remember," he urged, "just try a little. Miguelito [the Recorder] wants to know what sort of person Mina was; more or less smart, astute, cruel, magnanimous. What did he have inside? Did he fight honestly on the battlefield or was he a man who changed his party, being somewhat dishonest? This is what Miguelito wants you to analyze, because being older than me, you lived closer to those events."

In this way the discussion turned to how the bandit played one political party off against the other to his personal benefit and how he was able to transform himself into animals and plants to avoid his enemies—all communicated in a matter-of-fact, unromantic way, so unlike the attempts begun by intellectuals and students in the 1980s to apotheosize Mina as a (meta)symbol of resistance, and always with this swerve and flow process intermingling what Euesbio Cambindo, to his despair, saw as farce with fact, mythology with reportage.

Old Age and the Ancients

It early on occurred to us listening to the tapes that this process of swerve and flow was largely on account of don Tomás Zapata's venerable age and the tricks aging plays with memory. He himself would stop and say with some remorse that his memory was poor. But then, as we shall see later, his memory for ritualized speech, for his poetry, was well nigh perfect. What is more, we had to consider whether these very "tricks" that age plays with memory might not be as revelatory as the absence of tricks. Doing tricks could be just what the obsessions of the past need so as to get the old *Aufhebung* going.

It also occurred to us that in "accessing" the elite Western tradition, the old man was trying to impress the Recorder, the educated foreigner, the *inglés*—the Englishman—as he came to be known. By peppering his remarks with ancient Greek philosophers, for instance, was not the old peasant merely showing off and hence betraying philosophy with sycophancy? Was he not merely aping the intelligentsia of the cities, the upper classes, and old Europe?

To be sure, this suspicion was tempered when we realized the great and genuine respect in which don Tomás held the ancients, together with a measure of fond familiarity. But as we thought about the implications of the aping argument, we realized that, first, there is a sense in which *all* thought is derivative, and second, that it was not all that uncommon at that time in Puerto Tejada—according to the Recorder's notes—to every now and again come across in the late afternoons, lounging on street corners, middle-aged or elderly men (who surely had spent very few years in school) arguing about Socrates or Plato, as if they lived just around the corner. Then again the authority of the ancients can be used in wildly different ways. To invoke the ancients is not necessarily to invoke conformity with the present setup. The great revolutionary theorist, Karl Marx, for instance, owed some of his key economic distinctions, such as the distinction between use value and exchange value, to Aristotle and peppered his *Capital* with quotations from the ancients, while Bertolt Brecht based his fundamental distinction between epic and dramatic theater on Aristotle's *Poetics*. And these were modern European theorists with an eye not on the past but on the future.

We also had to consider that the aping argument really does not tell one all that much because neither the intelligentsia nor the upper classes are that uniform and therefore do not provide just one model or one canon to ape but several, often antagonistic, ones. And then what is one to make of the strikingly different style of thought exhibited by Eusebio Cambindo as compared with Tomás Zapata? Here was a man perhaps also trying to impress the *inglés,* yet far from adulating the ancients as he was impatient with don Tomás for failing to keep to the straight and narrow of what he conceived of as the historical record. So how do we explain two very different styles of thought as the one reaction to the Recorder's presence? But, then, what was that presence?

STORYTELLER, HISTORIAN, COLUMBUS

In a well-known essay Walter Benjamin says the storyteller can be seen as located at the junction where the traveler returns to those who never left.[2] This puts emphasis on situation as much as storyteller, the story emerging from a meeting of persons on different trajectories, bringing the faraway to the here and now. We assume that the Recorder's presence was bound to and defined by this nexus, complicated by the fact that this must have been, to some extent, also an encounter with History in the figure of the old, blind man, iconic of the wisdom stored in the opacity of the past's pastness. In listening to the tapes and studying the notes, we remembered the Director's puzzlement as to how the old man might have felt at being in this position. (Was this because we were putting the Director in a similar situation?)

This was made vivid at one point early on in the tapes where Tomás said to the Recorder and Eusebio Cambindo, "Good! Before anything else I want to clear up for you the history of Columbus. I could see that you didn't understand me, and this is what I wanted to tell you: this existed, but in private. When Columbus came it then passed into history. No longer did it remain in private. Now it had passed into history. This is what Miguel [the Recorder] is coming to do too; getting hold of things that were in private, so as to take them into history. That's what I wanted to tell you about Columbus."[3]

"There's so many things forgotten," commented Eusebio. "That's why one goes to an old person who can give a summary of more or less how things were."

"Sí, señor. Because before things were written down in books like the Sacred Scripture, it came by tradition, what they called the tradition of the ancients, with one old person telling another . . . and it's this tradition which Miguel is acquiring for history."

Eusebio said it would be too tiring to get through everything in one day and that he and the Recorder would return later. "Let me make it clear," he said, "that there's no danger whatsoever, no social danger at all."

"No! I understand what sort of person he is."

"These are affairs that. Clearly. Miguel is making a computation of the anterior life of the country, maximally of the Negroes, . . . what sort of treatment they received from their masters in the epoch of slavery, if your father or grandparents were slaves . . . "

"Exactly," affirmed Tomás. "He's an investigator. Precisely. For instance, you can't lie to an investigator. You have to say the truth."

IN ACCORD WITH WHAT IS WRITTEN

According to the fieldnotes supplied by the Director, the Recorder returned thereafter on his own many times and tape-recorded his conversations with don Tomás, questioning him about slavery and abolition. The Recorder seems to have assumed a chain of oral tradition to which the old man was privy. The recording would thus be a continuation, a plumbline of magnetic tape hurled into the abyss of history, then hauled in, wet with the sticky weight of dripping speech. Had not don Tomás himself said that what the Recorder was doing was recovering "the tradition of the ancients," just like in the times before books like the sacred Scripture came into being?

But don Tomás would always confound this expectation by stating he was working from the book. It was the ultimate double bind; the authority of the oral tradition privileging the authority of the text. In the beginning was the word, maybe. But here it was endorsing sacred script(ure).

"I'll tell you according to what's written," he would say. "I'm going to tell you what I understand in accord with what's written. After the war of Independence they got together and made themselves owners of the land, but during the war they had to fight and they fought united, the three parties fought united–Conservative, Liberal, and the priests—against the Spanish. But once they'd achieved victory they left the poor in the cold, and the land was partitioned amongst the heavyweights, the rich. They partitioned it amongst the rich Conservatives, the rich Liberals, and the rich priests. And the poor? The poor they abandoned! Nothing! Thus the poor began to rebel and join with someone called José Hilario Lopez and when the rich got wind of the fact that the poor were after land, then they imposed politics—*la política*—so there would be no unity between the poor. Thus came politics and thus came hatred of the one against the other so that nobody ever got any land!"

"After Independence there arose a man called, whom I have studied. Are you listening?"

"Yes."

"To support José Hilario Lopez and the rights of the poor."

"Without land?"

"Sí, señor. There arose Napoleon Bonaparte. This man fought the good fight."

"Here in Colombia?" asked the Recorder.

"Yes. He fought good."

"Here?"

"Yes."

"Or in Europe?"

"Here in Colombia. At that time there existed the Concordat. The Concordat consists in that the priest has the same power as the mayor, and thus the law of the church had more power than civil law and had many people placed in the Inquisitions. And Napoleon Bonaparte succeeded—this was in Spain—succeeded [in] destroying one of these prison houses. In these houses they had a Virgin together with the judges. They would take everything a person owned and the person would wither away because these prisons were underground. They would order you to kiss the Virgin and as you stepped out towards her along a pavement so she moved and opened her eyes, and when you went to kiss her she opened her arms and you were cut to pieces that fell to the ground because they were knives. So when Napoleon triumphed he made those judges go and kiss the Virgin. They screamed they couldn't go, but he forced them, and then he placed a stick of dynamite and blew up that house of Inquisition because Napoleon was fighting to destroy the Concordat. Concordat comes from concordance, two different people agreeing on a single thing. But he was not able, although he diminished it greatly. You can't destroy it because it's so well put together . . . "

We chuckled over this astute but geographically disorienting history of Napoleon as we sat in the mottled light drifting through the unwashed windows of the Prague archive. But we felt a little uncomfortable, wondering if maybe the laugh was not on us, that we who were sitting in judgment were, in that laughter, having our own bases of judgment judged.

Don Tomás's was a life-world in which the art of storytelling was very much alive, while at the same time the written text was accorded great prestige. Could it be that his ability to evoke the past, condensing it into brilliant and eccentric image fragments of commentary and counsel, was predicated on just this overlap of storytellers and books?

POET OR HISTORIAN?

The strangest thing of all was the old man's disposition to answer questions about the past by reciting verse. So natural was this, so in keeping with the old man's formal mode of address, that the Recorder at first failed to realize that he was being answered in verse. The tape on which we first picked this up began typically enough with the Recorder's persistent questions about land tenure and marriage after the abolition of slavery. "Free unions were more common than marriage," don Tomás was saying. "But then came the war."

"What war?"

"The War of One Thousand Days [1899–1901]. After the war was over it was said that men were scarce and that therefore anybody living in a free union had [by orders of President Reyes] to get married.

> Están los enamorados muy enojados con Reyes
> que con sus rígidas leyes
> los obliga a ser casados
> si no arreglan su conciencia de aquí a fins de mayo,
> sean liberales o godos los manda pal Putumayo.

> Lovers all over are mad at Reyes
> who, with his Draconian measures
> forces them into marriage
> If their conscience is not in order by the end of May, Oh!
> Whether Liberals or Goths, they'll be shipped off to the Putumayo.

"Si, señor. The Putumayo was a jungle. It was serious. Anyone who resisted marriage got sent to the Putumayo."

It was snowing in Prague. The archive was miserably cold. We tried to imagine don Tomás and the Recorder sitting there in the heat of that dusty plantation town with its open sewers, the old man tremulous, the Recorder anxiously awaiting the response to his next question.

"Tomás, do you remember well what happened the ninth of April?"

It must have been don Tomás's talking about the War of One Thousand Days that made the Recorder ask this, because the ninth of April (1948) is code for the notorious *Violencia* that began at noon of that memorable day with the assassination of the populist, Liberal party leader, Jorgé Eliécer Gaitain. To speak of *La Violencia* in middle- and upper-class Colombia or Latin America is somewhat like raising the specter of Auschwitz or Hiroshima in the sense that for a brief moment someone draws the curtain on something unspeakably violent and evil, then draws the curtain closed again, not knowing what to say. Peasants from the two political parties, more like religious war machines, the Liberal party and the Conservative party, were pitted against each other for over a decade (the time span varies, and one could say the *Violencia* never stopped) in acts of grotesque violence highlighting the mutilated body and resulting in some 200,000 deaths over an eight-year period (in a total national population of around nine million). The Conservative party held control of the state, the army, and the police.

Don Tomás curtly answered, "Sí, señor!"

"Can you tell me about it?"
"Sí, señor." And once again the response was verse.[4]

Blessed God, what is to be done about Zambrano's government
We are already like two beasts, brother killing brother
Since Zambrano came, the town began to shiver and to shake
They stripped us ripe for the plucking, not even a needle remained
Defenseless, because on the ninth of April, the knives had marched off
    behind the gun
Oh My! What a problematic time for the black folk!
With a gun at the door; "Hands up you fuckers!
Cowards. Your courage flees, you don't dare to fight
Screw the damn blacks, and the Liberal party too
Long live Doctor Laureano Gómez
Elected president of Colombia
We are going to wipe you out; even your shadow."
Strutting in tranquility, the *chulavitas*[5] took over with the Military Police
Breaking doors and signs, whooping their battle cries
When they bumped into people on the street
With the flat of the machete they tenderized them, just short of killing,
To don Anselmo Cetro, it happened; at five in the morning on his way to
    work they got him good
To Dionisio Mercado—to disarm him of his machete,
    they shot and left him; mouth shut tight, body fried
To don Manuel Pizarro it happened that the MPs took his 400 pesos
When the man saw himself lost he went directly to the town mayor
    [Zambrano], and the mayor said to him:
"Get out of here you bum before I have you shot!"
When the man understood he'd lost his entire economy,
All he could do was repeat "God Bless the Virgin Mary."
To Felix María Acosta, the MPs paid a visit
And the money in his trunk disappeared in an instant
One night they set off so joyous in their lorry,
But it got stuck at the corner and so they went to worry
The daughters of Evaristo Ospina. But since at first this didn't work out
They rolled down the ditch to relax at Josefa's, that bitchy bitch
Raving like madmen
They got those daughters, filling their mouths with shit
Saying to each other, "Oh! We'll be bringing back the dough!"
But it didn't work out that way, cos' on seeing the soldiers in droves
Them cute little blacks slipped wraithlike into their cocoa groves,
    wandering, massing, wandering
Until they got to the road
Where the jeep, 'cos of a ditch, disgorged its passengers
"And now those blacks are firing on me like I'm a wounded bear
Run! Run! Compañeros! This black fella's gonna kill me
Leap. Flying into the jeep. Oh! The pain!

Already I've been shot. Look here at the wound!
If we don't get outa here real quick, the game is up."
So the pale heroes come back to Puerto Tejada
At the hands of the sweet black folk, how many came wounded!
I've got to tell you Zambrano, Ol' buddy o' mine
Never, never, can I go off with you again
Because brought from afar, life's just too fine.
"You come right along, but not with any ambassadors
If you try to be brave, we'll kick you along."
And off he went propelled by the flat of the machete
To be dumped with rifle butts inside the jail.
"You've got to pay two thousand pesos to get yourself free
And if you don't, you'll go to eternity!"
And so, to free him of his doleful song
From this poor citizen too, they got their due
And, speaking with valor, Zambrano came up with an idea.
"I'm going to Villa Rica with all my means of State."

So Spoke the Means of State

If you go to Villa Rica then we'll come, Sire,
And if those blacks try anything, we'll finish them with fire
Into their jeep they clambered and off to Villa Rica
To Manuel Bedoya's they came by saying,
"A thief got in here and we're after him."
On hearing these words, Bedoya replied,
"Nobody has come. I'm the only one who dwells within."
"Don't deny that a gangster's inside
If you don't let us in, then we'll spray you by God!"
"I won't open my door 'cos this store's mine
Whosoever touches my door I'll gut with lead."
After many shots, well, they got what they wanted
Cos' Bedoya was all alone and they numbered forty
They subdued him, made him prisoner, and took him to Zambrano.
"You have to pay me two thousand
And if not, then right here we'll kill you." So to set himself free
He put his hand to his pocket. "Here! Take it, and don't make such a fuss."
Then they were on their way to Jesús Giraldo's
"We've come for two friends, on account of don Zambrano."
"Why are you taking me away if I've got no debts?
I'm here in my agency awaiting my people."
Now surely they will kill me 'cos I always tell the truth
Because my pen keeps writing even when I stop to think of proof
And if, through my writing, enemies come aswarming
I feel fortified; and not only on account of this warning
By the way, I must inform you, I never had a teacher
Yet just as the tiger is known because of its stripes,

So you get to know a person by the shapes their writing takes,
Here stop the verses written by my hand [*mano*]
Thus came and went the government of Marco Polo Zambrano

He stopped here. Only later, after hearing different tapes, did we realize that this poem goes on and on. There is a cycle of verse for each of the military mayors imposed on the town at that time. The poem could end with any one of them. The poem is endless. The poem is epic. This happened, then that happened, and it could have happened differently.

But it is very much a lyric poem, too, not in the sense of the emboldened "I" passionately enthused with revelation of selfness but in the sense of music in the verbal line. And we are crestfallen at the size and shape of our failure, at our inability to render either the rhyme or the rhythm in the English language. The pain of the failure goes further than this inability to translate the music per se, because it is the conjunction of the music with the verbal sense, the combinatory effect of the world of music with the world of the image (as *The Birth of Tragedy* would have it), that is jeopardized—and not just the music alone. The intelligence and skill of the poet cannot survive our translation, and this sober reckoning surely makes us pay keener attention to the task of the anthropologist in the figure of the Recorder. Poor soul, doomed to failure in a practice given over to the contrast of difference, desperate for a language of mediation.

As the weeks went by, the old man increasingly responded in verse to the Recorder's questions about the past. From questions *about the past* to *speaking of the past* to *speaking the past* is but a series of fine lines, yet how different the end point is compared with the beginning. While *questions about the past* smacks of interrogation, of the past as much as of an informant, and rather magically assumes the necessity no less than the capacity for distancing the subject from the object of inquiry, hence the existence of an objectified knowing, *speaking the past* detours amiably around these wishful assumptions. It was poetry, for some reason, that provided just this epistemological ease, and once loosed, it flooded. There were so many poems! Poems for Mother, for the wife who had just died, poems about land disputes in the 1930s.

Tengan presente señores lo que les voy a contar.
Los enemigos de los pobres no les deben olvidar.
El asunto es bastante grave que mucho lo admiraran
Los amigos de don Lisandro, te le digo consejero
Este tierra la compró Manuel María Carbonero
Deseaba don Lisandro de este tierra posesión
Y le dijo al juez Ernesto Pino, apenitas media acción.

Listen hard my friends, to what I'm about to recite.
The enemies of the poor, you must never put out of sight.

The case is a serious one of interest to many people,
Not least the friends of don Lisandro, who will later says it's feeble.

And so it continues with precise accounting of boundary lines, names of
judges, defendants, plaintiffs, witnesses, each speaking in his own voice. The
poet sets scenes, to such an extent that the poem appears like a dramatic
script moving from the courts to the land to prison, encompassing the cor-
ruption of the state-legal apparatus.

"Seeing as you've brought the tape recorder," said don Tomás, "I'd like
to recite a history, a Farewell by Doctor Laureano Gómez [Conservative
party president of Colombia, expelled to Spain because of the nature of his
involvement in La Violencia]. I'm going to recite this composition so that
we might understand that not everything written is certain. In studying universal history I came across a guy saying that this or that part had been corrected, . . . that he had to correct this and that because it was badly put. He
said that over the long haul history is subject to the conflict of writing." He
paused. "I never knew Doctor Laureano Gómez personally," he continued.
"I knew him from his picture."

He then recited his Farewell, *Adiós Colombia, The Benighted,* which
recorded the history of the expulsion of the deposed leader, the rise of Ospina Pérez, the coup led by General Rojas Pinilla, and the implications of
this coup for restrengthening the Liberal party. Each famous personage
would speak in his own voice. The ending was ominous, Laureano Gómez
declaiming, "Well, now I leave Colombia, but I have to come back, I'll return as president so as to occupy power forever." But this poem was immediately followed by "The Death of the Conservative Party," which works
around the image of the burial of a corpse, the corpse of the party, offici-
ated by mocked figures of leading party politicians carrying out their ritual
duties. "Yes it's dead, the Conservative party, and now its being buried / And
those who read these verses must never, never, forget / . . ." is how this
poem begins and ends with the announcement of the birth, from death, of
a baby—the newly invigorated Liberal party.

El niño está muy hermoso, se parece una maravilla
El Liberalismo nació en manos de Rojas Pinilla
Estos versos así escritos son de un humilde poeta El niño del Liberalismo
     estuvo mamando teta.

There was a lot of laughter when he thus finished, the Liberal poet
poking fun at Liberalismo and at himself, too, resurrecting new life from
the death of the enemy, yet avoiding histrionics.

Asked by the Recorder the meaning of P.M. in this poem, don Tomás
replied, "The Police, the military police," and without pause continued with
another of his verses, not about the police but, in mock serious terms, bib-

lical and colloquial, on the wrongness of stealing, the exposure of the poor
to theft, the necessity for the poor of all races to unite, and the power for
justice that he, don Tomás Zapata, a black man, packs with his poetic pen.

Señores hay que respetar lo ajeno, y mirarlo con prudencia
Porque si la autoridad se da cuenta, quedaremos en verguenza
Si pensamos no robar, es un noble pensamiento
pues, robando se quebranta el septimo mandamiento.
Si piensas que esto es mentira y en lo que te digo miento,
Andate directamente al Antiguo Testamento.

and so it goes, till the end

Muchos se distinguen porque mi pluma aquí se asome
Y quieren saber mi nombre, soy Thomás Zapata Gómez.
El que se encuentre capaz que contrarrestar mi pluma
Lo que entiendo no es postizo, esto lo heredo de cuña.
No conozco ni una escuela, tampoco Universidad
Y el que a dudar lo tuviere mi pluma contestara.
Que unos nacemos donados del cuarto don que es de ciencia
Que a donde hay entendimiento de mucho vale nobleza,
¡Señores! No estamos en los tiempos bárbaros en que la ignorancia se cruce
Estamos en el siglo veinte que es el siglo de las luces
La verdad yo se la digo aún cuando seas más bonito
Apenas quedaran diciendo ve que diablo este negrito
Pues si hubieramos sabido que ese demonio escribía
No hubieramos cometido semejantes picardías.
Siempre vemos en Colombia hartos hombres sin conciencia,
Que roban a donde pueden, digo esto con experiencia.
Unamonos pués los pobres sin distingos de colores,
A ver si así nos libramos hoy de tantos salteadores.
Los salteadores de hoy día por todas partes se cruzan
Buscando el lado al pobre porque a este siempre le hurtan.

Tomás Zapata Gomez.

The Director, an admirer of Bertolt Brecht, liked this verse. He pulled
out a copy of John Willett's *Brecht in Context* and began to read from an essay showing the influence Kipling had had on Brecht. Both poets were
steeped in the language of the Bible and the hymn book, notes Willett, by
Horace and other Latin poets. Both "were basically unliterary" in a way that
other "socialist" poets such as Aragon, Becher, and Neruda were not, with a
respect, writes Willett, for the direction of a person's actions rather than the
quality of his or her feelings. Intended for action, the work of both poets is
marked by its "popular forms, clear language, rough rhythms, and 'gestic'
or syncopated linebreaks."[6]

The Director continued reading where Willett quotes Kipling.

But it will take a more mighty intellect to write the Songs of the People. Some day a man will rise up from Bermondsey or Bow and he will be coarse but clear-sighted, hard but infinitely and tenderly humorous, speaking the people's tongue, steeped in their lives and telling them in swinging, urging, dinging verse what it is that their inarticulate lips would express. He will make them songs. Such songs! And all the little poets who pretend to sing to the people will scuttle away like rabbits.[7]

And Willett sees this as a prescription close to Brecht's later aims.

But as the Director pointed out, in his spoilsport way, don Tomás would never compose a poem like Kipling's "When 'Omer smote his bloomin lyre" because that would be disrespectful of Homer and the ancients. It would take a poet from the educated classes to put that into the mouth of the uneducated Poet of the People. What Brecht and Kipling found in "ordinary speech" was a language they in part invented, a vigorous Creole language mediating class mixture that could be turned against the quite different pretensions of literary languages.

THE VOICE OF THE PEOPLE

Coming from an as yet unexamined intellectual and poetic location on the poverty-stricken margins of burgeoning agribusiness, these verses invite us to do more than identify them as the soul of the people or the true voice of America. Indeed, the constant process of what the Recorder called "flow and mix, flow and swerve," juxtaposing the often labyrinthine complexities of local history with authors canonical to the Western tradition, such as Plato and Pythagoras, and mythological figures, such as Leda and Zeus, should be sufficient to check such knee-jerk responses like nostalgia and authenticity projected onto "the Latin American peasant," "the descendants of the African slaves," and so forth. Far from reflecting a continuous tradition or even creating one, mix and swerve suggests an art of interruptions, of cultural and temporal montage.

We would like to somehow get around the seductive power of nostalgia and authenticity, not by denying their power or ruling them out by fiat but by speculating on our need for them and why they should be so intimately part of our being in the world. We would like to point out that this voice of don Tomás Zapata is a very powerful contribution to the construction of America precisely because, being of "the people," it is also a reworking of the Western canon that it holds in great esteem and on which it is so dependent—in its own way. Not least noteworthy in this reworking is a stress, at once dignified and ironic, heartfelt yet mischievous, on the need of the poor to organize against the classes that are supposed to identify most closely with that very canon and be its living embodiment into the future. (Not for nothing was Bogotá called "the Athens of America.")

Yet at the same time there are significant parallels, perhaps complicities, between this economically poor Colombian peasant, descendant of slaves from Africa, and the Western canon. Apart from his obvious respect for the ancient philosophers and Greek mythology, and so forth, and the enjoyment his understanding of them affords him, there is the fact that his personal style—his dignity and measured tone, his confidence and directness—has an aristocratic, nonauthoritarian, resonance, the sort of character we might mean when we talk of nobility of character, humble yet assured, down to earth and direct yet more concerned with ends than with utility—what Georges Bataille philosophizes as "sovereignty" as opposed to mastery.[8] Perhaps, then, this can be usefully rephrased: the old man uses an aristocratic style associated with the learned elite of yesteryear, so as to critique the elite and the system of laws and property on which it rests.

When we see the nature of the impact that commercialized mass culture now exerts in Latin America, no less than in the so-called developed world, to the extent that extraordinarily violent and sexist Hollywood film is routinely shown to captive yet generally eager audiences via video monitors in interurban buses, and to the extent that the heavy metal music subculture defines the ideals of young men in the drug-saturated and homicidal barrios of Medellín, (somewhat misnamed) the cocaine capital of the world—then we can gauge the degree to which don Tomás's way of thinking, style of being, clothing, forms of address, bearing and body movement, has not only been left long behind but to what degree it might seem to share far more with the culture of the elite of yesteryear than with the poor, both rural and urban, of today.

But there is more to it than this, for what the old man speaks from is not so much an elite culture that he imitates but a peasant culture of great formality and measured, rhythmical speech in which persons are acutely sensitive to inequality of moral standing and to slights of honor. The moral world in don Tomás Zapata's verses is this world of great formality and sensitivity with respect to the person. It is an ideal that lived in speech, especially the speech of address of the person, which is what the poet strives for as the implicit power carrying the line. It is no less aristocratic than it is statist, no less aristocratic than it is popular. And in some ways its time is now gone, even though the memory may be strong as carried in the form.

THE VOICE OF THE PAST

We were struck by the old man's ability to remember his verses that could go on for maybe twenty minutes at a time. Because the Recorder's notes indicate that what we might call collective memory in this town was of a very short span indeed, we wondered, and we found the Director of the Prague archive to be wondering also, whether in fact history would be kept alive without these epics—assuming that the poet had some sort of real audience. Otherwise people seemed to live immersed in the present, a fact that never ceased to surprise the Recorder who had naively assumed, first of all, that history was a necessary and positive value, and second, that a "peasant village" in Latin America—shades of one hundred years of solitude—being "of the past" would hence have a high degree of consciousness of the past. We could sense the shock in his later notes when we came across the huge scrawl in his notes covering an entire page–*from Nietzsche, "life in any true sense is impossible without forgetfulness."*[9]

We wondered if the old man frequently recited his poems or whether he was isolated and lost until fate brought him and the Recorder together? We began to suspect that were it not for the Recorder coming to town, the poet could well have remained silent in his last year of life, politely ignored by his neighbors as an eccentric talent to be taken for granted. What a sight that must have been, the two lonely historians face to face in the sun-drenched, cement-covered patio with old burlap bags and the excreta of chickens, the old black blind man, a year before his death, and the young white "Englishman" with his tape recorder. Was the old man, then, living in some sort of time warp, alone with his verses rattling inside his head?

In this vein we also wondered, after consultation with the Director, whether the Recorder and the poet jointly created a sort of "playground"— "between illness and real life," as Freud referred to the transference scenario in his 1914 paper, "Remembering, Repeating and Working Through," a playground in which repetition is allowed to expand in almost complete freedom such that remembering can eventually take the place of repeating.

What we were rather taken aback by was the thought that the poet and the Recorder had *jointly* created something special, an intercultural transference space made out of poetry as a playground of memory and language, bound to the repetition of formal rhyme and meter. It was our hunch that in its very repetition and character as ritual, the poetry provided a type of repetition that, instead of blocking, facilitated a type of remembrance.

Far from being a neurotic repetition due to resistances that could be exposed through the transference space, and far from being the practice of an analyst listening to a madman, this "playground" was a two-way street with two analysts or two madmen, simultaneously existent or switching off, whichever way you care to take it, creating a transference space not so much of two individuals as of world histories brought into a serendipitous overlap for a certain, small period of time. Surfacing in this intercultural space provided by the accident of the Recorder's arrival, it was the very repetition of the poetry, its aesthetic of repetition, that provided the constant that is one way of trying to live with, if not temporarily outwit, the nervousness of the cultured being that is the nervous system of violence, upheaval, and phantasmagoria of twentieth-century Colombian rural existence.

BLINDNESS AND WRITING

We could not stop thinking of the poet's blindness, apparently caused by cataracts late in life. Perversely romantic as it may seem, we wondered whether blindness in some way magnified either his powers of memory or his need to remember, plunging him into an interior world of the past, remembrance becoming a sort of hypertrophied sensory or emotional tool compensating for the atrophy of sight. We started to realize, however, that instead of emphasizing the vision turned inward, the more important issue was the need and the means for expression of that thwarted vision—hence the poems, the objects of and for recollection.

What concerned the Recorder in this regard, if we are interpreting his notes correctly, was the confusion set up in his own mind by the poet's continual emphasis on writing and reading. Here he was, a virtual epitome of the "oral tradition," reciting poem after poem, yet it was writing—his own writing—and books—history books and the Bible—that he underlined as the source of inspiration and legitimation. "*Según las letras . . .* " (According to the printed word . . .) is how he would begin, not to mention frequent references to the weight of his pen and how he had no option but to keep on writing, and so forth.

It is surprising that the Recorder never seems to have recorded whether the old man did indeed write down his verses. But we do know that the old man had learned to read, although he never spent a day in school. We wondered if he had ever come across those amazing newspapers that the Recorder had found in the National Library of Colombia, in Bogotá. Dated 1916 (when Tomás Zapata was 26 years old), both newspapers claim to be of Puerto Tejada. There was the *Cinta Blanca* (White Ribbon), "fortnightly organ of general interest," and what looks like its opposition, *El Latigo* (The Whip), "epidemic publication, not familiarized with the endemic of the nation, arriving when you spy it." This in 1916, when the population of the town could hardly have been more than 2,000 adults, with difficult communication to the city of Cali, no roadway, most goods moved by bamboo rafts, and a large degree of illiteracy.[10] What is even more astonishing than the fact that two newspapers could be published in the town at that time—making us revise all our preconceptions of the development of print and culture in the Latin American countryside—are the covers of *El Latigo,* stark woodcuts diplaying virulently anticlerical and politically radical cartoons, underlain by rhyming verse!

As a child, don Tomás had badly wanted to read. He told the Recorder how one day he had asked his stepfather for three *reals* to buy a book, but his stepfather whipped him instead, saying reading was for girls. He then secretly saved the money and went to the weekly market in Santander and found a man selling books.

Tú eres mi vida, oh muerto!
Sin tí qué fuera de mi suerte?
Contigo negocio en toda parte
Con lo craso, lo imbécil e ignorante.

En la plaza de mercado
un burro de hábito y cruz,
con santidad e indignado,
a un niño obsequió una coz;
porque voceaba *El Perrero*;
El Perrero, si señor

Pero es el caso, lector,
que cuando el burro talar
atacaba al voceador,
de manera singular,
agótese la edición,
del *Látigo*, si señor.

" 'Have you got the book Mantillo, Number One?' I asked."

"Yes."

"How much?"

"Three *reals*."

"Sell me one and teach me the first lesson."

"I gave him the three *reals* and he gave me the book and he taught me the ABC for the first time in my life, then a second time, then a third time, then a fourth time, and then he left me there and wandered away selling his stuff. So I struggled and when I forgot a letter I would go back to the marketplace and he would teach me that letter."

We could not but be reminded of this feat when we came across the old man's poem that we found toward the end of a tape marked "January 1970." It is what he called "A composition I made for a young girl going for the first time to school":

Adiós querida niña, te alejas de este hogar
Mañana cuando partas, no vayas a llorar
Te espera un neuvo ambiente, la puerta del saber
Que elevera tu alma a un más alto nivel
Y tu hermanita Adela se queda sin consuelo
Que por tí pide bendiciones al Santo Dios del Cielo
Mañana cuando vuelvas a este querido hogar
Trayendo la semilla que ya debes sembrar
Pues tú hermanita Adela te ha de acompañar
Por llanos y montañas que han de trabajar
Jesucristo fué maestro en las tribus de Juda
Y el que tenga vocación, esto debe sembrar.

Farewell dear child, leaving home
Tomorrow when you go, don't cry
For there's a new world awaiting through the gates of knowledge
And while your soul will be uplifted
Your little sister Adela remains without comfort
Asking benediction for you from the Lord above
Tomorrow when you return to this dear home
Bringing with you the seed you need to sow
Your sister, Adela, will be there to help you
Through the valleys and mountains that have to be worked
Jesus Christ was teacher among the tribes of Judah
Whoever has the vocation, this is what has to be sown.

More than a gift, such a rhetorical gem stands ritually like a talisman, signaling and offering warranty of safety through a rite of passage. With its promise of education, the school elevates the soul. Such a generous view of the ideal of formal education is only likely to come, we are tempted to say, from a person who had never been to school, and surely it is a view deeply shared by Colombia's peasant farmers whose respect for the local school is boundless. More than that, we wondered if the poet's attitude toward the world of letters and poetic forms was the result of just this misrecognition, just this generosity and idealism.

PEASANT FARMING AND EPIC POETRY

Indeed, might not his position as a reader who never went to school, a peasant farmer with one foot in the market economy and the other foot in subsistence, might not this marginality vis-à-vis formal institutions of state, economy, and culture be the "structural condition" of his mix and swerve, flow and mix, of high culture and popular culture? Might not this marginality with respect to the state and the market, this marginality trembling with contradiction and ambivalence, with its own mix of pain and desire, blindness and insight, be precisely the spiritual source of the epic, a poetic form bearing witness to the lived effects of formalization—of the rationalization of the mind, of the body, of social and economic life? Perforce the poetry that fills this conflictual locus will also bear the brand of law, the state's mighty instrument of formalization, as we see clearly in Tomás Zapata's output with its endless civil suits over jurisdiction of land, police who take the law into their own hands, town mayors who resort to violence, and presidents who make laws to force marriage instead of free unions. Certainly we can read the *Odyssey*, as Robert Fitzgerald so pithily describes it, as "about a man who cared for his wife and wanted to rejoin her."[11] But we can read it in a more historically pungent way embedded in philosophical problems of representation and the mythological basis of modern reason. We can see it as the pre-Socratic ur-tale of mimetic forms of knowing succumbing to the impersonality of capital and the modern state, the epic rendition of how yielding to the particulate sensuousness of worldly detail through imitation is turned against itself in the vast story of worldly progress known as the domination of nature (and no doubt this vast story is still Fitzgerald's story of a man who cared for his wife and wants to rejoin her). This is how Horkheimer and Adorno read Homer in their *Dialectic of Enlightenment,* a book of special interest for peasant poetry if we care to define the poetic as that art of mimetic signification that delights in taking relations of sound and sense, nature and culture, to their outermost limits where signs hover in the fragility and power of artifice exposed. And if poetry is that signifying practice that thus exposes or has the potential to expose signifying practice, is it not a form of sympathetic magic, too, of like affecting like, of contagion along the sympathetic chain where ideas become forceful presence using correspondences to outwit and even dominate reality? Frazer of *The Golden Bough* sees magic in this way, and Benjamin scrutinizes Baudelaire's poetry with this very much in mind, too, concluding that the correspondences are scored in that poet's work as an attempt to preserve experience in a crisis-proof form, but that nevertheless the poetry is formed by a ready acceptance of failure, in the face of the shock force of modernity, to maintain this crisis-proofing.[12] With particular poignancy these observations touch on the issue of peasant memory and the forward march of machine- and chemical-based agribusiness in Latin America.

HISTORY AS EPIC

We find these verses entertaining, unusual, and significant as epic poetry. But we do not want to analyze them formally, in themselves, so to speak, for their formulas of construction, as the Homeric epic and poetry in general has been so long subjected—as if "form" was some sort of trick of meter and

rhyme facilitating the reach of memory, as if it is our task to find their secret.[13] Nevertheless, we do consider questions of form to be essential insofar as they apply to our own forms of expression—how we work word and
image pertaining to the past, no less than how we right here and now in this
text unfolding work word and image into a hybridinal text laminating,
swerving, jumping, and mixing the epic poet from over there and back then
with the textual streams possible for over here right now. If form was a
mnemonic device for the epic poet, then how much more has form of a
quite different sort become for creating the naturalistic illusion of the real
on the part of our modern historians! And how urgent this becomes for historiography; how urgently the poet's verse and commentary perturb our his-
toriographic confidence. By opening up the range of possibilities for doing
history, these verses threaten us with unnameable dangers. By the same token, they excite us.

If the historian gains power by standing apart, this epic poet gains power
from embodiment within—an embodiment that, precisely because it is *poetic* and hence self-consciously performative, precisely because it lies so close
to the fault lines of language and the evocative power of speech, turns out
to be a mobile location within and outside of time. We also see how this creates a curious reverse movement; by laying claim to a profound kinship with
a particular moment to which it gives voice, the verse is able to stand apart
from that moment and erode its momentousness.

We can safely assume that for *professional historians*—a somewhat telling,
even ominous appellation—these verses would be dismissed as history, in
the sense of historiography, and would be cautiously embraced as history in
the sense of raw material from the past that the modern historian has a license to store and analyze, plunder and appropriate for the "telling detail,"
the "voice of the past," the "authenticating seal." Yet in categorizing it as
booty (also known as "data"), surely the professional historian is desperately
trying to deny the way such verse defamiliarizes the historian's task and so
has to be classified as art, not science. Nietzsche's words come to mind here
where he addresses the curious cultural power that flows toward those
whose job it is to judge the past. In *The Use and Abuse of History*, he writes, "As
judges you must stand higher than that which is to be judged; as it is you
have only come later."[14] He goes on to say, "The guests that come last to the
table should rightly take the last places; and will you take the first? Then do
some great and mighty deed—the place may be prepared for you then, even
though you do come last."[15] Speaking of great deeds, what fun it would be
if our historians were quick witted enough, were brave enough and adept
with language and image, so that they, too, instead of perfecting the culturally contrived performance of objectivity, could sing us their verses—
verses that gambol with truth's pretensions and the illusions of sobriety
wrought by the endless duplicity of language.

With reference to the great historians of the nineteenth century, and by implication all attempts to write histories, Hayden White says that the status of their works "as models of historical narration and conceptualization depends, ultimately, on the preconceptual and specifically poetic nature of their perspectives."[16] Given the profound resistance to this view, we think it necessary once again to examine historiography as poetry, both in White's capacious yet precisely formulated sense of the poetic as an aesthetic infrastructure of the historical text and in the apparently more literal sense of historiography written or spoken in poetic form like that of don Tomás. Can we really say his verses are equivalent to writing a history?

For the Director of the archive, Tomás Zapata's poetry was not merely aesthetic embellishment—art beautifying reality—but was another way of archiving the past. He was particularly struck by the way don Tomás would spontaneously respond *in verse* to questions about the past meant to elicit *facts*, for instance, questions about marriage customs, the development of private property in land, the *Violencia*. It is of added interest that this spontaneously erupting versifying response to questions intended to elicit historical facts was a response to an outsider, a stranger—an *investigator*, as he was at one point called—and that this encounter was seen by don Tomás as compelling truth-saying in a mighty, almost cosmic, transition of the status of historical knowledge from a private to the public world—akin to Columbus's "discovery" of America. Can we assert that repetition—of the verses as much as the history they put into words—acquired a qualitatively new status, from the private to the public world, thanks to the encounter of the two different types of historian, the investigator and the versifier, the one who searched for an informant and the other who searched for an audience?

This puts Benjamin's storyteller in a different and, we feel, more comprehensive light than his own essay, which isolates the encounter between two individuals sharing more or less the same class and culture position such that any difference in experience nevertheless still presupposes both the ability to exchange experience and a wide range of common cultural reckoning. Such would be the case, for instance, of the encounter between the peasant who rarely left the region and the artisan or servant returning to the village after years in the cities. But equally important to modern world history, if not as frequent, is the encounter between strikingly different narrators—like the poet and the Recorder—different on just about any criterion you care to select; economic class, urban/rural, skin color, generation, education, diet, body build, understanding of labor, of gossip, of sorcery. When the Grimm brothers published their stories, for instance, they created in effect a mediation between bourgeois and peasant, a mediation that effectively purified the peasant as a type on whose back all sorts of lofty universals could be packed. Likewise, when Benjamin writes on the art of the storyteller, he, in fact (and this seems never to have been pointed out), writes of a premodern, peasant and artisan, form, as worked in the texture of the published work not of a peasant or an artisan but of Nikolai Leskov, a writer and commercial traveler—in other words, a salesman. The art of the storyteller then transpires as Leskov's voice partly imitating and partly mediating the world of the Russian artisan and peasant.

This mediation between bourgeois and peasant has of course been crucial to the stories that anthropologists have built all their work on since E. B. Tyler published his *Primitive Culture* in 1872, if only because in the field (that sonorous phrase) it is always by means of stories (occasionally termed "cases") that "information," whether on "kinship" or on "mythology" or "economics," or whatever, is in fact transmitted to Columbus, the Investigator, the Recorder, whose job it is to further mediate to the bourgeois reader. More could be said about this mediating function crucial to modernity because it has been precisely the role of the peasant and the primitive to endorse the ur-nature nurturing not only narrativity but modernity's sense of literality—the experiential notion that makes metaphor effective. Modernity's peasant, like modernity's primitive, functions to bring the ancients into the realm of the living no less than the body into the realm of the mind. Language itself rests on this otherwise transparent yet necessary fiction of a bodily link between sign and referent, a link established by the history of class forms in the world historical movement from country to city.

LIVING THROUGH, LOOKING BACK

We kept coming back to one feature, which at first seemed merely technical and rather unimportant but which later assumed dense complexity. This was the fact that the chronicler, as in don Tomás's case, tends to be recording what is going on at the time of the recording or shortly thereafter, while the recorder-as-historian, through the salvage operation stimulating the aged body of the eyewitness, don Tomás Zapata, is recording the past in all its living pastness. And even when the chronicler such as don Tomás is recording what happened many years before, it will be based on an eyewitness account or something approaching such an account set in a lived present.

But as time goes by, as the chronicler ages or dies, this record of the lived present ages, too. It slips over the weir of the present into the stream of time to become history. It passes into history as datum and at the same time becomes a history. This is more than a confusion of words—history as the past, history as the record of the past—because it is precisely as confusion that it exercises a special quality of force speaking from within as well as outside events, speaking as expression and as commentary.

This quality of the present passing into history bestows on the chronicle—and its associated form, the epic—the potential to achieve what Freud singled out as the key feature of memory in psychoanalysis. Commenting on the implications of repetition among people suffering from traumatic neuroses and shock, Freud wrote in 1921, much as he had written about hysteria with Josef Breuer at the beginning of his career in 1893, that the analyst must get the patient to "re-experience some portion of his forgotten life, but must see to it, on the other hand, that the patient retains some degree of aloofness, which will enable him, in spite of everything, to recognize that what happens to be reality is in fact only a reflection of a forgotten past."[17] What we wish here to emphasize is the double action of being part of and being distant from, of being immersed in an experiential reality and being outside that experience. We might say that the quality of pastness in the past has to be registered in the very repetition, no less than the acute, experiential presence of the memory experienced as actual. Repetition can be a sign of resistance to the emergence of memory. But in certain social situations and for certain groups in certain epochs, it could also be a technique for archiving the past.

Indeed, repetition became for Freud in his later writing more than a sign of repression. More than a sign, it was an end in itself, a profound compulsion beyond the pleasure principle, a predisposition to death and suffusion of mind and soul in the inorganic crust of time where there is no history, at least not human history. In people suffering from shock after a terrible fright, repetition took the form of recurring nightmares perhaps, suggested Freud, to create the anxiety that was lacking at the time of the fright—it being his argument that anxiety acted as a stimulus shield preventing fright from creating shock, that is, from imploding the psyche and causing collapse of mental and physical structure. The curious thing for our discussion of the meaning of history is that this stimulus shield—the mark of modernity—is made up of a consciousness so prone to rapid processing of stimuli that it undermines both memory itself and the ability to experience (*Efahrung*, which includes the ability to be changed by experience).

This makes us wonder about the function of repetition in poetry, understanding poetry in the plain and popular sense of rhyming verse in which words and the rhythms of grammar and image move from speech to song. Truly here is where a modern high culture and popular culture clash and where suspicion toward don Tomás's verses is most easily aroused. Listen to the disdain for rhyming poetry, as opposed to "free verse," in this confident 1911 futurist manifesto of the musician Francesco Balilla Pratellar. "Free verse is the only one," he declaims, for "not being bound by the limitations of rhythm and of accents monotonously repeated in restricted and insufficient formulas." And he correctly, in my opinion, emphasizes the rhythm of rhyming poetry as a dance rhythm, that is, where words become incarnate. Listen to his contemptuous dismissal of dancing words. "The rhythm of dance: monotonous, limited, decrepit, and barbarous, will have to yield its rule of polyphony to a free polyrhythmic process."[18] Which was close to Baudelaire's point, too, in the foreword to *Paris Spleen*. "Which one of us," he asked, "has not dreamed of the miracle of a poetic prose, musical, without rhythm and without rhyme, supple enough and rugged enough to adapt itself to the lyrical impulses of the soul, the undulations of reverie, the jibes of conscience?"[19] Clearly, don Tomás's verse shares little with this version of modernism. Yet is it not also as much a poetry of shock as futurism and Baudelaire whose poetry was defined by Benjamin as the site where aura disintegrated because of the shock experience of the modern?[20]

Is it not one of the functions of steady, relentless rhythm, no less than simple rhyme, to extol repetition for repetition's sake? When we specify the poetry as epic poetry, we add another type of repetition, that of repeating the past—in verse. The even tone, a certain emotional flatness, at times, the jocularity, wit, and ironies, do not so much oppose the repetition of the nightmare as scoop it up and reorient its forces, channeling the anxiety of the stimulus shield into an understanding of the past that comes from being both within and outside it.

When we identify Tomás Zapata's poetry as epic verse and wonder about its status as historiography, we recall Benjamin's essay on the storyteller in which he states that Mnemosyne, the remembrer, was the muse of the epic art among the Greeks and that the epic forms a creative matrix from which a range of very different forms have emerged—the story, the novel, and what we today call histories. This observation provokes one into thinking about similarities no less than differences among such disparate forms of putting the past in words. In this regard, recall White's contribution to the analysis of forms of writing history, in which he distinguishes between annal, chronicle, and modern forms of historiography. What is intriguing about the epic form, a form intimately related to the annal and the chronicle and thus a form we are likely to think of as antiquated, is that it is nevertheless in some respects extraordinarily modernist as well. Indeed, it can be seen not only as an expression of the art of memory but, applied in modern times, as an aesthetics of shock. And nobody made this clearer for the twentieth century than Brecht, whose poetry and dramatic direction of what he chose to call "epic theater" in this regard has still to be given its due—in good part, because it was "accepted" before it was understood. Here was where the poet "in dark times" strapped himself to the ultimate double bind, repeating well-known histories in the theater, the dark house of illusion, to display illusion making. The often cited "alienation effect" could be striven for in many ways, but essentially it meant showing through a curious succession of effects occasioned by a shock sufficient to jar but not overwhelm the intellect, such that one moved in and out of a lived experience.

VIOLENCE

What really set us back on our heels and led to the writing of this work was don Tomás Zapata's response to the *Violencia*. Here was the "voice of the people," of the oppressed, the voice of the victim. Here was the voice "from within." What aching void of silence, of pain beyond words, it would fill!

But instead of a private voice, what we find is an eminently public one. Instead of emotional involvement, we find distancing. Instead of tension and a subsequent catharsis, we find a more or less endless story with a grand flourish of a conclusion, the poet-storyteller making sure to reintroduce himself as the "untragic hero."

> Seguro me mataran porque digo la verdad
> porque mi pluma se impone mientras yo pueda pensar
> ya no me peudo aguantar y por eso ya aquí escribo
> por el peso de mi pluma muchos serían enemigos
> me siento capacitado no solamente para esto
> y de paso les aviso que nunca tuve maestro
> si al tigre se le conoce por sus pintas que no es una
> al hombre se le conoce por el peso de su pluma
> Aquí termina mis versos escritos ya por mí mano
> en esta forma fue el gobierno de Marco Polo Zambrano

Here we are far from the magical realism of those Latin American and Caribbean writers, climbing to the stars on the backs of what they take to be peasant fantasy. We are far from the attempts at clinical exactitude to be found in reports by groups like Amnesty International. We are also far from the emotionally overwhelming first-person accounts of the *Violencia* in the north of the Cauca valley to be found in Alfredo Molano's extraordinary and heavily edited transcripts in *Los años del tropel*.[21] To the contrary, in don Tomás's hands the epic as spontaneous response to the demands for memory purges the sensational—both from the real horror of the *Violencia* as well as from the attempts thereafter through the decades to talk and write about it. He puts on a show, thereby showing showing. Unlike the histories composed by professional historians, his works are simultaneously both within and without the reality proffered, therewith indicating its modes of realization. He not only exposes his personal "values" but achieves the even more important task of exposing as exoskeleton the physicality and soulfulness of the medium of thought—language itself—thereby manifesting the imaginative infrastructure of all our works, any and every rendering of the past. His is eminently an art form drawing attention to itself as art, as rite, together with the self-mockery, never letting us forget for a moment that just as historiography is contrived, so shock can to some extent be outshocked—by being repeated in predictable rhyme, steady rhythm, and turned over by humor so its belly can be scratched while its claws gyrate in mindless, albeit menacing, meanderings. In today's world in which the Colombian *Violencia* is no longer restricted to the rural poor of Colombia but is, instead, in so many ways a worldwide phenomenon, we take this to be a singularly important contribution to the "construction of America," no less than it is a construction "by America" driven by the quincentenniality of history's obsessions.

This epic art form, however, presupposes no less than it deserves an audience. And who is that audience? There is no record of don Tomás reciting his poems to his neighbors in Puerto Tejada. And although we presume that happened, we are nevertheless haunted by the image of him sitting alone with his verses rattling inside his skull. What we do know is that twenty years later in another part of the world, it is we who form, for however brief a time, an audience—thanks to the blunderings of the mysterious Recorder and the good counsel of the Director of the Prague archive. Through the archive, an encapsulated site of remembrance has been created, a site enacted in the mis-en-scène of this writing based on fragments resurrected by the Director—bits of tapes and scattered notes, clips of time brought glowing from dark files. This site is one of transference (in Freud's sense of psychoanalytic technique) between past and present. Here repetition is allowed to play "in almost complete freedom" such that the obsessions driving history "are at every point accessible to our intervention,"[22] so long as we recognize, in the words of the angel of redemption, that history is the subject of a structure whose site is not homogeneous, empty time, "but time filled by the presence of the now."[23] It was the angel's fervent hope that against all odds the leap into the past would be into "the open air of history" and not in the arena where the ruling class gives its commands. To accomplish this, we have found it necessary to construct a closed archival space layered with the debris of the past from which such a leap may occur, and it is this space—every bit as much as the space of marginal peasant existence alongside agribusiness—that has to be recognized and drawn into the equation of how it is that we construct the past while being constructed by it.

ACKNOWLEDGMENTS

This chapter was written for a conference organized by the Colombian Association of Anthropologists in Bogotá, Colombia, in 1992, to mark the quincentenary of Columbus's voyage to America, and I wish to thank the association for their kind invitation. This seemed a fitting occasion for what I most wanted to do, simply to reveal to the public more of the poetry of an old peasant farmer, Tomás Zapata, I had known in western Colombia who had died in 1972. Because his poetry was so obviously epic, it raised a host of questions about ways of representing the past and about the philosophy of history—questions that have dictated the very form and imaginary mis-en-scène of this chapter. In considering these questions I have been inspired by the work of Klaus Neumann, as in his book *Not the Way It Really Was: A View of the Tolai Past.*

NOTES

1. *"Dijo que la historia a lo largo estaba sometido al conflicto del escritor."* Tomás Zapata, Puerto Tejada, Colombia, 1972.

2. Walter Benjamin, "The Storyteller," in *Illuminations,* ed. Hannah Arendt, 83–110 (New York: Schocken, 1969), on 84–85.

3. "Esto existía pero estaba en privado, pero cuando ya Colón vino, entonces ya pasó a la historia, ya esto no quedo en privado; esto ya pasó a la historia. Eso mismo viene haciendo Miguel; sacando unas cosas que están en privado para llevarlos a la historia. Esto era lo que yo les quería decir de Colón."

4. This poem was translated into English with the assistance of Juan Carlos Tafur of Bogotá.

5. *Chulavitas* was a name given to the paramilitary assassins recruited by the Conservative party. Chulavita is the name of a neighborhood (*vereda*) in the department of Boyaca from where at first many such assassins were forthcoming. "The most terrible came from Boavita and Chulavita," wrote Eduardo Franco Isaza in his memoir, *Las guerrillas del llano* 2d ed. (Bogota: Libreria Mundial, 1959: 2), "so that this latter *vereda* earned the horrific honor of bestowing its name on the horde." The Recorder's notes state that his informants remember that the *chulavitas* were generally *"indios"* or "mestizos," recruited from the highlands of Narion, certainly not blacks. They were more commonly referred to in this area as *pájaros* (birds) and have been seen as forerunners of the *sicarios* or hired assassins said to be frequently employed by the cocaine cartels (and other interests) in Cali and Medellín today. Dario Betancourt and Martha L. Garcia, *Matones y cuadrilleros: Origen y evolución de la violencia en el occidente colombiano* (Bogotá: Tercer Mundo, 1990): 20–22.

6. John Willett, "The Case of Kipling," in *Brecht in Context: Comparative Approaches* (London and New York: Methuen, 1984): 44–58.

7. Ibid., 50.

8. Georges Bataille, *The Accursed Share,* vol. 3 (New York: Sovereignty Zone Books, 1991).

9. Friedrich Nietzsche, *The Use and Abuse of History,* trans. Adrian Collins (Indianapolis: Bobbs Merrill, 1981): 7.

10. The government's national census for 1938 shows 958 people above the age of 30 living in the town who could read and 689 who could not read.

11. Homer, *The Odyssey,* trans. Robert Fitzgerald (Garden City and New York: Doubleday Anchor, 1963): 497.

12. Walter Benjamin, "Some Motifs in Baudelaire," pp. 105–154 in *Charles Baudelaire: A Lyric Poet in the Era of High Capitalism,* 111–117, 139–140.

13. Albert B. Lord, *The Singer of Tales* (New York: Atheneum, 1978).

14. Nietzsche, *The Use and Abuse of History,* 40.

15. Ibid.

16. Hayden White, *Metahistory: The Historical Imagination in Nineteenth-Century Europe* (Baltimore: Johns Hopkins University Press, 1973): 4.

17. Sigmund Freud, *Beyond the Pleasure Principle, Standard Edition of the Complete Psychological Works of Sigmund Freud,* 18:9 (London: Hogarth Press, 1960–1974).

18. Francesco Balilla Pratella, "Futurist Music: Technical Manifesto," in *Futurist Performance,* ed. Michael Kirby and Victoria Nes Kirby, 160–165 (New York: PAJ Publications, 1971): 164, 162.

19. Charles Baudelaire, "To Arsene Houssaye," in *Paris Spleen,* trans. Louise Varese (New York: New Directions, 1970): ix-x.

20. Benjamin, "Some Motifs in Baudelaire," 152–154.

21. Alfredo Molano, *Los años del tropel: Relatos de la Violencia,* (Bogotá: CEREC, 1985).

22. Sigmund Freud, "Remembering, Repeating and Working Through," Standard Edition, 12:154.

23. Walter Benjamin, "Theses on the Philosophy of History," in *Illuminations,* 261.

FIFTEEN

Crushed Glass, or, Is There a Counterpoint to Culture?

E. Valentine Daniel

Not long ago it was the privilege of anthropologists to celebrate and take credit for weaning the concept of "culture" from the clutches of literature, philosophy, classical music, and the fine arts—in other words, from the conceit of the humanities. Our discipline's founding father initiated this emancipatory project, I believe, unbeknown to himself. He rescued the concept from its joint monopoly by the opera house, on the one hand, and the petri dish, on the other. Sir Edward Burnett Tylor (1878) proffered a definition:

> Culture or Civilization, taken in its widest ethnographic sense, is that complex whole which includes knowledge, belief, art, morals, law, custom, and any other capabilities and habits acquired by man as a member of society.

For all its unwieldiness, its omnibus character, and despite its embeddedness in the evolutionary paradigm of the day to which Tylor himself paid ample homage, the definition generated the now-famous view that culture is relative, it defines the *human* condition, that all human beings have it, or rather that it has them, and that one human being's culture is no better or worse than another's. To be fair, it was Franz Boas who, though never offering a definition of his own, breathed life into the implications of the Tylorean definition by putting it into the practice of his craft.[1] Of course, I am sure he did not foresee the silliness into which relativism, freed of its original polemical context, was to degenerate a generation later. And then there was Bronislaw Malinowski, who, though never calling himself a cultural anthropologist, introduced the discipline's methodological *sine qua non,* participant-observation.

The humanities, for its part, was vaguely aware of the scandal brewing in anthropology, but, perhaps chalking it down to eccentricity (something many an English anthropologist and a few Americans were guilty of), it was content to continue refining the Arnoldian view of culture[2] in practice if not in theory. History shared much of the prejudice of the humanities.[3] To support my argument with an extreme case, take, for instance, that most prestigious of think tanks, the Institute for Advanced Study at Princeton. It has four schools: Mathematics, Physics, History, and the Social Sciences. At "The 'tute,' " as some of the locals call it, "History" means European history. European history is more historical, not in the sense of temporality but in the sense of an imputed cultural richness; "cultural," in the Arnoldian sense. Even more to the point, historians of classical Greek and Rome are the "real historians" there, and by the time we get beyond the Renaissance, "History" begins to lose its empyrean dignity. Thus we find the only French social historian, whose work happens to be centered around the eighteenth to nineteenth century, housed in the Social Sciences. But even among the "less than sterling" historians who chose to write on the more recent past, the Arnoldian viewpoint persisted in only a slightly different form. Their histories, for the most part, privileged the scripted voices of the powerful and the "cultured." If this bias is true of European historiography, it is even truer of those working on the histories of non-European peoples, up to and including the very latest of historiographies, colonial history. Oral history, even when available, would be suspect and would most likely be relegated to that degenerate form, "folklore."

Speaking of European social historians, however, it is to some of these that the anthropological concept of culture began to make sense and in whose works its implications have been the most profound; more profound, I think, than in anthropology itself. Tylor's name was rarely invoked, and the phenomenon in question was called "social" rather than "cultural." But as it was to subsequently become clear, the sense in which "social" was employed was more akin to "culture" than to the concepts of "social" and "society" that were employed by British structural functionalists. It was "social" in the Durkheimian sense that was to influence the *Annales school* of history, especially through Marcel Mauss. The move beyond the history of the Middle Ages to the creation of a space for what came to be known as early modern history was simultaneously the move from ecclesiastical history to *histoire seriale*.[4] Marc Bloch's two-volume work *Feudal Society* (1961) was to become an anthropological canon in the sixties and seventies. Culture found its counterpart in the *longue duree* of history.[5] On the English side, history from below was to find its finest embodiment in E. P. Thompson's classic, *The Making of the English Working Class*. The strikingly similar influence of "culture" on European historian Carlo Ginzburg, on the one hand, and the Americans Robert Darnton and Natalie Zemon Davis, on the other, is remarkable. What distinguishes all these historians is their ability to "hear" the voices not of those who were bearers of Culture (with a capital "C") but of those who found themselves embedded in culture (with a small "c"), those whose voices were inscribed in minuscule: the witches, the women, the shepherds, the serfs and peasants, the poor, the popular and the public.

Enter cultural studies and its counterpart, literary study. Scholars in cultural studies, like the anthropologists and the social historians I have referred to, began to take seriously the culture of the neglected. In this case it was the culture, mainly in the West, of the many over that of the privileged few. If the Arnoldian definition were a decanter, students in cultural studies chose to study and appreciate the dregs, not the sublimate. Their topics of interest included, among others, the media, film, billboard advertisements, reggae and rap, potters and punks, gangs and televangelists, wine, beer, and cheese. "Culture," in Raymond Williams's words, became "ordinary."

If cultural studies, paralleling anthropology's turn away from the privileged West, thumbed its nose at the high, the mighty, and the refined, literary study thumbed its nose at conventional literary criticism by emulating anthropology (at least some branches of anthropology) in emphasizing the context in which texts are written and, more important, in which they are read.

The story I have told thus far may sound as though all is triumphant in anthropology: its goals reached, its intentions vindicated. Anthropologists teach; others, sooner or later, learn. Alas, it is not so. Allow me to backtrack a bit to Roger Keesing's review essay of over twenty years ago and in the interest of convenience recommit all his sins of slight—of Linton, Lowie, Kluckhohn, Kroeber, White, and most regrettably, Sapir. Keesing divided the culture theorists into two broad camps: the adaptationalists and the ideationalists. Marvin Harris and a few archaeologists were the leading spokesmen of the former, while the major subdivisions among the ideationalists were headed by the cognitivists, the Lévi-Straussian structuralists, the Schneiderian symbolists, and the Geertzian interpretivists. The adaptationalists *de rigueur,* who had attempted to define culture as merely adaptation to economic, demographic, technological, and ecological forces, have by now, for all practical purposes, fallen by the wayside. Human beings turned out to be as incorrigibly maladaptive as they were adaptive, and the way they went about being adaptive and maladaptive was as capricious as the proverbial weather in certain temperate zones. As for the cognitivists, their early high hopes of finally making the culture concept scientific—and that, too, by not having to resort to analogies from the physical or biological sciences but by identifying it as a system of rules along linguistic lines—fell faster than they rose. Brent Berlin and Paul Kay's *Basic Color Terms* (1969) was the last "love story" that came out of those heady days of ethnoscience. Cognitive anthropology survives today in a much more modest yet vital form in the fields of ethnobiology, cognitive psychology, and similar subfields. Structuralism, which, in one of its extensions, came paradoxically close to a kind of biologism—with the imputed binary structure of the mind seeking homology with the bicameral structure of the brain, triune-brain notwith-standing—has been superseded by poststructuralism and postmodernism in intellectual circles. Schneiderian insights, articulated in increasingly con-fused, confusing, and quaint astronomical terms,[6] were both better stated and overwhelmed by Michel Foucault's writings where the focus shifted to *epistemes* and epochs. Schneiderian anthropology's disregard for history, its essentialism, its unabashed idealism, its hypernominalism, and its absolute disregard of questions of power, rendered it parochial and largely irrelevant in the 1980s. It is not that Foucault was innocent of at least some of these apparent drawbacks, but the range of his power and intellect converted them into interestingly defended assets.[7] For Geertz, too, culture was sym-bolic. But as against Schneider, however, he played down the *systematicity* of culture. He belittled the cognitivists' emphasis on the rule-governedness of culture. He found structuralism's commitment to universalize Culture and to locate it in the "human mind" dangerously close to biologism. (I, for one, am not against making a place for both "Culture" and "culture" but am wary of structuralist construction of it.) As against all these co-ideationalists (if we accept Keesing's label in this regard), Geertz was committed to taking "cul-ture" from out of the private, especially from within people's minds or heads, and recognizing it as public. And then there is the persistent pres-ence of Geertz's prose style in his brand of interpretive anthropology. I be-lieve that this, more than any other single factor, more even than the Weberian and Diltheyan roots of his interpretive anthropology, is responsi-ble for the wide appeal his writings have had, especially in the Humanities. What is of lasting significance in this aspect of Geertz's work is the un-apologetic incorporation of the ethnographer with and in the ethnography. Once, when asked about ethnographic objectivity by one who still believed that there was an objective/scientific prose, Geertz replied, "I don't want anyone to mistake any of my sentences as having being written by anyone else but by me."[8] Every line bore his signature. Thus "culture" was no longer something out there to be discovered, described, and explained but rather something into which the ethnographer, as interpreter, entered. "Self-indulgence!" cried the traditionalists. "Not enough reflexivity!" cried the new reflexivists. But culture had become dialogic, less in the much-heralded Bakhtinian sense but more in the lesser-known Peircean sense, a sense in which the consequences of conversation is shot through with "tychasm."[9] Tychasm was Peirce's neologism for that element of chance contained in the "play of musement"—a free kind of doing, much like Lord Siva's *leelas'* "mindless" eroticisms and asceticisms, acts of wanton love and wanton war, and the cosmic dance that spans it all—that is more funda-mental than either the gentle persuasion of *agapism* or the mechanistic necessity of *anancasm*.

It is *this* dialogic aspect of culture, culture not as a given but as something made or, rather, co-created anew by anthropologist and informant
in a "conversation," that I in my own work attempted to elaborate (1984). I
argued for a conversation in which what was generated, exchanged, and
transformed consisted not only of words but the world of nonverbal signs as
well, not only of symbols—those arbitrary or conventional signs—but also
of icons and indexes and a whole array of other, more or less motivated,
signs. Built into a semiotic conceptualization of culture is an argument
against a certain kind of essentialism. Given the silliness of some of the
forms of relativism that are on the prowl in anthropologyland and beyond,
it behooves me to stress that the antiessentialism I advocate is not directed
at what is essentially human—a debatable and refinable list that should include, besides language, a sense of dignity, a need to love and to be loved,
the capacity to reason, the ability to laugh and to cry, to be sad and to be
happy. My antiessentialism is directed against those who advocate *essential*
differences between and among cultures, or rather, against those who believe that the differences are essential and more or less everlasting.[10] The
Schneiderians are most guilty of this kind of essentialism. Their position
may best be described as essential relativism, which is fundamentally irrational and immoral—a charge I do not have the time to explicate but which
will become clear to anyone who ponders a little on the moral implications
of such a position. What I envisage is a dynamic relativism that does not es-
sentialize differences but believes in the essential humanity of humankind,
a humanity that is not merely biological but Cultural (with a new kind of
capital "C"). Most cultural anthropologists, in focusing their accounts on
culture with a small "c", have been guilty of neglecting, even if not denying,
the importance of this kind of "Culture."

At this point allow me to interject what appears to be a radical critique of
such a semiotic view of culture. The charge is that the governing metaphor
in such a view, "conversation," exalts consensus at the expense of contestation. One response to this charge is an elementary one. "Conversation" entails communication or even communion in the widest sense of those terms,
a sense that includes agreements and disagreements, consensus as well as
contestation; but on shared grounds. Such a defense is neither very inge-
nious nor thoroughly ingenuous. For it is true that most cultural accounts
in anthropology have given scant attention to contestations, even if they
were only a subset of a larger consensual matrix. Yet, the "contestators" must
concede the argument in principle. But the critique in question suffers from
a more serious infirmity. It suffers from what we may, following Hobbes, di-
agnose as "bagpipitis," "a going along with the prevailing windy cant, with
whatever passes for [radical] *afflatus,* [becoming] indistinguishable from
the tamest of *bienseance*" (Hill 1991: 17). Contestation itself has become a
cliché, a call to combat with phrases "on tap," an obliging mannerism, part

of a higher-order consensus. Both consensualists and contestators sleep in the same bed of complaisance.

Furthermore, regardless of whether we see ourselves as consensus theorists or as contestory types, and even as we concede that we are culture co-making processualists rather than culture-finding essentialists, we cannot afford to be unaware of our collective logocentric inclinations, our privileging of language over labor, words over acts. True, the culture-making that the ethnographer or the poet engages in parallels the culture-making of the artisan or the farmer. Both are engaged in trimming the excess and in coaxing the stubbornly unproductive to yield. And in both domains, there are the craftsmen and the hacks, both of whom have a bearing on the production of culture. The significant divide, however, is not between the consensus theorists and the contestatory ones but between those who privilege the word—a group to which most academic scholars belong—and those who privilege the deed. I introduce the deed here to facilitate our movement to culture's edge, to what I shall call its counter-point. Words are symbols, which, even at the edges, pull one toward culture's center. Deeds, even when culturally centered, "habitus" notwithstanding, threaten to push against culture's limits. The deed I shall employ for making this point clear is the act of violence. But first I must return to my story about the culture concept.

This brief diversion, apart from other matters, was also intended to make the caveat about essentialism clearer. What, then, do we have? A series of paired terms: culture as given and culture as emergent, culture as reality and culture as realizing, culture as essentially relative and culture as relatively (and dynamically) essential. The second in each of these paired terms could hold its own, even if only by means of various adjustments and equivocations. The first would falter. But for those of us who advocate the second set of terms and thereby think that we are on the winning side, it is too early to gloat. There is a worm in the apple, a bomb in the banana.

The problem lies at the core of the culture concept itself. The problem lies in what Tylor called "that complex whole." For the essentialists, the whole is an existent, a done thing, a thing of the past. For the processualists, "the whole" is something toward which the culture-makers and culture-seekers move. It lies in the future. The movement is toward this realizable entity, a foretaste of which is provided in what the hermeneutician calls "understanding." The dialectic is what guides one toward it. In other words, there is a teleology to the cultural process. You and I may not live long enough to see its completion, its *summum bonum,* but it is moving toward such an end, however long that end may be deferred. It is this logic and this faith on which culture, emergent, dynamic, and processual, is built.

Regardless of the difference, both ideas of "culture"—culture as essence and culture as process—partake of a Kantian cum Hegelian project. With respect to Kant, I have in mind the implications of his *Critique of Aesthetic Judgment,* whereby we are invited to see the beautiful as the sublime[11] and wherein when we contemplate an object and find it beautiful, there is a certain harmony between the imagination and the understanding which leads us to an immediate delight in that object. That whole which we call culture is supposed to end up, in anthropological analysis, to have a certain harmony, not unlike the Kantian object of beauty. If we can only make it true, then we will also have made it beautiful. Or is it the other way around? In our monographs, how much time do we spend "rounding it all up," especially through the crafting of a closing statement or conclusion? This ideal is most poignantly captured in W. B. Yeats's description of a poem's reaching this moment of the sublime in a letter of September 1936 to Dorothy Wellesley: "a poem comes right with a click like a closing box." So would we like our cultural accounts, our monographs, our arguments, to end in a moment of beautiful finality.

Ah beauty! For John Keats, "the aesthetic impulse is encapsulated in the coldness and sterility of his Grecian Urn" (Shaviro 1990: 10). The point is made even better yet by Steven Shaviro's reading of that marvelous poem by Emily Dickinson. First the poem:

> I died for Beauty—but was scarce
> Adjusted in the Tomb
> When one who died for Truth, was lain
> In an adjoining room—He questioned softly, "Why I failed?"
> "For Beauty," I replied—
> "And I—for Truth—Themself are One—
> We Brethren, are," He said—
>
> And so, as Kinsmen, met a Night—
> We talked between the Rooms—
> Until the Moss had reached our lips—
> And covered up—our names—

Now to Shaviro's interpretation:

> It is only insofar as they are ironically "Adjusted in the Tomb," assigned their fixed boundaries under the power of death, that beauty and truth are one. "I died for beauty": does this mean that the speaker and her interlocutor died for the sake of beauty and truth (as martyr or witness)? Or, more perversely, did they choose to die *in order that* they might thereby attain truth and beauty? A desire for death is perhaps the hidden *telos* of beauty and truth. (1990: 11)

The desire to find culture, either as a present reality or as a deferred ideal, to find it in any case, as a coherent whole, true and beautiful, is the desire to find a corpse. The work of culture becomes the "lifeless residue in which the process of creation is lost," the spark of tychasm denied (ibid., 10).

The same moral is conveyed in a well-known folktale in South Asia. It probably has a common Indo-European origin. There was once a young man whose quest for truth was insatiable. He crossed the seven seas, climbed every mountain, dared the wildest of jungles, and traversed several deserts until he finally came to a cave where he found a toothless old hag, dressed in rags, with matted hair, holding a chain of beads in her gnarled hands with overgrown fingernails. To the young man's surprise and delight, the old woman spoke. She uttered her words with caution and care, pausing to make every syllable true. After a spellbinding session of truth-hearing, the young man worshiped the old woman, thanked her profusely, and pleaded with her to allow him to do something for her in return for having so kindly and so completely slaked his thirst for truth. "Yes," replied this woman, this font of all truth. "You can do me a favor. When you return to your people, tell them that I am beautiful; will you please?"

You may well object, holding that all this about the sublimation of truth and beauty in an objectified culture may be true enough of the essentialists but not true of the processualists. You may even be kind enough to count me among those exempt from the charges in question because, in *Fluid Signs,* I described the fixing of culture as something that is forever deferred. And to the heckler who might say, "But where in your book is chance?" my supporters could have chanted, *"Passim, passim, ubique!"* I might have gloated in agreement, had I not confronted the task of writing an ethnography, or rather, an anthropography of violence (Daniel: Forthcoming). So I must demur. The culture concept, even in its processual mode, relies on a unifying metaphysical process called the dialectic. Culture totalizes. Culture is the emergence of higher and increasingly more adequate agreement from less adequate and less developed contradictions. At a more concrete level, a level in which my own fieldwork in Sri Lanka on the anthropology of violence is implicated, we see this Hegelian hope expressed in theories of the state. According to this view of the world, there is a metaphysical process that transforms tribal life, which is primitive and inadequate, into the more adequate and evolved rational nation-state. But the international and intranational strifes of the day and the violence they spawn have made a mockery of this hope. The contradictions inherent in the concept of the nation-state, constructed with the help of an imagined national past, demonstrate most clearly the operation of this exclusionary teleology. In nationalist discourse, the question is not who is a Sri Lankan or who an Englishman but who is a *true* Sri Lankan and who a *true* Englishman. Mythohistories are invoked to help recast and relive an idealized past that is "constantly undermined by current and changing realities." And it is in these very imperfections—or, more correctly, in the perception of these "surpluses" or "excesses" as imperfections—that "nationalisms find their succor and sabotage" (Daniel, Dirks, and Prakash 1991: 6). Nationalism is a horripilation of culture in insecurity and fright; it is as much the realization of the power in culture as the lack thereof. In either case, culture is not power-neutral.

All this is not to deny the successes of culture's recuperative and appeasing capabilities. Marx's celebrated "opiate" is only one—even if the most poignant—case in point. Marxism itself, like the Hegelianism it turned on its head, is another case in point. Call it cultural or culturoid. Culture does make sense, even beauty, and sometimes, truth. But its totalizing mission and capacities are what is in question. And to question such capacities is not to invoke their opposite (whatever that may be) as the solution. All of which brings me back to the subtitle of this chapter: Is there a counterpoint to culture?

Let me hasten to warn you, however, that the counterpoint to culture I have in mind must go beyond Bach and, ergo, beyond Wertheim who metaphorized Bach in a hope-filled paper on social change (1974). The counterpoint I speak of is something that resists incorporation into the harmony of a still higher order of sound, sense, or society. It resists the recuperative powers of culture; it runs parallel without ever crossing the dialectic. It resists normalization, in the Foucaultian sense of that term.

Allow me to indicate more clearly what I have called the counterpoint of culture by the only way I know how: by intimation, by example. The example is violence, though violence is not the only event that is constituted of the culturally unrecuperable surplus I speak of. Let me plunge into ethnography and tell you of an event that was described to me by two brothers. It concerns the senseless deaths of two men and the suffering of two survivors. These two brothers narrowly escaped being killed by a gang of Sinhalese youth during the 1983 anti-Tamil riots in a northeastern village in Sri Lanka. However, they saw their elder brother and father being murdered.[12]

Selvakumar is twenty-two years old and works as a teller in one of the local banks. When it was arranged for me to interview Selvakumar on the events that led to his father's and brother's deaths, I was not warned that whenever he recalled these events he suffered episodes of loss of consciousness. The day of my interview with him was no exception. During our interview, which lasted for over four hours, Selvakumar lost consciousness thrice. The first time he lost consciousness was after the first half hour of the interview, and it took twenty-five minutes for him to recover. On the second and third occasions, he remained unconscious for about ten minutes each time. During these episodes his pulse and temperature fell sharply, his color drained to an ashen gray, he responded neither to pinpricks nor smelling salts, and he lost control of his bladder. By a *Siddha* physician's orders, a warm poultice of medicinal herbs was applied to his temples and forehead and his lips were moistened with *tippili* tea. When Selvakumar regained consciousness he did not remember having lost consciousness.

What follows is a partial description of what happened on "that day," as he calls it.

> That day my father and the chairman [of the Urban Council] went to the police and told them that we had heard with our own ears that this Gunasene had collected the other boys in the soccer team and had obtained long knives and sticks and that they were planning to come and cut up all the Tamils in this housing settlement. This Gunasene had already served some time in jail. He is not from this area. He is from Nawalapitiya, from where you come. He has been here for many years though. This place, this housing colony was in really bad shape when my father moved in. But he organized the place. He cleaned up the well, cleared the jungle, and cut drains for the rainwater to flow. My brother. Oh, my brother they killed him. They killed him and I couldn't even help. I was afraid. They beat him to death: "thuk," "thuk." [He passes out. My attempts to terminate the interview are brushed aside by others.]

Later:

> The police inspector told the chairman that if we had a complaint we should take it to the navy post. So my father and the chairman went to the navy post. The sentry did not let them through at first. They waited there all morning. Then the commander's car came. He must have been going into town. The chairman waved him to a stop. They asked him if they could talk to him for a moment. The chairman had known him personally. "Say what you have to say. I have a lot of work." "Can we go into your office?" the chairman wanted to know. "There is no time for that," replied the commander. So my father and the chairman told him what they had heard. The commander told them that they did not have any right to approach him on such matters and that he should have taken his complaint to the police station. They told him that they had already been there and the Police Inspector had told them to come to him [the commander]. "If you are so smart, why don't you control your own people," said the commander to the chairman. My father and the chairman walked back to the police station. On the way, another man, a Tamil, told us that some Sinhalese from Vavuniya had also joined Gunasene's gang and that he had heard Gunasene say to the boys not to worry, that he had taken care of the police. My father and the chairman walked back to the police station. We were met there by Nitthi [Selvakumar's younger brother], who came to tell us that all the Sinhalese taxi drivers were telling the Tamil taxi drivers that they were going to be killed today. There were no taxis in the Tamil taxi stand. They [the Sinhalese taxi drivers] had told my younger brother that the rain had delayed things a little, but when it stopped to be prepared for "Eelam."[13] It was raining heavily. The inspector finally came out and said, "So what, the commander did not want to see the tigers?" The chairman said, "Look, you know all these boys. You know this man. They are good people. They have lived with the Sinhalese in peace. They are neither tigers nor bears. There are rowdies who are threatening to kill them" He said like that. The inspector laughed and said, "Looks like the tigers are afraid. They have become pussycats." The other constables joined in and laughed. "Why don't you go to

Appapillai Amirdhalingam?[14] He will take care of you. What do *you* say? (He was talking to my brother). They tell me that you are the big man in the area. What, are you afraid too?" My brother did not say a word. He just clenched his teeth and looked down and walked away. All the constables were laughing. [Then he said] "Now go home and take care of your women and children. And beware! If any of you dare call a Sinhalese a rowdy. I am warning you. That is how you start trouble." Then what was there to do? The chairman went to his home, my father and I came home and shut the doors and put bars against them. Then the rains stopped.

Then they came. About half an hour later. My father was old and not as strong as he used to be. He was not feeling well in his body. But my brother was very strong. He was a big man. He was a good soccer player. That was something else this Gunasene had against him. He used to play soccer with us. We heard this loud noise at a distance. It sounded like a hundred saws were sawing trees at the same time. They were shouting something in Sinhalese. Nitthi looked out through the crack in the front door and told us that there were two navy personnel standing on the side of the road. We felt relieved. Our neighbor, she is a Sinhalese woman who is married to a Tamil. Her husband works in Anuradhapura. He is a government servant. He used to come once in two weeks. So this little girl, about three years old, used to spend most of her time in our place. This woman treated my mother like her own mother and she used to leave this child with us. That day this child was with us. And the gang started coming closer and closer. My sister and my mother were hiding. Where can they hide? The house has only three rooms. They were in the kitchen behind the firewood. Then suddenly there was silence. All the shouting stopped. Nitthi looked through the crack in the door and the two navy personnel were talking to Gunasene. Then we saw the navy personnel leave. My father told my younger brother to bar the two windows. But then we heard footsteps in the mud outside. Then they started pushing down the door. My father had fallen to the ground. My brother was still holding the door. But they used crowbars to break it. I ran into the kitchen out of fear. Another gang broke through the kitchen door. They surrounded the house. But the men who entered through the kitchen door didn't look for us in the kitchen, they walked on into the front room. Then I heard the beating. My mother and sister took the child and ran out of the back door into the fields. Then I heard the beating again. I slowly stood up and looked through the kitchen door into the front room. Nobody saw me. They were looking at the ground. I knew it was my brother on the ground. I wanted to help him. There was a knife in the kitchen. I wanted to take it and run and cut them all up. But I was a coward. I was afraid. My brother would have certainly done that for me. [He becomes unconscious. He is laid flat on the floor on a mat. A single tear trickles down his cheek. The man who had arranged this interview tells me, "The boy can't cry. That is the trouble."]

Later:

Then someone said, "The old man is out there near the well." They looked out and laughed. "He is trying to draw water." They said things like that and were making fun of him. Some of them moved out, and now I could see my brother. They had cut him up. My younger brother had fainted behind the stack of firewood. I left him there and ran into the field. Someone shouted, "There, over there, someone is running." I sat down behind some old tires. I must have fainted. When I woke up it was dark. There was smoke coming from where our house was. They had set their torches to it. I went looking for my mother and sister in the dark.

Nitthi is sixteen. He believes that he was in school, waiting for the rains to stop, when his father and brother were killed and his house was set on fire. Most of the time he has total amnesia about the events of that day. There are two exceptions. The first is when he wakes up with a start from a nightmare. From the time he wakes up he begins to describe certain events of that awful day in great and minute detail. And then, as suddenly as he was awoken, he falls back onto his mat and falls asleep. In the second typical occasion, he too loses consciousness during the day, like his brother does, but he then wakes up, not into his wakeful amnesia but into detailed recall. The recalling and retelling lasts for about a minute and then he falls asleep. He may sleep for several hours before waking up again. What follows is several of Nitthi's accounts taped by his brother for me during several episodes. The statements are Nitthi's but are drawn from four different "dream episodes" and two separate "postunconsciousness" episodes. I was asked by the family not to play back the tapes to Nitthi. I have, with Selvakumar's help, edited the tape so as to arrive at a narrative that makes reasonable chronological sense. Apart from rearranging the utterances for such a purpose, the editing is limited to omitting the highly repetitive utterances (ranging from exclamations such as "*Aiyo*" to phrases and full sentences) and those sounds that made no sense to either Selvakumar or me. In this edited version, shifts from utterances drawn from one episode to those drawn from another are marked by the first word of the changed episodic utterance being rendered in boldface type.

The middle hinge is coming loose. They are pushing the door. Someone is kicking the door. Listen. **He** has put his foot down now. Now he is lifting it out of the mud. Now he is kicking the door. **Kick,** Kick, Kick. Now he is resting his foot again in the mud. It is like a paddy field outside. For all the kicking the door is not loosening. . . . **The** bottom hinge is still holding. The screws in the top hinge have fallen. The wood is splitting. A crowbar is coming through. **It** appears that father has been poked in the back. He can't breathe. He has fallen down. **My** elder brother has turned around and is trying to hold the door back with his hands. **I** see his [Gunasene's] toes from under the door. I know them from seeing him play soccer. He has ugly toes. Mud is being squeezed from in between his toes. **Knives** are cutting through the wood of the window. There is smoke coming through the window. **Gunasene** is shouting, "Not yet, not yet" [*dämma epā, dämma epā*]. **My** brother's leg moving. It is moving like the goat's leg. [He is supposed to have witnessed the slaughtering of a goat when he was younger.] **The** front door is open and they are going around to the back. They are going to the back to kill my father. Look through the door. The two navy men are near the dhobi's house [a house at some distance across the main road]. My eyes are filling with tears. The navy men look like they are very close. I squeeze my eyes. The navy men are far away again, near the dhobi's house. **Father** is crying. "Give me some water for my son, Sami. Kill me but give my son some water. Let me give my son some water. The son I bore, the son I bore, the son I bore . . ." **Piyadasa** is asking, "How are you going to draw water like this, lying in the mud? Stand up to draw water from the well; like a man." They are all laughing. **Karunawathi** has come. The tailor boy has come. [The tailor boy is telling her] "They ran to the field with your child. They are alright. Don't go. They might follow you." **They** are kicking my father. Karunawathi is shouting, "Leave that old man alone. Leave him alone. He is almost dead." "We know your man is a Tamil too. And we'll do the same thing to him if we find him." Karunawathi is crying: "What a dreadful shame/tragedy this is" [*Mona aparādeda mēka*]. **Someone** is calling the men to the front. They want someone to drag my big brother to the road and leave him there. Listen! Karunawathi is drawing water from the well. She tells the tailor boy, "He is dead."

I was not able to meet Gunasene. He was in police custody. However, I was able to find out two things about him. First, he was not from Nawalapitiya, where I had spent part of my childhood, but from a neighboring town called Kotmale. Second, using a police constable as a messenger, he had sent Selvakumar Rs.500 and a message, the gist of which (according to Selvakumar) was,

> What has happened has happened. Let us forget what has happened. This money is for you to rebuild your house. You can stay in our house if you want until you finish building your house.

Social scientists, yours truly included, have tried to understand or even to explain communal violence in Sri Lanka. The grandest, and in many ways, the most admirable, attempt so far in this regard is the one put forth by Bruce Kapferer (1988). It sought to understand Sinhala against Tamil violence in terms of Sinhala cultural ontology. He argued that Sinhala-Buddhist ontology required that it hierarchically encompass and dominate a subdued antithesis, in this case, the Tamils. Were such a contained antithesis to rebel from within, it was seen as demonic, and Sinhala Buddhism was called upon to exorcise this demon by ritual. The available ritual in the context of ethnic rebellion was violence. Such is a rough and shoddy summary of *Legends of People, Myths of State*. The thesis is perfectly Hegelian, except of course for its arrival not at a *summum bonum* in equipoise but at an ontology condemned to violence. The only problem was that no sooner had this and similar theses been put forth than Tamil violence rose to match Sinhala violence. Furthermore, violence was no longer interethnic but intraethnic, with more Tamils killing Tamils and Sinhalese killing Sinhalese than Sinhalese killing Tamils or Tamils killing Sinhalese.

I must pause to emphasize here that my description of a violent event in which Tamils were victims and Sinhalese the aggressors is fortuitous. Conditions in 1983 and 1984 when I did fieldwork on this topic yielded more tales of Sinhala on Tamil violence. Rest assured that there followed plenty of equally gory examples of violence in which Sinhalese were the victims.

The point is this. Violence is an event in which there is a certain excess: an excess of passion, an excess of evil. The very attempt to label this excess (as indeed I have done) is condemned to fail; it employs what Georges Bataille called "*mots glissants*" (slippery words). Even had I rendered faithfully, without any editing, the words—both coherent and incoherent—of Nitthi, I would not have seized the event. Everything can be narrated, but what is narrated is no longer what happened.

I have also interviewed young men who were members of various militant movements and who have killed a fellow human being or human beings with rope, knife, pistol, automatic fire, or grenade. "You can tell a new recruit from his eyes. Once he kills, his eyes change. There is an innocence that is gone. They become focused, intense, like in a trance." Such was the account of a veteran militant, who has since left the movement in which he fought. Violence, like ecstasy—and the two at times become one—is an event that is traumatic, and interpretation is an attempt at mastering that trauma. Such an attempt may be made by victim (if he is lucky to be alive), villain, or witness. We who are either forced or called on to witness the event's excess either flee in terror or are appeased into believing that this excess can be assimilated into culture, made, in a sense, our own. Regardless of who the witness is—the villain, the surviving victim, or you and me—the violent event persists like crushed glass in one's eyes. The light it generates, rather than helping us see, is blinding. Maurice Blanchot, in *Madness of the Day*, writes thus:

> I nearly lost my sight, because someone crushed glass in my eyes. . . . I had the feeling I was going back into the wall, or straying into a thicket of flint. The worst thing was the sudden, shocking cruelty of the day; I could not look, but I could not help looking. To see was terrifying, and to stop seeing tore me apart from my head to throat. . . . The light was going mad, the brightness had lost all reason; it assailed me irrationally, without control, without purpose. (Quoted in Shaviro 1990: 3)

More ethnography.

Piyadasa (a pseudonym) is a Sinhalese in his late twenties. I knew him as a young boy who played soccer in the town of Nawalapitiya, where I grew up. He lived in a village near Kotmale and used to ride the bus back and forth to his school with Tamil schoolchildren who came to Nawalapitiya from the tea estates. At times, after a game of soccer, he and his bus-mates would feel so famished that they would pool all their small change, including their bus fares, to buy and eat buns and plantains from the local tea shop. Then they would start walking up the hill to Kotmale, all of six miles. His village now lies buried under the still waters of a reservoir built by the Swedes as part of the Mahaveli River damming project.

In 1983, the *pantaram* (the boy who makes garlands) of the local Hindu temple was killed. I was informed by another Sinhala man, a close friend of one of my brothers, that Piyadasa was among those who had killed the *pantaram* and that he too had wielded a knife. I visited Piyadasa, who has been resettled in the north-central province, and asked him to describe to me what had happened. He excluded himself from having directly participated in the violence but was able to give me a detailed account of the event. The following are a few excerpts.

> He was hiding in the temple when we got there. The priest, he had run away. So they started breaking the gods. This boy, he was hiding behind some god. We caught him. Pulled him out. So he started begging, "*Sāmi*[15] don't hit. *Sāmi* don't hit." He had urinated. He pleaded, "Oh gods that you are, why are you breaking the samis?" They pulled him out to the street. The nurses and orderlies were shouting from the hospital balcony. "Kill the Tamils! Kill the Tamils!" No one did anything. They all had these long knives and sticks. This boy was in the middle of the road. We were all going round and round him. For a long time. No one said anything. Then someone flung at him with a sword. Blood started gushing [*Ō gālā lē āvā*]. Then everyone started to cut him with their knives and beat him with their sticks. Someone brought a tire from the Brown and Company garage. There was petrol. We thought he was finished. So they piled him on the tire and set it aflame. And can you imagine, this fellow stood up with cut up arms and all, and stood like that, for a little while, then fell back into the fire.

The constant shifting from the including "we" to the excluding "they" is noteworthy. This was in the early days of my horror-story collecting, and I did not know what to say. So I asked him a question of absolute irrelevance to the issue at hand. Heaven knows why I asked it; I must have desperately wanted to change the subject or pretend that we had been talking about something else all along. "What is your goal in life?" I asked. The reply shot right back: "I want a VCR."

I have struggled to understand this event, to speak *about* it, and thereby to master it. But I have literally been struck "speechless." I am not alone, quite clearly. During my work in 1983–84 and since, in Sri Lanka, India,

Europe, and North America, I have met many witnesses of the excess of violence who have been stricken likewise. Shaviro puts it eloquently when he describes such a silence as "not a purity before or beyond speech. It does not indicate calm or appeasement. It is rather a violent convulsion, a catastrophe that overwhelms all sound and all speaking" (1990: 84).

There are, to be sure, interpretations of such events that friends and "friendly texts" offer me, but no sooner than I seize them, they escape the grasp of my understanding. There are times when I think that I do understand. But, to return in closing to the optic, there remains a blind spot in all such understandings, of which Bataille says,

> There is in understanding a blind spot: which is reminiscent of the structure of the eye. In understanding, as in the eye, one can only reveal it with difficulty. But whereas the blind spot of the eye is inconsequential, the nature of understanding demands that the blind spot within it be more meaningful than understanding itself. To the extent that understanding is auxiliary to action, the spot within it is as negligible as it is within the eye. But to the extent that one views in understanding man himself, by that I mean the exploration of the possibilities of being, the spot absorbs one's attention: it is no longer the spot that loses itself in knowledge, but knowledge which loses itself in it. In this way existence closes the circle, but it couldn't do this without including the night from which it proceeds only in order to enter it again. Since it moved from the unknown to the known, it is necessary that it inverse itself at the summit and go back to the unknown. (1988: 110–111)

"In this darkness and this silence," there is neither ontology nor epistemology, hermeneutics nor semiotic, materialism nor idealism, and most important, neither culture nor Culture. Herein lies (C/c)ulture's counterpoint, a slippery word in its own right. The counterpoint of which Wertheim wrote almost twenty years ago was a counterpoint of hope and human emancipation. He described it as a "tiny and apparently futile beginning" that had the capacity to "evolve into a powerful stream leading humanity, or part of it, toward evolution and, in more extreme cases, revolution" (Wertheim 1974: 114). The counterpoint of which I have written here is one that resists all evolutionary streams, whether of action or of thought. It will and should remain outside of all (C/c)ulture, if for no other reasons than to remind us that (a) as scholars, intellectuals, and interpreters we need to be humble in the face of its magnitude, and (b) as *human beings* we need to summon all the vigilance in our command so as to never stray toward it and be swallowed by its vortex into its unaccountable abyss. The first is a sobering point that concerns observation, the second is a cautionary one that concerns participation: the twin terms that, hyphenated, constitute the *sine qua non* of the anthropological method. It is time for cultural anthropology to lose both its Hegelian conceit and its Malinowskian innocence.

NOTES

This is a modified version of a talk delivered as the Second Wertheim Lecture at the University of Amsterdam in the summer of 1991.

1. See Stocking (1968).

2. See Arnold (1932).

3. I owe thanks to Prof. Eric Hobsbawm and, especially, to Dr. Miri Rubin for substantive discussions of this and the following paragraph. The responsibility for errors in interpretation is entirely mine.

4. See Le Roy-Ladurie (1974, 1979).

5. See Braudel (1976).

6. For instance, consider this: "It should be stressed that these concepts rest on the premise that any symbol has many meanings, on the premise that symbols and meanings can be clustered into galaxies, and on the premise that galaxies seem to have core or epitomizing symbols as their foci"; or this: "I am now dealing with a galaxy [American culture] in which coitus is the epitomizing symbol." Schneider (1976: 218 and 216, respectively).

7. See, in particular, Foucault (1972, 1973, 1980).

8. Overheard from a conversation between Geertz and this other scholar during which I was present.

9. One of C. S. Peirce's several neologisms that he triangulates with anancasm (the force of mechanical necessity) and agapism (loving lawfulness/mindfulness). See Peirce 6:302.

10. If the essentialist treatments of cultures are wanting and deserving of interrogation, so do comparable treatments of "class" and "gender." In this regard, see Scott (1988: II) but also the back-and-forth between Scott and Laura Lee Downs (1993).

11. As far as the interesting distinction that Kant draws between the beautiful and the sublime, and insofar as he aligns the former with women and the latter with man, it is but one step away from the Shivaist resolution of the dichotomy in the androgynous unity of Shiva and Shakti in the form of Ardhanarisvarar.

12. The killings took place in April 1983. My interview with Selvakumar was in December of the same year.

13. "Eelam" is the name that Tamil separatists have given to their separate nation-state.

14. The sarcastic allusion to "tigers" is in reference to the Tamil militant separatists, the Liberation Tigers of Tamil Eelam. Mr. Amirdhalingam was the head of the Tamil United Liberation Front, which had constituted in 1975 of the former (major Tamil) Federal party and several smaller parties and groups. In its 1976 platform, the TULF proclaimed the right of self-determination for the Tamils, even if that were to entail the formation of a separate state. In August 1983, the constitution was amended so as to outlaw parties advocating secession. Members of parliament were required to take an oath of allegiance to the new constitution. The elected members of the TULF refused, and consequently the party was outlawed and the members lost their seats in the legislature, leaving the Tamils largely unrepresented.

15. *Sāmi* means god.

REFERENCES

Arnold, Matthew.
    1932. *Culture and Anarchy*. Cambridge: Cambridge University Press.
Basso, Keith M., and Henry N. Selby, eds.
    1984. *Meaning in Anthropology*. Albuquerque: University of New Mexico Press.
Bataille, Georges.
    [1954] 1988. *Inner Experience*. Albany: State University of New York Press.
Berlin, Brent, and Paul Kay.
    1969. *Basic Color Terms*. Berkeley, Los Angeles, and London: University of California Press.
Blanchot, Maurice.
    1977. *The Madness of the Day*. New York: Station Hill Press.
Bloch, Marc.
    1961. *Feudal Society*. 2 vols. London: Routledge and Kegan Paul Ltd.
Boas, Franz.
    [1896] 1940. *Race, Language and Culture*. New York: Macmillan.
Braudel, Fernand.
    1976. *The Mediterranean and the Mediterranean World in the Age of Philip the Second*. 2 vols. New York: Harper and Row.
Daniel, E. Valentine.
    1984. *Fluid Signs: Being a Person the Tamil Way*. Berkeley, Los Angeles, and London: University of California Press.
————. Forthcoming. *Charred Lullabies: Chapters in an Anthropology of Violence*. Princeton: Princeton University Press.
Daniel, E. Valentine, Nicholas Dirks, and Gyan Prakash.
    1991. "Nationalizing the Past: A Proposal for a Workshop." Ms.
Darnton, Robert.
    1985. *The Great Cat Massacre*. New York: Basic Books.
Davis, Natalie Z.
    1975. *Society and Culture in Early Modern France*. Palo Alto: Stanford University Press.
Downs, Laura Lee.
    1993. "If 'Woman' Is Just an Empty Category, Then Why Am I Afraid to Walk Alone at Night? Identity Politics Meets the Postmodern Subject." *Comparative Studies in Society and History 35* (2): 414–451.
Foucault, Michel.
    1972. *The Archaeology of Knowledge*. New York: Pantheon.
————. 1973. *Order of Things: An Archaeology of the Human Sciences*. New York: Random House.
————. 1980. *Power/Knowledge: Selected Interviews and Other Writings, 1972–77*. New York: Pantheon.
Geertz, Clifford.
    1966. *Person, Time and Conduct in Bali: An Essay in Cultural Analysis*. Yale South East Asia Program, Cult. Rep. Ser. No. 14.

———. 1967. "The Cerebral Savage: On the Work of Claude Lévi-Strauss." *Encounter* 28: 25–32.

Ginzburg, Carlo.
1982.   *The Cheese and the Worms.* New York: Penguin.

Harris, Marvin.
1968.   *The Rise of Cultural Theory.* New York: Crowell.

Hill, Geoffrey.
1991.   *The Enemy's Country.* Stanford: Stanford University Press.

Kapferer, Bruce.
1988.   *Legends of People, Myths of State: Violence, Intolerance and Political Culture in Sri Lanka and Australia.* Washington, D.C.: Smithsonian Institution Press.

Keesing, Roger.
1974.   "Theories of Culture." In *Annual Review of Anthropology,* ed. B. J. Siegel et al. Palo Alto: Annual Review.

Le Roy-Ladurie, Emmanuel.
1974.   *The Peasants of Languedoc.* Urbana: University of Illinois Press.

———. 1979. *Montaillou: The Promised Land of Error.* New York: Random House.

Peirce, C. S.
1934.   *Collected Papers.* Cambridge: Belknap Press.

Schneider, David M.
1976.   "Notes toward a Theory of Culture." In *Meaning in Anthropology,* ed. Keith H. Basso and Henry A. Selby. Albuquerque: University of New Mexico Press.

Scott, Joan W.
1988.   *Gender and the History of Politics.* New York: Columbia University Press.

———. 1993. "The Tip of the Volcano." *Comparative Studies in Society and History* 35(2).

Shaviro, Steven.
1990.   *Passion and Excess.* Gainesville: Florida State University Press.

Stocking, George, Jr.
1968.   *Race, Culture and Evolution.* New York: Free Press.

Thompson, E. P.
1966.   *The Making of the English Working Class.* New York: Vintage.

Tylor, Sir Edward B.
[1878] 1974.   *Primitive Culture.* New York: Gordon Press.

Wertheim, W. F.
1974.   *Evolution and Revolution.* Baltimore: Penguin.

CONTRIBUTORS

John Borneman is a member of the Department of Anthropology at Cornell University. He is the author of *Belonging in the Two Berlins: Kin, State, Nation* and editor of *East Meets West in the New Berlin* and *Gay Voices from East Germany.*

E. Valentine Daniel teaches anthropology at the University of Michigan in Ann Arbor. He is the author of *Fluid Signs: Being a Person the Tamil Way* and a forthcoming book on the anthropology of violence entitled *Charred Lullabies: Chapters in an Anthropography of Violence.* He has edited several books, the latest of which is *Mistrusting Refugees,* also to be published by the University of California Press.

Nicholas B. Dirks is a member of the Departments of History and Anthropology and Director of the Center for South and Southeast Asian Studies at the University of Michigan in Ann Arbor. He is the author of *Hollow Crown: Ethnohistory of an Indian Kingdom,* and the editor of *Culture and Colonialism.* He is currently working on a book about the colonial construction of caste and religion in India, as well as writing a series of essays concerning the postcolonial genealogies of modernity and tradition in South Asia.

Paul Friedrich is a member of the Departments of Anthropology, Linguistics, and Social Thought and is an Associate in Slavic Languages and Literatures at the University of Chicago. He has done fieldwork among the Tarascans in Mexico, the Nayars of India, and Russian dissidents. He has published many works on poetics, semantics, and related aspects of language and culture, notably, *The Language Parallax,* and he recently finished another book, *Music in Russian Poetry.*

Clifford Geertz is Harold F. Linder Professor of Social Science at the Institute for Advanced Study, Princeton. He has carried out fieldwork in Indonesia and Morocco and is the author of *The Religion of Java, Islam Observed, The Interpretation of Cultures,* and *Works and Lives.*

Marilyn Ivy teaches anthropology at the University of Washington in Seattle. She has written on mass culture, modernity, and the politics of knowledge, and Japanese national culturalism, themes she also examines in her book, *Discourses of the Vanishing: Modernity, Phantasm, Japan.* Her recent work concerns the relationship among media representation, criminality, and bourgeois sensibility in contemporary Japan.

Mary N. Layoun is a member of the Department of Comparative Literature at the University of Wisconsin at Madison. She teaches and writes about modern literatures and cultures, nationalism and gender, politics and culture, disciplinary histories, and institutional politics and pedagogy. Her books include *Travels of a Genre: Ideology and the Modern Novel* and, recently, *Boundary Fixation?*—a comparative study of the contradictions of modern nationalism and of Greek, Palestinian, and Cypriot cultural responses to nationalism-in-crisis.

David Lloyd teaches English at the University of California, Berkeley. He is the author of *Nationalism and Minor Literature: James Clarence Mangan and the Emergence of Irish Cultural Nationalism.* He is co-editor of *Nature and Context of Minority Discourse* and has written numerous essays on aesthetics and cultural politics. His most recent book is *Anomalous States: Irish Writing in the Postcolonial Moment.*

Zita Nunes is a member of the Departments of English and Comparative Literature at Columbia University. She has written on the literatures of the Americas and is currently working on Brazilian modernism and race.

Jeffrey M. Peck is a member of the Center for German and European Studies at Georgetown University. He has published articles on the history and status of German studies in America, the development of cultural studies, racism and ethnicity, and East German responses to the Holocaust. He has just finished a collaborative book of interviews and a video documentary on German Jews who returned from exile in Allied countries to live in East and West Berlin entitled *Sojourners: The Return of German Jews and the Question of Identity in Germany.*

Dan Rose teaches at the University of Pennsylvania where he is a member of the Departments of Anthropology and Landscape Architecture. He has contributed to literary anthropology in the recent collections *Anthropology and Literature* and *Anthropological Poetics,* and at the University of Pennsylvania Press, he edits the series in Contemporary Ethnography. His ethnographic inquiry includes the community of ultra-large corporations in the United States and abroad, and it is to the formation of capitalist culture worldwide that he brings a poetic of inquiry. Two of his artists' books have been collected by the Museum of Modern Art. He is the author of *Patterns of American Culture, Living the Ethnographic Life*, and *Black American Street Life*.

Azade Seyhan teaches German and comparative literature at Bryn Mawr. She is the author of *Representation and Its Discontents: The Critical Legacy of German Romanticism*. She writes on romantic theory, cultural criticism, and minority cultures in Germany.

Susan Stewart teaches poetics and literary theory at Temple University. Her books include *Nonsense, On Longing, Crimes of Writing*, and two volumes of poetry, *Yellow Stars and Ice* and *The Hive*.

Arlene A. Teraoka teaches German at the University of Minnesota. Her research interests include contemporary German literature, culture studies, minority literature in German, and German drama. Her book on the East German playwright Heiner Muller appeared in 1985; more recently, she has completed a book on the discourse of the Third World in East and West German literature.

Michael Taussig teaches anthropology at Columbia University. He is the author of *The Nervous System; Shamanism, Colonialism, and the Wild Man: A Study in Terror and Healing; The Devil and Commodity Fetishism in South America*; and *La Esclavitud y Libertad en el Valle del Río Cauca*.

Margaret Trawick teaches anthropology at Massey University in New Zealand. She has published on South Asian medical systems and practices, Tamil poetry and song, the anthropology of emotion, and gender relations. Her most recent book is *Notes on Love in the Tamil Family*. She has just begun research on ethnic politics in the South Pacific.

Index

Designer: U.C. Press Staff
Compositor: BookMasters Inc.
Text: 10/12 Baskerville
Display: Baskerville
Printer: Haddon Craftsmen, Inc.
Binder: Haddon Craftsmen, Inc.